Moral Love Songs

and Laments

Middle English Texts

General Editor

Russell A. Peck
University of Rochester

Associate Editor

Alan Lupack
University of Rochester

Advisory Board

Rita Copeland
University of Minnesota

Thomas G. Hahn
University of Rochester

Lisa Kiser
Ohio State University

Thomas Seiler
Western Michigan University

R. A. Shoaf
University of Florida

Bonnie Wheeler
Southern Methodist University

The Middle English Texts Series is designed for classroom use. Its goal is to make available to teachers and students texts which occupy an important place in the literary and cultural canon but which have not been readily available in student editions. The series does not include those authors such as Chaucer, Langland, the Pearl-poet, or Malory, whose English works are normally in print in good student editions. The focus is, instead, upon Middle English literature adjacent to those authors that teachers need in compiling the syllabuses they wish to teach. The editions maintain the linguistic integrity of the original work but within the parameters of modern reading conventions. The texts are printed in the modern alphabet and follow the practices of modern capitalization and punctuation. Manuscript abbreviations are expanded, and u/v and j/i spellings are regularized according to modern orthography. Hard words, difficult phrases, and unusual idioms are glossed on the page, either in the right margin or at the foot of the page. Textual notes appear at the end of the text, along with a glossary. The editions include short introductions on the history of the work, its merits and points of topical interest, and also include briefly annotated bibliographies.

Moral Love Songs

and Laments

Edited by
Susanna Greer Fein

Published for TEAMS
(The Consortium for the Teaching of the Middle Ages)
in Association with the University of Rochester

by

Medieval Institute Publications

WESTERN MICHIGAN UNIVERSITY

Kalamazoo, Michigan –1998

Library of Congress Cataloging-in-Publication Data

Moral love songs and laments / edited by Susanna Greer Fein.
  p. cm. -- (Middle English texts)
 Includes bibliographical references.
 ISBN 1-879288-97-4 (alk. paper)
 1. Didactic poetry, English (Middle) 2. Christian poetry, English
(Middle) 3. Devotional literature, English (Middle) 4. Love
poetry, English (Middle) 5. Laments--England. I. Fein, Susanna
Greer. II. Series: Middle English texts (Kalamazoo, Mich.)
PR1203.M67 1998   97-49951
821'.05083823--dc21   CIP

ISBN 1-879288-97-4

©1998 by the Board of the Medieval Institute

Printed by CPI Group (UK) Ltd, Croydon CR0 4YY

Cover design by Elizabeth King

For my father

Martin Greer

Contents

Acknowledgments

In the course of preparing this edition I received help from many institutions and individuals. Support for the research underlying this project has been generously granted by the Division of Research and Graduate Studies of Kent State University. I am grateful to the Research Council for an Academic Year Award granting release time and also for travel funds to work at libraries in Great Britain.

I thank the librarians and archivists who graciously responded to my requests for materials or helped me during visits to their collections: in Oxford, the Bodleian Library (M. N. Webb, Assistant Librarian; Mark Purcell, Senior Library Assistant; and Susan Harris, Printed Book Photography), Corpus Christi College Library (Christine Butler, Librarian), Balliol College Library (Penelope Bulloch, Librarian, and Alan Tadiello, Assistant Librarian), and Jesus College Library (D. A. Rees, Archivist); in London, the British Library, and the Lambeth Palace Library (Melanie Barber, Deputy Librarian and Archivist); in Cambridge, the Cambridge University Library, the Trinity College Library (David McKitterick, Librarian; Alison Sproston, Sub-Librarian; and Jonathan Smith, Manuscript Cataloguer), and the Pepys Library, Magdalene College; in Hurst Green, Lancashire, the Stonyhurst College Library (Rev. F. J. Turner, Librarian); in Edinburgh, the National Library of Scotland; in San Marino, California, the Huntington Library (Mary L. Robertson, Curator of Manuscripts, and Thomas V. Lange, Curator of Early Printed Books and Bindings); in Rochester, the Robbins Library (Alan Lupack, Curator) of the University of Rochester; in Boston, the Widener Library of Harvard University; in Washington, D.C., the Library of Congress; and in Kent, the Kent State University Library.

In particular, I acknowledge the following colleges and libraries for granting permission to base my editions upon copies of the poems found in their manuscripts: the Principal and Fellows, Jesus College, Oxford, for MS 29 (*Love Rune*); Lambeth Palace Library, London, for MS 853 (*In a Valley of This Restless Mind*); the Bodleian Library, Oxford, for MS Eng. poet. a.1 (*The Dispute between Mary and the Cross*), Addit. MS A 106 (*The Four Leaves of the Truelove*), MS Bodley 596 (*The Bird with Four Feathers*), and MS Douce 322 (*Pety Job*); the Master and Fellows, Corpus Christi College, Oxford, for MS 237 (*The Sinner's Lament*).

I am grateful for opportunities to have presented portions of this work at the Medieval Association of the Midwest Meeting, the Early Book Society Meeting, the International Congress on Medieval Studies at Kalamazoo, and the Kent State

University Institute for Bibliography and Editing (IBE). Among those who offered information and advice, I am pleased to thank Linne Mooney, Helen Phillips. Hoyt Duggan, Martha Driver, Derek Pearsall, and John J. Thompson, as well as my IBE colleagues, S. W. Reid and Allan Dooley. As always, I must acknowledge Tony Edwards's help with a bibliographic detail, as he directed my attention to a possible fragment of *The Bird with Four Feathers*. For a close review of my editions of *Pety Job* and *Bird*, I am much indebted to Ian Doyle, who shared generously the fruits of his own research. *The Four Leaves of the Truelove* edition originated as part of my dissertation, for which I owe much to the discerning guidance of Morton Bloomfield and Larry Benson. Among my own students, I am pleased to acknowledge the help and interest of Terry Shears, Nancy Burian, Arlene Hilfer, Catherine Rock, Kirsten DeVries, Brenda Weingartner, and especially Susan Butvin, who served for a time as my research assistant. My husband David and children Elizabeth, Carolyn, and Jonathan graciously lived with this book in process and cheerfully assisted in more ways than they know.

I am indebted to Russell A. Peck and the TEAMS Middle English Texts Board for encouraging this project, and particularly to Russell for his thorough review of my texts and notes. I also thank Melissa Bernstein for her careful reading of the manuscript against its sources; Karen Saupe, for help with the TEAMS format; and Jennifer Church, for preparing the volume for publication. At Rochester. Alan Lupack gave it a careful last reading, and at Kalamazoo, Thomas Seiler gave it its final review.

Lastly, I acknowledge my profound gratitude to the editors who have preceded me in working out many of the intricacies of these lyric survivals, most especially to Carleton Brown, Karis Ann Crawford, F. J. Furnivall, F. Holthausen, Carl Horstmann, Israel Gollancz, J. Kail, Richard Morris, Felicity Riddy, Rossell Hope Robbins, G. V. Smithers, and Magdalene M. Weale, whose names and styles became familiar companions and aids as I followed their leads and attempted to emulate their learning.

Moral Love Songs and Laments

Introduction

"Meditation," according to Hugh of Saint Victor, "is the concentrated and judicious reconsideration of thought, that tries to unravel something complicated or scrutinizes something obscure to get at the truth of it."[1] The authors of the poems in this volume designed them as forms that conceal truths accessible to those willing to delve them studiously and devoutly. The lyric becomes an object perceived in meditation, which, when properly used, promises to be spiritually efficacious. These poets saw poetry as a deliberative process leading to religious renewal: sacred images sequenced for the thoughts and emotions they arouse, correlated to tenets of redemptive theology, and situated to invite God's grace to enter a reflective reader's responsive heart.

These moral love songs and laments thus illustrate how, in the devout medieval English sensibility, doctrine was vitally connected to affective receptivity. One may grasp intellectually the theology of redemption and grace, but only through one's heart-felt response to God's offering of love (in Incarnation and Passion) may one gain these rewards. High emotionalism marks these poems' penitential lyricism. Narrative moods range from love-longing and passion to bitter grief and sorrowful lament, feelings that devolve from the intimately personal state of being God's created creature, individually answerable to divine law and love. Whatever emotion holds sway, these lyric songs anatomize the human side of love and raise its expression to the godly sphere, either as one's yearning for God or as God's reciprocal love for humankind.

In so writing the loftiest human emotions upon the divine realm, the poets joined in trying to express the sublimity of their topics through a perfected art, an art that sought form melded precisely to content. Our distance in time and culture from these writers has obscured the seriousness and delight of their accomplishments. The poems printed here — *Love Rune, In a Valley of This Restless Mind, The Dispute*

---

[1]Hugh of Saint Victor, "The Soul's Three Ways of Seeing," in *Selected Spiritual Writings*, trans. a religious of the Community of St. Mary the Virgin (London: Faber and Faber, 1962), p. 183.

between *Mary and the Cross*, *The Four Leaves of the Truelove*, *The Bird with Four Feathers*, *Pety Job*, and *The Sinner's Lament* — all share the fate of relative obscurity, even among specialists of medieval English verse. Their elusiveness in the canon may be attributed to a variety of perceptions and misperceptions: they have seemed too lengthy to classify with traditional lyrics, too didactic and artifice-ridden to appeal to moderns, too charming to be more than simply an ornamental exercise, or too lacking in narrative logic or verisimilitude even to be worth reading. Their unassuming presence in editions or anthologies prepared from the 1860s onwards has not led to general recognition of their artistic merits, perhaps because modern readers are rather far from the mindset of those who originally created a demand for the kind of mental stimulation and spiritual caretaking these texts supply.

With medievalists now in wide agreement on how rooted in the material and visible world was a theology centered on divine incorporealization, we can better understand how a culture of learned and popular devotionalism could have bred a poetics of incarnation. In accordance with a firm belief in Christ the Word made flesh to save mankind, several moral poets attempted to create from the Word so conceived the verbal means to flesh out signs and patterns of redemption for an audience eager to add such texts to their devotional lives. The sacred enigmas buried in these poems sometimes seem to be so curious as to be implausible; however, to a devout English reader of the time, for whom reading was a step toward God, the nuggets to be found in these texts were emanations of the divine, the reward that came from frequent perusal. Even if a reader failed to "get" every part of the pattern, the talismanic power of the incarnational poem was probably thought to be enough by itself to allow the balm of grace to flow into a reader of sufficient devotion.

Recent commentators on *Pearl*, the masterpiece of English devotional poems, have given us ways to understand how an incarnational aesthetic might operate in verse. The poetics of the Pearl-poet is, according to John Fleming, rather more akin to the theological art of Dante Alighieri than to the English prosodics of a long-line alliterative poet.[2] In particular, the centuple structure of *Pearl* (its 101 stanzas) links it with Ubertino da Casale's *Arbor vitae crucifixae Jesu* in a "mysterious tradition, at once open and hidden" that formalizes "the idea of penitential consolation . . . through numerological convention" (pp. 96–97). Ubertino, a Franciscan contemporary of Dante, also incorporated in his work the dialogic motif of Mary in debate with the Cross, in a version that may have partially influenced the highly original English rendering printed here. Fleming supplies the term *incarnational verse* to describe

---

[2]John V. Fleming, "The Centuple Structure of the *Pearl*," in *The Alliterative Tradition in the Fourteenth Century*, ed. Bernard S. Levy and Paul E. Szarmach (Kent, Ohio: Kent State University Press, 1981), p. 82.

2

"certain patterns of poetic intentionality" that offer "visible demonstration" of "abstract and ideal truths" and that are "as relevant to the readers of these poems as to their writers" (p. 97).

Another recent writer on *Pearl*, Britton Harwood, delineates its diptych form, rendered in chiastic symmetries that present the poem, ultimately, as a "devotional object."[3] Each half collates with the other, he argues, and is read both sequentially and in simultaneity, in analogy with diptychs created in ivory in the Pearl-poet's day, where "the right-hand term of an opposition would stand in a superior relation to the left-hand one" (p. 65). The poem itself thus becomes "something to be seen"; more than a bauble, it is like the eucharistic wafer, a "figure for the opposition between time and eternity" (p. 72). Although he deals differently with the content of *Pearl*, Harwood, like Fleming, perceives that the poem is to be apprehended in its whole, shaped form.

Eugene Vance sorts the threads of philosophical and theological thought that likely would have influenced the Pearl-poet's "poetics" of the soul's participation in God's oneness, from Plato and Plotinus to Augustine and Dionysius the pseudo-Areopagite. It is in Dionysius that Vance identifies "a Hellenistic Platonism radically revised as Christian theology" that offered to the Pearl-poet "a powerful counterbalance to Augustine's emphasis upon man's distance from an ineffable God."[4] Dionysius stressed instead both "the active potential of the human soul" and also *reciprocation on the part of an enamoured and extroverted God*" (p. 141):

> Eros is a structuring principle in the cosmic process of participation. . . . Thus, God participates as the partner of humanity in this eros, and God's ecstasy is a downward movement of love through Christ. Simultaneously, human eros reverts upwards through its own ecstasy. . . . [T]hrough the eucharist, the incarnate Christ is revealed to us perfectly, making communion with God and his mysteries possible. (p. 142)

Dionysius's ninth-century translator, John Scot Eriugena, used the term *theosis* to denote "the transformation in humans that comes through participation in divine love" or "the deification of what is created" (p. 143). Such transformation could also

---

[3]Britton J. Harwood, "*Pearl* as Diptych," in *Text and Matter: New Critical Perspectives of the Pearl-Poet*, ed. Robert J. Blanch, Miriam Youngerman Miller, and Julian N. Wasserman (Troy, N. Y.: Whitson, 1991), p. 61. See too the spatial analysis of Cary Nelson, "*Pearl*: The Circle as Figural Space," in *The Incarnate Word: Literature as Verbal Space* (Urbana: University of Illinois Press, 1973), pp. 25–49.

[4]Eugene Vance, "*Pearl*: Love and the Poetics of Participation," in *Poetics: Theory and Practice in Medieval English Literature*, ed. Piero Boitani and Anna Torti (Cambridge: D. S. Brewer, 1991), p. 141.

mark a poem thought to be created through the Word, a kind of poetics evidently espoused by both Dante and the Pearl-poet. Vance ends his analysis, like Harwood, with the eucharist, seen now as the means of human participation with the cosmic eros. Through it the priest reveals Christ "uche a day" and the lover gains the consolation he seeks, participating in God's reciprocated love: "Poetic discourse, then, has found its proper pearl and its proper Prince" (p. 147).

By whatever name we call it — incarnational verse or poetics of participation — an aesthetic of sacred forms and types made sensible to the mind that dwells in devout meditation can be seen, to varying degrees, in the moral love songs and laments presented here. Dionysius was translated again in the twelfth century, and yet again in the thirteenth, then by Robert Grosseteste, an English scholar whose writings must have been familiar to his contemporary and fellow Franciscan Thomas of Hales, author of *Love Rune*. Later, the fourteenth-century poet of *The Dispute between Mary and the Cross* cited Dionysius's authority (whom he confused, as was common in contemporary practice, with Saint Denis).

Evidence for a practice of locating divine emanations in well-crafted words can also be adduced from other sources. It is well known that the relics and icons of saints were thought to be, like God's biblical Word, supernaturally imbued with the sacred essence of their origins. Efficacious icons did not have to be images, though: they could consist of words instead. Prayers (the Pater Noster especially), charms invoking the Trinity, Christ, or the Cross, and even saints' lives were believed to be possessed of spiritual powers. A devout person's contact with these texts, if occurring in a mode of exceptional receptivity, might allow God's grace to enter his or her being. To give a simple example, a fifteenth-century verse prayer that invokes Christ's name and Passion is composed in precisely thirty-three words, "mystecally representyng xxxiij yerys of the age of owr lord Jesu Cryst"; it is to be recited in a given pattern upon five colored beads of the rosary; and doing so will gain the speaker (according to a scribal note) an indulgence of 5,425 years, this number equivalent to the total number of wounds Christ received.[5] The text of the prayer is important to the petitioner, but so is the form composed in thirty-three words, for it memorializes and makes "mystecally" present Christ's wounded, thirty-three-year-old body, and it is through this sacrificed body (physically commemorated through handled beads and voiced prayer) that the petitioner hopes his own body and soul will be saved.

Medieval medical practitioners also routinely relied on the healing efficacy of prescribed charms and prayers. There are many instances of spiritual leechcraft

---

[5]John C. Hirsh, "A Fifteenth-Century Commentary on 'Ihesu for Thy Holy Name,'" *Notes and Queries* 17 (1970), 44–45.

worked through iconic texts, always with an intriguing emphasis placed upon the words' literal powers as objectified things sacred in themselves. Jocelyn Wogan-Browne notes a practice designed to protect the unborn and their expectant mothers: "Holy names [were] invoked via inscription on scraps of parchment tied to the bodies of pregnant women, or [were] carved on apples for their ingestion."[6] The written words — their semantics and sequencing — originated in a tradition that was the province of the expert practitioner. For the needy patient their efficacy worked not through her reading them, but rather through her wearing or eating them. In such instances, a written text's "ability to function as a species of contact relic" is felt by both practitioner and patient to be coextensive with its literate meaning (p. 43).

While the poetic texts in this volume are not charms, prayers, or saints' lives, they do invoke through remarkable structural techniques, typological shadings, and biblical echoes, the names and signs sacred to Christianity. Often embedded as enigma, such forms were clearly founded on the poets' belief that they helped to summon God's presence, as in prayer, and that emanations of divine grace could thus be conveyed to the meditant reader. That poets structured their poems on the shape of the Cross or enigmatically enclosed in them several namings of God suggests the very serious spiritual mission that they expected such verse to fulfill in the life of a reader. Such poetry was not merely to be read (as we might be prone to think of reading as a simple straight-once-through process), but rather *consumed* metaphysically, so that it might bring "sowlehele" to the devout, penitent user. One needs to picture the meditant man or woman retreating regularly to a private spot, reading a text through many times over an extended period, quite likely committing it to memory, and pausing over its words and verbalized images to make connections, find patterns, discover signs and meanings, participate with compassion in its depiction of holy suffering, and absorb its objectified shape, that is, what it becomes when perceived whole rather than as a series of discrete signifiers.[7]

---

[6]Jocelyn Wogan-Browne, "The Apple's Message: Some Post-Conquest Hagiographic Accounts of Textual Transmission," in *Late Medieval Religious Texts and Their Transmission: Essays in Honour of A. I. Doyle*, ed. A. J. Minnis (Cambridge: D. S. Brewer, 1994), p. 49.

[7]The literature on how medieval readers read devotional texts and who these readers were is vast and varied. Sources I recommend include: Margaret Aston, "Devotional Literacy," in *Lollards and Reformers: Images and Literacy in Late Medieval Religion* (London: Hambledon, 1984), pp. 101–33; C. A. J. Armstrong, "The Piety of Cicely, Duchess of York: A Study of Late Mediaeval Culture," in *For Hilaire Belloc: Essays in Honour of His 72nd Birthday*, ed. Douglas Woodruff (London: Sheed & Ward, 1942), pp. 73–94; John C. Hirsh, "Prayer and Meditation in Late Mediaeval England: MS Bodley 789," *Medium Ævum* 48 (1979), 55–66; Ann M. Hutchinson, "Devotional Reading in the Monastery and in the Late Medieval Household," and George R. Keiser, "'Noght How Lang Man Lifs; Bot How Wele': The Laity and the Ladder of Perfection," both in *De Cella in Seculum:*

Moral Love Songs and Laments

Friar Thomas of Hales, author of the thirteenth-century *Love Rune*, coaxes a devout reader to decipher the secret runes he has inscribed upon the poem's refined verbal surface. To dig deeply for buried meaning, the Franscican author implies, will bring rich reward. A shimmering treasure in verse, *Love Rune* belongs with the select group of medieval English poems of exceptional polish and perfection, such as *The Dream of the Rood* and *Pearl*. The mystic message of this rune-poem is offered in sexualized metaphors that yoke love to divine wisdom. The frame — an epistolary "love rune" from a friar counselor to a maiden — makes a gendered circumstance the pretext for a love counsel of the highest order, veiled with rich allusions to the Annunciation, Solomon's Temple, and the mystic Jewel that connotes both the Godhead and the mortal virginity that brings mystic access. Hidden at the center of the rune (its fiftieth line) is an image of the Cross, sign of its message of love from an incarnate, masculine Wooer. Thomas's language is courtly and elegant, with a subtle bawdy punning that stays within the parameters of a divine wooing conveyed through an earthly Gabriel-like friar.

Christ woos the reader rather more directly in the delicate and lovely *In a Valley of This Restless Mind*, a fourteenth-century lyric richly evocative of the love language found in Canticles. Christ is both male and female, both lover and mother, as he reaches out, wounded, to "Mannis Soul," seeking to stabilize the restless wandering of the lost narrator, whose persona merges imperceptibly with that of the reader. The narrator is transformed from seeker to sought, from male adventurer scouring the landscape for a "truelove" to a receptive, feminized soul led to her seduction. Consummation of this union produces an offspring, the same soul now converted and become a babe sucking the pap of Christ as Mother, nestled in the wounded heart, and ready to be reared on adversity. Metaphors of human sexuality and kinship — amid a strangely fluctuating sense of gender — underlie this love appeal from Christ, who is shown to be the androgynous, languishing Lover of each soul prepared to receive him.

Interchanged familial roles also direct the religious and aesthetic logic of *The Dispute between Mary and the Cross*, where, again, God's crucified body comes to

Perfection," both in *De Cella in Seculum: Religious and Secular Life and Devotion in Late Medieval England*, ed. Michael G. Sargent (Cambridge: D. S. Brewer, 1989), pp. 145–59, 215–27; Sixten Ringbom, "Devotional Images and Imaginative Devotions: Notes on the Place of Art in Late Medieval Private Piety," *Gazette des beaux-arts* 73 (1969), 159–70; Vincent Gillespie, "*Lukynge in haly bukes: Lectio* in Some Late Medieval Spiritual Miscellanies," *Analecta Cartusiana* 106 (1984), 1–27; Mary Carruthers, "Memory and the Ethics of Reading," in *The Book of Memory: A Study of Memory in Medieval Culture* (Cambridge: Cambridge University Press, 1990), pp. 156–88. For additional discussion and bibliography, the reader is referred to the introductions to each poem.

signify the ultimate locus of divine Love. A debate is carried on while Christ hangs — nailed, bleeding, and silent — between the disputants, Mary and the speech-endowed Cross. Here God's display of love is felt to be exceptionally violent and gruesome, with the two holy observers unable to agree upon how it should be viewed. Mary sees her Son torn and tortured, and grief fills her with pain, lament, and reproach against the Cross. In response, the dispassionate Cross explains how it is itself a second "mother" to Christ, bearing him now as Mary formerly did and aiding him in a wrenching birth for all humanity. *Dispute* is a talismanic cross-poem that uses startling, rapidly shifting, metaphysical metaphors to underline its message of Love enacting a cosmic change. As Christ suffers in body, the Cross serves up the eucharistic bread carved on its "board" and the wine pressed in its "wine-press." Symmetrically arranged speeches offer the meditant reader a verbalized sign of the Cross, useful for warding off the devil and for attaining God's promise of redemption.

Another efficacious Cross materializes in *The Four Leaves of the Truelove*, an alliterative poem whose meditational function is overtly couched in a medicinal metaphor. Here Christ is true Husband, benevolent Parent, and caring Doctor of the soul. Sacred history is a series of knottings and unknottings, culminating in the Triune God's union with Mary, which leads to Christ's birth and death, and man's redemption. The incarnational story focuses upon a four-way union — Mary joined to Trinity — a union that embodies Truelove. The sign for this incarnational promise exists in nature: herb truelove, a cruciate, four-leaf plant. In the frame narrative a maiden sick with love-longing seeks the herb, hoping for a secular easement of her pain, but instead of finding the herb, she receives its consolatory lesson from a heaven-sent, speech-endowed turtledove, whose sermon recreates the shape of the Cross. Meekly grateful and consoled, the maiden-soul has been cured by Truelove, the long-sought herb administered in pure form through words (*grace* comes to mean both "herb-grass" and "grace"), at a dosage prescribed by the Physician Christ.

The Bird with Four Feathers also contains a loquacious bird giving a four-part disquisition. Probably slightly later in date than both *Dispute* and *Truelove* (c. 1400), *Bird* is told in the style of a penitential refrain poem. Stanzas of varying length (eight, twelve, sixteen, or twenty lines) conclude on the chirpy Latin line *Parce michi, Domine!*, "Spare me, Lord!" As the naïve narrator pursues his desire to understand what this cryptic line means, he is drawn to question the bird and listen to her long complaint over four lost feathers — Youth, Beauty, Strength, and Riches. The lament of an injured female bird becomes, curiously, the narrative of a foolish man. Guided by pity, the narrator listens and absorbs the sad story as an exemplum for his own life. The only remedy is penitence — as the refrain reiterates — and the reward is to see God's face, whose secret lineaments are embedded in various strategically placed namings of God in the bird's speech. Rather than be fooled by life's gifts into trusting

7

in one's own powers, one must discern and rely on the sovereign Lord, font of a much-needed mercy.

Pety Job was written some fifty years later than *Bird*, but some copyists or booksellers seem to have regarded it a companion to the earlier poem because of their shared refrain. This beautiful and powerful lyric is a rich paraphrase of — with impassioned departures from — the nine lessons of the Dirge, taken from the Office of the Dead. The Latin source passages are drawn from the speeches of Job, with their profound questions and ruminations on the essential nature of mortal existence. In *Pety Job* the intensely personal and psychological ramifications of the penitent's condition — never free of remorse, never without consciousness of sin, perpetually in a state of self-abnegation before God — are probed with the precision of a surgeon while the strangely disembodied, timeless lyric voice offers an incessant plea for mercy. The tonal beauty of *Pety Job* — ever at odds with its self-denying ethos — shows the frightening tension of a lucid self-awareness that would but may not escape itself. *Pety Job* is the gem of fifteenth-century penitential lyrics.

The final poem presented here is *The Sinner's Lament*, a late penitential poem with a history of misidentification as tangled as is its intricate web of manuscript affiliations and variant texts. The lyric purports to be the voiced lament of a sinner who has died with no hope for salvation. He speaks from beyond the grave, warning the living to avoid his foolish mistakes. The work survives in two versions, the better of the two unprinted until now. In the known version the sinner is a nobleman who sinned in gluttony, avarice, and lust; it thus betrays a bias of class as well as gender (women are not included in the targeted audience). The newly discovered version has the sinner regret his sinning in all seven vices, and the poet addresses humanity in general — rich and poor, men and women. This longer text is more finely structured by halves — the sinner's mistakes in life, his pains after death — with a midpoint that slyly inverts his gluttonous failure to fast into the worms that now feast on him. The basic, imagistic outline of the poem — a suffering body who calls on passers-by to look upon him in remembrance of their own souls' states — recalls and inverts the sacred sign of *corpus Christi* on the Cross, the meditative focus of so many other poems.

From *Love Rune* to *The Sinner's Lament*, these poems span at least two hundred years, with their differing styles reflective of changing milieus, traditions, and ideas among moral lyricists in this long period in England. From Thomas of Hales's early Franciscan piety, with clear debts to the affiliated prose texts of the Katherine group and *Ancrene Wisse*, to the *Lament* poet's damned soul, whose feverish plight reflects the purgatorial anxieties of a later age, these seven poems sketch out in miniature the changing audiences and tastes that fostered medieval English devotional verse. What holds them as a group is their poets' shared desire to provide a means for grace to devout readers prepared to meditate upon these poetic objects of devotion. The poems lead the receptive soul into an apprehension of and participation in the love freely given by God, manifest in sacred signs that the poets make mentally "visible," sensiently immediate, and affectively moving, just as they and their readers believed God to have made his love visible to humankind through living in the flesh and dying on the Cross.

Abbreviations

AN   Anglo-Norman

EETS   Early English Text Society

ME   Middle English

MED   Middle English Dictionary

MS(S)   manuscript(s)

OE   Old English

OED   Oxford English Dictionary

OF   Old French

ON   Old Norse

List of Plates

Thomas of Hales, *Love Rune*

Introduction

The jewel-like lyric presented here is to be read in the spirit of a riddle or conundrum, one that imparts a mysterious, holy wisdom to be lived and learned by heart. Thomas of Hales, the author of *Love Rune*, calls himself not a maker of verse but the worker of a *ron* (line 2). The Anglo-Saxon term suggests an intricate verbal construction containing hidden meanings accessible only to the initiated or chosen. Such art was thought to follow the way of God, for as Hugh of Saint Victor wrote, God speaks by riddles, darkly and in secret, because "in this way truth keeps the faithful busy in searching it out, and at the same time continues hidden, lest it be found by unbelievers" (p. 134). Although the poem is not titled in its sole extant copy, the poet's simple, cryptic phrase in line 2 describes the elegant amulet that follows. *Love Rune* meets the multiple promise of its title: it is an artful song, counsel, and mystery about love.

The single surviving copy of the poem has a Latin incipit that provides a circumstance for the poem: *Here begins a certain song which Brother Thomas of Hales of the order of Minorites composed at the request of a young girl dedicated to God.* The opening stanza repeats this circumstance but is written in first-person address to the reader. Therefore only through the incipit do we know that "Ich" is Thomas of Hales, friar Minor. The incipit also provides scholars the first attested link between an English religious lyric and the Franciscan movement of the early thirteenth century. The Friars Minor constituted a new Franciscan order licensed in England in 1224. From that year until well into the fifteenth century the friars had an enduring, wide-ranging effect upon the development of English lyric expression. The Franciscans followed their founder, Saint Francis of Assisi, who wanted them to be *doctors de trobar* or *jonguleurs Dei*, "God's troubadours." The Friars Minor saw it as their mission to preach to the general populace, cutting their evangelical messages from popular cloth, that is, song, proverb, story, and verse (Hill [1964], p. 330; Jeffrey, pp. 12–32; Brewer, p. 44; Swanton pp. 246–48).

The poet names the current king of England, Henry III (line 82), a great benefactor of the Franciscans who generously endowed all their communities in England (Hill [1964], p. 325). The king's mention dates the composition of *Love Rune* to between 1224 and 1272, Henry's last regnal year. A narrower range can be postulated from other evidence: an anecdote in a book of friars' exempla mentions that Thomas of Hales was, with another boy (Adam de Maddelay), a chorister at St. Mary's, Hereford. Both boys later became friars. The anecdote can be dated to the second quarter of the thirteenth century (Hill [1964], pp. 327–30). With Thomas located in Hereford, his entry into the Franciscan order might have been linked to the career of Ralph of Maidstone, who in 1239 resigned as Bishop of Hereford (a position he had held since 1234), to become a simple friar. Thomas may have entered the order during the relatively short period of Maidstone's bishopric, or perhaps he followed Maidstone's example in 1239. If so, the dates for the writing of *Love Rune* would be narrowed to 1234–72.

The author was a native of either Hailes in Gloucestershire (which the southwestern dialect of the sole surviving text supports) or Hales Owen located then in Shropshire, now in Worchestershire.[1] What little else is known of his career comes from two letters in which Thomas is named, first as a friendly acquaintance of Adam Marsh and perhaps as a member of the London house, and second as one of four friars (along with Adam Marsh) writing to Fulk Basset, Bishop of London (1244–58). Adam Marsh was a prominent Franciscan from 1232 until his death in 1259, and he was a close friend of Robert Grosseteste, Bishop of Lincoln and head of the Franciscan School at Oxford. The fragmentary evidence thus shows that Thomas had some important cosmopolitan connections, that "c. 1252–56" he "was associated with, and associating with, notable Franciscans, probably in London."[2]

Three of Thomas's writings are extant in three languages: an Anglo-Norman sermon, a Latin prose life of Mary, and the English *Love Rune*. Manuscripts may preserve more of his works, particularly sermons, but there survive no further attributions to his name. Like *Love Rune*, the other works written by Thomas seem to be directed in large measure toward an audience of women (Horrall [1986], pp. 296–98). His *Vita sancte Marie* enjoyed a fairly wide distribution, particularly in England and German-speaking areas of Europe, to judge from thirteen extant manuscripts, and it was skillfully translated into Middle English in the late fourteenth or early fifteenth century. *Love Rune* was also still known in late fourteenth-century England, when it was modernized, probably for another female audience, under the title *Of Clene Maydenhod*.[3] This descendent poem survives in the Vernon Manuscript,

---

[1] On the place-name Hales, see C. Brown, p. 198; Dickins and Wilson, p. 103; Hill (1964), pp. 329–30; and D'Angelo, p. 236.

[2] Hill (1964), pp. 326–27. See also Horrall (1986), pp. 288, 295–98; D'Angelo, p. 237; C. Brown, p. 198.

[3] On how the two poems compare, see Wells (1914), pp. 236–37.

near similar modernizations of two early thirteenth-century anchoritic texts, *Ancrene Wisse* and *The Wooing of Our Lord*.

The sole surviving copy of *Love Rune* appears in one of the important early Franciscan miscellanies, Oxford, Jesus College MS 29, dated late thirteenth century.[4] Many medieval English lyric collections appear in manuscripts attributable to the Franciscans or to their influence, and individual lyrics are often traceable back to such collections. Among the contents of Jesus College MS 29 are the Middle English *Owl and the Nightingale, Proverbs of Alfred, A Moral Ode* (or *Poema Morale*), and eleven poems that survive only in this book. The copy of *Love Rune* found here, however, does not duplicate what is stated to be its original form: a roll. In the last two stanzas the poet instructs the maiden to turn to the poem often, by "drawing it forth," unrolling the document "open and without seal," and singing it in a "sweet voice" (lines 194–95, 202–03). The physical instructions have led scholars to conclude that the verses were originally written on a roll and perhaps were accompanied by musical notation (Hill [1964], pp. 322–35; Woolf [1968], pp. 57–58).

The Franciscan endeavor to appropriate art forms with wide secular appeal clearly resides in the fine, persuasive tones of *Love Rune*. While the runic notion and the love-song formula tap popular streams, it is unknown whether *Love Rune* was written for a general audience. The purported audience is a single maiden, and the circumstance, if generalized to a larger circle, would seem most appropriate to friars like Thomas and those individuals (lay or cloistered) whom they served as confessors. The rune has a private meaning meant for the specified female reader, but it also conveys a public valence, as in a generalized way the message extends to the maiden's community of women (line 198) and to the friars who compiled and read books such as Jesus College MS 29.

The term *luve ron* appears once elsewhere in a work that predates the lyric, a work that Thomas may have known. In *The Life of Saint Katherine* the phrase corresponds to the term *amatoria carmina* in the Latin source, and it appears in the context of Katherine's disinterest in social activities:

This mild, gentle maiden, this lovely lady of blameless behavior, did not delight in any frivolous games or foolish songs. *She did not learn or long for any love songs or love stories,*[5]

---

[4]On the history of Jesus College MS 29, see Hill (1963), pp. 203–13; and on affiliated English manuscripts, see Jeffrey, pp. 205–11.

[5]The early ME passage reads: "Nalde ha nane ronnes ne nane luve runes leornin ne lustnen" (ed. Eugen Einenkel, EETS, o.s. 80 [1884; rpt. Millwood, N. Y.: Kraus, 1975], p. 7; in Latin: *non amatoria carmina videre aut audire volebat*).

but she always had her eyes or her heart on Holy Writ, and most often both together. (trans. Savage and Watson, p. 263; italics added)

Although Katherine avoids love runes, she can understand the *deme runes* (hidden secrets) that pertain to God. Central to Katherine's character is her access to wisdom so profound that she outshines fifty masters of philosophy. She gathers this wisdom not just through a training in *hali writ* but also from a life of virginal solitude: "she kept to herself — and thought always to herself — a maiden in maidenhood, as she sat in a chamber in her family house" (p. 263). When the philosophers acknowledge her sapiential superiority, they perceive that it flows directly from the recesses of God's mind, which they state themselves unable to fathom:

> For as soon as she called on Christ and named his name, and the great strength of his sublimity, and then showed clearly *the depth and the secret mystery of his death on the Cross,*[6] all our worldly wisdom went away, so that we were afraid of his majesty. (p. 273; italics added)

Elsewhere the wisdom to which Katherine has access is termed (by her) an unknotted knot — that is, a riddle revealed — which is hers because she is "knotted" to Christ in marriage.[7] The key to Katherine's knowledge lies in her oneness with Christ; through her virgin body she possesses his unbroken image, and thus by a physical state she gains a direct line to godly wisdom (pp. 267–68).

The Life of Saint Katherine belongs to a group of well-known Middle English prose texts composed from about 1200 to 1230 for the spiritual direction of religious women living as anchoresses in the West Midlands of England. Accompanying *Saint Katherine* are two more saints' legends, those of Saints Margaret and Juliana. These texts comprise one cluster of works associated with *Ancrene Wisse* (*A Guide for Anchoresses*). Other related pieces are *Sawles Warde, Holy Maidenhood,* and *The Wooing of Our Lord*. This literature is animated by a unified belief in the sanctity of virginity and the enclosed life, especially for women. The spiritual guidance found in these works is shaped by gender; that is, it is literature for women, and often it is specifically a learned man's counsel going to a woman positioned as being in need of his tutelage and as gladly, passively accepting of his higher wisdom (Newman, pp.

---

[6]The ME author terms the mystery of God's Passion a *deme run*: "the deopschipe and te derne run of his death on rode" (ed. Einenkel, p. 62).

[7]She declares, "Ich habbe uncnut summe of theos cnotti cnotten" (ed. Einenkel, p. 54), and later describes her knotted espousal to Christ (p. 71). Hence, her eventual torture with "cnottede schurgen [scourges]" (p. 73) seems figuratively matched to the quality of her sainthood.

19–45). These instructions are imparted, however, with a view to empowering the female religious in her active espousal to God, a condition of joy she may achieve by diligently following the exercises in humility and models of saintly spirituality provided her.

In Thomas of Hales's *Love Rune* the situation found in *Saint Katherine* appears to be invoked for contrast. Acting quite unlike the chaste Katherine, a "maid of Christ" (*mayde Cristes*) has petitioned Brother Thomas earnestly and passionately (*yorne*) to make her a *luve ron* — a phrase easily read as "secret love message" — because she wants to learn how to take *another* true lover (lines 3–4). Apparently she cannot reconcile Christ's spiritual comforts with her physical longings. In his holy calling Thomas accepts the challenge of redirecting this potentially wayward soul toward the truest Lover she may hope to find. The *luve ron* becomes, consequently, not the secular advice the maiden seems to be asking for, but a song of the divine Love that awaits her when her desire is properly channeled, a song expressly like the one the brides of Christ will sing in heaven (line 203; Revelations 14.3–4). In its gendered discursive frame it resembles the anchoritic texts in the *Ancrene Wisse* group: a man gives counsel to a woman in spiritual need.

This framing fiction of *Love Rune* harbors an element hidden from view but latent in the circumstance and familiar to the audience. It is hidden because it is a sensitive subject: when a woman who belongs to God asks her spiritual counselor to advise her on a matter of love, it is strongly intimated that she has strayed from her spiritual lessons, mistaking the messenger for the message. Thomas's duty is to steer her gently, courteously, from a misguided infatuation with Thomas himself back to the correct path. In not addressing the lady's feelings directly, Thomas's private missive maintains a public propriety and guards the modesty and reputation of both parties.

Whether the situation was real or contrived, it was no doubt a snare that sometimes beset pious women dependent upon learned men for their religious counsel, and also a temptation for the men who gave the counsel. Gerald of Wales recounts how Gilbert of Sempringham, twelfth-century founder of the Gilbertines (a double house of monks and nuns), dealt with this problem in a dramatic way:

> Gilbert, . . . when an old man and, as Gerald put it, "most unsuited for the purposes of lust," was looked upon with lascivious eyes by one of his own nuns. Gilbert was horrified, and the following day, after preaching a chapter on the virtue of chastity, he disrobed entirely, walked around three times for all to see him, "hairy, emaciated, scabrous and wild," and then cried, evidently pointing to the crucifix, "Behold the man who should be duly desired by a woman consecrated to God and a bride of Christ." He then went on, pointing to himself: "Behold the body on account of which a miserable woman has made her body and soul worthy of being lost in Hell." (Constable, p. 222)

The *Ancrene* author warns of this danger in another way, stating that if a man were ever allowed to see the anchoress's face, he might in his weakness desire her carnally, which would make the anchoress responsible for his fall (pp. 68–69). He teaches the female reader about seductive men by giving her a sample scenario: "And he says she may confidently look upon holy men — yes, someone like him, with his wide sleeves" (p. 68). Aelred of Rievaulx, too, in a passage that the *Ancrene* author may be recalling, advises that the recluse's confessor be "an elderly man of mature character" and that "she should avoid looking at him and only listen to him with fearful reserve. Listening frequently to the same man's voice can be a cause of great danger to many people" (pp. 51–52). The writers of anchoritic rulebooks maintained a vigilant awareness of the bodily temptations latent in the close emotional bonds that would naturally develop between a holy man and his female charge.[8]

Thomas of Hales treats this danger besetting people of religious life by making it the framing fiction for a lyric extolling the virtues of the Holy Bridegroom. The situation need not have been real because it was well known and readily understood. Moreover, the maiden's unsaintly passion conforms to a misogynistic view that would have expected a woman to be unable to control her urges (McLaughlin, pp. 252–56) and a male counselor to be able to instruct her to a better way. Thomas assents to the maiden's request in order to produce a love message from God, adopting a role as God's emissary and becoming, properly, the woman's spiritual caretaker. Rosemary Woolf remarks that the narrator "acts as a paranymph for the divine bridegroom," fulfilling the ancient tradition of the friend who goes with the groom to fetch home the bride ([1968], p. 61). As such, Brother Thomas courteously declines to be the focus of the lady's attention, for, as he delicately puts the question to her at the end of his argument, "If one must choose between two things, does he not commit an evil if he should, without need, pick the worse and neglect the better?" (lines 189–92). The question pertains both to the lady's better choice and to Thomas's better action.

A private setting that the audience would have grasped carries, then, a portion of the encoded message. By a discreet indirection Thomas does not state his role in arousing the maiden's feelings, and thereby he preserves the maiden's dignity — and his own — even as he lovingly composes a love message of a higher purpose. Echoes of the Annunciation enlarge the meaning of this frame, turning the maiden into a

---

[8]Elkins details several examples of close spiritual friendships between religious men and women (pp. 19–60). The relationship of Christina de Markyate and Geoffrey of St. Albans gave rise to rumors of impropriety, which the writer of Christina's *vita* dismisses as false (Elkins, pp. 35–38). For other examples, see Fein, pp. 141–42; Newman, pp. 46–75; and P. Brown, pp. 140–59. On how friars exercised their pastoral care of men and women in gender-specific ways, see Coakley (1991, 1994).

figure for the human soul, wooed (as was Mary) by God, while the poet conveys words that portend a transforming miracle. Hence, whether the setting was a true circumstance or not matters little in how contemporaries would have read the poem.[9] It is written to impart truths universal to persons dedicated to Christ, and the specified genders underline a message that God's love for humanity — made immanent in Christ's male body — outshines any mortal attachment.

The heart of the poem — the words that Thomas delivers to the maiden — provides the rest of the runic meaning, the mysterious secret to be unlocked. Understanding this hidden meaning requires one to adopt a perspective used in Christian didactic writings, drawn from mystic terminology, that expresses the holiness of virginity in metaphors that are strongly sexualized. The virgin's status as a bride of Christ is literalized. In the writings on virginity spiritualized union with God comes to depend on the perpetuance of an "intact" body, a female maidenhead (the bride-soul figured as a woman) becoming the "seal" that carnally connects a virgin to Christ (compare *Holy Maidenhood*, pp. 228–29). In the tradition this union is physical even as it is figurative, since the doctrine extols the fleshly link that brings to a virgin knowledge of the incarnate and virgin Christ. The virgin who has saved her body for Christ is more sanctified than a widow or a wife in a hierarchy that places her just below the angels.[10]

The authors of virginity tracts seem often to take a special delight in sexual rhetoric, even in extraneous places, almost as if they are giddy with the license gained by immersion in an ascetic subject. A notable example is Aldhelm, an early eighth-century West Saxon bishop, who wrote the Latin treatise *On Virginity*. After a gracious greeting to ten named Anglo-Saxon nuns, he plunges into a prolix — and R-rated — Virgilian simile comparing his writing task to wrestling:

---

[9]This interpretation of the poem's setting as generic rather than specific differs from the mainstream of criticism, where there has been speculation as to the maiden's status (nun, recluse, or laywoman; see notes to lines 1 and 4). While there may have been a specific female who inspired the poem, it is important also to see how Thomas has contrived a common experience and how a recognition of the contrivance nuances the meaning of the rune that follows. On the allusion to the Annunciation, see Levy, pp. 123–34. An Annunciation hymn follows *Love Rune* in the manuscript.

[10]In *Sawles Warde* the holy confessors (like Thomas of Hales) appear to be even higher than the virgins (trans. Savage and Watson, pp. 218–19; ed. R. Morris, *Old English Homilies*, EETS o.s. 29, 34 [1868; rpt. New York: Greenwood, 1969], p. 261; see also Bugge, p. 118). On the doctrine and aesthetics of virginity in medieval thought, see Bugge; Atkinson, pp. 131–43; Bloch, pp. 93–112; and Wogan-Browne, pp. 165–94.

... one (athlete), smeared with the ointment of (some) slippery liquid, strives dexterously with his partner to work out the strenuous routines of wrestlers, sweating with the sinuous writhings of their flanks in the burning centre of the wrestling-pit. . . . (p. 60)

And so on, for many more lines. Aldhelm deliberately turns the notion of virginity into a trope of concealment, as when he declares of one martyr saint: "I shall not allow the virginal glory of the martyr Julian to lie hidden in the secret recesses of silence" (p. 99). The writer's act exposes the virgin in a way that seems almost to violate his sanctified state. Aelred of Rievaulx, the twelfth-century English Cistercian abbot, writes in explicit sexual terms in a treatise to his own virgin sister, asking her to imagine the Incarnation as if she were the Virgin Mary: "with what a fire of love you were inflamed, when you felt in your mind and your womb the presence of majesty" (p. 80; Fein, pp. 146–47). A pivotal mystical experience for the virgin recluse Christina de Markyate — a contemporary of Aelred — involves an erotic-maternal encounter with Christ "in the guise of a small child": "with immeasurable delight she held Him at one moment to her virginal breast, at another she felt His presence within her even through the barrier of her flesh" (*Life*, p. 119). Writing for a milieu close in time to Thomas of Hales, the author of *Holy Maidenhood* gives the enclosed virgin plenty of lusty imagery to contemplate. To give one striking example:

"Your father" is the name [of] that vice that begot you on your mother — that same nasty flaming of the flesh, that burning itch of the bodily lust before that sickening act, that bestial swelling, that shameless coition, that stinking and ugly act of filth. (p. 228)

Such imagery is supposed to steel the virgin in her adamancy against the married state, but it obviously opens the door to another kind of knowledge, one of which she is known to be carnally innocent.

Love Rune needs to be read as part of this lively tradition, long practiced by ascetics and monks, even as it infuses it with the fresh strains of a new Franciscan lyricism. In what is still one of the best summations of *Love Rune*, a reader wrote in 1907 that with "lofty devotion," "passionate yearning," and "deep seriousness," the poet conveys "through a medium tender and refined" a sense of "erotic mysticism."[11] Christ has an appeal that is palpably physical, with his humanation openly male in its ability to attract a maiden. He is depicted as more handsome, more rich, more powerful, more wise, and of course more amorous than any earthly suitor may hope to be. The allure of Christ outdoes the famous lovers Paris, Amadas, and Tristan, the supreme heroes Hector and Caesar (lines 65–70), and even, in power and

---

[11]*Cambridge History of English Literature*, p. 258. On the mixing of erotic and sacred love, see also Swanton, p. 248.

wealth, the sovereign ruler Henry III, King of England (lines 81–82, 102). Clothed in a material courtliness, Christ becomes the ultimate Lover-Knight proffering incomparable gifts (a castle and a gem) and wooing by means of the ultimate love song.

The gifts are of course supremely better than their earthly shadows: Solomon's temple possesses but a meager likeness to the castle (lines 113–20); a whole collection of precious gems fails to match the virtuous power of the valuable jewel called "Virginity" (*Maydenhod*), which the maiden must guard (*witen*) in the castle of her body (lines 153–76), a castle coextensive with God's mansion in heaven: "For the temple of God is holy, which you are" (1 Corinthians 3.17).[12] Thus while castle and gem symbolize body and virginity, they also denote the heavenly city, God's abode that exists inwardly and outwardly (compare Rogers, pp. 28–40). It is what Hugh of Saint Victor called the "inward dwelling" (p. 179), reached by contemplation, where one "glories inwardly in the Lord's hidden face" (p. 106). The *Katherine* author has Katherine describe it as a city of the heart, a gleaming metropolis of jewelled streets and joyous inhabitants that satisfies all desire (pp. 276–77).

What Katherine describes is the source of her wisdom, the deiform image that resides in her pristine body, derived from her "knotted" connection to Christ. This power also surfaces in the related *Life of Saint Juliana* when Juliana, beleaguered by a demon, calls for Christ's wisdom "silently in her heart" and is answered by a voice that gives specific instructions on how to bind the troublesome devil (pp. 312–13). Ruminating on Matthew 13.44, Hugh of Saint Victor pieces out the logic underlying the heart's power, in a passage that may have influenced *Love Rune*:

> The kingdom of heaven is likened to treasure hidden in a field. The kingdom of heaven is of course eternal life. But Christ is life eternal, Christ is also wisdom, and wisdom is the treasure. And this treasure was hidden in the field of the human heart when man was created in the image and likeness of his Maker. . . . The dust of sin cast on the heart of man concealed that precious treasure from our sight, and the outspread darkness of ignorance intercepted wisdom's light. . . . Solomon builds the temple for God, since by the wisdom of God the heart of man was made, that in it God might dwell as in a temple. . . . That treasure, therefore, is hidden in the field of our own heart. (pp. 102–03)

Within the heart lies wisdom, and wisdom is God.

Thomas of Hales's rune-poem both contains and conceals wisdom — the deepest wisdom of God. The way to access this wisdom (that is, to solve the riddle) is first to

---

[12]This passage opens the English Franciscan Robert Grosseteste's popular *Templum Dei*, a work dated c. 1220–30 (ed. Goering and Mantello, pp. 6–10), and one that Thomas probably was familiar with.

prepare oneself — by rejection of the world and contemplation of Christ's irresistible traits — and then to give oneself fully to the loving blandishments of the soul's espoused Husband. *Love Rune* enables the reader (figured as female) to take these steps and receive her mystic Lover each time she reads the poem, which she is instructed to do whenever she is struck by love-longing (lines 201–04). In a subtle reading Morton W. Bloomfield hints, provocatively, that the runic secret is sheltered like virginity itself; enclosed in a poetic frame and shielded from view, it "must be 'opened' to understand but . . . also must remain closed"; at the heart of the poem lies "wisdom" which "dwells in secret, in a holy of holies, in a temple, in the temple of man's mind" (p. 59). When Hugh of Saint Victor writes about writing about love, he shows a fascination with the paradox that this act entails:

> Perhaps in an excess of wantonness we wear a harlot's face, since we are not ashamed to compose something in writing about love, though these are matters that even the shameless are sometimes unable to express in words without a blush. . . . Our purpose is to probe and seek what we may know and — when we know — avoid that into which some others go and, knowing, may indulge therein. (pp. 187–88)

The contemplative life seeks knowledge of God and God's love; it probes the depths for wisdom. This intellectual action by a carnal virgin sexualizes the soul.

The runic meaning of *Love Rune* devolves from a play on the concepts of knowability and unknowability. The poet raises this theme early by stating the maiden's request for a lover who is *best wyte cuthe a freo wymmon* (line 6). The phrase *wyte cuthe*, highly ambiguous, is open to a variety of meanings: "best able to guard/ protect/keep/ know/advise a noble/single woman" or "best advisor known to a noblewoman" (a reading that implicates Thomas in the maiden's request). *Cuthe* (from *connen*) is a verb susceptible throughout the poem to a sexualized meaning of "know," while *witen* tends to waver between its two verbal definitions, "guard, protect" (virginity) and "know" (Christ the Bridegroom). Thus while ambiguous language seems to cloud knowability, the combined senses of these key words imply both an access to God's wisdom and a sensual enjoyment of God's love through a perfected contemplation of the image borne in one's own bodily wholeness.

Serving as a prompt for the virgin bride, Thomas's rune-poem leads the *mayde Cristes* to the bridal chamber of her Spouse and introduces her to the spiritual love-act. Modern readers have glanced away from Thomas's boldest statements because sexualized metaphors pertaining to God seem to be almost unthinkable in our age.[13]

---

[13]For a fascinating survey of many explicit images of Christ's sacred manhood in medieval and Renaissance art, which modern thinking has obscured, see Steinberg.

Introduction

Instead of uncovering the private meanings embedded in the poem, twentieth-century critics have tended to read them as they are clothed, seeing a gentle, didactic poem expressed in the elegant rhetoric of courtly love-verse. Influenced by the mystical love language of such writers as Hugh of Saint Victor and Bernard of Clairvaux, however, the writers of twelfth- and thirteenth-century virginity tracts were not shy in relegating to God the virility of a male Lover. Thomas of Hales adopts this language like the Franciscan he was, using the metaphor of sexuality within the metaphor of a secular love song. His punning on sexual meaning culminates in lines 153–84, where the pronouns *he* and *hyne* seem to indicate a neuter "it" (the choice of modest critics) referring to the maiden's virginity which must be *witen* ("guarded"), but the pronouns also possess a continuous double register, "He/Him," referring to Christ who is to be *witen* ("known") in ways nuanced as sexual. The friar's latent meaning culminates when the maiden is told, in a topos common to secular love-verse, that *thu hyne witest under thine hemme*, "you know Christ under your skirt" (line 167).[14]

This moment is potentially the most sublime offering the poem holds for the spiritually receptive reader. But the poet has hidden still more mysteries to be delved and explored, at least one of which is embedded in the formal shape of *Love Rune*. The poem numbers twenty-five eight-line stanzas (each scribally written as four double lines) with a final ten-line stanza (written as five lines). The first stanza addresses the reader; the last two address the maiden and close on a personalized prayer. These three stanzas constitute the frame as discussed above. The love rune proper, that is, the epistle written to the maiden, is composed of the twenty-three stanzas that fall in between (184 lines). The argument balances two motifs: *contemptus mundi* (with an elegaic sense of the losses caused by transience) and *sponsa Christi*. In Bloomfield's analysis the first topos covers eighty lines (9–88), the second ninety-six lines (89–184) (pp. 55–57; see also Swanton, pp. 247–48). This assessment misses, however, the true dividing line, which occurs, significantly, at line 100, or, looked at another way, the rune's central ninety-second line. Overall the 210 lines divide as follows: 100 + 100 + 10.[15]

The stanza containing the hundreth line is important, for it is the one that declares Christ as supreme — *the ricchest mon of londe* (line 97) — the most powerful and

---

[14]This phrase has been read by all commentators as "you should guard your virginity under your skirt" (see the note to line 167).

[15]Or, 50 + 50 + 5, as laid out in the MS; see Note on the Edited Text (below). Thomas of Hales's interest in numbers also appears in his sermon, "a meditation in the form of a figurative kissing of Christ's feet. . . . divided into ten," based on the ten talents of Matthew 25.14–20 (Legge [1935], pp. 227–28).

wealthy suitor a maid could desire. In this stanza of highest sovereignty,[16] the comparison extends to King Henry III, who must himself receive power from and bow before God. The hundreth line caps the centrality of this passage in the rune's central stanza:

> Alle heo beoth to His honde,
> Est and west, north and suth! (lines 99–100)

A sign of the Cross, delineated in the four cardinal directions, inscribes the center of the poem. It signifies God's redemptive power, the mysterious wisdom that the fifty pagan philosophers in *The Life of Saint Katherine* acknowledged to be beyond their ken. The mystery of the whole rests in Christ's Incarnation and Passion. Placing the Cross at the center sanctifies the rune and bids God to bring the power of his wisdom to its lines.[17]

Moreover, in a nexus of artful, half-hidden erotic metaphors, even the reference presenting *Love Rune* as if it were on an unsealed roll comes to be implicated. Thomas explains how the maiden may turn to this love song whenever she wishes to enjoy her espoused union with Christ: "Whenever you sit in longing, draw forth this same piece of writing; sing it in a sweet voice, and do everything as it directs you" (lines 201–04). The detail of a roll participates in allusions to the Annunciation, where a scroll is standard in artists' depictions, and also to the brides in Revelations, where rolls portend the song they shall sing. But, beyond these meanings, the roll is a suggestive medium for the poem, that may allude to the divine Wooer's masculinity. As a *writ* establishing marriage to Christ, *Love Rune* brings mystic ecstasy in material form. By establishing the poem's physical form (which need not have been literal) — that is, by causing a reader to imagine the poem as inscribed upon a roll — Thomas connects the poem's presence to its mystically encoded eroticism.

Thomas of Hales is indulging in a game that for him has a serious and sacred meaning. In knowing Christ to be the Word incarnate, he infuses the lyric with God's divine presence — by means of punning verbal signs, a Cross inscribed in the center, and perhaps even the document's physical shape. For himself he fashions a complex and aesthetically fascinating role. He is poet, friar-confessor, holy messenger, and go-

---

[16]The motif appears in *The Bird with Four Feathers*, another poem edited in this volume. On the tradition, see A. C. Spearing, "Central and Displaced Sovereignty in Three Medieval Poems," *Review of English Studies*, n.s. 33 (1982), 247–61.

[17]The cross holds a talismanic power in *Ancrene Wisse* and two of the fourteenth-century poems edited in this volume: *The Dispute between Mary and the Cross* and *The Four Leaves of the Truelove*. The practice is discussed in the introductions to those poems.

between for God. Unlike the fluctuating, yet simply dual, positionings of reader and narrator in the later poem *In a Valley of This Restless Mind*,[18] which portrays the soul's wooing as directly from God, the author of *Love Rune* enters as a *third party* — the religious advisor — who joins together as in marriage the two lovers, eager Bridegroom and modest bride. Thomas's interest here shades into a kind of voyeurism, especially when he colors his language with explicit, gendered images of heterosexual love. He not only leads the maiden to her Truelove; he provides verbal enticements to the act of lovemaking.

What is ultimately most interesting about Thomas's construction of *Love Rune* is the care with which he provides solutions to the veiled secrets in the poem. Despite modern obscurity, none of the double signifiers is truly hidden. If one is able to read in the frame the delicacy of the relationship between a male spiritual advisor and a female charge, and if one understands the mystic state to which a virgin's body was thought to give access, the rune quickly yields its secrets. Words like *cuthe* and *witen* recur in modulated contexts that add nuance to each repetition. The reference to a roll occurs *in* the poem, so that reading the verses from a book like Jesus College MS 29 does not alter how one would come to apprehend the love song in its mystic figural form.[19]

It appears, moreover, that the incipit is part of the original poem, because Thomas puns upon his own identity as a friar. Were it not for the incipit, this reference would be private between himself and the maiden — and entirely lost to future readers. In lines 121–24 the poet depicts the fortitude of Christ's mansion, which "stands upon a fine hill / Where it shall never fall, / Nor may any *miner* (or friar *Minor*) ever undermine it, / Or cause the foundation to give way." The word translated "undermine" is *underwrot*, so that embedded in the double meaning is a humble apology for Thomas's meager writing. Neither may a military miner tunnel under God's fortress (a sexual image, since the fortress is also the castle of the virgin's body), nor may a friar Minor falsify through poor writing the worthiness of God. Thomas implicitly identifies himself with the unworthy miner who might try but would fail to solace the maiden's love-longing.

Thomas of Hales wrote what is now the first known English Franciscan lyric. As it turns out, the stroke of luck that records this fact may be due not only to the diligence of a scribe but also to the precision of the poet, who fashioned of his own

---

[18]Edited in this volume.

[19]The poem is also referenced as a song in the text and in the incipit. This reference, like the one to a document roll, participates in the poet's extensive allusions to Revelations. On the poem as a *cantus* on an unsealed roll, see notes to lines 194–202, 196, and 203.

Franciscanism both the mode and the meaning for a mystical love-song, one that deftly masquerades as a private missive from a man to a woman.

Note on the Edited Text

The presentation of *Love Rune* in eight-line stanzas (210 lines) follows modern convention. The layout in Jesus 29 appears to indicate a somewhat different perception of the poem's line length by the scribe, who copies Thomas's poem in one hundred and five *double* lines, the beginning of each stanza marked by a colored capital. The scribe has, moreover, positioned the poem so that its midpoint (lines 99–100/MS 50) occurs at the bottom of the middle verso, and the compliment to Henry III (lines 101–02/MS 51) occurs at the top of the middle recto. The poet probably conceived of the rune as one hundred lines in length (twenty-five stanzas) plus a five-line coda (balanced spatially by the incipit). As with the inscribed Cross, a central number fifty would reflect the Crucifixion, that is, Christ's five wounds. This actual layout may indicate that the original poem was planned for inscription in a manuscript, which suggests, further, that the reference to a roll is primarily figurative.

Select Bibliography

Manuscript

Oxford, Jesus College MS 29, Part II, fols. 187a–188b. C. 1270. [Franciscan miscellany of Anglo-Norman and English texts with some Latin.]

Editions

Brown, Carleton, ed. *English Lyrics of the XIIIth Century.* Oxford: Clarendon, 1932. Pp. xxiv, 68–74, 198–99.

Dickins, Bruce, and R. M. Wilson, eds. *Early Middle English Texts.* New York: Norton, 1951. Pp. 103–09, 216–20.

Dunn, Charles W., and Edward T. Byrnes, eds. *Middle English Literature.* Second ed. New York: Garland, 1990. Pp. 156–362.

Introduction

Kaiser, Rolf, ed. *Medieval English: An Old and Middle English Anthology*. Third ed. Berlin: Rolf Kaiser, 1958. Pp. 219-21.

Morris, Richard, ed. *An Old English Miscellany*. EETS o.s. 49. 1872; rpt. New York: Greenwood, 1969. Pp. 93-99.

Edited Extracts

Cook, A. S., ed. *A Literary Middle English Reader*. Boston: Ginn, 1915. Pp. 239-40. [7 stanzas.]

Manly, John Matthews, ed. *English Poetry (1170-1892)*. Boston: Ginn, 1907. Pp. 10-12. [17 stanzas.]

Sisam, Celia, and Kenneth Sisam, eds. *The Oxford Book of Medieval English Verse*. Oxford: Clarendon, 1970. P. 13. [2 stanzas.]

Translations

Fr. Cuthbert, O. S. F. C., trans. In *A Mediæval Anthology*. Ed. Mary G. Segar. London: Longmans, Green, 1915. Pp. 49-55. [19 stanzas.]

Pancoast, Henry S., trans. In *Medieval English Prose and Verse*. Ed. Roger Sherman Loomis and Rudolph Willard. New York: Appleton-Century-Crofts, 1948. Pp. 63-65. [16 stanzas.]

Stone, Brian, trans. *Medieval English Verse*. Second ed. New York: Penguin, 1971. Pp. 51-56.

Weston, Jessie L., trans. *The Chief Middle English Poets: Selected Poems*. Boston: Houghton Mifflin, 1914. Pp. 343-45.

Textual Commentary

Holthausen, F. "Zu Morris' Old English Miscellany." *Archiv für das Studium der Neueren Sprachen und Literaturen* 8 (1892), 369-70.

Thomas of Hales's Other Known Works

Horrall, Sarah, ed. *The Lyf of Oure Lady: The ME Translation of Thomas of Hales' Vita sancte Marie*. Middle English Texts 17. Heidelberg: Carl Winter, 1985. [Latin life of Mary.]

Legge, M. Dominica, ed. "The Anglo-Norman Sermon of Thomas of Hales." *Modern Language Review* 30 (1935), 212–18.

Related Latin Works

Aelred of Rievaulx. "Rule of Life for a Recluse." Trans. Mary Paul Macpherson. In *Treatises; The Pastoral Prayer*. Cistercian Fathers Series 2. Spencer, Mass.: Cistercian Publications, 1971. Pp. 43–102. [Prose treatise on the anchoritic life by a twelfth-century English Cistercian abbot, written as a letter to his recluse sister.]

Albertus Magnus. *Book of Minerals*. Trans. Dorothy Wyckoff. Oxford: Clarendon, 1967. [A lapidary.]

Aldhelm. *De virginitate*. Trans. Michael Lapidge and Michael Herren. In *Aldhelm: The Prose Works*. Cambridge: D. S. Brewer, 1979. Pp. 51–132. [Prose treatise on virginity by a sixth- to seventh-century English abbot, written as a letter to the nuns of Barking Abbey.]

Grosseteste, Robert. *Templum Dei*. Ed. Joseph Goering and F. A. C. Mantello. Toronto: Pontifical Institute of Mediaeval Studies, 1984.

Hugh of Saint Victor. *Selected Spiritual Writings*. Trans. a Religious of the Community of St. Mary the Virgin. Intro. Aelred Squire. London: Faber and Faber, 1962.

Osbert of Clare. *Letters*. Ed. W. W. Williamson. London: Oxford University Press, 1929. Pp. 135–53. [Letters 40 and 41 on virginity; author was a twelfth-century prior of Westminster.]

Life of Christina of Markyate: A Twelfth Century Recluse. Ed. and trans. C. H. Talbot. Oxford: Clarendon, 1959. [Narrative of twelfth-century Englishwoman dedicated to Christ who escapes her family's desire to have her married.]

Introduction

Related Middle English Works Earlier than *Love Rune*

Prose works composed 1200–25, printed in Anne Savage and Nicholas Watson, eds. and trans., *Anchoritic Spirituality: "Ancrene Wisse" and Associated Works* (New York: Paulist Press, 1991). Individual works are:

Ancrene Wisse. Pp. 41–207. [A rule for anchoresses.]

Holy Maidenhood. Pp. 223–43. [Argues for virginity by showing the ills of marriage.]

Saint Juliana. Pp. 306–21.

Saint Katherine. Pp. 259–84.

Saint Margaret. Pp. 288–305.

Sawles Warde. Pp. 209–21. [Allegory of the body as castle of the soul, drawn from Hugh of Saint Victor's *De anima.*]

Wooing of Our Lord. Pp. 245–57. [Love song to Jesus.]

Related Middle English Works Contemporary with *Love Rune*

Select contents of Oxford, Jesus College MS 29, printed in Richard Morris, ed. *An Old English Miscellany*, EETS o.s. 49 (1872; rpt. New York: Greenwood, 1969). Individual works are:

A Litel Soth Sermon. Pp. 187, 189, 191.

A Moral Ode. Pp. 58–71.

An Orison of Our Lord. Pp. 139–41.

Death. Pp. 169–85 [alternating with text from MS Cotton Caligulo A.ix].

Doomsday. Pp. 163, 165, 167, 169.

Long Life. Pp. 157, 159.

On Serving Christ. Pp. 90–92. [Precedes *Love Rune.*]

The Annunciation of the Virgin Mary. P. 100. [Follows *Love Rune.*]

The Passion of Our Lord. Pp. 37–57.

The Castle of Love. Ed. Kari Sajavaara. "The Middle English Translations of Robert Grosseteste's *Chateau d'Amour.*" *Mémoires de la société néophilologique de Helsinki* 32 (1967), 5–434. [Original poem composed in Anglo-Norman, c. 1230–53; translated into English c. 1300.]

The Harley Lyrics. Ed. G. L. Brook. Fourth ed. Manchester: Manchester University Press, 1968.

Love Rune

The Owl and the Nightingale. Ed. J. H. G. Grattan and G. F. H. Sykes. EETS o.s. 119. 1935; rpt. Millwood, N. Y.: Kraus, 1975. [Appears in Jesus College MS 29.]

The Thrush and the Nightingale. Ed. Carleton Brown. In *English Lyrics of the XIIIth Century*. Oxford: Clarendon, 1932. Pp. 101–08, 207–08.

Were Beth They biforen Us Weren. Ed. Carleton Brown. In *English Lyrics of the XIIIth Century*. Oxford: Clarendon, 1932. Pp. 85–87, 202–03.

Related Middle English Works Later than *Love Rune*

A Talking of the Love of God. Ed. Carl Horstmann. In *Yorkshire Writers*. Vol. 2. London: Swan Sonnenschein, 1896. Pp. 345–66. [Fourteenth-century descendent of *The Wooing of Our Lord*; appears in Vernon MS.]

The Four Leaves of the Truelove. Printed in this volume. [Fourteenth-century stanzaic alliterative poem; a maiden is counseled to seek God instead of an earthly lover.]

Of Clene Maydenhod. Ed. F. J. Furnivall. In *The Minor Poems of the Vernon Manuscript*. Vol 2. EETS o.s. 117. 1901; rpt. New York: Greenwood, 1969. Pp. 464–68. [Fourteenth-century descendent of *A Love Rune*; appears in Vernon MS.]

Pearl. Ed. E. V. Gordon. Oxford: Clarendon, 1953. [Important fouteenth-century poem, with imagery of gems, brides of Christ, and virginity.]

Criticism of *Love Rune*

Bloomfield, Morton W. "Thomas of Hales' 'A Love Rune' (1250–1270): A Christian Didactic Poem." In *Europäische Lehrdichtung: Festschrift für Walter Naumann zum 70. Geburtstag*. Ed. Hans Gerd Rötzer and Herbert Walz. Darmstadt: Wissenschaftliche Buchgesellschaft, 1981. Pp. 49–60.

Brewer, Derek. *English Gothic Literature*. New York: Schocken, 1983. Pp. 44–45.

Cambridge History of English Literature. Cambridge: Cambridge University Press, 1907. Pp. 258–59.

Introduction

D'Angelo, Benito, O. F. M. "English Franciscan Poetry before Geoffrey Chaucer (1340?–1400)." Trans. Luke M. Ciampi, O. F. M. *Franciscan Studies* 21 (1983), 218–60, especially 229, 235–39.

Hill, Betty. "The 'Luue-Ron' and Thomas de Hales." *Modern Language Review* 59 (1964), 321–30.

Horrall, Sarah. "Thomas of Hales, O. F. M.: His Life and Works." *Traditio* 42 (1986), 287–98.

Kane, George. *Middle English Literature: A Critical Study of the Romances, the Religious Lyrics, "Piers Plowman."* London: Methuen, 1951. Pp. 116–17.

Levy, Bernard S. "The Annunciation in Thomas de Hales' *Love Ron*." *Mediaevalia* 6 (1980), 123–34.

Manning, Stephen. *Wisdom and Number: Toward a Critical Appraisal of the Middle English Religious Lyric.* Lincoln: University of Nebraska Press, 1962. Pp. 122–24.

Pearsall, Derek. *Old English and Middle English Poetry.* London: Routledge & Kegan Paul, 1977. Pp. 97, 141.

Rogers, William Elford. *Images and Abstractions: Six Middle English Religious Lyrics.* *Anglistica* 18. Copenhagen: Rosenkilde and Bagger, 1972. Pp. 22–40.

Saintsbury, George. *A History of English Prosody from the Twelfth Century to the Present Day.* Vol. 1. London: Macmillan, 1906. P. 56.

Schofield, William. *English Literature from the Norman Conquest to Chaucer.* Second ed. 1931; rpt. New York: Phaeton Press, 1969. Pp. 439–40.

Swanton, Michael. *English Literature before Chaucer.* London: Longman, 1987. Pp. 246–49.

Wells, John Edwin. "'A Luue Ron' and 'Of Clene Maydenhod.'" *Modern Language Review* 9 (1914), 236–37.

––––––. *A Manual of the Writings in Middle English, 1050–1400.* New Haven: Yale University Press, 1916. Pp. 390, 406, 529–30, 852.

Woolf, Rosemary. *The English Religious Lyric in the Middle Ages*. Oxford: Clarendon, 1968. Pp. 61–62.

Related Studies

Atkinson, Clarissa. "'Precious Balm in a Fragile Glass': The Ideology of Virginity in the Later Middle Ages." *Journal of Family History* 8 (1983), 131–43.

Bloch, R. Howard. "The Poetics of Virginity." In *Medieval Misogyny*. Chicago: University of Chicago Press, 1991. Pp. 93–112.

Brown, Peter. *The Body and Society: Men, Women, and Sexual Renunciation in Early Christianity*. New York: Columbia University Press, 1988.

Bugge, John. *Virginitas: An Essay in the History of a Medieval Ideal*. The Hague: Martinus Nijhoff, 1975.

Coakley, John. "Friars as Confidants of Holy Women in Medieval Dominican Hagiography." In *Images of Sainthood in Medieval Europe*. Ed. Renate Blumenfeld-Kosinski and Timea Szell. Ithaca: Cornell University Press, 1991. Pp. 222–46.

———. "Friars, Sanctity, and Gender: Mendicant Encounters with Saints, 1250–1325." In *Medieval Masculinities: Regarding Men in the Middle Ages*. Ed. Clare A. Lees. Minneapolis: University of Minnesota Press, 1994. Pp. 91–110.

Constable, Giles. "Aelred of Rievaulx and the Nun of Watton: An Episode in the Early History of the Gilbertine Order." In *Medieval Women*. Ed. Derek Baker. Oxford: Basil Blackwell, 1978. Pp. 205–26.

Cornelius, Roberta D. *The Figurative Castle: A Study in the Medieval Allegory of the Edifice with Especial Reference to Religious Writings*. Bryn Mawr: Bryn Mawr College, 1930.

Elkins, Sharon K. *Holy Women of Twelfth-Century England*. Chapel Hill: University of North Caroline Press, 1988.

Fein, Susanna Greer. "Maternity in Aelred of Rievaulx's Letter to His Sister." In *Medieval Mothering*. Ed. John Carmi Parsons and Bonnie Wheeler. The New Middle Ages 3. New York: Garland Press, 1996. Pp. 139–56.

Introduction

Hill, Betty. "The History of Jesus College, Oxford MS. 29." *Medium Ævum* 32 (1963), 203–13.

Jeffrey, David L. *The Early English Lyric and Franciscan Sprituality.* Lincoln: University of Nebraska Press, 1975.

Legge, M. Dominica. *Anglo-Norman Literature and Its Background.* Oxford: Clarendon, 1963. Pp. 114, 227–28, 351.

McGinn, Bernard. "The Language of Love in Christian and Jewish Mysticism." In *Mysticism and Language.* Ed. Stephen T. Katz. Oxford: Oxford University Press, 1992. Pp. 202–35.

McLaughlin, Eleanor Commo. "Equality of Souls, Inequality of Sexes: Woman in Medieval Theology." In *Religion and Sexism.* Ed. Rosemary Radford Reuther. New York: Simon and Schuster, 1974. Pp. 213–66.

Millett, Bella. "Women in No Man's Land: English Recluses and the Development of Vernacular Literature." In *Women and Literature in Britain, 1150–1500.* Ed. Carol M. Meale. Cambridge: Cambridge University Press, 1993. Pp. 86–103.

Newman, Barbara. *From Virile Woman to WomanChrist: Studies in Medieval Religion and Literature.* Philadelphia: University of Pennsylvania Press, 1995.

Robertson, Elizabeth. *Early English Devotional Prose and the Female Audience.* Knoxville: University of Tennessee Press, 1990.

Steinberg, Leo. *The Sexuality of Christ in Renaissance Art and in Modern Oblivion.* New York: Pantheon/October, 1983.

Wogan-Browne, Jocelyn. "The Virgin's Tale." In *Feminist Readings in Middle English Literature: The Wife of Bath and All Her Sect.* Ed. Ruth Evans and Lesley Johnson. London: Routledge, 1994. Pp. 165–94.

Woolf, Rosemary. "The Theme of Christ the Lover-Knight in Medieval English Literature." *Review of English Studies*, n.s. 13 (1962), 1–16.

Love Rune

Incipit quidam cantus quem composuit frater Thomas de Hales de ordine fratrum Minorum ad instanciam cuiusdam puelle Deo dicate. [1]

	A mayde Cristes me bit yorne	*of Christ earnestly asked me*
	That Ich hire wurche a luve ron,	*make a love rune (see note)*
	For hwan heo myhte best ileorne	*By which she; learn*
	To taken onother soth lefmon,	*true lover*
5	That treowest were of alle berne,	*men*
	And best wyte cuthe a freo wymmon. [2]	
	Ich hire nule nowiht werne,	*I will not at all deny her*
	Ich hire wule teche as Ic con.	*as I am able*
	Mayde, her thu myht biholde	*here you*
10	This worldes luve nys bute o res,	*is nothing but a rash delirium*
	And is byset so felevolde,	*beset with manifold [evil]*
	Vikel and frakel, and wok and les.	*Fickle; vile; weak; false*
	Theos theines that her weren bolde	*These thanes (i.e., men); here*
	Beoth aglyden so wyndes bles;	*Have passed away like a gust of wind*
15	Under molde hi liggeth colde,	*earth they lie*
	And faleweth so doth medewe gres.	*wither like meadow grass*
	Nis no mon iboren olyve	*There is no man born alive*
	That her may beon studevest,	*here; be steadfast*
	For her he haveth seorewen ryve,	*many sorrows*
20	Ne tyt him never ro ne rest;	*Nor does he ever attain peace or rest*
	Toward his ende he hyeth blyve,	*hastens quickly*
	And lutle hwile he her ilest;	*a short while; endures*
	Pyne and deth him wile ofdryve	*Suffering; drive away*
	Hwenne he weneth to libben best.	*When he hopes to prosper*

---

[1] *Here begins a certain song which Brother Thomas of Hales of the order of Minorites composed at the request of a young girl dedicated to God*

[2] *And best able to protect (or advise) a noblewoman (see note)*

Love Rune

25	Nis non so riche, ne non so freo,	*none so powerful; noble*
	That he ne schal heonne sone away!	*soon [go] away from here*
	Ne may hit never his waraunt beo	*warrant [against death]*
	Gold ne seolver, vouh ne gray;	*fancy variegated nor gray fur*
	Ne beo he no the swift, ne may he fleo,	*Be he never so swift; flee [death]*
30	Ne weren his lif enne day —	*Nor guard his life a single day*
	Thus is thes world, as thu mayht seo,	
	Al so the schadewe that glyt away!	*Entirely like; glides*

	This world fareth hwilynde:	*changes constantly*
	Hwenne on cumeth, another goth;	*When one*
35	That wes bifore nu is bihynde;	*[He] Who was ahead now*
	That er was leof nu hit is loth.	*Who once was beloved now is despised*
	Forthi he doth as the blynde	*Therefore; acts*
	That in this world his luve doth;	*Who; seeks*
	Ye mowen iseo the world aswynde —	*may see; languish*
40	That wouh goth forth, abak that soth!	*While grief advances, truth retreats*

	Theo luve that ne may her abyde,	*The love; abide*
	Thu treowest hire myd muchel wouh	*You trust it with; grief*
	Al so hwenne hit schal toglide —	*Until the time when it shall pass*
	Hit is fals and mereuh and frouh	*unstable; weak*
45	And fromward in uychon tide!	*unruly; each season*
	Hwile hit lesteth is seorewe inouh;	*lasts; sorrow enough*
	An ende, ne werie mon so syde,	
	He schal todreosen so lef on bouh.[1]	

	Monnes luve nys buten o stunde:	*lasts but a fleeting moment*
50	Nu he luveth, nu he is sed,	*Now; tired (of his love)*
	Nu he cumeth, nu wile he funde,	*depart*
	Nu he is wroth, nu he is gled;	*angry; glad*
	His luve is her, and ek alunde;	*also elsewhere*
	Nu he luveth sum that he er bed;	*formerly fought*
	Nis he never treowe ifunde —	*found to be true*
55	That him tristeth, he is amed!	*Whoever; trusts; mad*

---

[1] *In the end, however thoroughly a person may guard [himself], / He shall die like a leaf on a bough*

Love Rune

	Yf mon is riche of worldes weole,	*worldly good fortune*
	Hit maketh his heorte smerte and ake;	*smart and ache*
	If he dret that me him stele,	*dreads; someone will rob him*
60	Thenne doth him pyne nyhtes wake.	*worry keeps him awake at night*
	Him waxeth thouhtes, monye and fele,	*His thoughts grow; numerous*
	Hw he hit may witen, withuten sake.	*How; protect; sin*
	An ende hwat helpeth hit to hele?	*In the end conceal*
	Al deth hit wile from him take.	*death will take all of it*
65	Hwer is Paris and Heleyne	
	That weren so bryht and feyre on bleo?	*beautiful and fair in face*
	Amadas and Ideyne,	*Idoine*
	Tristram, Yseude, and alle theo?	*those*
	Ector with his scharpe meyne,	*powerful strength*
70	And Cesar riche of wordes feo?	*worldly wealth*
	Heo beoth iglyden ut of the reyne	*They have vanished; dominion*
	So the schef is of the cleo.	*Just as the sheaf is [cut] by the scythe*
	Hit is of heom al so hit nere,	*It is as if they never were*
	Of heom me haveth wunder itold.	*wonders have been told to me*
75	Nere hit reuthe for to here	*Is it not a pity to hear*
	Hw hi were with pyne aquold,	*painfully killed*
	And hwat hi tholeden alyve here?	*they suffered [while]*
	Al is heore hot iturnd to cold —	*their; turned*
	Thus is thes world of false fere!	*appearance*
80	Fol he is the on hire is bold.	*Foolish is he who here is bold*
	Theyh he were so riche mon	*Although; as powerful*
	As Henry ure kyng,	*Henry III (1216–72)*
	And al so veyr as Absalon,	*just as fair as*
	That nevede on eorthe non evenyng,	*never had; an equal*
85	Al were sone his prute agon;	*pride*
	Hit nere on ende wrth on heryng!	*In the end it was not worth a herring*
	Mayde, if thu wilnest after leofmon,	*long for a lover*
	Ich teche the enne treowe king.	*will teach you about a*
	A! Swete, if thu ikneowe	*knew*
90	The gode thewes of thisse childe —	*qualities*
	He is feyr and bryht on heowe,	*in appearance*

34

Love Rune

Of glede chere, of mode mylde,   *countenance; temperament*
Of lufsum lost, of truste treowe,   *amorous desire*
Freo of heorte, of wisdom wilde —   *Noble; strong of wisdom*
95 Ne thurhte the never reowe   *You would never regret it*
Myhtestu do the in His ylde!   *Were you to put yourself; protection*

He is ricchest mon of londe,
So wide so mon speketh with muth;   *As far as men speak with mouths*
Alle heo beoth to His honde,   *All are at His command*
100 Est and west, north and suth!
Henri, King of Engelonde,
Of Hym he halt and to Hym buhth.[1]
Mayde, to the He send His sonde,   *you; message (or messenger)*
And wilneth for to beo the cuth.   *desires to be known by you*

105 Ne byt He with the lond ne leode,
Vouh ne gray ne rencyan;[2]
Naveth He therto none neode,   *He has no need to do so*
He is riche and weli mon!   *powerful; prosperous*
If thu Him woldest luve beode,   *grant*
110 And bycumen His leovemon,
He broughte the to suche wede   *would bring you to; wedding*
That naveth king ne kayser non!   *As never had; emperor*

Hwat spekestu of eny bolde   *temple*
That wrouhte the wise Salomon   *was constructed by*
115 Of jaspe, of saphir, of merede golde, *jasper; sapphire; refined*
And of mony onother ston?
Hit is feyrure of feolevolde —[3]
More than Ich eu telle con!   *am able to tell you*
This bold, Mayde, the is bihote   *mansion; to you is promised*
120 If that thu bist His leovemon.   *become; lover*

---

[1] *He (Henry) holds [power] from God and bows to Him*

[2] *He asks with thee (i.e., in dowry) neither lands nor people, / Nor fancy furs or fine cloth*

[3] *It (i.e., the dwelling God will give you) is fairer by many times*

35

Love Rune

Hit stont uppon a treowe mote   *fine hill*
Thar hit never truke ne schal,   *Where; fall*
Ne may no mynur hire underwrot,
Ne never false thene grundwal;[1]
125   Tharinne is uich balewes bote,   *remedy for every sorrow*
Blisse and joye, and gleo and gal!   *mirth and song*
This bold, Mayde, is the bihote   *dwelling place; promised you*
And uych o blisse thar wythal.   *every; beyond that*

Ther ne may no freond fleon other,   *friend leave another*
130   Ne non furleosen his iryhte;   *lose his rights*
Ther nys hate, ne wreththe nouther,   *anger*
Of prude ne of onde of none wihte.   *pride; ill will*
Alle heo schule wyth engles pleye,   *Ultimately they; angels*
Some and sauhte in heovene lyhte.   *United and reconciled*
135   Ne beoth heo, Mayde, in gode weye
That wel luveth ure Dryhte?   *Lord*

Ne may no mon Hine iseo   *see Him*
Al so He is in His mihte   *Entirely as*
That may withuten blisse beo;   *Who*
140   Hwanne he isihth ure Drihte,   *sees*
His sihte is al joye and gleo!   *gladness*
He is day wythute nyhte!
Nere he, Mayde, ful freo   *privileged*
That myhte wunye myd such a knyghte?   *dwell with*

145   He haveth bitauht the o tresur   *committed to you one treasure*
That is betere than gold other pel,   *or fine cloth*
And bit the luke thine bur,   *bids you lock (look after); bower*
And wilneth that thu hit wyte wel.   *desires; you guard (know) it well*
Wyth theove, with revere, with lechur,   *Against thief; robber; lecher*
150   Thu most beo waker and snel —   *alert and vigilant*
Thu art swetture thane eny flur   *sweeter; flower*
Hwile thu witest thene kastel.   *defend your castle*

---

[1] *No miner may ever undermine it (her) / Nor cause the foundation to give way (or, no Minorite may falsify it through his meager writing — see note)*

36

Love Rune

	Hit is ymston of feor iboren —	*gemstone borne from afar*
	Nys non betere under heovene grunde;	*the lowest part of heaven*
155	He is tofore alle othre icoren;	*It (He); before all others chosen*
	He heleth alle luve wunde.	*heals*
	Wel were alyve iboren	
	That myhte wyten this ilke stunde,	
	For habbe thu hine enes forloren,	
160	Ne byth he never eft ifunde.[1]	

	This ilke ston that Ich the nemne	*describe for you*
	"Maydenhod" icleoped is.	*"Virginity"; is called*
	Hit is o derewurthe gemme,	*a precious*
	Of alle othre, he berth that pris,[2]	
165	And bryngeth the withute wemme	*without blemish*
	Into the blysse of paradis.	
	The hwile thu hyne witest under thine hemme,[3]	
	Thu ert swetture than eny spis.	*You are sweeter than any spice*

	Hwat spekstu of eny stone	*What may you say*
170	That beoth in vertu other in grace —	*That possesses power or grace*
	Of amatiste, of calcydone,	*amethyst; chalcedony*
	Of lectorie and tupace,	*cock-stone; topaz*
	Of jaspe, of saphir, of sardone,	*sardonyx*
	Smaragde, beril, and crisopace?	*Emerald; beryl; chrysoprase*
175	Among alle othre ymstone,	*gemstones*
	Thes beoth deorre in uyche place.	*precious; every*

	Mayde, al so Ich the tolde,	*as I have told you*
	The ymston of thi bur	*your bower*
	He is betere an hundredfolde	
180	Than alle theos in heore culur;	*their colors*
	He is idon in heovene golde,	*set in the gold of heaven*
	And is ful of fyn amur.	*refined love*

---

[1] *Fortunate are [they who are] born alive / Who might this same condition guard (know) / For once you have lost it (Him), / It (He) is never found again*

[2] *Among all others, it (He) bears the prize (i.e., is the best)*

[3] *While you guard it (know Him) under your skirt*

Love Rune

Alle that myhte hine wite scholde,   *who; guard it (know Him) shoula [do so]*
He schyneth so bryht in heovene bur!   *bower of heaven*

185 Hwen thu me dost in thine rede   *asked my advice*
For the to cheose a leofmon,
Ich wile don, as thu me bede,   *wish to select; asked*
The beste that Ich fynde con;
Ne doth he, Mayde, on uvele dede
190 That may cheose of two that on,
And he wile withute neode
Take thet wurse, the betere let gon? [1]

This rym, Mayde, Ich the sende,
Open and withute sel.   *Openly; seal*
195 Bidde Ic that thu hit untrende,   *I request; unroll*
And leorny bute bok uych del
Herof that thu beo swithe hende. [2]
And tech hit other maydenes wel:
Hwoso cuthe hit to than ende,   *Whoever knows it to the end*
200 Hit wolde him stonde muchel stel.   *afford him much help*

Hwenne thu sittest in longynge,
Drauh the forth this ilke wryt: *Draw forth this same writ*
Mid swete stephne thu hit singe,   *Sing it with a sweet voice*
And do al so hit the byt.   *everything as it directs you*
205 To the he haveth send one gretynge: *you*
God Almyhti the beo myd,   *be with you*
And leve cumen to His brudthinge   *allow [you] to come to His bridal*
Heye in heovene, ther He sit!
And yeve him god endynge   *give*
210 That haveth iwryten this ilke wryt. Amen.

---

[1] *Does he not [commit], Maiden, an evil deed, / Who may choose one of two things, / If he should, without need, / Pick the worse [of the two] and neglect the better?*

[2] *And learn each part of it without book (i.e., memorize it) / So that you may be very expert in [knowing] it*

Notes

Abbreviations:

MS   Oxford, Jesus College MS 29.
M   Morris edition (1872).
B   Brown edition (1932).
DW   Dickins and Wilson edition (1951).
K   Kaiser edition (1958).
DB   Dunn and Byrnes edition (1990).

Oxford, Jesus College MS 29 is the sole record for *Love Rune*. Each stanza, written in double lines, begins with an enlarged capital. These initials alternate in color, red or blue. After the incipit in red, the poem begins midway on a recto, fills a verso/recto opening, and ends midway on the next verso. The last ten lines are copied as one stanza in five lines. Inscribed by a thirteenth-century scribe who writes in a neat, compact hand, the poem is occasionally corrected by a later hand. The following notes record the second hand's corrections and the relatively few emendations and variant readings in the five editions.

1   *mayde Cristes*. The phrase meaning "Christ's maid" is synonymous with *puella Deo dicate* in the Latin heading. What these phrases indicate of the woman's status is uncertain, except that she is a virgin. If she was a real person, she may have been a nun — a Minoress or Poor Clare (Hill [1964], p. 321; D'Angelo, p. 237), a lay recluse (Millett, pp. 97–98), or merely a pious laywoman under the friar's instruction. Bloomfield remarks that the maiden "may be no one at all but a poetic construct" (p. 55). For another possibility, see the note to line 4, and for a discussion of the circumstance stated in the incipit and this stanza, see the Introduction to *Love Rune*. The gendered context of the work — pious instruction from a religious man to a woman in need of guidance — has a long tradition; such works often focus on the subject of virginity; see Newman, pp. 19–45.

2   *luve ron*. The exact meaning is uncertain. *Ron* ("rune") would seem to combine a range of senses: "song," "message," "secret," and "riddle"; the whole phrase *luve ron* suggests a private message between lovers or a love poem with a

private meaning. The phrase *luve runes* is the translation of Latin *amatoria carmina* in *The Life of Saint Katherine* (ed. Eugen Einenkel, EETS, o.s. 80 [1884; repr. Millwood, N. Y.: Kraus, 1975], p. 7). The poet's plan to "wurche" a love rune suggests the intricacy of verbal composition in interlocked rhyme and sense, and it hints at a secret message to discover. In *The Harley Lyrics* (ed. Brook) the word *roune* appears four times as a noun: a love song (4.38, p. 33); a song that pleases women (6.62, p. 36); a birdsong, seen as amorous and cryptic, and animal sounds, seen as secretive (11.2, 11.29, pp. 43–44; according to Peter Heidtmann, "the hidden meaning of audible sounds" ["The *Reverdie* Convention and 'Lenten is Come with Love to Toune,'" *Annuale Mediaevale* 12 (1971), 88]). It also appears twice as a verb: the reader's whispered naming of the poet's lover, which is hidden in a pun (3.30, p. 32); the private sweet-talking whispers between men and women (6.41, p. 36). A later alliterative poem, *Summer Sunday*, also calls its own form runic (ed. R. H. Robbins, *Historical Poems of the XIVth and XVth Centuries* [New York: Columbia University Press, 1959], p. 100).

Only a few commentators have given close attention to what the term means in this poem. For Bloomfield, *luve ron* suggests a hidden "wisdom" within a framed structure, something to be unlocked like the treasure of virginity itself (pp. 59–60; on the gnostic concept that virginity confers knowledge of God, see Bugge, pp. 120–22). Levy believes that the poem is a veiled message in likeness to the Annunciation (p. 125; see notes to lines 103 and 205). The rune is elucidated in several of the following notes. See especially notes to lines 100, 123, 127, 153–84, 167, 181, 189–92, and 194–202.

4   *onother soth lefmon.* This phrase sets up the situation as if it were ordinary, but the word *onother* is startling after the poet has stated the maiden's dedication to Christ. One wonders if the phrase *mayde Cristes* has a generic, neutral meaning, that is, "virgin made in the image of Christ" (see note to line 1). That the virgin should so much as express a desire not directed to God reveals her virginal status to be endangered (Bloch, pp. 97–101).

5   *treowest.* First *t* is interlined by the second hand.

6   *wyte cuthe.* The language is very ambiguous. M and B take the phrase *wyte cuthe* as an infinitive plus a past participle as adjective, "best able to keep (or guard) a noblewoman," an adjectival phrase in parallel with *treowest* (so Swanton, p. 246). As a verb *witen* has two quite different meanings ("guard, keep, preserve" and "know, advise"), and either may be meant here. Punning

upon both verbs occurs in lines 148, 152, 158, 167 (note), and 183. Another interpretation would read *wyte* as a noun ("advisor") and *cuthe* as the past participle, "best advisor known to a noblewoman." (In a reading close to this one, Stone takes *wyte* as the noun *wight*, "man," but the spelling is improbable; compare *wihte* at line 132.)

The word *cuthe* suggests, in the courtly language of the poem, a friendly acquaintance with the potential for amorous intimacy. It is used in a similar way at line 104, to refer to Christ's wooing desire to be *cuth* by the maiden. At line 199, it is the poem itself that should be *cuthe* to the end, that is, known by heart. The word appears to be used thrice strategically — at beginning, middle, and end — to develop a theme of how one may know God through words and desire. See *MED connen* v., senses 3–5.

The ambiguity of the phrase *wyte cuthe* is important, for it initiates a theme — the desire for "knowing" through counsel or experience — even as it shows that received wisdom is difficult to unlock. The phrase is very hard to pin down because it is made to comprehend several possible meanings: the advising role of Thomas, the possessive or protective role of a husband or of God, the need to guard something the woman has (virginity), and the potential of someone sexually "knowing" her.

6   *freo*. Best translated "noble," as DW suggest: "The virgin addressed is obviously a nun, who in the ME period would almost certainly be of gentle birth" (p. 217). Another meaning may, however, be present — "free, unattached" — since Thomas seems to be inviting the question of why a woman dedicated to Christ would seek *onother soth lefmon* (see note to line 4). The word recurs in different contexts at lines 25, 94, and perhaps 143 (an emendation; see note).

13   *theines*. Means "men" generically, but, with its primary sense "servants, attendants," it implies men who are subject to higher authority (God or death). Compare *Death*: "Hwer beoth thine theynes / That the leoue were?" (line 177; ed. Morris, p. 179).

her. Swanton translates as "formerly," but the modern sense "here" fits this word here and in line 9.

bolde. The modern meaning "bold, proud" is primary here, but this is another word that unfolds with repetition in the poem (like *cuth*, note to line 6); it recurs at lines 80, 113 (note), 119, and 127 (note). The word has two areas of meaning that come into play: (1) the adjective describing a range of qualities generally deemed masculine: "brave, heroic, confident, forward, rash, sturdy, strong" (*MED bold* adj.); and (2) the noun for a sturdy "building, temple, stronghold" (*MED bold* n.). The word denotes male activity, implicit if not overt, here and in two Harley lyrics (ed. Brook): *The Fair Maid of Ribblesdale* (7.6, p. 37) and *An Old Man's Prayer* (13.19, p. 46); see T. L. Burton, "'The Fair Maid of Ribblesdale' and the Problem of Parody," *Essays in Criticism* 31 (1981), 288. Compare too the phallic sense of *boldhede* in *The Owl and the Nightingale*, line 514 (ed. Grattan and Sykes, p. 16).

Thus the word here may be translated "bold, proud, with masculine bravado," a meaning that underscores the futility of brazen confidence in the face of mortality.

15   Saintsbury praises Thomas of Hales's poetic skill, noting the newness of such natural versified rhythms in English:

> It is inexpressible what a joy the first occurrence of such rhythms as [line 12], of such an internal rhyme as [line 15] gives one. The very bones of an Englishman under the cold mould itself ought to start and tremble at the hearing of them. (p. 56)

20   *ro ne rest*. Written in the corrector's later hand. For the collocation, see *MED ro* n.(4), sense (b).

23   *ofdryve*. "to drive (something) away, dispel" (*MED*); this rare word, not recorded in OE, is documented only here and once in a fifteenth-century text.

24   *best*. Taking this word to modify *weneth* rather than *libben*, DW translate: "When he has the greatest expectation of life" (p. 217). The sense is very close by either interpretation.

25   *riche*. The word denotes power as well as wealth; see *MED riche* adj.

28   *vouh ne gray*. The phrase, derived from OF *vair et gris* ("variegated fur and gray fur") and common in thirteenth-century ME verse, appears several times elsewhere in Jesus College MS 29: *The Passion of Our Lord*, line 66; *A Moral Ode*, line 357; and *Doomsday*, line 28 (all ed. Morris, pp. 39, 70, 164). DW

explain that the first kind of fur comes "from the grey back and white belly of a sort of squirrel, the second from the grey back alone" (p. 197). *See MED fou* adj. as n., sense 2, and *grei* n.(2), sense (a).

30   *enne*. "a single one"; see *MED on* num., sense 4(f), "the space of one day, a single day," and compare line 88.

32   *Al so*. So MS; DW: *Al-so*; DB: *Also*. The phrase, meaning "just as, as" is written as two words here and at lines 43, 73, 83, 138, 177 and 204; see *MED also* adv., senses 4b.(b) and 5b.

33   DW offer a colloquial translation: "This world is full of ups and downs."

35   *is*. So MS; K: *hit is*.

39   *Ye*. This use of the second-person plural pronoun is unique in the poem and may be an error for *Thu*. If not, Thomas's usually intimate tone of address to the maiden is here more generalized as he expounds on the transience of life.

       aswynde. The word is from OE *aswinden*, "waste, away, perish, be ruined," as all editors agree (see also *MED*). Manning, however, would read it as the phrase *as wynde*, "as wind," and he uses it to locate six images from nature that have biblical overtones (p. 123).

43   *Al so*. So MS; DW: *Al-so*; DB: *Also*. See note to line 32.

44   *mereuh*. See *MED meruwe* adj., sense (c); this occurrence is the only one cited as a description for love ("unstable, variable"); more commonly the word is used for people ("frail").

47   *ne werie mon so syde*. Misconstruing the verb, Manly emends to *ne werie mon robe so syde*, "no matter how wide a robe a man may wear" (p. 11).

50   *sed*. MS: *sad*. The emended spelling, an attested form, is adopted for rhyme (see *MED sad* adj.). The word includes the sense "sated, satiated." DW note the break in the rhyme and suggest the emendation without actually adopting it (p. 218).

51   *funde*. For this verb, see *MED founden* v.(1), sense 2(a), "go away, depart, leave."

53   *alunde*. So B, K; MS: *a lunde*. Taking the word to be a past participle, the *MED* cites no other occurrences and compares it to the adverb *alunde*, "in the land," and the past participle *aloined*, "remote, estranged." DW provide a lengthy etymological note (p. 218).

54   *bed*. See *MED bidden* v., sense 7(d), "offer to fight, challenge."

55   *he*. So MS; B, K: *ne*.

56   *amed*. This word, derived from OE *ge-mæd(e)d*, is not recorded in texts later than 1300 (*MED amad* adj.).

57–64   The guarded treasure of this stanza is analogous to the treasure of heaven (see note to line 145) and the treasure of the maiden's virginity (lines 177–84). The wealth described here is, of course, the false kind, threatened by theft or decay (Luke 12.34).

59   *me*. "one, someone" (*MED*).

65–72   *Hwer is* . . . This stanza uses the *ubi sunt* formula ("Where are they [the great ones] now?"). Hector and Caesar are two of the nine worthies of the past, used to show the futility of worldly dominance. Thomas's emphasis is, however, on the pairs of famous worldly lovers, Paris and Helen, Amadas and Idoine, Tristram and Isolde, a focus "in consideration of his theme" (Brown, p. 199). Several commentators have praised the elegaic quality of *Love Rune*. See Woolf (1968), p. 62; Pearsall, p. 97; and Bloomfield, pp. 55–56. On the motif, see Wells (1916), pp. 389–90; Geoffrey Shepherd, "'All the Wealth of Croesus . . .': A Topic in the 'Ancren Riwle.'" *Modern Language Review* 51 (1956), 161–67; and Takami Matsuda, "The *Ubi Sunt* Passages in Middle English Literature," *Studies in English Literature* (Japan) 59 (1983), 65–81, especially 74.

67   *and Ideyne*. So DW, DB; MS: *& dideyne*, the initial *d* of *dideyne* deriving from an elision with *and*. Amadas and Idoine are the lovers of French romance. It

is possible that an adjective originally appeared before one of the names in this line. In an awkward attempt to correct the line length, M emends lines 67–68: *Amadas tristram and dideyne / yseude and all theo.*

68 *alle theo.* the sense wanted is "those" (compare *theos*, line 180), not "they" (compare lines 71, 99, 103).

69 *meyne.* For the meaning "physical strength, vigor," see *MED main* n.1.(a), the definition provided by B. DW's definition, "retinue," which DB follow, is unlikely given the context and rhyme-words (*MED meine* n.).

71 *ut of the reyne.* "out of dominion," that is, they have lost their former dominance. The *MED* cites this passage under the meaning "people of a kingdom, a king's subjects" (*regne* n., sense 2[b]), but the first meaning "sovereignty, dominion" is more appropriate to the context. Manning sees in lines 71–72 the last of six images that establish the "theme of the inevitability of natural decay, . . . the dominant theme of the first part of the poem" (p. 123).

72 *schef.* M emends this word to *scheft* and provides a far-fetched gloss for lines 71–72: "They have passed away as a shaft from the bowstring" (p. 95). Weston's translation follows this interpretation (p. 343). See, too, Holthausen's comment (p. 370).

   cleo. The meaning of this word is uncertain. The definition provided, "just as the sheaf is [cut] by the scythe" is the choice of most commentators. Bloomfield connects it to Revelations 14, the Son of Man with a sickle (pp. 56–57), which would tie the image to many other allusions to Revelations in *Love Rune.* The etymological problem is whether *cleo* derives from OE *clif, cleofu,* "hillside, clift," or from OE *clawu, clea,* "hook." Brown, perhaps following Manly, accepts the former, cites the word's appearance elsewhere in the MS (*A Moral Ode,* line 343, ed. Morris, p. 70), and translates: "as the sheaf from the hillside." This gloss is also adopted by Cook, and by Sisam and Sisam. If, as seems more likely, the word has the second derivation, there is no other documentation of its reference to a farm implement; the recorded usages signify a claw, a talon, a crosier, and an instrument of torture. See *MED claue* n.(1), sense 2.(b); Holthausen, p. 370; Kemp Malone, "Notes on Middle English Lyrics," *ELH* 2 (1935), 60; DW, p. 218.

73 *al so.* So MS; DB: *al-so;* B, DW, K: *also.* See note to line 32.

75   *here*. MS: *heren*. For this emendation, taken for the rhyme, compare the infinitive *to hele* in a rhyme position at line 63.

79   *fere*. Derived from OF *ofaire*, the word is rare in Middle English. The *MED* cites only three occurrences, this one being the earliest, the others dating from the fifteenth century (see *fere* n.[5]).

80   *the on hire is bold*. Literally translated "the one [who] here is bold." On the significance of the recurring word *bold*, see note to line 13.

82   Cook lengthens the line by inserting the word *noble* before *kyng*.

83   *al so*. So MS; DB: *al-so*; DW: *also*. See note to line 32.

        Absalon. David's son, noted for his beauty. See 2 Kings 14.25; and Chaucer's *LGW* Prol. F 249 (*Riverside Chaucer*, p. 595).

85   Malone reads this line as parenthetical (p. 60).

87   The *sponsa Christi* theme begins here, with Christ described as the lover the maiden should seek. One may note how Jesus is shown to fulfill all a woman may be thought to desire, and how his appeal lies, in large measure, in his physical, human traits: "Since the person of Christ is not only God but truly man, he displays all the desirable qualities of perfect humanity, and may be responded to as a true lover and the worthiest of suitors" (Swanton, p. 248; see also Bugge, pp. 87–90). Compare the presentation of Christ's appeal in the *Ancrene Wisse*:

> Let everyone now choose one of these two, earthly comfort or heavenly, whichever she wants to keep — because she must let go of the other. . . . Stretch out your love to Jesus Christ, and you have won him. Reach for him with as much love as you sometimes have for some man. He is yours to do all that you want with. (Trans. Savage and Watson, p. 197)

Courtly terms applied to Christ are typical of the anchoritic texts that preceded *Love Rune*, "expressly developed to meet the needs of women" and drawing "ultimately on the bride-imagery of the Song of Songs" (Swanton, p. 248). On the *sponsa Christi* motif, see also Bugge, pp. 90–96.

89   *ikneowe*. So Cook; MS: *iknowe*. The only occurrence of the word in the poem, the rhyme indicates this spelling.

90   *childe*. As DW point out, the term means "a youth of noble birth," which seems to have been something of a title for a young aspirant to knighthood, especially in romances and ballads. See *MED child* n., sense 6(a).

93   *lufsum lost*. Christ is depicted as having amorous desire for a human lover (i.e., the soul). The logic behind this depiction is that Christ endured the Passion to prove His love for humankind, so certainly he desires each soul in a way best expressed through the terms of passionate love. See Bugge, p. 82; and compare *In a Valley of This Restless Mind* (edited in this volume).

94   *of wisdom wilde*. "strong in wisdom." B glosses *wilde* as "filled" (that is, *vvilled*). The substitution of *v* for *f* is common in the MS, but not *w* for *f*. The *OED* glosses it as the adjective *wield*, "strong, powerful, mighty," which I accept here (see also DW, pp. 218–19). Wisdom is a central theme; see note to line 6.

95   *reowe*. So Cook; MS: *rewe*. Emendation is accepted for rhyme.

96   *ylde*. Cook emends to *hylde*. The word, from OE *hyldo*, carries a range of appropriate meanings, "grace, favor, protection." Swanton and DW translate it as "protection."

100   *Est and west, north and suth!* This line comes at the exact center of the *luve ron* composed by Thomas (lines 9–192). The four cardinal directions may be meant to invoke the sign of the Cross and thereby sanctify the rune, so that it may bring the Holy Bridegroom to the maiden. (On why the Passion should be invoked, see note to line 93.) If this interpretation is correct, the line is integral to the cryptic, runic nature of the poem (see note to line 2).

102   *Of Hym he halt*. DW translate this phrase as "he is his vassal," and they remark that it is "apparently a translation of the Latin legal formula *X tenet de Y*" (p. 219).

103   *sonde*. So all editors; MS: *schonde*. The MS reading offers an odd meaning: "shame, disgrace, insult" or "disgraced person" (from OE *sceand, scand, scond*). The word obviously wanted is *sonde*, "message"; see *MED sond(e)* n.

47

Love Rune

Here Thomas styles himself an emissary for God, a role analogous to that of Gabriel at the Annunciation. The poem that follows *Love Rune* in MS is *The Annunciation of the Virgin Mary* (ed. Morris, p. 100). On this aspect of the poem, see Levy, pp. 123–34.

104   *cuth.* "known by, acquainted with," with amorous implication. See note to line 6.

105   This line appears to refer to the custom of a dowry, which Christ does not demand. DW translate and comment: "'He demands no dowry with you'. But the convent generally did" (p. 219).

106   *rencyan.* The word refers to a kind of fine cloth, but its specific features are uncertain, except that it was "made in or associated with Reims" (*MED*). The only other occurrence of the word appears in a text of the same MS, *On Serving Christ* (c. 1300), line 70 (ed. Morris, p. 92). In both occurrences, the spelling in *-an* departs from the rhyme-words in *-on*.

108   *weli mon.* MS: *weli man*, with *i man* written by the second hand over an erasure. The vowel has been emended for the rhyme because everywhere else the spelling *mon* appears.

111   Manning reads this line as about each person's potential for grace: "To realize [his] capability [for eternal love], man must raise himself above the merely natural level through sanctifying grace, a gift which God freely bestows upon him" (p. 124).

113   *bolde.* "castle or mansion, dwelling place, abode" (*MED bold* n.). The figure of a castle carries several associated traditional meanings: Solomon's temple, the heavenly city, Christ's body, a human body, and (less meaningful in *Love Rune*) the Church. See Cornelius; Rogers, pp. 28–40; Bloomfield, p. 58 n. 8; and Swanton, pp. 247, 283 n. 43. Thomas of Hales's Franciscan contemporary Robert Grosseteste made the figure popularly known through his AN *Chateau d'Amour*, a work visibly influenced by the writings of Hugh of Saint Victor and Bernard of Clairvaux (Sajavaara, p. 62). Grosseteste used it, too, in *Templum Dei*, which begins with a meditation on 1 Corinthians 3.17, "For the temple of God is holy, which you are" (ed. Goering and Mantello, pp. 10, 29; see also 1 Corinthians 6.19). The castle of the body is the basic metaphor for *Sawles Warde* and a frequent figure in the *Ancrene Wisse*; see Savage and Watson, pp. 70, 133, 137, 190–91, 210, 217, 380 n. 82, 383 n. 99.

In *Love Rune* the choice of the word *bolde* adds an element of masculine dominance to the traditional castle figure: God's *bolde* (of which Solomon's temple is a type) will stand forever, while mere men who are *bold* will always wither like meadow grass. Given to the maiden (line 119), the *bold* of God becomes also a figure for her intact body, in which she may experience paradisaical joy; compare St. Katherine's description of the city in the heart (trans. Savage and Watson, pp. 276–77; the only instance of *bold* in *Katherine* appears in this passage [line 1649; ed. Einenkel, p. 81]). On the usage of *bold* in *Love Rune*, see also notes to lines 13 and 127.

114   *Salomon.* Solomon's temple is described in 3 Kings 6–8 (Douay-Rheims translation). It is both a figure for the heavenly mansion, and an embodiment of the moral that the best of what men may build is infinitely exceeded by God's edifice in heaven. The biblical account explains how God entered the temple in the guise of a cloud (3 Kings 8.10–12), and Hugh of Saint Victor uses the biblical passage to illustrate how God conceals the "treasure of the heart," i.e., His image in man (p. 102); Hugh's treatment of Solomon's temple has probably influenced Thomas of Hales.

115–16   These lines introduce an important imagery of gems, which is later to be associated with the maiden's virginity (lines 161–66). On the gems of Solomon's temple, see 3 Kings 7.9–10, where the specific stones are not named. Compare too the listed gems of the New Jerusalem in Revelations 21.18–21 and in the dreamer's vision at the end of *Pearl*, lines 985–1032 (ed. Gordon, pp. 36–37). Bloomfield also cites a letter on virginity by Osbert of Clare, twelfth-century Prior of Westminster, that names the "twelve stones of virginity from the Apocalypse" (p. 57).

119   *bold.* See notes to lines 113 and 127.

121   *mote.* The word, from OF *mote*, means "hill, eminence, mound," not "moat, ditch," a meaning not recorded before 1378 (*MED mote* n.; Malone, p. 60).

123   *mynur.* The primary meaning is "miner," describing a military activity: "one whose military function it is to undermine fortifications, tunnel into a town" (*MED minour* n.). All editors accept this reading; see also Swanton, p. 248. This passage is the earliest recorded instance of this usage, which is also found in Chaucer's Knight's Tale, *CT* I 2465 (*Riverside Chaucer*, p. 58). If *bold* is understood as the maiden's body, the miner figure becomes sexually charged.

The secondary meaning is a crucial pun. *Mynur* discreetly refers to Thomas the poet, a friar Minor (in the heading, *"de ordine fratrum Minorum"*). See *MED Menour* n. and adj. The poet is graciously deflecting the maiden's attentions from himself to Christ, their proper object (see Introduction). The innuendo is thus sexual even as Thomas politely declines: "No miner (or friar Minor) may undermine the castle of God that is given to you, maiden, by right." Shakespeare uses a similar pun in a comic exchange that quibbles on virginity in military figures; see *All's Well That Ends Well* I.i. 118–22 (*Riverside Shakespeare*, p. 506.)

123   *hire*. This word may mean either "it" or "her," and it participates in the pun on *mynur*.

       underwrot. "undermine," and possibly "underwrite, meagerly write." Thomas appears to extend the pun upon *mynur* (see note above) into this verb. If so, he modestly calls his writing inadequate to the purpose; God, however, will overlook it in His love for the maiden. Thus seen as a modesty topos, the pun maintains the courtesy of Thomas's refusal of the maiden. Nonetheless, the original meaning, "undermine," lingers, and if given Thomas as its subject, the word raises sexual thoughts even as Thomas refuses the offer.

127   *bold*. A masculine, vaguely phallic connotation may have been perceptible to the contemporary audience. Avoiding the "miner" or "Minor" (line 123), the maiden is given the *blisse* of God's *bold*. On the strongly implied physicality of God's love, compare notes to lines 87 and 194–202; on the usage of *bold*, compare notes to lines 13 and 113.

128   *thar wythal*. K, DB; MS: *thar wyth al*; M: *thar-wyth-al*; B, DW: *thar wyth-al*. See *MED ther-withal* adv., sense 3, "in addition to that."

138   *Al so*. So MS; DW: *Al-so*; DB: *Also*. See note to line 32.

142   See Revelation 21.25.

143   *freo*. MS: *seoly*; DW emend: *sley*. Emendation is indicated by the rhyme. The error may have originated in a confusion between scribal *f* and *s*. The word *freo*, "privileged" and also "out of the bondage of sin" (*MED fre* adj., senses 1a.[d] and 3a.), completes the question of how a *freo wymmon* should choose a *lefmon* (see note to line 6). The emended reading also accords with a

traditional view of virginity; compare Aldhelm: "virginity is freedom, chastity ransom, conjugality captivity" (trans. Lapidge and Herren, p. 75); and P. Brown, p. 86. The MS reading, faulty in rhyme, means "blessed." DW argue that *sley*, "skillful, dexterous," "would give a fair rhyme, though perhaps not quite so satisfactory a meaning" as *seoly* (p. 219). Holthausen suggests emendation of *ful seoly* to *ful of feo*, "wealthy" (p. 370).

144   On the figure of Christ as Lover-Knight, see Woolf (1962), pp. 1–16.

145   *tresur.* The idea that God gives each person a treasure when he or she relinquishes worldly possessions appears often in the Gospels; see Matthew 19.21, Mark 10.21, and Luke 12.33–34, 18.22. This treasure is not only the promise of heaven but the image of God in each soul, described as "this treasure in earthen vessels" (2 Corinthians 4.7; cited by Aldhelm, p. 74). A critical aspect of this treasure, because it is Christ's presence within, is profound wisdom, as described by Paul:

> . . . their hearts may be comforted, being instructed in charity, and unto all the riches of the fulness of understanding, unto the knowledge of the mystery of God the Father, and of Christ Jesus: In whom are hidden all the treasures of wisdom and knowledge. (Colossians 2.2–3)

This conception of treasure as wisdom buried within the soul of each human being, where there is both image and presence of Christ, is central to Thomas's poem, itself styled as an enigmatic message-box enclosing hidden wisdom (Bloomfield, p. 59); virginity itself may be thought the key to wisdom (Bugge, pp. 120–22).

146   *pel.* The definition is "fine cloth" often of royal purple (OF *paile*, from Latin *pallium*); see *MED pal* n., where *Love Rune* is listed under sense 1.(c). M, DW, and Malone (p. 60) correctly identify this meaning, while B glosses the word "fur" (see *MED pel* n.(2), and compare line 28). The word *pel* is not recorded before 1349, and it occurs in technical documents, such as wardrobe accounts, but not in poetry. Compare, too, Aldhelm: "virginity is gold, chastity silver, conjugality bronze; . . . virginity is the royal purple, chastity the re-dyed fabric, conjugality the (undyed) wool" (trans. Lapidge and Herren, p. 75).

147   *luke.* There are two verbal meanings evoked by this word, which, like *witen* (see note to line 6), is a clear pun. It means both "lock," *MED louken* v.(1), sense 1(b); and "guard, defend, watch over," *MED louken* v.(1), sense 1(b), and

loken v.(2), sense 12b. While editors and commentators have differed in translating the line (M, B, DW, DB: "lock, fasten, close"; Swanton: "look to"), no one seems to have caught the pun.

The different meanings matter. The one given by the editors, "lock, fasten," pertains specifically to physical virginity, which the maiden must keep hidden and intact. The second meaning, "watch over," also requires that the maiden be protective of her "bower," but treats the treasure more as something she may view and enjoy. These two meanings blend into the next line, with its equally ambiguous verb *wyte*.

148   *wyte*. Means either "guard" or "know"; see notes to lines 6 and 147, and 167.

149   *theove . . . revere . . . lechur*. MS *theoves . . . reveres . . . lechurs*. The rhyme indicates that the original of *lechurs* was the singular form; all three nouns have been emended to accord with this form.

151   The language comparing the maiden to a sweet flower is traditional in both love poetry (see, for example, *Annot and John*, lines 11–20 [*The Harley Lyrics*, ed. Brook, pp. 31–32]) and devotional descriptions of virginity, as in *Holy Maidenhead*: "Maidenhood is the flower that once completely cut down never blooms again" (trans. Savage and Watson, p. 228; see also Aldhelm, p. 74).

152   *witest*. See notes to lines 6 and 167.

153–84   *ymston*. The treasure in the castle of the body is now called a gemstone, named *"Maydenhod"* at line 162. The figurative notion that virginity is a gem has a long tradition (see Swanton, pp. 247–48; Rogers, pp. 28–40). St. Margaret in the *Katherine*-group legend calls out to Christ in prayer:

> "Lord, listen to me! I have a precious jewel, and I have given it to you — I mean my maidenhood, the brightest blossom in the body that bears it and keeps it well. Never let the evil one throw it in the mire. . . . Lord, defend me, and protect it always for yourself." (*Saint Margaret*, trans. Savage and Watson, p. 289)

In the anchoritic literature virginity, a gem, is closely identified with Christ himself:

> The eagle keeps in his nest a precious gem called "agate," . . . This precious stone is Jesus Christ, true as a stone, and full of every power over all gemstones. He is

the agate that the poison of sin never came near. Keep him in your nest, that is, your heart. (*Ancrene Wisse*, trans. Savage and Watson, pp. 98–99; compare p. 296)

Virginity becomes the mark of physical linkage to Christ in spiritual marriage, because Christ's image is unmarred in the virgin's intact body. The author of *Holy Maidenhood* so instructs the reader:

Do not break the seal [of virginity] that seals you both together (Canticles 4:12). . . . No wonder if what is so like God is lovely to him; for he is the loveliest thing and all unbroken, and always was and is more pure than anything, and loves purity more than anything. And what is a more beautiful thing and more praiseworthy among earthly things than the power of maidenhood, unbroken and pure, modelled on him?" (trans. Savage and Watson, pp. 228–29)

On this idea further, see Bugge's discussion of how the anchoritic texts are influenced by "the Christian gnostic tradition, wherein virginity is the image of the divine essence" (p. 120).

Consequently, in order to grasp the meaning of the *rune*, one must read the pronouns *He* and *Hine* in lines 155, 156, 159, 160, 164, 167, 179, 181, 183, and 184 in a double fashion: as the neuter pronoun "it" in reference to the gemstone virginity (as all editors and commentators have read these pronouns) *and* as the masculine "He" and "Him" in reference to Christ the Holy Gemstone, who actively desires, inhabits, and enjoys the body of the virgin.

157   *alyve*. So DW, K, DB; MS: *a lyve*; B: *a-lyve*.

158   *wyten*. See notes to lines 6 and 167.

167   *witest under thine hemme*. The pun always latent in the verb *witen* (note to line 6) comes forth in a sexualized way — "know God under hem" — beside the expected meaning — "guard virginity under hem." On sexualized language to describe union with Christ, see Bugge, 81–122, and McGinn, pp. 205–26. Bugge speaks of how virginity was thought to be "the first condition of intimate communion with God" (p. 121). Caroline Walker Bynum notes how Catherine of Siena was said to receive "the ring of Christ's foreskin" in mystic marriage (*Holy Feast and Holy Fast* [Berkeley: University of California Press, 1987], p. 246). Thomas has extended the erotic metaphors of mystical language by contextualizing them into what looks like a courtly love lyric. As McGinn comments, rather than be surprised (as we moderns tend to be), in the context of Christian mysticism "we should be scandalized not so much by the presence

of such erotic elements as by their absence" (p. 205).

The phrase *under thine hemme* invokes a motif in love poetry in which the poet enjoys imagining what is under a maiden's clothes and often expresses a desire to be there (under her skirt, in particular). The usual phrase is *under gore* ("skirt") or *under bis* ("linen"). The sexual meaning is unambiguous in *The Owl and Nightingale*, line 515 (ed. Grattan and Sykes, p. 16). See also *The Thrush and the Nightingale*, line 150 (ed. Brown, p. 106); and *The Harley Lyrics* 3.16, 3.17, 4.37, 5.38, 7.58, 7.79–84, 9.54–55 (ed. Brook, pp. 31–34, 38–39, 41). Here, while the imagined Lover is Christ, Thomas writes in the language of a love-poet who typically invites sexual thoughts of the lady.

168   *than*. So B DW, K, DB; MS: *that*.

170   *vertu*. This word has its technical sense, referring to an occult efficacy or curative power thought to inhere in a substance. Precious stones and plants were said to possess virtues, which were enumerated in lapidaries and herbals. See DW, p. 219, and Bloomfield, p. 59. For specific lapidaries, see Joan Evans, and Mary S. Serjeantson, eds., *English Medieval Lapidaries*, EETS o.s. 190 (1933; rpt. Millwood, N. Y.: Kraus, 1990); and Albertus Magnus, *Book of Minerals*, trans. Dorothy Wyckoff (Oxford: Clarendon, 1967).

grace. So all editors; MS: *pris*, written by a later hand where the scribe omitted the rhyme-word.

172   *lectorie*. This is the first recorded occurrence of the word in ME, and the only one spelled without the prefix *a-*. See *MED alectorie* n. and *lectorie* n. The word, derived from Latin *alectoria*, denotes a small, clear stone said to be found in a cock's gizzard.

tupace. So all editors; MS: *tupace ywys*, the second word written in a later hand.

175   *Among*. So M, DW, DB; MS: *A mong*; B: *A-mong*; K: *Amon*.

177   *al so*. So MS; DW, DB: *also*. See note to line 32.

181   Both Christ and the gem of virginity are described as set in gold, and Thomas the poet may be seen to be completing the "worked" love rune in a manner analogous to a goldsmith setting a gem. Compare the analogous idea of the

narrator — by extension the poet — as a *jueler* in the exquisitely wrought *Pearl*, lines 252–300 (ed. Gordon, pp. 10–11).

182   *fyn amur.* "A technical term used by Provençal poets" (Bloomfield, p. 59). Christ, the Lover-Knight who proffers love-gifts (a castle, a treasure, a gem) loves in noble, courtly fashion.

183   *wite.* See notes to lines 6 and 167.

184   *bur.* The term that has denoted the lady's body, in which she must guard her virginity (compare lines 147 and 178), now denotes heaven, shining with Christ's light (Revelations 21.23). Compare too the description of heaven in *The Wooing of Our Lord*: "You [Christ] loosed your prisoners and delivered them out of the death-house, and yourself took them with you to your jewelled bower, the abode of eternal joy" (trans. Savage and Watson, p. 250).

189–92   This rhetorical question, explaining the choice and making clear the proper answer, is so delicately expressed that it refers both to the maiden's proper choosing of Christ over Thomas *and* to Thomas's noble choosing to write the *luve ron* rather than assenting to the maiden's desire.

194   *withute sel.* Stone interprets the absence of a seal as Thomas's way of making the poem an open message rather than one that might be perceived as a love note (p. 56). This idea supports the notion that Thomas is discreetly deflecting the maiden's amorous desires even as he is making a *luve ron* that brings her God's *fyn amur.* Levy finds here an allusion to the scrolls in the iconography associated with the Annunciation (pp. 127–30). Allusions to Revelations may also be present: the opening of the scroll with seven seals (chap. 6) and the unsealed roll (chap. 10). Compare too the notion of virginity as the unbroken "seal" that keeps whole God's image in the soul (*Holy Maidenhood*, p. 228).

194–95   The poem is to be thought of as written upon an unsealed parchment roll. Hill argues that the original poem was in fact written on a roll, as were many other Franciscan lyrics ([1964], pp. 322–25; see also Woolf [1968], pp. 57–58). The reference may in fact be more figural than literal, as discussed in the Introduction.

199   *Hwoso.* So K; MS: *Hwo so*; B, DW, DB: *Hwo-so.*

199   *cuthe*. See note to line 6.

201   Millett notes that the maiden appears to be literate (in English, though probably not in Latin or French) and that she is pictured "in solitary but not silent meditation" (pp. 97–98).

203   The song the maiden will sing is both this poem (called a *cantus* in the incipit) and the "new song" of the hundred and forty-four thousand virgin brides of Christ in Revelations 14.3–4 (Swanton, p. 249; see also Bugge, pp. 117–18). The second hand has written *Item cantus* in the right-hand margin on the line that opens the next piece (*The Annunciation to the Virgin Mary*), directly below the *Amen* that concludes *Love Rune*.

204   *al so*. So MS; DW: *al-so*; DB: *also*. See note to line 32.

205   *he*. The pronoun is richly ambiguous. It refers to the message, the rune itself, or to the messenger, either Thomas its conveyor (and author) or God the Wooer (figured as ultimate Author). The line also contains an allusion to the Annunciation; see note to line 103 and Swanton, p. 249.

207   *brudthinge*. "bridal," from OE *bryd-þing*; according to the *MED* this is the only occurrence of the word in ME.

209–10 These lines are not differentiated from the preceding stanza in MS: they continue the rhymes, and the sole colored capital is the *H* of *Hwenne* (line 201). They do mark a dramatic shift to the poet. The preceding eight lines complete an image: the maid who sits in longing arrives as a bride before God who sits enthroned. The final two lines, Bloomfield writes, are "the last reminder of a submerged theme which runs through the poem. . . . Here we have the true conclusion which is the culmination and conclusion of the frame. It is the last reminder of death in the poem — the writer's own" (p. 55).

The formal structure of the first two hundred lines (twenty-five stanzas) of *Love Rune* suggests that the last ten lines serve as formal epilogue. See note to line 100.

In a Valley of This Restless Mind

Introduction

The poem that follows here has attracted some of the highest praise bestowed upon a Middle English religious lyric: Albert C. Baugh honors it as "the most beautiful,"[1] and Ann W. Astell, in a sensitive study of the Song of Songs in medieval literature, calls it "perhaps the finest of the vernacular poems inspired by the *Canticum*" (p. 145). It is routinely included in general anthologies of religious verse, but it has rarely been printed in specialized Middle English collections. The poem, entitled by its first line *In a Valley of This Restless Mind*, survives in two manuscripts from the early fifteenth century — one from Lambeth Palace, the other from Cambridge University Library. The earliest edition (Furnivall [1866]) prints both texts side by side. While the two versions are similar, there are often subtle differences in individual wordings, and an important variation in order of stanzas (the fourteenth and the fifteenth are reversed). Although scholars of the poem have preferred the Lambeth text and (usually) its order for the basis of their discussions, editors of general anthologies have most often printed the Cambridge version. When this disparity in modern reception is set against the poem's extraordinary qualities, a critical edition of the poem seems rather overdue.

In the Lambeth manuscript *This Restless Mind* follows the Marian lament *In a Tabernacle of a Tower*, another poem with the same refrain, which is taken from Canticles 2.5 — *Quia amore langueo*, "Because I am sick for love" — where it is spoken by the Bride to the Bridegroom. Beyond the shared refrain, these two poems agree in both stanzaic pattern and lyrical tone of intimate address. These correspondences, taken together, suggest the derivation of one from the other. The more uniquely original of the two poems is the one printed here, which is probably the earlier piece. The Marian poem has the Virgin utter her refrain-lament to a musing narrator from within a dreamlike vision. Here, it is a wounded lover-knight figure — Christ as Bridegroom — who suffers an exquisite longing for love, and who speaks from within a visionary place imagined with natural detail (valley and hill) yet

---

[1] *A Literary History of England* (New York: Appleton-Century-Crofts, 1948), p. 218. See also Gray (1972), p. 143; Woolf (1968), p. 187; Wimsatt (1978), p. 345.

interiorized in the narrator's "restless mind." The shifted assignation of the scriptural line from human Bride-Soul-Virgin to divine Bridegroom delivers a startling effect, as Mary-Ann Stouck has noted: "The effect of the change is to inform the whole poem with intensified feeling, since it implies not only a greater degree of love — Christ's capacity for love, as for suffering, being infinitely greater than man's — but also a startling insufficiency in Christ: He cannot be satisfied without man's love . . . . The feeling here is refined and engages our sympathy" (p. 3).

Like the narrator's restless mind, the poem's logical movement is fluid, emotive, ever-shifting. Lines of uneven length create a lyric echo of the Song of Songs. Terms for the beloved punctuate the lover's speech, initially in third-person descriptions given to the listening narrator, but, increasingly, in second-person expressions made directly to the female beloved, whom he identifies by name, Mannis Soule. The frequent endearments create an atmosphere of intimacy and loʋ ..gness, of overhearing — eventually of receiving — the most private murmurings and erotic blandishments of a lover while he woos and seduces his espoused. Christ the Bridegroom here makes love to the reader, approaching first through the distanced figure of Mannis Soule, then through the drawn-in narrator, and finally through direct address to "thow," the reader.[2] The tone of familiarity is intense: God is personified as a gentle, patient, persistent lover, waiting to gain a response, seizing upon any sign of affectionate reciprocation. The languishing voice of a loving Deity shapes the emotional texture of the poem.

In using the figure of Lover-Knight for Christ, the poet transfers attribution for Christ's wounds from the history of the Passion to the effects of an unrequited love for mankind. The metaphor is well-known in Middle English religious lyrics and meditations (Woolf [1962], pp. 1–16). Here, Christ is literally wounded for love, languishing in pain caused by his beloved, who, in return for his affection, has beaten him and forcibly dressed him in strange garments — a bloodied shirt, gloves embroidered with blood, shoes tightly buckled with nails. The reader is asked to reenvision the crucified Christ and his wounds through the language of courtly fashion and love etiquette.

The poet thus depicts the relationship of God and man in humanly sexual terms: Christ is the male suitor of the feminine soul (the *anima*). This representation merely prefaces, however, another, more startling figure of amorous kinship: Christ as the

---

[2]This method of gradual approach through a metamorphosing narrator has troubled at least one critic, Stevick, who judges the piece "not [to] be good poetry" because of "distracting shifts in the direction of direct address" and "contradictions" that frustrate logic (pp. 109–10; see also Speirs, p. 81). Wimsatt asserts, on the other hand, that in the context of a mystical, 'dream realm" "transitions from one role to another are easily made" ([1984], p. 83).

nurturing mother who shelters her infant Mannis Soule within her wounded side, nursing her with milk/blood from her "pap." Here is another expression of Christ's loving nature that found outlet in such affective writings as Julian of Norwich's *Shewings*, where Christ is tenderly referred to as "oure precyous moder Jhesu, he may fede us wyth hymselfe, and . . . he may homely lede us into his blessyd brest by his swet opyn syde, and shewe us ther in perty of the godhed and the joyes of hevyn" (pp. 123–25; see Stouck, pp. 3–4, 8). The juxtaposing of two quite differently gendered metaphors for Christ achieves, as Thomas D. Hill has noted, "an original and startling effect — a moment in which Christ's sexual nature is abruptly redefined" (p. 459). In fact, gendered definitions of behavior and kinship seem to govern a hidden movement within the poem's narrative of conversion. Astell believes that the poet imposes a feminized perspective upon the reader, that is, a sexualized perspective that connotes a receptivity for conversion. Many of the roles given to Christ are also specifically feminine, and as Astell notes, they form "an imagistic sequence from languishing to receptive lovemaking to pregnancy, nursing, and rearing" (p. 147). She interprets this figuratively feminine process as a means by which Christ models the response he seeks from his Bride.

One might take the interpretation of gendered roles in the poem a bit further by considering the key kinships represented by these roles. It seems that the essential natures of Christ, of the visionary narrator/reader, and even of the named bride Mannis Soule are each to some extent bigendered. The Soule is "man's," yet she is the feminized object of God's love-pursuit. The visionary wanderer of the opening is ostensibly like all male narrators who recite a lyric *chanson d'aventure* (Hill, p. 460). Yet when he meets the wounded man, he has found both the object of his search ("Truelove") and an alter-ego (reinforced when Christ's lamenting "I" supplants his narrating "I"). These correspondences implicitly identify him with both the masculine, love-seeking wooer *and* the feminized love-object, Mannis Soule. Christ is a courteous pursuer of his beloved, a hunter, and yet his courtship of Mannis Soule is remarkably passive and stationary, his wounded body laid out as an enticing "bait": seemingly more like a woman, "he draws his love to him by the beauty of his body" (Hill, p. 461). The gender-oriented positions of these three personages are all curiously interchangable and fluctuant.

What stabilizes the flowing in and out of sexual roles is the assertion of immutable familial relationships: Christ names Mannis Soule as his sister and his wife. These horizontal relationships betoken Christ's flesh-and-blood kinship to mankind. The marital bond creates, in addition, the potential for procreation, a possibility that in the poet's devotional framework suggests conversion. That, in fact, is what happens when Christ and Mannis Soule — Bridegroom and bride — consummate their spiritual marriage in the stanza break between lines 104 and 105. Conversion leads to a new kinship of vertical dimension, Christ as bigendered parent (Mother and reigning Father) and Soule as bigendered child (man and woman). Conversion brings revelation of the kinship in spirit (rather than flesh) that exists between God and Mannis Soule.

In joining with God, the soul is transformed from wayward sister flesh to docile spiritual child. The catalyst for the transformation is Christ's wounded side, a venerated site of holiness in *This Restless Mind*; it is, as James I. Wimsatt notes, "the source and place of contemplative bliss, which [the poet] has made the master image of the poem" ([1978], p. 343). In a very literal way the wound makes Christ's heart accessible to mankind. Whether Christ is to be seen as Lover or as Well of Grace, this point of access is crucially important to humankind. The tender scene of the soul's refuge and infantile repose in Christ's wound becomes yet another transition, this time to imagery of proper child-rearing. The newly birthed infant soul will eventually be weaned from "baby food" and fed with "adversity" (lines 117–19). The caring Parent will raise the child through strict, loving discipline, ever testing the trueness of its filial love.

Thus, the poet's seemingly bizarre blurring of gender lines can be seen to belong to a larger, anthropomorphized expression of God's relationship to humankind. Presented as a kinship, this relationship is complex and, in natural terms, irrational. The logic exists devotionally, as one may see in the poem that follows *This Restless Mind* in Lambeth 853. In seeking to know how he should "for kyndnes . . . luf [his] kyn" (line 17), the poet of *The Sweetness of Jesus* works through the familial and social roles of Jesus — father, mother, brother, sister, spouse, prince, king, friend — and concludes that he owes total fealty: "no thyng will he have iwys, / Bot trewluf for his travail" (lines 87–88). Another Middle English lyric of exceptional power, *Undo Thy Door, My Spouse Dear*, begins with the sexualized image of Christ imploring narrator-spouse (mankind) to unlock the door of his heart. The physically insertive act is reversed at the end, when the narrator appeals to Christ, whose "herte is cloven oure love to kecchen" (line 17), to "Perce myn herte with thi lovengge, / That in The I have my duellingge" (lines 21–22). The desire of Christ to enter man's heart reveals itself as man's need to be enclosed in Christ's wounded heart. The poem is ultimately about a complete change in one's being, that is, a spiritual giving up of the boundaries of self.[3] Similar ideas clearly direct the restless imagery of *In a Valley of This Restless Mind*.

The text printed here is based on the copy in Lambeth 853, a collection of religious

---

[3]See Edmund Reiss, *The Art of the Middle English Lyric* (Athens: University of Georgia Press, 1972), p. 129; Astell, pp. 154–58.

verse that dates from the mid-fifteenth century. The compiler of this manuscript exercised judgment as to the arrangement of poetic matter largely of a devotional nature. The poem falls within a group of four copied in the first quire: *Surge mea sponsa*, *Tabernacle*, *This Restless Mind*, and *Sweetness*. The effect of this sequence is to treat the poem as a lyrical companion — almost as a continuation — of *Tabernacle*. All four poems are songs of love-longing, and a narrative thread develops: Christ singing of love to the Virgin, the Virgin singing to mankind, Christ also singing to mankind, and, in response, mankind's declaration of love to Christ and a final plea for mercy. The second, slightly later manuscript, Cambridge University Library Hh.4.12, has *This Restless Mind* copied in the midst of works by the fifteenth-century poet John Lydgate, between *The Legend of Saint Austin at Compton* (an exemplum on tithing) and *The Debate of the Horse, Goose, and Sheep* (a beast debate with political overtones). Why the lyric was chosen to join this collection is not apparent, but the book's fascicular origin may provide some clue. In the fifteenth-century book trade, publishers would sometimes "have poems or groups of related poems copied in loose quires which would then be held in stock and bound up to the taste of specific customers."[4] Lydgate's works were often marketed in this fashion, and the Cambridge manuscript is one such book.[5]

The date of *In a Valley of This Restless Mind* is uncertain. Robert D. Stevick places it c. 1430, but Carleton Brown prints *In a Tabernacle of a Tower* as a lyric of the late fourteenth century, and Felicity Riddy groups both poems under this earlier date. If *Tabernacle* is accepted as the later poem, as several commentators have thought it to be, then *This Restless Mind* is surely a composition of the fourteenth century, perhaps close in time to *The Sweetness of Jesus*, its other companion in the Lambeth manuscript. *Sweetness* may be dated by its earliest manuscript to the mid-fourteenth century. The dialects of *Tabernacle* and *Sweetness* are, however, both more northern than is that of *This Restless Mind* — insofar as we have an accurate record of its original dialect in two fairly late manuscripts. The two texts that survive are in the more standard, southern dialect associated with London, a dialect into which many fourteenth-century texts were translated in the fifteenth century. To make comparison, *Tabernacle* survives in eight manuscripts, six in this dialect and two preserving

---

[4]Derek Pearsall, *John Lydgate* (London: Routledge and Kegan Paul, 1970), p. 75.

[5]It is interesting to note that the poem's sister piece *Tabernacle* was ascribed to Lydgate by an aged John Shirley, fifteenth-century publisher. Even though Shirley's knowledge of Lydgate's canon is usually reliable, scholars have not accepted the attribution: see Henry Noble MacCracken, *The Minor Poems of John Lydgate*, part 1, EETS e.s. 107 (rpt. London: Oxford University Press, 1962), pp. xxxi–xxxii; and Pearsall, p. 78.

features of the northern origin;[6] *Sweetness* survives in sixteen manuscripts, but only two retain the northern dialect.[7] The two texts of *This Restless Mind* do not, therefore, reliably indicate its date of composition or its author's dialect. If *Restless Mind* preceded *Tabernacle*, then it, too, probably originated in the north.

Note on the Stanza Form

Both manuscripts present the poem in sixteen eight-line stanzas, but in different order (two stanzas are reversed). Paragraph signs occur in the Lambeth MS at the fourth line of each stanza. The spatial arrangement used here is designed to accentuate (1) the syntactic break that occurs after either the fourth line (end of quatrain) or the fifth line (in tandem with the continued rhyme); (2) the lyrical echoes of the Song of Songs; and (3) the closing short-line Latin refrain. Astell also prints the poem in this form, an adaptation of Furnivall's presentation.

Select Bibliography

Manuscripts

London, Lambeth Palace Library MS 853, pp. 7–14. C. 1450. [Base text.]

Cambridge, Cambridge University Library Hh.4.12, fols. 41b–44a. C. 1475.

Editions

Both Manuscripts

Furnivall, F. J., ed. *Political, Religious, and Love Poems*. EETS o.s. 15. Second ed. 1903; rpt. Bungay, Suffolk: Richard Clay, 1965. Pp. 180–89.

---

[6]Felicity Riddy, "The Provenance of *Quia amore langueo*," *Review of English Studies*, n.s. 18 (1967), 429–33.

[7]Brown, *Rel. Lyr. XIV*, p. 262; on the manuscripts see Carleton Brown and Rossell Hope Robbins, *The Index of Middle English Verse* (New York: Columbia University Press, 1943), no. 1781.

Introduction

Based on Lambeth

Riddy, Felicity, ed. In *The Middle Ages (700–1550)*. Ed. Michael Alexander and Felicity Riddy. St. Martin's Anthologies of English Literature. Vol. 1. New York: St. Martin's, 1989. Pp. 416–21.

Based on Cambridge

Cecil, David, ed. *The Oxford Book of Christian Verse.* Oxford: Clarendon, 1940. Pp. 25–29.

Comper, Frances M. M., ed. *Spiritual Songs from English Manuscripts of Fourteenth to Sixteenth Centuries.* London: Society for Promoting Christian Knowledge, and New York: Macmillan, 1936. Pp. 167–71. [In modern spelling, based on Cambridge.]

Donaldson, E. Talbot, ed. *Poets of the English Language: I. Langland to Spenser.* Ed. W. H. Auden and Norman Holmes Pearson. New York: Viking, 1950. Pp. 30–34.

Duncan, Thomas G., ed. *A Selection of Religious Lyrics.* Oxford: Clarendon, 1975. Pp. 100–04. [Lambeth order.]

Gray, Douglas, ed. *A Selection of Religious Lyrics.* Oxford: Clarendon, 1975. Pp. 41–45, 125–27. [Lambeth order.]

Nicholson, D. H. S., and A. H. E. Lee, eds. *The Oxford Book of English Mystical Verse.* Oxford: Clarendon, 1917. Pp. 6–10.

Sisam, Celia, and Kenneth Sisam, eds. *The Oxford Book of Medieval English Verse.* Oxford: Clarendon, 1970. Pp. 357–60.

Stevick, Robert D., ed. *One Hundred Middle English Lyrics.* Second ed. Urbana: University of Illinois Press, 1994. Pp. 88–93. [Lambeth order.]

Edited Extracts

Chambers, E. K., and F. Sidgwick, eds. *Early English Lyrics.* London: Sidgwick and Jackson, 1926. Pp. 151–54. [12 stanzas, based on Lambeth.]

Cook, A. S., ed. *A Literary Middle English Reader.* Boston: Ginn, 1915. Pp. 439–40. [3 stanzas, based on Cambridge.]

Kaiser, Rolf, ed. *Medieval English: An Old English and Middle English Anthology.* Third ed. Berlin: Rolf Kaiser, 1958. Pp. 291–93. [10 stanzas, based on Lambeth.]

Reeves, James, ed. *The Cassell Book of English Poetry.* New York: Harper and Row, 1965. [11 stanzas, in modern spelling, based on Lambeth.]

Translations

Davie, Donald, trans. *The New Oxford Book of Christian Verse.* Oxford: Oxford University Press, 1981. Pp. 16–20. [Based on Cambridge, follows Gardner translation.]

Gardner, Helen, trans. *The New Oxford Book of English Verse, 1250–1950.* Oxford: Clarendon, 1972. Pp. 9–12. Also: *The Faber Book of Religious Verse.* London: Faber and Faber, 1972. Pp. 56–60. [Based on Cambridge, follows Sisam and Sisam edition.]

Segar, Mary G., trans. *A Mediæval Anthology.* London: Longmans, Green, 1915. Pp. 23–26. [12 stanzas, based on Lambeth.]

Watts, Nevile, trans. *Love Songs of Sion: A Selection of Devotional Verses from Old English Sources.* London: Burns Oates and Washbourne, 1924. Pp. 58–62. [Based on Lambeth.]

Weston, Jessie L., trans. *The Chief Middle English Poets: Selected Poems.* Boston: Houghton Mifflin, 1914. Pp. 347–49. [Based on Lambeth.]

Related Medieval Works

Bernard of Clairvaux. *On the Song of Songs.* Trans. Kilian Walsh and Irene Edmonds. 4 vols. Cistercian Fathers Series 4, 7, 31, 40. Kalamazoo, Mich.: Cistercian Publications, 1971, 1976, 1979, 1980.

In a Tabernacle of a Tower. Ed. Carleton Brown. In *Religious Lyrics of the XIVth Century.* Second ed. Rev. G. V. Smithers. Oxford: Clarendon, 1957. Pp. xii, 234–37, 286–87. [Companion poem in Lambeth.]

Introduction

Julian of Norwich. *The Shewings*. Ed. Georgia Ronan Crampton. TEAMS Middle English Texts Series. Kalamazoo, Mich.: Medieval Institute Publications, 1994. [Especially pp. 120–26.]

A Meditation of the Five Wounds of Jesus Christ. Ed. Carl Horstmann. In *Yorkshire Writers*. Vol. 2. London: Swan Sonnenschein, 1896. Pp. 440–41.

Rolle, Richard. *Prose and Verse*. Ed. S. J. Ogilvie-Thomson. EETS o.s. 293. Oxford: Oxford University Press, 1988. [Especially pp. 15–33, 42–63.]

Surge mea sponsa. Ed. Carleton Brown. In *Religious Lyrics of the XVth Century*. Oxford: Clarendon, 1939. Pp. 65–67, 305–06.

Sweet Jesus, Now Will I Sing. Ed. Carl Horstmann. In *Yorkshire Writers*. Vol. 2. London: Swan Sonnenschein, 1896. Pp. 9–24.

The Sweetness of Jesus. Ed. Carleton Brown. In *Religious Lyrics of the XIVth Century*. Second ed. Rev. G. V. Smithers. Oxford: Clarendon, 1957. Pp. 61–65, 262–63. [Companion poem in Lambeth.]

A Talking of the Love of God. Ed. Carl Horstmann. In *Yorkshire Writers*. Vol. 2. London: Swan Sonnenschein, 1896. Pp. 345–66.

Undo Thy Door, My Spouse Dear. Ed. Carleton Brown. In *Religious Lyrics of the XIVth Century*. Second ed. Rev. G. V. Smithers. Oxford: Clarendon, 1957. P. 86.

Criticism of *In a Valley of This Restless Mind*

Astell, Ann W. *The Song of Songs in the Middle Ages*. Ithaca: Cornell University Press, 1990. Pp. 143–54.

Brewer, Derek. *English Gothic Literature*. History of Literature Series. Ed. A. Norman Jeffares. New York: Schocken Books, 1983. Pp. 48–50.

Gray, Douglas. *Themes and Images in the Medieval English Religious Lyric*. London: Routledge & Kegan Paul, 1972. Pp. 143–45.

Hill, Thomas D. "Androgyny and Conversion in the Middle English Lyric, 'In the Vaile of Restles Mynd.'" *ELH* 53 (1986), 459–70.

Manning, Stephen. *Wisdom and Number: Toward a Critical Appraisal of the Middle English Religious Lyric.* Lincoln: University of Nebraska Press, 1962. Pp. 59–62.

Speirs, John. *Medieval English Poetry: The Non-Chaucerian Tradition.* New York: Macmillan, 1957. Pp. 80–81.

Stevick, Robert D. "The Criticism of Middle Engish Lyrics." *Modern Philology* 64 (1966), 108–10.

Stouck, Mary-Ann. "'In a valey of þis restles mynde': Contexts and Meaning." *Modern Philology* 85 (1987), 1–11.

Wimsatt, James I. "The Canticle of Canticles, Two Latin Poems, and 'In a va.ey of þis restles mynde.'" *Modern Philology* 75 (1978), 327–45.

——. "St. Bernard, the Canticle of Canticles, and Mystical Poetry." In *An Introduction to The Medieval Mystics of Europe.* Ed. Paul E. Szarmach. Albany: State University of New York Press, 1984. Pp. 82–88.

Woolf, Rosemary. *The English Religious Lyric in the Middle Ages.* Oxford: Clarendon, 1968. Pp. 187–91.

Related Studies

Beckwith, Sarah. "Limens, Boundaries and Wounds: Corpus Christi as Rite of Passage." In *Christ's Body: Identity, Culture and Society in Late Medieval Writings.* London: Routledge, 1993. Pp. 55–63.

Bynum, Caroline Walker. *Jesus as Mother: Studies in the Spirituality of the High Middle Ages.* Berkeley: University of California Press, 1982. Pp. 110–69.

Cross, J. E. "The Virgin's *Quia Amore Langueo.*" *Neuphilologische Mitteilungen* 73 (1972), 37–44.

Introduction

Dronke, Peter. "The Song of Songs and Medieval Love-Lyric." *The Medieval Poet and His World*. Storia e Letteratura Raccolta di Studi e Testi 164. Rome: Storia e Letteratura, 1984. Pp. 209–36.

Gillespie, Vincent. "Strange Images of Death: The Passion in Later Medieval English Devotional and Mystical Writing." In *Zeit, Tod und Ewigkeit in der Renaissance Literatur*. Ed. James Hogg. Salzburg: Institut für Anglistik und Amerikanistik, Universität Salzburg, 1987. Pp. 111–59.

Gray, Douglas. "The Five Wounds of Our Lord — I–IV." *Notes and Queries*, n.s. 10 (1963), 50–51, 82–89, 127–34, 163–68.

Heimmel, Jennifer P. *God is Our Mother: Julian of Norwich and the Medieval Image of Christian Feminine Divinity*. Salzburg: Institut für Anglistik und Amerikanistik, Universität Salzburg, 1982. Pp. 34–45.

McGinn, Bernard. "The Language of Love in Christian and Jewish Mysticism." In *Mysticism and Language*. Ed. Steven T. Katz. Oxford: Oxford University Press, 1992. Pp. 202–35.

Rubin, Miri. "Christ's Suffering Humanity." In *Corpus Christi: The Eucharist in Late Medieval Culture*. Cambridge: Cambridge University Press, 1991. Pp. 303–16.

Woolf, Rosemary. "The Theme of Christ the Lover-Knight in Medieval English Literature." *Review of English Studies*, n.s. 13 (1962), 1–16.

In a Valley of This Restless Mind

In a valey of this restles mynde,
    I soughte in mounteyne and in mede,   *meadow*
Trustynge a trewelove for to fynde,
    Upon an hil than Y took hede: *took notice*
5   A voice Y herde — and neer Y yede —   *nearer I approached*
        In huge dolour complaynynge tho: *sadness; then*
    "Se, dere Soule, how my sidis blede,   *See*
        Quia amore langueo."   *Because I am sick for love*

Upon this hil Y fond a tree,   *found*
10   Undir the tree a man sittynge,
From heed to foot woundid was he,
    His herte blood Y sigh bledinge: *heart's; saw*
    A semeli man to ben a king,   *handsome enough to be a king*
        A graciouse face to loken unto;
15   I askide whi he had peynynge,   *suffering (lit., paining)*
        He seide, "*Quia amore langueo.*

"I am Truelove that fals was nevere.   *who*
    My sistyr, Mannis Soule, Y loved hir thus.
Bicause we wolde in no wise discevere,   *in no way part company*
20   I lefte my kyngdom glorious.
    I purveide for hir a paleis precious;   *prepared; palace*
        Sche fleyth; Y folowe. Y soughte hir so,   *flees*
    I suffride this peyne piteuous,   *piteous pain*
        Quia amore langueo.

25   "My fair spouse and my love bright,
    I saved hir fro betynge, and sche hath me bet!   *beating; beaten*
I clothid hir in grace and hevenli light,
    This bloodi scherte sche hath on me sette!   *shirt*
    For longynge of love yit wolde Y not lette —   *give up*
30   Swete strokis are these, lo!

68

I have loved hir evere, as Y hir het,   *always; promised*
    Quia amore langueo.

"I crowned hir with blis, and sche me with thorn;
    I ledde hir to chaumbir, and sche me to die;   *bedchamber*
35   I broughte hir to worschipe, and sche me to scorn;   *honor*
    I dide hir reverence, and she me vilonye.   *indignity*
    To love that loveth is no maistrie;   *one that loves; hard task*
        Hir hate made nevere my love hir foo.   *foe*
    Axe me no questioun whi —   *Ask*
40   *Quia amore langueo.*

"Loke unto myn hondis, Man:
    These gloves were yove me whan Y hir soughte —   *given to me*
Thei ben not white, but rede and wan,   *are; discolored*
    Onbroudrid with blood. My spouse hem broughte.   *Embroidered*
45   Thei wole not of; Y loose hem noughte.   *will not come off*
        I wowe hir with hem whereevere sche go —   *woo; goes*
    These hondis for hir so freendli foughte,   *as a friend*
        Quia amore langueo.

"Merveille noughte, Man, though Y sitte stille: *Marvel; motionless*
50   Se, love hath schod me wondir streite,   *shod; very tightly*
Boclid my feet, as was hir wille,   *Buckled*
    With scharp naile, lo! Thou maiste waite   *nails; You may know*
    In my love was nevere desaite —   *deceit*
        Alle myn humours Y have opened hir to —
55   There my bodi hath maad hir hertis baite,   *has been made bait for her heart*
        Quia amore langueo.

"In my side Y have made hir neste.
    Loke in: How weet a wounde is heere!   *wet*
This is hir chaumbir. Heere schal sche reste,
60   That sche and Y may slepe in fere.   *sleep together*
    Heere may she waische if ony filthe were;   *wash; any*
        Heere is sete for al hir woo.   *shelter; woe*
    Come whanne sche wole, sche schal have chere,   *welcome*
        Quia amore langueo.

65	"I wole abide til sche be redy;	*wait*
	I wole hir sue if sche seie nay;	*pursue; say*
	If sche be richilees, Y wole be gredi,	*uncaring· forward*
	And if sche be daungerus, Y wole hir praie.	*aloof; entreat*
	If sche wepe, than hide Y ne may —	*withdraw*
70	Myn armes her highed to clippe hir me to:	*here raised; embrace*
	Crie oonys! Y come. Now, Soule, asay!	*once; attempt [it]*
	Quia amore langueo.	

	"I sitte on this hil for to se fer.	*so that I may see far*
	I loke into the valey my spouse to se.	
75	Now renneth sche awayward, yit come sche me neer,	*she runs away; nearer*
	For out of my sighte may sche not be.	
	Summe wayte hir prai to make hir to flee,	*await their prey*
	I renne bifore and fleme hir foo.	*run; drive away her enemy*
	Returne, my spouse, ayen to me!	
80	*Quia amore langueo.*	

	"Fair love, lete us go pleye —	
	Applis ben ripe in my gardayne;	
	I schal thee clothe in a newe aray;	*fashion*
	Thi mete schal be mylk, hony, and wiyn.	*food; wine*
85	Fair love, lete us go digne —	*dine*
	Thi sustynaunce is in my crippe, lo!	*bag*
	Tarie thou not, my fair spouse myne!	*Delay*
	Quia amore langueo.	

	"Iff thou be foul, Y schal thee make clene;	
90	If thou be siik, Y schal thee hele;	*sick*
	If thou moorne ought, Y schal thee meene.	*at all; comfort*
	Whi wolt thou not, fair love, with me dele?	
	Foundist thou evere love so leel?	*loyal*
	What woldist thou, spouse, that Y schulde do?	*do you wish*
95	I may not unkyndeli thee appele,	*accuse*
	Quia amore langueo.	

	"What schal Y do with my fair spouse	
	But abide hir, of my gentilnes,	*wait for her, out of courtesy*
	Til that sche loke out of hir house	*body*

100   Of fleischli affeccioun? Love myn sche is!

        Hir bed is maade: hir bolstir is blis;   *bolster*

           Hir chaumbir is chosen, is ther non moo.   *none other [like it]*

        Loke out on me at the wyndow of kyndenes,

           Quia amore langueo.

105   "My love is in hir chaumbir. Holde youre pees!

        Make ye no noise, but lete hir slepe.

      My babe Y wolde not were in disese;   *discomfort*

        I may not heere my dere child wepe;

        With my pap Y schal hir kepe.   *breast; feed her*

110   Ne merveille ye not though Y tende hir to: *attend*

        This hole in my side had nevere be so depe,   *been*

           But *quia amore langueo.*

      "Longe thou for love nevere so high,

        My love is more than thin may be:[1]

115   Thou wepist, thou gladist, Y sitte thee bi —   *rejoice*

        Yit woldist thou oonys, leef, loke unto me,   *dear one*

        Schulde I alwey fede thee.

           With children mete? Nay, love, not so! —   *baby food*

        I wole preve thi love with adversité,   *prove (i.e., test)*

120   *Quia amore langueo.*

      "Wexe not wery, myn owne wiif.   *Grow*

        What mede is it to lyve evere in coumfort?   *reward*

      In tribulacioun I regne moore riif,   *powerful*

        Oftetymes, than in disport —   *pleasant times*

125   In wele and in woo Y am ay to supporte![2]

           Than, dere Soule, go not me fro!

        Thi meede is markid whan thou art mort,   *reward; determined; dead*

           Quia amore langueo."

---

[1] *No matter how exaltedly you may long for love, / My love is greater than yours may be*

[2] *In gladness and in woe I am forever able to support [you]!*

Notes

Abbreviations:

Manuscripts:

L   MS Lambeth 853. [Base text.]
C   MS Cambridge University Library Hh.4.12.

Editions based on L:

Fu[L]   Furnivall (1903). [A diplomatic text.]
CS   Chambers and Sidgwick (1926). [Omits stanzas 4, 6–8.]
Ka   Kaiser (1958). [Omits stanzas 8–9, 12–13, 15–16.]
Re   Reeves (1965). [Omits stanzas 12–16.]
Wi   Wimsatt (1978). [Fragmentary; adopts C order.]
Ri   Riddy (1989).

Editions based on C:

Fu[C]   Furnivall (1903). [A diplomatic text.]
Co   Cook (1915). [Omits stanzas 4–16.]
NL   Nicholson and Lee (1917).
Com   Comper (1936).
Ce   Cecil (1940).
Do   Donaldson (1950).
SS   Sisam and Sisam (1970).
Gr   Gray (1975). [Adopts L order.]
St   Stevick (1994). [Adopts L order.]
Du   Duncan (1995). [Adopts L order.]

Variants from C are listed in the following notes, as are the emendations made by editors (aside from modernized spellings). Most editions based on one MS incorporate some readings from the other one; these editorial decisions are recorded below.

72

1   *a valey of this.* C: *the vaile of.* The overt psychologizing of the landscape, as part of the narrator's "restless mind," is exceptional among early English lyrics. Stouck describes this opening as "marvelously evocative, Dantesque," and glosses the valley as the narrator's "state of separation from God, but . . . not so far from Him as to be in a state of sin." She finds the scene "reminiscent of courtly love dream visions" and compares it to Chaucer's *Book of the Duchess* (p. 9). The traditional *chanson d'aventure* opening may cause one both to visualize the narrator as a man about to embark on a love adventure (Hill, p. 460) and to expect an overheard dialogue or complaint (Gray [1975], p. 126). Beyond these conventions, however, the figure of lovelorn seeking strongly evokes the lyric voice heard in Canticles (see, for example, 3.1–2, 4.6, 5.6, and 6.1).

2   *mede.* L: *myde*; C: *mede*, adopted by CS, Ka, Re, Ri. On the punning development of the word, from the site of searching to the sought-for reward, see note to line 122.

3   *a trewelove.* The narrator is engaged in the same sort of ambiguous search as is the lovelorn maiden in the opening of *The Four Leaves of the Truelove.* He seeks "*truelove*," an abstract (and divine) quality, or a secular lover, or, in the naturalism of the setting, a cross-shaped plant (herb Paris) known by this popular name and commonly sought as a sign of good luck in love. As in *Truelove*, the end of the search is found to exist unambiguously in the figure of Christ crucified.

4   *Y took.* C: *toke I*, adopted by Re.

6   *huge.* C: *gret.*

7   *how.* Adopted by Com; omitted in C.

8   Canticles 2.5 (2.8, Vulgate). A contemporary gloss of the phrase exists in Richard Rolle's *Form of Living* (ed. S. J. Ogilvie-Thomson, pp. 15–25), further elaborated in *Ego dormio* (pp. 26–33). See also the phrase as refrain in *In a Tabernacle of a Tower* and allusions to it in English couplets embedded in Latin homilies (ed. Carleton Brown, *Register of Middle English Religious and Didactic Verse*, vol. 1 [Oxford: University Press for the Bibliographical Society, 1916], p. 131).

9   *hil.* C: *mownt.* The hill with the tree is to be associated with the Cross on

Calvary. In the topography of the poem, it contrasts with the valley (perhaps the "shadow of death," Psalm 23.4). The narrator's discovery of it signifies his moving closer to God. The hill remains a focal point throughout, a locus of stillness, unlike the wandering — by restless narrator and Mannis Soule — that takes place around it.

10   *the*. C: *thys*.

10–11   Here the secular signifiers for "truelove" dissolve into sacramental ones of increasing religious valence: a search for the cruciform plant (or, an earthly lover) leads to the Tree-cross, and then to the prostrate, wounded stranger (the five wounds and Cross coalesce in meaning and form). On the iconographic theme "Christ in distress," see Woolf (1968), p. 188, and Deirdre Kessel-Brown, "The Emotional Landscape of the Forest in the Mediaeval Love Lament," *Medium Ævum* 59 (1990), 244–45.

12   *sigh*. C: *saw*.

13   *ben*. Adopted by St; C: *be*.

14   *graciouse*. This word is important. It bears both its courtly sense of refinement as well as its full religious weight, "filled with grace." It is the narrator's looking into the stranger's face that brings about his own expression of compassion and initiates the erotic encounter. Here is where the narrator, as Mannis Soule, begins to respond to Christ's love. (There is the possibility of an herbal pun, too; compare *Truelove*, note to line 515.)

        loken. C: *loke*.

15   *whi*. C: *how he* (adopted by Watts).

17   The stranger, who identifies himself by the name Truelove, has assumed Christ's features. Even as he names himself as "the one the speaker seeks," he is also the alter-ego of the narrator, that is, "someone who searches and languishes for love even as he does" (Astell, pp. 147–48).

18   On the Bride as sister, see Canticles 4.9–12 and 5.1–2.

19   *we*. C: *I*, adopted by Wi (and Watts).

19   *discevere*. C: *dissevere*, adopted by Wi.

21   *for hir a paleis*. C: *hyr a place full*; Gr, Du: *hyr a paleis*; Re: *her a palace full*. The references to Christ's Incarnation ("leaving his kingdom") and to heaven (a "palace") are couched in courtly terms.

22   C: *She flytt I folowyd I luffed her soo*, adopted by Wi, Re (and Watts). Segar's modernized text mimics the preterites of C: *She fled, I followed*.

23   *I suffride this peyne*. C: *That I suffred thes paynes*; Re: *That I suffered this pain*.

25   *spouse . . . love*. C: *love . . . spouse*, adopted by Re.

25–26   The lines contain resonances of the Canticles account of the Bride, who is fair (1.8, 1.16, 5.9, 6.1) and who suffers beatings from the watchmen as she seeks the Bridegroom (5.7).

26 ff.   These vividly contrastive reproaches of Christ are based on the *improperia* in the liturgy for Good Friday. Astell sees a purifying effect in these reproaches (p. 148). See also Stouck, pp. 6–7; and Wimsatt (1978), pp. 336–37.

28   *scherte*. Adopted by St; C: *surcote*. A symbolic reference to Christ's scourged back and wounded side. Gray notes that each manuscript provides a reading that fits with the Lover-Knight motif, but he prefers *surcote* as "the more obviously knightly word" ([1975], p. 126).

29   *longynge of love yit wolde Y*. C: *langyng love I will*. St, following C, emends *will* to *wol*.

30   *are*. C: *be*; St: *ben*. The *r* in L is misformed, causing Fu[L] to read *axe*; Ka, Ri print *are*. The letter lacks the diagonal descender present in the scribe's *x* elsewhere. The scribe may have intended to write a capital *R* (an example appears in L, top of p. 113).

31   *hir evere, as Y hir het*. C: *over als I hett*; Fu[C] emends: *ever als I hett*, which all editors of C adopt.

39   C: *Ask than no moo questions whye*; Re: *Ask me then no question why* (as in Segar's translation).

40   C: *But* precedes the refrain. Stouck notes that here and at line 49, Christ addresses the narrator and audience directly, while he consistently refers to the Soul in third person; she feels that this rhetoric keeps narrator and soul distinct (p. 9). The distinctions are not, however, so clear-cut; the boundary lines of individual identities are constantly shifting and blurring. Christ's first words addressed the narrator (and reader) as "dere Soule" (line 7), so in naming his beloved "Mannis Soule" (line 18), he implicitly ties her identity to that of the narrator/reader. These addresses to "Man" repeat the effect.

41–45   The gloves symbolize Christ's wounded hands. This image may derive from medieval christological commentaries upon Canticles (Wimsatt [1978] p. 337 n. 34).

42   *yove*. C: *geven*; St: *yeven*.

43   *ben*. Adopted by St; C: *be*.

44   *hem*. Adopted by St; C: *them*.

        broughte. Adopted by Do; C: *bowght*, an interesting variant that alludes to the sacramental meaning of Christ's suffering.

45   *wole*. Adopted by St; C: *wyll*.

        loose. Adopted by Com; C: *lefe*.

        hem. Adopted by St; C: *them*.

46   *hem*. Adopted by St; C: *them*.

47   *for hir so freendli*. C: *full frendly for hyr*.

50   *Se*. C: *My*.

        schod. C, adopted by Ri; L: *sched*.

51   *Boclid*. C: *She boklyd*.

52   *naile*. C: *nailes*, adopted by Re.

52   *lo!* Adopted by Do; C: *well*, adopted by Re.

54   *Alle.* C: *For all.*

        myn humours. C: *my membres*, adopted by Re, Wi, Ri (and Watts). Hill explicates the C reading: "Christ speaks of 'opening' his 'membres' for 'mannys soule', and the *locus* of erotic contact is the wound in Christ's side, an opening within which Christ and 'mannys soule' may enjoy erotic contact" (p. 461). The reading in L is also sensual, although maybe less erotic; the *humours* denote Christ's bodily fluids — that is, blood, water, and milk — accessible through the wound. As in lines 58–61, the emphasis in L is on the wetness of God's wounds, in which the soul will be washed and reborn, as in baptism. Eucharistic meanings are also implicit; see Rubin, pp. 302–06.

55   C: *My body I made hyr hertys baite*, adopted by Re, Wi. Wimsatt reads lines 54–55 as the transition point between a "Passion meditation" and "Christ's active wooing of the soul" ([1978], p. 337). On this striking figure, Gray comments, "The poet's bold imagination does not shrink from extreme images" ([1972], p. 144).

57   The meditation upon the Passion and Christ's crucified body have been leading to this climactic entering into that body through the wound. Even as Christ describes this spot where the Soul will find refuge, he urges the narrator/reader (the two are now merged) to "look in" and visualize it. On the meaningful symbolism of such devotion, see Beckwith, pp. 58–63.

        neste. The allusion is to Canticles 2.14 ("My dove in the clifts of the rock, in the hollow places of the wall"), which medieval commentators interpreted as the Bride-Soul making her nest in Christ's wounded side; see Eric Colledge, *The Mediaeval Mystics of England* (London: John Murray, [1962]), pp. 11–13; Gray (1963), pp. 85, 129; Wimsatt (1978), pp. 338–40. Citing the mystical meanings attached to the Canticles verse by Bede and Bernard of Clairvaux, Stouck claims that the English poet's aim is more purely devotional than mystical: "The associations are primarily with refuge and retreat rather than with upward-moving contemplation" (p. 7). Wimsatt maintains, however, that *This Restless Mind* is one of the rare Middle English poems that is wholly mystical ([1984], p. 82).

58   *in.* Adopted by St, Du; C: *in me.*

58   *weet*. C: *wyde*, adopted by Re, Wi, Ri (and Watts). But *weet*, like *humours* in line 54, emphasizes the wound as a site in which the soul may bathe and cleanse herself (line 61). Wetness also is compatible with the blended sexual imagery that the poet attaches to the sacramental wound of Christ: erotic lovemaking, gestation in the womb, breastfeeding.

61   Washing in the blood of Christ's wounds, removing the filth of natural birth and sin, is the subject of *A Meditation of the Five Wounds of Jesus Christ* in Oxford, Univ. Coll. MS 97. The meditant is asked to contemplate each wound in order and "clecch up the watir" from each "well." The devotional exercise culminates in the fifth wound:

> Out of the largest and deppest welle of everelastyng lif, in the moste opene wounde in Cristys blessed syde, cleech up deppest and hertyliest watir of joye ard blisse withouten ende, biholdyng theere inwardly how Crist Jhesu, God and man, to brynge thee to everlastynge lyf, suffrede that harde and hydous deeth on the cros and suffrede his syde to be opened and hyself to be stongyn to the herte with that grisly spere, and so with that deelful strook of the spere theere gulchide out of Cristys syde that blysful floode of watir and blood to raunsone us, watir of his syde to wasshe us, and blood of his herte to bugge us. For love of thise blessede woundes, creep in to this hoot baath of Cristys herte-blood, and theer bathe thee. (ed. Horstmann, p. 441)

See also the bathing allegory in *Ancrene Wisse*, Pt. 7: "[The Lord] makes a bath of his blood for us . . . he loves us more than any mother her child' (ed. and trans. Bella Millett and Jocelyn Wogan-Browne, *Medieval English Prose for Women* [Oxford: Clarendon, 1990], p. 119); and in *A Talking of the Love of God*, pp. 347–48.

62   *sete*. C: *sucour*. On the meaning "abiding place for soul," see *MED sete* n.(2), sense 4.(b).

63   *whanne sche wole*. C: *if she will*.

65   *wole*. Adopted by St; C: *will*.

65–80   Stouck sees in these stanzas an expression of "Christ's mercy, protectiveness, and love-longing" (pp. 3–4, 8), comparable to the conception of Christ found in Julian of Norwich's *Shewings* (see especially pp. 123–26, 150–51).

66   *I wole hir sue if.* Adopted by SS, Gr; C: *I will to hyr send or.* St, following C, emends *will* to *wol*, *or* to *er.*; Do, following C, emends *or* to *if.*

67   *wole.* Adopted by St; C: *will.*

       gredi. Adopted by NL, Do; C: *redy*, adopted by Ri. *Gredi* may be translated "forward, overanxious." Seger in her translation substitutes the word *steady.*

68   *daungerus.* A descriptive word drawn from the conventional language of court poetry. Other examples are *leel* (line 93) and *unkyndeli* (line 95). See Gray (1972), p. 144; Wimsatt (1978), p. 340; and Stouck, p. 3.

       wole. Adopted by St; C: *will.*

69   *wepe.* C: *do wepe*, adopted by Ri.

       hide Y ne. C: *byd I*, adopted by Ri; Re: *bide I ne.* Riddy glosses the phrase in C as "I beg [her] to stop." The meaning for *hide*, "withdraw," is common in biblical language. See *O.E.D. hide* v.[1], sense 1.c.

70   *her highed.* L: *her hired*; C: *ben spred*, adopted by Re, Ri. Riddy notes that Christ's spread arms evoke the "posture of the crucifixion as well as that of embrace" (p. 419). S substitutes a modernized gloss: *are outstretched.* The verb *hiren* in L does not yield good sense, but the verb *highed* ("raised") would accord with C. An error of *r* for yogh (= *gh*) is plausible. Christ's arms upon the Cross were likened to a mother's ready embrace in several meditative treatises from fourteenth-century England: see especially *A Talking of the Love of God*, p. 347; *The Monk of Farne*, ed. Hugh Farmer (Baltimore: Helicon, 1961), p. 64; and other texts cited by Heimmel, pp. 38–45. The pose is compared to a lover's embrace in the fourteenth-century English hymn *Sweet Jesus, Now Will I Sing* (ed. Horstmann, p. 15, lines 181–84). The two ideas — love embrace, maternal embrace — are combined in the English translation of Aelred of Rievaulx's *De institutione inclusarum* appearing in the Vernon MS (ed. John Ayto and Alexandra Barratt, EETS o.s. 287 [London, 1984], p. 35, lines 380–83).

       me. Adopted by SS; omitted in C.

71   *Soule.* C: *sowle*, misprinted by Fu[C] as *soule*. It is possible to interpret the speaker of *Y come* in either of two ways, as the soul's cry or as Christ's response.

Modern punctuation forces a choice, and I have taken the words to be Christ's faithful answer. Compare Isaiah 30.19: "at the voice of thy cry, as soon as he shall hear, he will answer thee." Editors who have agreed: Re, SS, Ga, Gr, Ri; those with the other interpretation: NL, CS, Ce, Do, Du. Furnivall, who printed both texts, punctuated both ways. Astell finds in this line a revelatory identification of listener with Bride: "Now [Christ] no longer speaks to the man about his Bride; rather, he speaks to his Bride in the man" (p. 150).

73   *this.* C: *an.*

73–80   Even as this stanza allows development of an image of Christ as hunter. the Soul as his prey, the activity and passivity of the two roles are strangely blended. Christ's pursuit is active (line 22), yet his method is to lie in wait, his body as bait (line 55). Here he sits and observes his spouse's running movements, even as he "runs before" her as protector (line 78). Eventually the Soul's restless movements are housed (line 99) and then chambered (line 105), as she grows still and sleeps within the wound. The Soul too is a kind of hunter, in causing the wounds of Christ. On the imagery of hunting and of movements in the poem, see Hill, pp. 460–61, and also Wimsatt (1978), p. 340. (For an opinion that the logic is flawed, see Stevick, p. 110.)

74   *into the valey.* C: *to the vayle.*

       to. Adopted by St; C: *I.*

75   *yit come sche me neer.* C: *now cummyth she narre,* a reading parallel to the line's first half (and adopted by Segar). Du, following C, emends *cummyth* to *come.* The L reading is the more subtle one, with its idea that even as the soul flees "awayward," she sometimes approaches nearer. The soul seems to know less about her path than does Christ who observes her.

76   *be.* So Ri; L: *flee.* The line in C reads: *Yet fro min eye syght she may nat be.*

77   *hir*[1]. Adopted by St; C: *ther.*

       to[2]. Omitted in C.

77–78   "Some await their prey to make her flee [into capture], but I run in front of her, in order to vanquish her foe (i.e., to save her from capture)." The imagery of masculine hunter is conflated with the actions of a divine protector. The mention of others (*Summe*) evokes the contrastive actions of ordinary lovers or hunters — or even the devil (her foe) as hunter.

78 *bifore and fleme*. C: *tofore to chastise*; St: *to-fore to fleme*.

79 *Returne*. Adopted by St; C: *Recover*.

    spouse. C: *soule*. This variation between the two manuscripts recurs at lines 85 and 94.

81 *Fair love*. C: *My swete spouse*.

    lete us go pleye. Adopted by St; C: *will we goo play*.

81–104 Christ's words to Mannis Soule in stanzas 11–13 enact a process of seduction; she is now "near enough for Christ to address her directly in passionate and richly charged imagery drawn from the *Canticum canticorum*" (Hill, pp. 461–62). On the scriptural imagery, see Wimsatt (1978), pp. 340–41. Stouck finds little mystical rigor in these stanzas, because they "stress the ease, comforts, and rewards of meditation rather than its demanding nature by insisting on the passive nature of the Soul" (p. 9). However, the ease felt here is only transitional; after the union of Christ and Bride, the espoused Soul will be constantly tested by adversity (line 119).

82 See Canticles 5.1: "Let my beloved come into his garden, and eat the fruit of his apple trees."

83 *thee clothe*. Adopted by St; C: *clothe the*. Wimsatt suggests echoes from Canticles 5.3 and 5.7, but Riddy points to the stronger portrayal of new garments in Revelations 19.8, where the Bride of the Lamb is "arrayed in fine linen, clean and white: for the white linen is the righteousness of saints."

84 Canticles 5.1: "I am come into my garden . . . I have eaten . . . my honey; I have drunk my wine with my milk."

85 *Fair love*. C: *Now dere soule* (adopted by Watts).

    digne. C: *dyne*, adopted by Wi. The spelling is influenced by OF.

86 *crippe*. Adopted by Gr; C: *skrypp*, adopted by Wi (and Watts). *Crippe*, a rare variant of *scrippe*, "bag, pouch, pilgrim's wallet," is adopted in Gray's edition based on C ([1975], p. 127). It serves as another figure for Christ's wound (Wimsatt [1978], pp. 341–42). Astell notes an allusion to the Eucharist (p. 151).

87 *thou not, my*. C: *not now*; Ri: *thou not*.

89 *thee make*. C, Com, Gr: *make*; St, SS, Du, following Fu[C], emend: *make thee*. Other editors (NL, Ce, Do) adopt this emendation of C without comment.

89–91 The contrasts within these lines, in which Christ explains the healing, cleansing powers of his blood, recall in form the *improperia* of stanzas 4 and 5.

91 *moorne ought*. C: *owght morne*.

   thee meene. Adopted by Ce, St, Du; C: *bemene*; Com emends: *thee be-mene*.

92 *Whi wolt thou not, fair love*. C: *Spouse why will thow nowght*. Fu[F] mistakenly prints *faire* for *fair*. Com, Ce, Du emend C's *will* to *wilt*. St emends *will thow* to *wyltow*.

93 *Foundist thou evere*. C: *Thow fowndyst never*.

94 C: *What wilt thow sowle that I shall do*; St emends *wilt thow* to *wyltow*.

95 *not unkyndeli*. C: *of unkyndnes*.

97 *do*. C: *do now*.

   fair. Omitted in C.

98 C: *Abyde I will hyre jantilnesse*. Com blends the two MS readings: *But abide her will of my gentleness*.

99 *Til that sche loke*. C: *Wold she loke onys*, adopted by Wi. Com blends the two MS readings: *Till that she look once out of her house*.

100 *affeccioun*. C: *affeccions*. The "house of fleshly affection" refers to the body and its desires.

100   *Love myn sche is*. C: *and unclennesse*. The half-line variant in C continues the idea of worldly corruption.

101   *blis*. Adopted by Do, SS; C: *in blysse*, adopted by Wi.

102   *is ther non moo*. C: *suche ar no moo*, adopted by Wi. Using C as evidence, I interpret the phrase in L to mean that the chamber is incomparable. R and CS punctuate the phrase as a question, and do not gloss its meaning.

103   *on me*. Omitted in C, and by Ri.

           at the. Com emends: *of thy*.

           wyndow. C: *wyndows*, adopted by Wi. Canticles 2.9: "Behold, he standeth behind our wall, looking through the windows, looking through the lattices." Wimsatt explains that "'Our wall' was usually seen as the house of the body, the windows as the senses or the eye of reason" (1978), p. 342.

104–09 The silent space between these stanzas "marks the moment of conversion" (Hill, p. 462). Another aspect of Christ is revealed; He changes from Bridegroom to nurturing Mother. The Soul, initially in erotic contact with Christ's wound, becomes the infant nursing her (or his) mother's breast. A metaphoric impregnation, gestation, and birth has occurred in the space of lines 103–05, and now "the wound in Christ's side becomes the breast which feeds the soul with spiritual milk" (Wimsatt [1978], p. 343). On the concept of Jesus as mother, central to the piety of Julian of Norwich and the author of the *Ancrene Wisse*, see discussions in Bynum, pp. 129–35; Heimmel, pp. 34–45; Woolf (1968), pp. 189–91; Stouck, pp. 8–9; and Astell, pp. 152–53. A further source comes from commentaries on Canticles 1.3, "where the bride speaks of 'remembering thy breasts more than wine.' The commentaries discuss the beneficent milk which flows from these breasts" (Wimsatt [1978], 343). Bernard of Clairvaux calls it "the milk of inward sweetness" (*On the Song of Songs*, vol. 1, p. 58; see also Hill, p. 462).

105   *love*. Adopted by Com; C: *spouse*.

           hir. Omitted in C.

           youre. St: *thy*. See note to line 106.

105–20 The order of stanzas 14 and 15 is reversed in C. Gray, who edits C, adopts the order of L; Hill's interpretation, based upon Gray's text, thus follows the order of L, not C (as he mistakenly states, p. 466 n. 3). Wimsatt, using his own text based on L, prefers the order of C (1978), p. 336, n. 25.

106 *ye.* Omitted in C; compare also line 110. Taken with *youre* (line 105), the three pronouns of formal address in this stanza distance the reader from the intimacy taking place between Christ and Mannis Soule. The trope of narrator has disappeared; it has yielded partially, as Mannis Soule, to God's intimacy, and it has also remained partially distanced as the voyeuristic reader. Christ's rhetorical shift to pronouns of intimate address in stanza 15 ("thow," "thee," "thin") marks his final drawing in of the reader. It is an appeal to the reader to let go of the boundaries of self that distinguish between Mannis Soule, narrator, and reader, and that separate him (and her) from God. See also Canticles 2.7 and 8.4 (formal pleas not to awaken the Bride).

107 *Y wolde not were in.* C: *shall sofre noo.*

108 *may.* R emends: *wolde.*

109 *With.* C: *For with.* The reference to Christ's breast appears to have embarrassed Segar in 1915; she prints, without comment, a substituted line: *With watchful care I shall her keep.*

110 *Ne merveille ye not.* C: *No wondyr.*

111 *be.* C: *ben.*

113 *Longe thou for love.* C: *Long and love thow.*

114 *My love is.* C: *Yit is my love.*

115 *wepist . . . gladist.* C: *gladdyst . . . wepist.*

116 C: *Yit myght thow spouse loke onys at me.*

116–18 All previous editors have read these three lines as a single sentence, joining lines 117–18 into a question. Lines 116–17 should instead be read as a declaration of Christ's constancy: "I will always take care of you." Compare Julian of Norwich:

> For He [Jesus] hath not all to don but to entendyn about the salvation of hir Child. It is His office for to saven us. It is His worship to don it, and it is His will we knowen it . . . (p. 126)

The rest of the stanza declares the parental manner: not perpetually fed baby food, the maturing soul will be reared with adversity. On the "food of children," see discussions by Wimsatt (1978), p. 344; and Stouck, pp. 4, 8–10. Heimmel offers a good summary of biblical passages on God's parental rearing of the soul, pp. 8–11.

117 *Schulde.* C: *Spouse shuld.*

118 *children.* C: *childys.*

119 *wole preve thi.* Adopted by St; C: *pray the*; SS, Gr, Du: *preve thi*; Do: *preve thee.*

121 *wiif.* C: *dere wyfe.*

122 *mede.* The promise of receiving a sought-for reward, mentioned here and in line 127, reshapes, in retrospect, the meaning of the narrator's opening search "in mounteyne and in mede." There is a subtle pun upon *mede*, "meadow," and *mede*, "reward."

it to lyve evere. C: *aye to lyffe.*

123 *In.* C: *For in.*

regne. C: *ryn.* The variant has led several C-based editors to a different interpretation. SS, Ga gloss *ryn more ryfe* as "run (to help) more quickly"; Do as "run more often."

124 *Oftetymes.* L: *Ofttymes*; C: *Ofter tymes*, adopted by Wi. The meter would seem to require that a medial syllable be pronounced.

125 C: *In welth in woo ever I support.*

126   *Than, dere Soule.* C; L: *Myn owne wiif.* The reading in L repeats the first line of the stanza. C's reading is better, directing the discourse back to the opening "narrator" — by now whatever remains distinct in this persona has merged with the reader. Nonetheless, this figure for wayward, restless, truth-seeking mankind was addressed as "dere Soule" in the first stanza (line 7).

        not. C: *never.*

128   C: *In blysse* is added before the refrain. SS, Gr, Du omit the phrase.

The Dispute between Mary and the Cross

Introduction

The Dispute between Mary and the Cross is an invented debate between the two
most intimate participant-observers of the Crucifixion: Christ's sorrowing mother and
the non-human Cross. Christ is present too, of course, but he never speaks, not even
to utter his own last words, which are reported to Mary by the Cross (line 271).
Jesus's figure is entirely passive, with only the blood flowing from his wounds giving
motion to his body. God's bleeding serves as both spectacle and poetic focal point.
It is the source of Mary's pain, the Cross's occupational *raison d'etre*, and the
meditant's subject for contemplative horror and veneration. Christ's body in torture
is the sacrificial object to be named and renamed, defined and redefined by the two
disputants.[1]

The verbal texture of *The Dispute between Mary and the Cross* reveals a remarkable
poet obsessed with language and, especially, with typological and metaphysical
wordplay. At these skills he is so startlingly adept that his verbal pyrotechnics may
be worthily compared to those of the Pearl-poet or of William Langland. We have
here a distinct style of pun and metaphor, one shaped by an aesthetic of physical
literalism, violent semantic conjunction, and rapid imagistic transmutation.[2] Words
and visuals shift radically, sometimes at dizzying speed, often typologically or
associatively, usually with a transcendent effect, as if the veil of words were constantly
being ripped to reveal the holiest of meanings. Intensity informs both technique and
content, as the poet verbally dissects Christ's bleeding body on a wooden cross-beam
for all latent signs.

In one remarkable stanza, for instance, Adam's bite of the apple collapses in time
to become Christ's deep side-wound, a radical revision of the fruit-on-a-tree figure

---

[1]The reenvisioning of God's tortured body through a series of imaginative figures exists, as
well, in Richard Rolle's meditation on the Passion: *Meditation B*, ed. Ogilvie-Thomson, p. 74,
lines 195–250. Similes for the wounds liken them to heavenly stars, a net, a dovehouse, a
honeycomb, a book, and a meadow of flowers. Of these figures, only the book also appears in
Dispute. See also Gray (1972), pp. 122–45.

[2]O. S. Pickering has detected the poet's style in three other poems (listed in the Select
Bibliography; see Pickering [1978, 1997]).

that conflates sin, sacrifice, eucharist, and redemption (stanza 10). This revelatory figure typifies how the poet (in the words of the doctrinal Cross) continually reconstitutes images of graphic gore as figures of eucharistic nourishment, bills of pardon, or other types of redemptive exempla. The *Dispute* poet asks the meditant reader to confront the Passion as a paradox of body-torn spectacle and whole-bodied redemption. He grounds religious meaning in the physical, an incarnational aesthetic that extends even to how the poem is structured, its distinctive design being two shapes superimposed: a Cross and a maternal human body. By means of poetic form, the poet makes manifest the physical nature of the two disputants while also advancing a theological argument of twin motherhood and double birth.

A look at the frame formed by stanzas 1 and 40 illustrates the poet's method of naming and renaming through pun, contrast, and unfolded meaning. In the opening stanza Mary names Jesus her "Fruit," now removed from her body and nailed to "Rode-treo." She calls the Cross a disgraceful "pillori" for felons who is harming her innocent son (lines 1–13), her womb's fruit now turned into a tree's fruit. The maternal/arboreal analogy sets off a dazzling flux of fructuous images in subsequent stanzas, from the apple of Eden to the grape of eucharistic wine. Eventually, too, the Cross will revalue the name "pillori" it receives here from Mary by naming itself the "piler" (pillar) that shows humanity the vertical way to salvation (line 150). In reconfiguring the Cross both architecturally and linguistically, the poet's verbal sleight illuminates one of many holy transformations occurring through Christ's Passion.

The pathos of the first stanza — a scene of human torture told in the injured voice of distraught maternal sorrow — is similarly transmuted and wholly inverted in the last stanza. Christ's lacerated body is now seen to be merely a garment, borne (and born into) expressly "to blede." Thus clothed in royal red garments, he rides a "stokky stede," the wooden "stock" of the Cross revealed as the sturdy mount of a heroic Knight, who rides this instrument to save people from the devil and lead them in triumph to Judgment. In a post-Resurrection world the roadmap to the afterlife has been newly configured. Formerly there was but one path, the one to hell; now there are two ways, one pointed to hell, the other to heaven. A person may choose between opposites, a choice drawn literally in the Cross's symmetrical pointings — up or down, right or left — and made possible by three mediating, physical agents: Jesus's blood, Mary (who imparted to him that blood), and the Cross (where the blood was shed). The final stanza thus inscribes Mary's opening tones of woe and reproach inside a larger sphere of triumph and joy.

Introduction

The poetic debate is itself symmetrically shaped like the Cross,[3] with the disputants opposed in emotional register (compassion/dispassion), gender (female/male, by pronoun), and species (human/nonhuman). In forty thirteen-line stanzas they speak in balanced turns, three speeches each: eight stanzas for Mary, nine for the Cross, three for Mary (first half); then, three for the Cross, nine for Mary, and eight for the Cross's winning position (second half). The resultant mirrored ratio, 8:9:3|3:9:8, is probably meaningful: 2^3 and 3^2 and 3, numbers of duality (as in the debate) and trinity. Meditation upon these lengths might suggest a cruciform shape, with a vertical base of eight units, a horizontal crossbar of nine, and a topmast of three. One manuscript of the three that preserve *Dispute* (MS Royal 18 A.x) includes marginal notations to mark the changes in speakers, which may indicate that the poem was, at least in some settings, read aloud in opposing voices. Moreover, while the disputants are meant to be contrasts, they also come to be, in religious essence, alike: both are "mothers" for God and mankind (lines 450–51, 491), and both are trees, which in Mary's case means the human lineage she embodies (line 478). The poet builds poetic argument on chiastic opposition and analogy, and as he does so, he models the poem on the familiar and sacred shape of a cross.

Modern readers should not hesitate to apprehend this seemingly arcane shaping of the poem, for the poet shows that he did not expect it to be obscure. At the poetic midpoint he displays the figure through the Cross's words:

> "Ladi, to make the devel dredi,
> God schop me a scheld, schame to schilde,
> > Til Lomb of Love dyede,
> > And on me yeld the gost with vois.
> > I was chose a relik chois,
> > The signe of Jhesu Cristes Crois;
> > > Ther dar no devel abyde." (lines 254–60)

The center of the poem is a defining moment, and here the Cross triply names himself as a shield, a choice relic, and a sign that wards off the devil. In the thirteenth-century *Ancrene Wisse*, a late version of which is found near *Dispute* in the Vernon MS, a figure of the crucifix as a shield is developed:

> In a shield there are three things, the wood, the leather and the painting. So it was in this shield: the wood of the cross, the leather of God's body, the painting of the red blood that

---

[3]My analysis of poetic structure is based on the forty-stanza poem found in the Vernon and Simeon MSS. The Royal MS possesses twenty-eight stanzas and is apparently an abridgement of the version found in Vernon/Simeon.

colored it so beautifully. . . . After a brave knight's death, his shield is hung high in church in his memory. So is this shield, that is, the crucifix, set high in church . . . to bring to mind Jesus Christ's chivalry, which he performed on the cross. (trans. Savage and Watson, p. 192)

The Cross is made the shield of Christ the Lover-Knight, the same figure for Christ that appears at the end of *Dispute*.

Crucial, too, in the Cross's self-representation is the notion that it defends Christians against the devil, a popular understanding of the Cross's power that was readily adapted to religio-magical purposes. Medical charms from medieval England were punctuated liberally with cruciform signs to be physically gestured by the practitioner as a way to enhance the charm's potency. They might also include Cross-inspired asseverations by the four apostles, or by a house's four corners, as in John the carpenter's "white *pater-noster*" in Chaucer's Miller's Tale (I 3478–85).[4] Again, the *Ancrene Wisse* provides some of the best analogous passages on the Cross as a devil-repelling talisman, as it guides anchoritic readers (and possibly, by the time it appears in the Vernon MS, lay readers) in their devotions to the Cross, including, for example, a prayer by which to bless one's bed before retiring:

> The cross + makes all evil flee.
> The cross + restores everything.
> By this sign of the cross +
> may all evil flee far away.
> And by the same sign +
> may whatever is good be preserved. (p. 65)

Elsewhere, the author explains how to use the Cross as a weapon against the devil:

> Hold it up against the enemy, show it to him clearly. The sight of it alone puts him to flight. For it both shames him and terrifies him out of his wits. (p. 155)

Such an act of self-defense is meant quite literally, for the devil lurks behind every temptation felt physically in the body: "Drive your knees sharply down to the earth and lift up the staff of the cross and swing it in four directions against the hell-dog: this is nothing else than to bless yourself all around with the sign of the holy cross" (p. 154). Attacks from the devil required vigorous defense.

---

[4]See, for example, Gray (1974), pp. 56–71; the charm edited by Theodore Silverstein, *English Lyrics before 1500*, York Medieval Texts (Evanston: Northwestern University Press, 1971), p. 124; and the charms in Ralph Hanna III, "*The Index of Middle English Verse and Huntington Library Collections*," *Papers of the Bibliographical Society of America* 74 (1980), 235–58.

Introduction

The practices recommended in *Ancrene Wisse* persist in many later texts that attest to a cultic adoration of the Cross as well as an abiding belief in its efficacious powers. From the thirteenth to the fifteenth centuries, the behaviors associated with these beliefs filtered increasingly into the lay population. In prescribing a set of devotional practices for a layman, a fifteenth-century clerical writer exhorts him to "make the sign of the Cross at the head, at the feet, at the hands, and at the side" of his bed every morning when he rises (Pantin, p. 398). At supper he is to fashion a Cross upon the wooden table from five bread crumbs, allowing no one but his wife to perceive what he is doing (p. 400). The five crumbs in this shape would recall the five wounds of Christ. At the same time, the writer asks the devout man *not* to "climb up to the Cross" in church, apparently discouraging a zealous practice of laypersons kissing the rood, which church officials thought either a risk or a nuisance (pp. 399, 404). Henry VI made a devotional custom of beginning each meal with "a certain dish which represented the five wounds of Christ as it were red with blood" (qtd. by Pantin, p. 408).

Why did the *Dispute* poet affix a Cross-sign at the center and further invoke it in the oppositional structure? Viewed against the popular tradition of devotion to the Cross, the answer is obvious. The poem is itself an emblematically shaped crucifix designed to shield the reader and ward off the devil. The poet leads the reader to meditate on the words of the holy disputants and the image of Christ bleeding, and — as in any other devotion to the Cross — to learn how to be saved. The practice of embedding a crucifix in poetry is not unique to this poet. It exists meaningfully in Thomas of Hales's *Love Rune* and in *The Four Leaves of the Truelove* (both appearing in this volume). Numerous Middle English religious poets position, without any deeper structuring, an image of the Crucifixion at the center of their verses.[5] A brief verse tale found in MS Ashmole 61, *The Legend of the Crucifix*, uses a chiastic structure to present an exemplum of reconciliation between two long-time enemies: the older knight repents his hatred at the one-quarter point, the two make peace at midpoint, and the younger knight is embraced and kissed by a momentarily animated

---

[5]See, for example, the centers of William Herebert's *Thou Wommon boute Vere* (lines 25–30, the Crucifixion); *The Sweetness of Jesus* (lines 60–61, Christ's vanquishing of the devil); and the Rolle-type *Lament over the Passion* (lines 13–16, Christ nailed and hung on Cross) (all ed. Carleton Brown, *Religious Lyrics of the XIVth Century*, second ed. rev. G. V. Smithers [Oxford: Clarendon, 1957], pp. 18–20, 61–65, 94–95). See also the lyric *Jhesu That Hast Me Dere Iboght* (ed. Brown, pp. 114–19); Pezzini, pp. 37–38; Rubin, pp. 302–08; and Weber, pp. 133–36, 250 n. 8.

crucifix at the three-quarters point.[6] Discovering poetic content matched to a cruciform shape was probably relatively routine for readers expecting a poem to be a useful meditational device. The *Dispute* poet is unusual, however, in declaring so emphatically the shape of the verbal token, that is, by conjuring, in the Cross's own words, that choice sign that scares off the devil.

The second figure verbally "made flesh" in *Dispute* — a maternal body giving birth — is somewhat more startling to discover, and it was doubtless less common in verse than was an embedded crucifix. The key places are stanzas 19 and 21, which surround the crucifix stanza quoted above. Stanza 19 recounts, in Mary's voice, the collective plea of the Old Testament prophets to be delivered "Out of the wildernesses ston" (line 237). This plea for release from a hard place, similar to a fetal struggle to be born, is answered by God's Incarnation in Mary, expressed as the stony "Mount of Syon / Becom Man" (line 239–40). Deliverance from stone required stone made flesh, with the rhyme-words *ston* and *bon* coming to seem divinely ordered. The prophets facing rocky barriers in the wilderness were unable to "bore" into "hevene blis" until "blod brac up the yate" (lines 243–47). Their release from exile and entry into heaven is visualized as a burrowing through a bloodied opening. The configuration enacts a birth, with the second disputant Mary — herself a virgin — being the archetypal mother who inspires the poetic figure of parturition.

In stanza 21 the speaking Cross must complete the explication begun by Mary. The imagery of stones dissolves when the gate breaks open, but another figure, the "Lomb of Love," remains, unifying stanzas 19–21. The prophets prayed for the "Lomb" to deliver them from the lion and the stone, and in response the incarnate God delivered them. Mary wonders why, if men were so much in need of the mild Lamb, did they and the Cross harm her child. The Cross responds that when the Lamb of Love died, he (the Cross) became the "relik chois," and he then explains the logic of redemption in spatial terms, that "Hevene yates weore keithed clos [shut tight] / Til the Lomb of Love dyede"; now "mon is out of bondes brouht, / And hevene dores undone!" Heaven's gates open as soon as the Cross reveals his essence and mission: it is he who has enabled the Lamb to die (Christ's last words also appear in stanza 21). The resultant image is thus of two figures superimposed: a crucifix upon the open ground of a gate newly ajar. The latter figure is maternally construed, that is,

---

[6]A compiler's devotional preoccupation with the Passion seems to unify the diverse mix of texts put together in MS Ashmole 61. The Ashmole *Charter of Christ* appears with a drawing of a shield bearing Christ's five wounds, and the *Northern Passion* ends with an exhortation "to have Christ's Passion in mind as a 'warant', or shield against the Devil" (Blanchfield, p. 83). For other crucifixes that greet and embrace the faithful, see Camille, pp. 213–14.

Mary (with maternal Cross) opens the gate that Eve had closed.[7]

This working out of the doctrine of redemption in terms of embodied signs is part of an incarnational aesthetic that merges meaning with form. The poet makes literal the Cross's efficacy. But how can he justify a literalism of birth, especially when the mother in question — Mary — did not herself experience natural parturition? The answer rests in biblical doctrine, and, as with the Cross's explanation of its own sign, the poet carefully expounds this figure so that the reader will be sure to apprehend that a birth has occurred. In stanza 35 the Cross paraphrases Christ's words to Nicodemus: "I say to thee, unless a man be born again, he cannot see the kingdom of God" (John 3.3). Each Christian must be born twice, first bodily and then spiritually through baptism. In historical terms, the Christian progresses from a first birth into the old law of the Jewish patriarchs, to a second birth into the redemptive law of Christ. The prophesied passage from old to new inspires the birthing configuration of stanzas 19–21.

Beyond this doctrinal explanation, however, the birthing metaphor is grounded in the experience of Christ as an embodied man. The piety of the poem links Nativity and Passion, both being birthing events for the God who took flesh. The first birth is joyous, painless, and shared with Mary, a human mother who remains (miraculously) a virgin. The second birth through the Cross is, in contrast, filled with the labor pains of both mother and son, as God cataclysmically dies in body and mankind is redeemed. Mary feels the brunt of this torturous "birth" emotionally and physically, while the Cross bears the part of encumbered pregnancy, but it is Christ who is the actual Parent who births a new life for humanity.[8] The figure of the patriarchs

---

[7]Compare a ME couplet: "The gates of para[d]is thoruth Eve were iloken [locked] / And thoruth oure swete Ladi agein hui beoth nouthe open [they are now open]" (ed. F. J. Furnivall, *Political, Religious, and Love Poems*, EETS o.s. 15, second ed. [1903; rpt. Bungay, Suffolk: Richard Clay, 1965], p. 257).

[8]I know of only a few other lyrics that represent this tradition through birthing metaphors. *Stand Wel, Moder, under Rode*, a *planctus* that has Mary in dialogue with Christ, portrays the Passion as a painful second birth with both mother and son the sentient participants. What appears at the center of this poem is Christ's request that his mother "let" him die (lines 31–36; ed. Silverstein, pp. 12–14). The idea is not that Jesus dutifully wants his mother's permission, but that his death is parallel to his conception: for both, God requests and gains the freely willed acquiescence of a humble Mary. See Love's *Mirror*, ed. Sargent, pp. 25–26, 178; and Weber, pp. 37–46, 125–33. Another lyric from the thirteenth century, *Jesu Cristes milde moder* (ed. Silverstein, pp. 17–19), has an interesting quartered structure based on birth: at the one-quarter point Mary and Christ feel the sword-wound (a kind of mutual impregnation with pain and sorrow); at midpoint she must yield to his death (with language that recalls her birthing of Jesus); at the three-quarter point there appears an astonishing figure of the Resurrection (one that violates Scripture) in which Christ glides whole through the stone sealing the tomb (a

escaping the wilderness merges in meaning with the triumphant Harrowing of Hell.

Implicit in the birthing image is the notion of God entering and departing the realm of finite time, and also of humans occupying a space in time either before or after the Crucifixion. It is therefore not surprising to find the poet considering time in ways both subtle and precise. That the depictions of Adam, Moses, and the wandering prophets occur before the midpoint of the poem is surely indicative of the old law. Here too are the Virgin's allusions to the Nativity — her lullings of the Holy Infant and her wrapping him gently — prefigurements of the grotesque reversals enacted in the Crucifixion. After the midpoint — the moment of second birth through the Passion — allusions shift to New Testament and future events: Paul's conversion of Dionysius, the Last Judgment, and most interestingly, a trio of newly converted Jews, who come to postfigure the Three Magi. The tale of the three Jews (stanzas 24–26) combined with an adjacent exposition on Christ as the Shepherd of Christians (stanza 23) forms a "new" Nativity story to accompany the maternally birthing Cross.

The highly charged image of Christ's body on the Cross is thus perpetually shifting as to what it signifies. It varies according to who explains it (Mary or Cross) and according to chronology (before or after Christ's momentous death). It also fluctuates by a dazzling associative process that seems to suggest that the sacramental made visible — through image, through words — eludes the natural laws of matter. A two-stanza sequence densely plays upon the body-as-parchment figure that must have been well known from *The Charter of Christ*, a poem reworked in many forms and surviving in many manuscripts.[9] Here, the figure is far from stable: Jesus's wounded body is, alternatingly, a shrine, a written pardon, eucharistic bread, a book; the Cross is the post for the pardon, the table under the bread, the wooden covers of the book, the altar displaying the open book (stanzas 15–16). In another instance of radical figural and linguistic dislocation, an argument near the end of the poem may be deciphered only when one comes to understand that each of five instances of the word *kuynde/kende* possesses a different signification: "creatures," "natural wits," "kindred," "heritage," "mankind" (lines 386–403).

There are at least two points at which the poet's fantasy appears to have strained a scribe's duller, more narrowly orthodox mind. The textual evidence suggests that the Vernon compiler (or a predecessor) had trouble accepting the boldness of some of the imagery attached to the vibrantly animated Cross. Here is where an editor is

---

reversal of Christ conceived in Mary's virgin womb). I am indebted to Nancy Burian for bringing this last figure to my attention; see also Weber, pp. 137–40.

[9]A version appears in the Vernon MS near *Dispute* (ed. Furnivall, *The Testament of Christ*, pp. 637–57); for the many other extant and variant texts, see Spalding.

grateful for the variant Royal text — and sorry for the stanzas that are missing from it. The passages in question both occur in the second half of the poem and refer to the Cross's agency in the events during and after the Passion. In the first instance the Cross declares itself to have been "baptized" in Christ's blood (stanza 34), a non-human participation in a sacrament that might well have taxed a clerical redactor's willingness to transmit a metaphor. The Vernon/Simeon text contains altered pronouns so that the passage becomes a safe, pastoral explication of baptism — entirely ordinary and therefore entirely out of character for this poet of brilliant images. The second instance is similar. The Cross explains the legalistic role *it* will have at the Last Judgment, how it will present its *own* bill of grievance against mankind for their part in the Crucifixion, which is described from the viewpoint of one who actually felt the nails (stanza 37). This self-fashioning of the Cross could be another uncomfortable moment for a redactor. It has been "corrected" in the Vernon/ Simeon text by removal of all the first-person pronouns. The effect is to render the identity of the plaintiff(s) general and vague.

That these changes occurred in the Vernon/Simeon texts suggests that the time-honored rhetorical device of personification faced skepticism in some late fourteenth-century circles, perhaps particularly when used for a devotional text having such sacred figures as agents. The poet, who appears to have been aware of potential resistence, ends the poem by explaining that the Cross "evere yit hath ben def and dom" and that the point of this apocryphal telling with its "faire [rhetorical] flour" is "to drive the devel abak" (lines 500–06). Even though *The Dream of the Rood* was well out of memory, a reputable model for giving the Cross a voice existed in Geoffrey of Vinsauf's *Poetria nova* (c. 1200), where the piece illustrating prosopopeia has an eloquent Cross exhorting Christians to go off on crusade.[10] Moreover, when the *Dispute* poet makes the disclaimer, he simultaneously asserts that his story is grounded in *eye-witness* truth (lines 495–97). He seems to be arguing that the subject has a paradoxical and profound "not-true-but-still-true" status. The Cross did *not* speak; nonetheless, what it says here *is* true. The poem-as-Cross is a *worded* Cross that repels the devil and points to salvation, just like the true Cross, even if the historical Cross never spoke any words to Mary.[11]

While *Dispute* is the first extant rendering of a Mary/Cross debate in English, the concept appears in medieval writings in many languages. There are at least two Latin, two Italian, two Old French, one Old Provençal, one Anglo-Norman, and one Middle

---

[10]Trans. Margaret F. Nims (Toronto: Pontifical Institute of Mediaeval Studies, 1967), pp. 32–34.

[11]More discussion of this stanza appears in the note to lines 495–507.

Dutch versions. In addition, there are two more Middle English versions that date after *Dispute*, one by Walter Kennedy and one by Deguilleville's anonymous translator. The Middle English *Dispute* and at least three other versions appear to be indebted to Philippe de Grève's *Crux de te volo conqueri* (Yeager, pp. 54–55; Holthausen, pp. 22–26). *Dispute* is, however, considerably longer, using de Grève's poem as a "point of departure for original rhapsodic amplification" and effectively leaving it behind somewhere in stanza 11 (Lawton, pp. 154–55). While the Dutch version by Jacob van Maerlant is written in thirteen-line stanzas and also indebted to de Grève, it bears no real resemblance to *Dispute* (Lawton, pp. 156, 168–69). The more interesting analogues are the Anglo-Norman poem and the two Old French poems, especially Guillaume de Deguilleville's *Pèlerinage de l'ame*. This broad area of possible influence needs more study, especially in light of the evidence that the *Dispute* poet had close knowledge of French.[12] The degree to which Franciscans reworked and promulgated the form also deserves attention, since the continental Mary/Cross debates are so often found in Franciscan collections.[13]

Within Middle English literature *Dispute* has other interesting associations. In metrical terms, it is one of the earliest extant poems in the thirteen-line stanza that developed as a more formally alliterated form in the late fourteenth century. A poem in a near-identical stanza, *The Festivals of the Church*, follows *Dispute* in the Royal MS. In the Vernon and Simeon MSS *Dispute* appears just before *The Pistel of Swete Susan*, a more alliterative thirteen-line poem. The structural likeness of *Dispute* and *The Four Leaves of the Truelove* — both forty stanzas, both built on cruciform and birthing figures — is very intriguing, and *Truelove* has the stanza closest to that of *Susan*. These correspondences seem to indicate some commonality of purpose and audience. Other works in the Vernon and Simeon MSS appear to bear a close aesthetic relationship to *Dispute*, in particular, *The Lamentation of Mary to Saint Bernard*, *The Debate of the Body and the Soul*, and the *The Testament of Christ*. The texts known as *The Middle English Harrowing of Hell* and *The Gospel of Nicodemus* may also belong in the group of seminal writings, since the Christian event vividly depicted there, conceived as a fissure in time from old to new law, informs the dramatic structure by halves in both *Dispute* and *Truelove*. In the Middle English corpus, there is, of course, a vast amount of meditative and mystical literature on the

---

[12]The poem contains several French words that are quite rare in English; see, for example, notes to lines 38, 136, 368, and 372. There is also a mention of St. Denis at line 393.

[13]The AN poem, too, survives in an interesting miscellany (British Library Addit. MS 46919) collected by Franciscan Friar William Herebert of Hereford. This work remains still unprinted. Although Lawton does not study its similarities to *Dispute* in depth, his remarks are useful (pp. 156–57).

Introduction

Passion. David Lawton believes that the *Dispute* poet's debt to Richard Rolle and the Vernon *Talking of the Love of God* "approaches the explicit" (p. 157). The poet actually names the mystical theologian Dionysius (line 393), whose influence was known through *The Cloud of Unknowing* and other English writings. In a few places there seems to be a debt to a well-known devotional text, the Pseudo-Bonaventuran *Meditationes vitae Christi*, which Nicholas Love translated as *The Mirror of the Blessed Life of Jesus Christ*.

For a period of several centuries the concept of Mary and the Cross in debate possessed a theological vitality that medieval preachers and moral writers found useful to tap. A comparison of Mary's maternity to the Cross's redemptive function clearly had an appeal both intellectual and popular. Peter Yeager sees the tradition as "the expression of a deeply felt spiritual reality" and "the actualization of a pattern potentially available" in medieval Christianity (pp. 62, 64). In *Dispute* an English poet intriguingly opposes the values of the *planctus* with those of sober moral instruction. While Mary's heightened emotionalism is designed to soften the heart of the meditant with empathy and compassion, the Cross's logical intellectualism confirms the legalistic economy of a sacrificing God. For the medieval Christian both of these responses are correct, but each purely by itself may be found deficient. The understanding symbolized by the Cross and by the Incarnation that took place in Mary is about a truth found in the reconciliation of things — of divinity and humanity — inherently opposed but joined in one form.

Note on the Edited Text

In the notes that follow the edited text I present a chart showing the degree of variance between the Vernon/Simeon and Royal versions of *Dispute*. Often the sense of the shorter version in Royal is inferior to the Vernon/Simeon text. In some instances, however, metaphors or wordplays that are typical of the poet's style seem to be more sharply preserved in Royal. Where the rhetorical flourishes are blurred in Vernon/Simeon but apparently preserved in Royal, I have emended with reference to the Royal text. Other emendation has been made rarely but where needed to restore rhymes, sense, or alliteration. As regards the latter feature, nearly all lines have at least two alliterating words; when this trait is lacking and a word from Royal supplies it, I have often accepted Royal as evidence of a better reading. Individual emendations are recorded and discussed in the notes.

Select Bibliography

Manuscripts

Vernon MS: Oxford, Bodleian Library MS Eng. poet. a.1, fols. 315b–316b. C. 1390. [Base text; copied in triple columns by Vernon/Simeon scribe B.]

Simeon MS: London, British Library Addit. MS 22283, fols. 124b–125b. C. 1390. [Copied in triple columns by Vernon/Simeon scribe A.]

London, British Library Royal MS 18 A.x, fols. 126a–130b. C. 1450. [Marginal notations mark changes in speakers.]

Facsimile

Doyle, A. I., intro. *The Vernon Manuscript: A Facsimile of Bodleian Library, Oxford, MS. Eng. Poet. a.1*. Cambridge: D. S. Brewer, 1987.

Editions

Furnivall, F. J., ed. *The Minor Poems of the Vernon Manuscript*. Part 2. EETS o.s. 117. 1901; rpt. New York: Greenwood, 1969. Pp. 612–26. [Vernon MS.]

Morris, Richard, ed. *Legends of the Holy Rood: Symbols of the Passion and Cross Poems*. EETS o.s. 46. 1881; rpt. New York: Greenwood, 1969. Pp. 131–49, 197–209. [Vernon and Royal MSS.]

Probable Latin Source

Philippe de Grève (d. 1236). *Crux de te volo conqueri*. Ed. G. M. Dreves. In *Analecta hymnica medii aevi*. Vol. 21, no. 14. 1895; rpt. New York: Johnson, 1961. Pp. 20–22. [Author was Chancellor of the University of Paris c. 1218–36.]

Introduction

Other Medieval Mary/Cross Dispute Poems

Ben vorrei piangere quando mi rimembro. Extracts printed in: Giuseppe Rondoni. "Laudi drammatiche dei Disciplinati di Siena." *Giornale storico della letterature italiana* 2 (1883), 286–93. [Fourteenth-century Italian poem with dramatic interaction, associated with Franciscanism.]

Croix, je me vueil a toy complaindre. Ed. A. Långfors. "Notice du manuscrit français 17068 de la Bibliothèque Nationale." *Romania* 43 (1914), 21–27. [Old French poem.]

Crux dura quid fecisti. Included in: Ubertino da Casale [Thirteenth-century Spiritual Franciscan from Tuscany]. *Arbor vitae crucifixae Jesu*. Intro. Charles T. Davis. Monumenta politica et philosophica rariora. Ser. 1, no. 4. Turin, 1961. Bk. 4, cap. 25. [Twelfth-century Latin didactic poem with several variants, one of which is a dialogue between Mary and Christ. For another version, see Sticca, pp. 71–77.]

Coment Nostre Dame e la Croiz disputerant sanz nule voiz. London, British Library Addit. MS 46919, fols. 79a–80a. [Unpublished Anglo-Norman poem in a miscellany compiled by Franciscan William Herebert of Hereford (d. 1333); see extracts in Paul Meyer, "Notice et extraits du ms. 8336 de la bibliothèque de Sir Thomas Phillipps à Cheltenham," *Romania* 13 (1884), 521–22; MS described in *Library Catalogue of Additions to the Manuscripts, 1946–50*, vol. 27 (London: The British Library, 1979), pp. 197–206.]

Deguilleville, Guillaume de. "Altercation piteous entre l'arbre verd et l'arbre sec." Ed. Jakob J. Stürzinger. In *Le Pélerinage de l'ame de G. de Deguilleville*, vv. 5931–6166, 6617–78. London: Roxburghe Society, 1985. [French moral poem composed between 1330 and 1358, translated into English c. 1413, and printed by Caxton in 1483. See *The Pilgrimage of the Soul*, ed. Rosemarie Potz McGerr (New York: Garland, 1990), p. xlix.]

E . . . alem tot enviro. Ed. Paul Meyer. In *Daurel et Beton: Chanson de geste provençale*. Société des anciens textes français 75. Paris: Firmin Didot et cie, 1880. Pp. lxxix–lxxxv. [Old Provençal poem by Franciscan author; incomplete.]

Kennedy, Walter. *The Passioun of Christ*, vv. 1093–1162. Ed. J. A. W. Bennett. In *Devotional Pieces in Prose and Verse*. Scottish Text Society. Third ser., no. 23. Edinburgh: William Blackwood & Sons, 1955. Pp. 42–45. [Fifteenth-century Middle English poem; indebted to Philippe de Grève.]

Molto si dolea sovente. Ed. Giuseppe Mazzatini. In *Inventario dei manoscritti italiani delle biblioteche di Francia.* Vol. 3. Rome, 1888. Pp. 254–57. [Italian poem; indebted to Philippe de Grève.]

van Maerlant, Jacob. *Ene Disputacie van onser Vrouwen ende van den heiligen Cruce.* Ed. Johannes Franck. In *Mittelniederländische Grammatik.* Leipzig: T. O. Weigel, 1883. Pp. 172–79. [Thirteenth-century Middle Dutch poem in 46 13-line stanzas; indebted to Philippe de Grève.]

Middle English Poems Apparently by the Same Author

All ʒe Mowen Be Blyth and Glade. Ed. O. S. Pickering. "A Middle English Poem on the Eucharist and Other Poems by the Same Author." *Archiv für das Studium der Neueren Sprachen und Literaturen* 215 (1978), 281–310. [Written in similar stanza, appears in Oxford, Bodleian Library Additional MS C 280, fols. 125a–127b.]

The Festivals of the Church. Ed. Richard Morris. In *Legends of the Holy Rood: Symbols of the Passion and Cross Poems.* EETS o.s. 46. 1881; rpt. New York: Greenwood, 1969. Pp. 210–21. [Written in similar stanza; follows *Dispute* in Royal MS 18 A.X, fols. 1306–46 (lacks end).]

Whon Grein of Whete Is Cast to Grounde. Ed. Carl Horstmann. "Proprium Sanctorum: Zusatz-Homilien des MS Vernon fol. CCXV ff. zur nördlichen Sammlung der Dominicalia evangelia." *Archiv für das Studium der Neueren Sprachen und Literaturen* 81 (1888), 83–85. [Written in similar stanza, appears in Vernon MS, fols. 215b–216a.]

Related Middle English Works

Ancrene Wisse. Ed. and trans. Anne Savage and Nicholas Watson. *Anchoritic Spirituality: "Ancrene Wisse" and Associated Works.* New York: Paulist Press. 1991.

The Bird with Four Feathers. Printed in this edition. [Multiple namings of God concealed in a numerological text; appears near *Dispute* in Royal MS.]

The Cloud of Unknowing. Ed. Patrick J. Gallacher. TEAMS Middle English Text Series. Kalamazoo, Mich.: Medieval Institute Publications, 1997. [English mystical work influenced by theology of Dionysius the pseudo-Areopagite, named in *Dispute*, line 393.]

De tribus regibus mortuis. Ed. Ella Keats Whiting. In *The Poems of John Audelay.* EETS o.s. 184. 1931; rpt. Millwood, N. Y.: Kraus, 1988. Pp. xxiv–xxvii, 217–23, 256–59. [Alliterative poem in 13-line stanzas.]

The Debate of the Body and the Soul. Ed. Thomas Wright. In *The Latin Poems Commonly Attributed to Walter Mapes.* Camden Society 16. London, 1841. Pp. 334–46. [Debate poem appearing in Vernon, Simeon, and Royal MSS.]

The Four Leaves of the Truelove. Printed in this edition. [Forty 13-line alliterative stanzas; second birth at midpoint; meditative focus on Mary's compassion and the Cross.]

Jhesu That Hast Me Dere Iboght. Ed. Carleton Brown. In *Religious Lyrics of the XIVth Century.* Second ed. Rev. G. V. Smithers. Oxford: Clarendon, 1957. Pp. 114–19. [Passion lyric to be said "at every Cros"; asks that Christ "write" the Cross in the heart of the petitioner.]

The Lamentation of Mary to Saint Bernard. Ed. Carl Horstmann. In *The Minor Poems of the Vernon Manuscript.* Part 1. EETS o.s. 98. 1892; rpt. New York: Greenwood, 1975. Pp. 297–328. [Passion narrative affectively recounted by Mary to Bernard of Clairvaux, from Vernon MS.]

Legend of the Crucifix. Ed. Carl Horstmann. In *Altenglische Legenden, neue Folge.* Heilbronn: Von Gebr. Henninger, 1881. Pp. 339–40. [Short tale with cruciate structure and animate Cross, from MS Ashmole 61.]

Love, Nicholas. *Mirror of the Blessed Life of Jesus Christ.* Ed. Michael G. Sargent. Garland Medieval Texts 18. New York: Garland, 1992. [Especially the meditation on the Passion, pp. 161–90.]

Meditation on the Passion; and of Three Arrows on Doomsday. Ed. Carl Horstmann. In *Yorkshire Writers.* Vol. 1. London: Swan Sonnenschein, 1895. Pp. 112–21. [Meditation on the Passion, influenced by Richard Rolle.]

The Middle-English Harrowing of Hell and Gospel of Nicodemus. Ed. William Henry Hulme. EETS e.s. 100. London: Kegan Paul, Trench, Trübner, 1907.

The Dispute between Mary and the Cross

Pearl. Ed. E. V. Gordon. Oxford: Oxford University Press, 1953.

The Pistel of Swete Susan. Ed. Russell A. Peck. *Heroic Women from the Old Testament in Middle English Verse*. TEAMS Middle English Texts Series. Kalamazoo, Mich.: Medieval Institute Publications, 1991. Pp. 73–108. [Written in 13-line alliterative stanzas; follows *Dispute* in Vernon and Simeon MSS.]

Stand Wel, Moder, under Rode. Ed. Theodore Silverstein. *English Lyrics before 1500*. York Medieval Texts. Evanston: Northwestern University Press, 1971. Pp. 12–14. [Mary's lament addressed to Christ.]

Rolle, Richard. *Meditation B*. Ed. S. J. Ogilvie-Thomson. In *Richard Rolle: Prose and Verse*. EETS o.s. 293. Oxford: Oxford University Press, 1988. Pp. 69–83. [Meditation on the Passion.]

The Testament of Christ. Ed. F. J. Furnivall. In *The Minor Poems of the Vernon Manuscript*. Part 2. EETS o.s. 117. 1901; rpt. New York: Greenwood, 1969. Pp. 637–57. [Imagery of Christ's body as inscribed parchment; follows *The Pistel of Swete Susan* in Vernon MS.]

Criticism of *The Dispute between Mary and the Cross*

Brewer, Derek. *English Gothic Literature*. New York: Schocken, 1983. Pp. 59–60.

Fein, Susanna Greer. "Form and Continuity in the Alliterative Tradition: Cruciform Design and Double Birth in Two Stanzaic Poems." *Modern Language Quarterly* 53 (1992), 100–25.

Holthausen, F. "Der mittelenglische Disput zwischen Maria und dem Kreuze." *Archiv für das Studien der Neueren Sprachen und Literaturen* 105 (1900), 22–29.

Lawton, David A. "The Diversity of Middle English Alliterative Poetry." *Leeds Studies in English* 20 (1989), 153–62.

Pickering, O. S. "Middle English Metaphysical Verse? Imagery and Style in Some Fourteenth-Century Religious Poems." In *Individuality and Achievement in Middle English Poetry*. Ed. O. S. Pickering. Woodbridge, Suffolk: Boydell and Brewer, 1997. Pp. 85–104.

Introduction

Schofield, W. H. "The Nature and Fabric of the Pearl." *PMLA* 19 (1904), 200.

Taylor, George C. "The English 'Planctus Mariae.'" *Modern Philology* 4 (1907), 1–33. [Lists the common motifs.]

Utley, Francis Lee. "Dialogues, Debates, and Catechisms." In *A Manual of Writings in Middle English, 1050–1500*. Ed. Albert E. Hartung. Vol. 3. New Haven: Connecticut Academy of Arts and Sciences, 1972. Pp. 684–85, 841–42.

Woolf, Rosemary. *The English Religious Lyric in the Middle Ages*. Oxford: Clarendon, 1968. Pp. 252–54.

Yeager, Peter. "The Dispute Between Mary and the Cross: Debate Poems of the Passion." *Christianity & Literature* 30 (1981), 53–69. [Discusses medieval analogues.]

Related Studies

Aston, Margaret. "Devotional Literacy." In *Lollards and Reformers: Images and Literacy in Late Medieval Religion*. London: Hambledon, 1984. Pp. 101–33.

Beckwith, Sarah. *Christ's Body: Identity, Culture and Society in Late Medieval Writings*. London: Routledge, 1993.

Bennett, J. A. W. *Poetry of the Passion: Studies in Twelve Centuries of English Verse*. Oxford: Clarendon, 1982.

Blake, N. F. "Vernon Manuscript: Contents and Organisation." In *Studies in the Vernon Manuscript*. Ed. Derek Pearsall. Cambridge: D. S. Brewer, 1990. Pp. 45–59.

Breeze, Andrew. "The Charter of Christ in Medieval English, Welsh and Irish." *Celtica* 19 (1987), 111–20.

Bynum, Caroline Walker. *Holy Feast and Holy Fast: The Religious Significance of Food to Medieval Women*. Berkeley: University of California Press, 1987.

Camille, Michael. *The Gothic Idol: Ideology and Image-Making in Medieval Art*. Cambridge: Cambridge University Press, 1989.

Doyle, A. I. "The Shaping of the Vernon and Simeon Manuscripts." In *Studies in the Vernon Manuscript*. Ed. Derek Pearsall. Cambridge: D. S. Brewer, 1990. Pp. 1–13.

Glasscoe, Marion. *English Medieval Mystics: Games of Faith*. Harlow, Essex: Longman, 1993.

Gray, Douglas. "Notes on Some Middle English Charms." In *Chaucer and Middle English Studies in Honour of Rossell Hope Robbins*. Ed. Beryl Rowland. Kent: Kent State University Press, 1974. Pp. 56–69.

———. *Themes and Images in the Medieval English Religious Lyric*. London: Routledge and Kegan Paul, 1972.

Kaske, R. E. "A Poem of the Cross in the Exeter Book: 'Riddle 60' and 'The Husband's Message.'" *Traditio* 23 (1967), 41–71.

Keiser, George R. "The Middle English *Planctus Mariae* and the Rhetoric of Pathos." In *The Popular Literature of Medieval England*. Ed. Thomas J. Heffernan. Knoxville: University of Tennessee Press, 1985. Pp. 167–93.

Pantin, W. A. "Instructions for a Devout and Literate Layman." In *Medieval Learning and Literature: Essays Presented to Richard William Hunt*. Ed. J. J. G. Alexander and M. T. Gibson. Oxford: Clarendon, 1976. Pp. 398–422.

Pearsall, Derek. *Old English and Middle English Poetry*. London: Routledge and Kegan Paul, 1977.

Pezzini, Domenico. "The Theme of the Passion in Richard Rolle and Julian of Norwich." In *Religion in the Poetry and Drama of the Late Middle Ages in England*. Ed. Piero Boitani and Anna Torti. Cambridge: D. S. Brewer, 1990. Pp. 29–66.

Rhodes, J. T. "The Body of Christ in English Eucharistic Devotion, c.1500–c.1620." In *New Science Out of Old Books: Studies in Manuscripts and Early Printed Books in Honour of A. I. Doyle*. Ed. Richard Beadle and A. J. Piper. Aldershot, Hants: Scolar Press, 1995. Pp. 388–419.

Rubin, Miri. *Corpus Christi: The Eucharist in Late Medieval Culture*. Cambridge: Cambridge University Press, 1991.

Introduction

Secor, John R. "The *Planctus Mariae* in Provençal Literature: A Subtle Blend of Courtly and Religious Traditions." In *The Spirit of the Court*. Ed. Glyn S. Burgess and Robert A. Taylor. Cambridge: D. S. Brewer, 1983. Pp. 321–26.

Spalding, Mary Caroline. *The Middle English Charters of Christ*. Bryn Mawr College Monograph 15. Bryn Mawr: Bryn Mawr College, 1914.

Stanbury, Sarah. "The Virgin's Gaze: Spectacle and Transgression in Middle English Lyrics of the Passion." *PMLA* 106 (1991), 1083–93.

Sticca, Sandro. *The "Planctus Mariae" in the Dramatic Tradition of the Middle Ages*. Trans. Joseph R. Berrigan. Athens: University of Georgia Press, 1988.

Turville-Petre, Thorlac. "'Summer Sunday,' 'De Tribus Regibus Mortuis,' and 'The Awntyrs off Arthure': Three Poems in the Thirteen-Line Stanza." *Review of English Studies*, n.s. 25 (1974), 3–15.

Weber, Sarah Appleton. *Theology and Poetry in the Middle English Lyric: A Study of Sacred History and Aesthetic Form*. Columbus: Ohio State University Press, 1969.

The Dispute between Mary and the Cross

Disputacio inter Mariam et Crucem secundum Apocrafum.[1]

1

Oure Ladi freo · on Rode-treo	*noble; Rood-tree (Cross)*
Made hire mone.	*complaint*
Heo seide, "On the · the Fruit of me	*She; you (Cross)*
Is wo-bigon!	
5 Mi Fruit I seo · in blodi bleo	*see; bloody state*
Among His fon!	*foes*
Serwe I seo · the veines fleo	*Sorrow; separate*
From blodi bon!	*bone*
Tre, thou dost no trouthe	*Cross, you perform no faithful act*
10 On a pillori my Fruit to pinne!	*By pinning my fruit to pillory*
He hath no spot of Adam sinne.	*Adam's*
Flesch and veines nou fleo atwinne!	*now come apart*
Wherfore I rede of routhe.	*Therefore I am mournful*

2

"Cros, thi bondes schul ben blamed —	*bonds (i.e., nails), must be*
15 Mi fayre Fruit thou hast bigyled.	*beguiled*
The Fruites Mooder was nevere afamed —	*Mother; defamed*
Mi wombe is feir, founden unfuyled.	*fair; undefiled*
Chyld, whi artou not aschamed	*are you*
On a pillori to ben ipiled?	*stripped (lit., peeled)*
20 Grete theves thus weore gramed,	*punished*
And dyede for heore werkes wyled.	*their wicked deeds*
In mournyng I may melte!	*be overwhelmed*
My Fruit, that is so holi halwed,	*holy and hallowed*
In a feeld is fouled and falwed;	*withered*

---

[1] *Disputation between Mary and the Cross according to Apocrypha*

25	With grete theves He is galwed,	*thieves; gallowed*
	And dyeth for monnes gelte.	*dies; guilt*

3

	"For grete theves galwes were greid,	*gallows; prepared*
	That ever to robbyng ronnen ryf;	*Who were always bent on robbery*
	Whi schal my Sone on the beo leid,	*should; you; laid*
30	That never nuyyed mon nor wyf?	*harmed*
	A drinke of deth, sothliche seid,	*truly said*
	Cros, thou yevest the Lord of Lyf;	*give*
	His veynes tobursten with thi breid.	*burst asunder; torment*
	Mi Fruit stont nou in a strong stryf!	*stands; violent strife*
35	Blod from hed is hayled,	*is flowing*
	Fouled is my fayre Fruit,	
	That never dude tripet ne truit;	*malicious trick nor wrong*
	With theves that loveden ryot and ruit,	*riot and disorder*
	Whi schal my Sone be nayled?	

4

40	"Thorwh jugement thou art enjoynet	*are legally enjoined*
	To bere fooles ful of sinne;	*To bear [only] foolish sinners*
	Mi Sone from the schulde beon ensoynet,	*should have been excused*
	And nevere His blod uppon the rinne.	*never [should]; run*
	But nou is Truthe with tresun teynet,	*Truth (= Christ); contaminated*
45	With theoves to honge fer in fenne,	*filthily*
	With feole nayles His limes ben feynet.	*cruel; falsified*
	A careful Moder men mai me kenne!	*Mother full of care; call*
	In bales I am bounde.	*woes*
	That Brid was of a Mayden born,	*Child; Virgin*
50	On a theoves tre is al totorn;	*completely torn*
	A broche thorwout His brest born	*spear borne through his breast*
	His holi herte hath wounde.	*has wounded*

5

	"Tre, thou art loked bi the lawe	*bound by*
	Theoves, traitours on the to deye;	*on you to die*
55	But now is Trouthe with tresun drawe,	*drawn [on the Cross]*
	And Vertu falleth in vices weye;	*Virtue (= Christ); vice's path*
	But Love and Treuthe, in sothfast sawe,	*to tell the truth*

On a Treo traytours hem teye; *traitors tie them*
Vertu is with vices slawe; *slain*
60 Of alle vertues Crist is keye.
  Vertu, swettore then spices, *sweeter than*
    In fot and hond bereth blodi prikke; *foot and hand; prickings*
    His hed is ful of thornes thikke;
    The Goode hongeth among the wikke; *wicked*
65   Vertu dyeth with vices!

6

"Cros, unkynde thou schalt be ked, *unnatural; known*
Mi Sone Stepmoder I the calle: *call you*
Mi Brid was born with beestes on bed, *Child; beasts*
And be my flesch my Flour gan falle; *from; flower; did fall*
70 With my brestes my Brid I fed;
Cros, thou yevest Him eysel and galle! *give; vinegar*
My White Rose red is spred, *is covered with red (spattered)*
That fostred was in fodderes stalle. *stall of fodder (i.e. manger)*
  Feet and fayre hondes,
75   That nou ben croised, I custe hem ofte, *crossed; kissed*
    I lulled hem, I leid hem softe. *laid them down softly*
    Cros, thou holdest hem hihe on lofte, *nigh aloft*
    Bounden in bledyng bondes!

7

"Mi Love ilolled up in thy leyr! *left to dangle; lair*
80 With cradel bond I gan Him bynde. *cradle cloth I used to wrap him*
Cros, He stiketh nou on thi steir, *sticks now upon thy staircase*
Naked ayeyn the wylde wynde. *against; wind*
Foules fourmen heor nestes in eyr, *Birds form*
Foxes in den reste thei fynde,
85 Bot Godes Sone, in hevene Heir,
His hed nou holdeth on thornes tynde. *tined (i.e., sharp)*
  Of mournynge I may mynne! *Of mourning I must speak!*
    Godes hed hath reste non, *has no rest*
    But leoneth on His scholder bon,
90   The thornes thorwh His flesch gon;
    His wo I wyte hit sinne. *I think it a sin*

108

8

"Cros, to slen hit is thi sleiht;   *it is your trick to slay*

Mi blody Brid thou berest fro blis.   *bear away from joy*

Cros, thou holdest Him so heih on heiht   *high in height*

95   Mi Fruites feet I mai not kis!

Mi mouth I pulte, my sweore I streiht   *thrust forth; neck; stretched*

To cusse His feet, soth thing hit is: *kiss*

The Jewes from the Cros me keiht;   *pulled*

On me thei made heore mouwes amis. *wrongfully made menacing faces*

100   Heore games and heore gaudes,   *[With] Their; trifles*

The Jewes wrouhten me ful wo.   *caused me much anguish*

Cros, I fynde thou art my fo;

Thou berest my Brid, beten blo,   *black and blue*

Among theose fooles fraudes!"   *foolish frauds*

9

105   **Cristes Cros** yaf onswere: *gave answer*

"Ladi, to the I owe honour;   *you*

Thy brihte palmes nou I bere;   *triumphs (see note)*

Mi schyning scheweth thorw thi Flour; *brilliance shows*

Thi feire Fruit on me ginneth tere;   *does tear*

110   Thi Fruit me florischeth in blod colour, *I make your Fruit flourish*

To winne the world that lay in lere;   *is doomed to destruction*

That Blosme blomed up in thi bour.   *bower (i.e., womb)*

Ac not for the alone,   *But*

But for to winne all this werd,   *world*

115   That swelte undur the develes swerd, *perishes; devil's sword*

Thorw feet and hond God let Him gerd, *God let Himself be stabbed*

To amende monnes mone.   *misery*

10

"Adam dude ful huge harmes   *caused enormous injury*

Whon he bot a bite undur a bouh;   *bit a bite; bough*

120   Wherfore thi Sone hath sprad His armes *As a result; spread*

On a Treo tyed with teone inouh;   *injury enough*

His flesch is smite with dethes tharmes, *worms (lit., entrails)*

And swelteth heerin a swemly swouh;

His breste is bored with dethes swarmes,[1]
125 And with His deth fro Deth He drouh   *He draws from Death*
    Alle His leove freondes.   *dear friends*
    As Ozie spac in prophecie   *Isaiah spoke*
    And seide, 'Thi Sone, Seinte Marie —
    His deth slouh Deth on Calvarie —   *slew*
130   Yaf lyf withouten endes.'   *Gave*

11

    "The stipre that is under the vyne set   *post*
    May not bringe forth the grape;
    Theih the Fruit on me beo knet,   *Although; is attached*
    His scharpe schour have I not schape.   *agony: inflicted*
135 Til grapes to the presse beo set,
    Ther renneth no red wyn in rape;   *from grape stalks (see note)*
    Nevere presse pressed bet: *Never did a press press better*
    I presse wyn for kniht and knape.   *knight and servant*
    Upon a blodi brinke,
140   I presse a Grape with strok and stryf;   *stroke and strife*
    The rede wyn renneth ryf.   *runs rife*
    In Samaritane God yaf a wyf   *Samaria; woman*
    That leof licour to drynke.   *precious*

12

    "Ladi, love doth the to alegge   *causes you to allege*
145 Thi Fruit is prikked with speres ord;   *point*
    On Cros, withouten knyves egge,   *a knife's edge*
    I kerve Fruit of Godes hord.   *carved; from God's hoard*
    Al is al red, rib and rugge,   *back (see note)*
    His bodi bledeth ayeyn the bord;   *upon the board*
150 I was piler and bar a brugge;   *pillar; bore a bridge*
    God is Weie, witnesse of Word.   *as Scripture witnesses*
    God seith He is sothfast Weye:
    Mony folk slod to helle slider —   *slid; slippery*
    To hevene mihte no mon thider   *go thither*

---

[1] *And [He] is overcome by a swooning state of unconsciousness [preceding death]; / His breast is impaled by death's swarming attacks (see note)*

155   Til God dyed and tauhte whider   *where*
     Men drawen whon thei deye.   *should go*

13

    "Moyses hath fourmed in his figour   *rhetorical figure*
    A whit lomb — and non other beste —   *beast*
    Schulde be sacred ur Saveour,   *[likened to] our sacred Saviour*
160   And be mete of mihtes meste;   *food of most esteem*
    I was that cheef chargeour,   *chief platter [of] that [food]*
    I bar flesch for folkes feste.   *meat; the people's feast*
    Jhesu Crist, ure Creatour,
    His flesch fedeth lest and meste.   *[those] least and most [in rank]*
165   Rosted ayeyn the sonne,   *sun*
    On me lay the Lomb of Love —
    I was plater His bodi above,   *[for] his body*
    Til feet and hondes al toclove —   *[became] wholly cloven*
     With blood I was bironne.   *drenched*

14

170   "Yit Moyses in rule this reson rad: *commandment; decreed*
    Ete your lomb in sour vergeous;   *bitter juice*
    Sour vergeous mai make the soule glad —
    Sore serwe for sinne is your sous —   *Deep sorrow for sin; sauce*
    Sour vergeous maketh the devel adrad,   *afraid*
175   Fer he fleccheth fro Godes spous.   *far; flees; i.e., the soul*
    Beo a staf ye stondeth sad   *By; reverently*
    Whon ye fongen flesch in Godes hous.   *partake of meat*
     That staf is Cristes Crouche: *Cross*
     Stondeth stifli bi that stake   *steadily*
180   Whon that ye fongen flesch in cake;   *eucharistic bread*
     Then schal no feond maystri make   *gain control*
     Youre soules for to touche.

15

    "For pardoun scheweth be a schrine,   *appears by means of*
    Brede on bord with nayl is smite;
185   Rede lettres write be lyne,

111

The Dispute between Mary and the Cross

    Bluwe, blake, among men pite.[1]

    Ur Lord I likne to this signe: *liken*

    His bodi uppon a bord was bite,   *stabbed/consumed (pun)*

    In briht blod His bodi gan schyne;   *shine (as a reliquary)*

190   Hou wo Him was no wight may wite,   *How He suffered may no man know*

       Red upon the Roode.   *Red/read (pun)*

    Ur pardoun brede from top too to,[2]

    Writen hit was, with wonder wo,   *with wonarous woe*

    With rede woundes and strokes blo,   *bruising strokes*

195   Ure Book was bounden in bloode.

16

    "Adam stod up in stede,   *[his] place*

    In bitter galle his gost he dreint;   *spirit; drowned*

    Ayeyn that galle God yaf us mede,   *mead/reward (pun)*

    With swete merci bitter is queynt.   *bitterness is quenched*

200   His bodi was Book, the Cros was brede,   *wooden book-cover*

    Whon Crist for us theron was cleynt.   *thereon was fastened*

    No mon gat pardoun with no bede   *prayer*

    Weor he nevere so sely a seynt   *humble a saint*

       Til Book on bord was sprad.   *displayed*

205   With sharpe nayles dunted and drive,   *pounded and driven in*

       Til feet and hondes al torive,   *completely split*

       His herte blod ure Book hath yive,   *has given*

       To make ur gostes glad."

17

    Cristes Cros yit spac this speche: *continued to speak*

210   "Furst was I presse, wyn to wringe;

    I bere a brugge, wei to teche,   *bridge to show the way*

    Ther semely aungeles sitte and synge: *where lovely*

    'Lord of Love and Lyves Leche,   *Doctor of Life*

    For The was set sely sacrynge   *[this] blessed sacrifice*

---

[1] *A tablet on a board is struck with a nail (or: Spread out broadly on a board, smitten with a nail); / Red letters written by line, / [With] Blue and black, tacked among men*

[2] Three interpretations are possible: (1) *Our bread of pardon from top to toe*; (2) *Our tablet of pardon from top to toe*; (3) *Our pardon spread out from top to toe*

215 To winne the world that was in wreche.'	*wretchedness*
The Cros was brede, pardoun to bringe.	*book-cover*
Pardoun in Book is billed.	*recorded*
What is pardoun uppon to minne?	*How is pardon defined?*
Hit is foryivenes of dedly sinne —	
220 Whon blod was writen on Cristes skinne,	*skin*
Pardoun was fulfilled."	

18

Oure Ladi seide, "Cros, of thi werk,	
Wonder the not theih I be wrothe;	*Be not amazed that I am upset*
Thus seide Poule, Cristes clerk,	*Paul*
225 'The feolle Jewes, with false othe,	*treacherous; oath*
Jewes ston-hard in sinnes merk,	*stone-hard in dark sins*
Beoten a Lomb withouten lothe,	*without a qualm*
Softur then watur undur serk,	*[Who was] Softer; shirt*
Meode, or milk medled bothe.'	*[Or] Mead; intermingled*
230 The Jewes weoren harde stones;	
Softur then watur, or eny licour,	*any liquid*
Or dewz that lith on the lilie flour,	*dew; lies*
Was Cristes bodi, in blod colour;	
The Jewes brisseden His bones.	*shattered*

19

235 "And mony a prophete gan make mon,	*did complain*
And seide, 'Lord, send us Thi Lomb	
Out of the wildernesses ston	
To fende us from the lyon cromb.'	*defend; lion's claw*
Of mylde, Mount of Syon	*From a gentlewoman (Mary); Zion*
240 Becom Mon, in a Maydens womb,	
Made a bodi, with blessed bon:	*Was made [into]*
In a Maidens blod Thi bodi flomb.	*shone like fire*
At barreres weore debate:	*barriers there was obstruction*
Thorwh stones in the wildernes,	
245 Men mihte better ha crepet, iwis,	*People; have crept, truly*
Then bored into hevene blis,	*forced a way (bored)*
Til blod brac up the yate.	*broke open the gate*

20

      "Sin monnes sone was so nedi   *Since man's son (i.e., people); needy*

      To beo lad with Lomb mylde,   *led by*

250   Whi weore gylours so gredi   *beguilers so overeager*

      For to defoule my faire Childe?

      Cros, whi weore thou so redi

      To rende my Fruit feor in fylde?"   *tear; further in filth*

      "Ladi, to make the devel dredi,   *in order to; fearful*

255   God schop me a scheld, schame to schilde,[1]

        Til Lomb of Love dyede,

        And on me yeld the gost with vois.   *yielded His spirit with His final words*

        I was chose a relik chois,   *chosen [to be]; precious*

        The signe of Jhesu Cristes Crois;

260   Ther dar no devel abyde.   *dares; remain near*

21

      "Moni folk I fende from heore fos,"   *defend; foes*

      Cristes Cros this sawes seide.   *saying*

      "Hevene yates weore keithed clos   *gates; proclaimed shut*

      Til the Lomb of Love deyede;

265   This is write in Tixt and glos.   *gloss (i.e., commentary)*

      Aftur Cristes deth prophetes preide.   *prayed*

      Til the Lomb of Love dyed and ros,   *Until; arose*

      In helle pyne monkynde was teyde.   *pain; tied*

        At houre of hiye none,   *nones (three o'clock)*

270   The Lomb of Love seyde His thouht:

        'Nou is folfuld that wel is wrouht.'   *fulfilled*

        A mon is out of bondes brouht,

        And hevene dores undone!

22

      "With the Fader that al schal folfille,

275   His Sone to hevene is an help;

      I was piler and stod ful stille.

---

[1] *God fashioned me as a shield, to protect against shame*

After othur yiftes now gostes yelp.[1]
The fend, that all this world wolde kille,
His swerd he pulte up in his kelp;   *thrust; clawed hand*
280   To helle he horlede from that hille,   *hurled [himself]*
Beerynge as a beore whelp.   *Bellowing; bear cub*
    A beore is bounden and beted;   *beaten*
    Cristes Cros hath craked his croun;   *cracked*
    The Lomb hath leid the lyoun adoun;
285   The Lomb is Lord in everi toun;
    So Cristes blod hath pleted.   *settled the case legally*

23

"In Holy Writ this tale is herde,   *recorded (lit., heard)*
That goode yiftes God us yaf;
God seith Himself He is Schepherde,
290   And uche an heerde bihoveth a staf: *each shepherd must have*
The Cros I calle the Heerdes yerde.   *Shepherd's staff*
Therwith the devel a dunt He yaf,   *blow; gave*
And with the yerde, the wolf He werde;   *restrained*
With duntes drof him al todraf."   *blows drove him entirely away*
295   The Cros this tale tolde,
    That he was staf in the Heerdes hond;
    Whon schep breken out of heore bond,   *their flock (lit., bond)*
    The wolf he wered out of lond,   *drove*
    That devoured Cristes folde.

24

300   Yit seide the meke **Marie**:
"Roode, thou reendest my Rose al red!
Threo Jewes coomen from Calvari   *Three; came*
That day that Jhesu tholed ded;   *suffered death*
Alle thei seiden thei weore sori,   *They all said*
305   Fordolled in a drouknyng dred; *Mentally enfeebled by a debilitating fear*
Thei tolden hem alle wherfore and whi   *them (i.e., each other)*
Heore hertes were colde as lumpyng led.   *lumpish lead*

---

[1] *[Joining] With the Father who will fulfill all [that is promised], / His Son [come] to heaven is a help; / I was a pillar and stood very still (i.e., providing a vertical pathway from hell to heaven) / The dead souls now cry out for more gifts (i.e., deliverance)*

The furste heore tale tolde:
'Whon Crist was knit with corde on a stok,   *tied; stock (= Cross)*
310   His bodi bledde ayein that blok;   *were driven*
Thorw feet and hondes, nayles gan knok.   *did; grow cold*
Then gan myn herte to colde.'

25

"The secounde seide, 'Nay, not that
That dude serwe into myn herte schete,   *did sorrow; shoot*
315   But whon the Roode ros and doun was squat,   *was set down. violently*
The nayles renten His hondes and feete;   *tore*
Thorwout His helm, the harde hat,   *head; skull*
The thornes into His flesch gan threte;   *did afflict [Him]*
His joyntes unjoynet I tok good gat.   *[Of] His; I took heed*
320   Tho weop I water and teres leete —   *Then wept; tears let fall*
To care I was enclyned.
In cloddres of blod His her was clunge;   *clots; hair. clumped*
The flesch was from the bones swonge;   *hanging*
Druiye drinkeles was His tonge;   *Dry and without drink*
325   His lippes tocloven and chyned.'   *split and cracked*

26

"The thridde seide, 'This thouhte me lest   *I thought least*
Of theose peynes and other mo;   *others*
This peyne thouhte me peyne mest: *seemed to me the most painful*
Al His flesch He let of-flo!   *allowed to be flayed off*
330   His mylde Moder stod Him nest,   *next to Him*
Loked upward, and hire was wo;   *she was woeful*
A swerd swapped hire thorw the brest;   *struck*
Out of the Cros the knyf com tho!
This siht sauh I myselve —   *saw*
335   The swerd of love thorw hire gan launce —   *did pierce*
Heo swapte on swownyng thorw that chaunce;   *She fell swooning; event*
To scornen hire thei gan daunce,
Jewes by ten and twelve.'

27

"Sin Jewes made so muchel mon   *Since; such great lament*
340   To seon my Brid bounden in brere,   *a crown of thorns (lit., briar)*

116

The Dispute between Mary and the Cross

In sad serwyng moste I gon   *sorrowing*
To seon blodi my Chyldes chere!   *face*
Fadres and modres that walken in won   *together*
Schul love heore children beo skiles clere;   *their; in fitting ways*
345 Theose two loves weore in me al on: *existed as one in me*
For fader and moder I was here.

Theose two loves in me weore dalt —   *dealt*
I was fader of His flesch,
His moder hedde an herte nesch;[1]
350 Mi serwe flowed as water fresch;
Weopyng and wo I walt.   *[With] Weeping; was downcast*

28

"In me weore tacched sorwes two: *implanted*
In the Fader mihte non abyde,   *none (i.e., no sorrows)*
For He was evere in reste and ro,   *peace*
355 Joyned in His joyes wyde.   *Unified; all-encompassing*
I serwed sore, for to sei so;   *grieved sorely*
I say whon that my Derlyng deyde;   *saw*
With duntes He was to deth ido;   *blows; brought to death*
Upon a Tre His bodi was teyde.   *fastened*
360 Whon Trouthe is told and darted,   *drawn and pierced (see note)*
Of alle joyes God is welle;   *the source*
Ther mihte no serwe in Him dwelle —
I serwed sore, as clerkes telle;
Mi pyne was not departed.   *pain*

29

365 "The hattore love, the caldore care,   *hotter; colder*
Whon frendes fynde heore Fruit defoyled!   *despoiled*
The dispitous Jewes nolde not spare   *cruel; would not desist*
Til trie Fruit weore tore and toyled;   *excellent; torn; made weary*
Never mayden mournede mare!
370 I sauh my Child ben surded and soyled —   *vilified; dishonored*
Myn herte toclef with swerd of care —   *cleft to pieces*
I sauh my Brid with blod bemoyled,   *anointed*

---

[1] *[And yet as] His mother [I] had a compassionate heart*

117

As Symeon seide beoforn.
The swerd of serwe scharp igrounde   *sharply ground*
375   Schulde yive myn herte a wounde —
In more wo then I was bounde   *than*
Nevere buirde hath born.   *Never a woman has borne*

30

"The dede worthily gan wake,   *dead with strength did awaken*
The dai turned to nihtes donne,   *duskiness of night*
380   The merke mone gan mournyng make,   *darkened moon*
The lyht outleop of the sonne,   *light leapt out*
The temple walles gan chivere and schake,   *did shiver and shake*
Veiles in the temple atwo thei sponne.   *ripped apart*
Cros, whi noldestou not crake   *would thou not crack*
385   Whon rihtful blod on the was ronne?   *righteous; you was shed*
And kuyndes losten heore kende,   *creatures; their natural wits*
Whon my Fruit on the was fast.   *fastened*
Cros, whi weore thou not agast?
Thow stod stif as eny mast,   *any*
390   Whon Lyf left up His ende.   *i.e., when Christ died*

31

"Whon that Prince of Paradys
Bledde bothe brest and bak,   *[from] breast and back*
An hethene clerk was Seint Denys: *heathen; Dionysius (see note)*
He seide: 'This world wente al to wrak!'   *has gone entirely to ruin*
395   He sauh the planetes passen out of plais,   *saw; move out of position*
The briht sonne gan waxen blak;
The clerk, that was so wonderly wys,   *wondrously*
Wonder wordes ther he spak.   *Marvelous*
Denys, this grete clerk, seide,
400   'The Day of Doom draweth to an ende,
Al ur kuyndes hath lost ur kende,   *our kindred; heritage*
Til God, that dyed for uch a kuynde,   *each person*
For monneskuynde deyde.'   *mankind*

32

"Foules fellen out of heore fliht;   *flight*
405   Beestes gan belwe in everi binne;   *did bellow; stable*

Cros, whon Crist on the was cliht,   *fastened*
Whi noldestou not of mournyng minne?"   *make sounds of mourning*
The **Cros** seide, "Ladi briht,
I bar ones thi Fruit for monnes sinne   *once*
410   More to amende monnes riht   *restore mankind's right*
Then for eny weolthe that I gan winne.   *did win*
    With blod God bouhte His brother:
Whon Adam Godes biddyng brak,
He bot a bite that made us blak,   *black [with sin]*
415   Til Fruit weore tied on Treo with tak —   *tack*
    O Fruit for another!   *One; [exchanged] for*

33

"Sin Cristes Cros that kepeth yifte   *upholds that gift*
Graunted of the Fadres graunt,   *grace*
I was loked: I schulde uplifte   *I was obligated: I had to lift up*
420   Godes Sone and Maydenes Faunt;   *Infant*
No mon hedde scheld of schrifte.   *[yet] had the shield of confession*
The devel stod lyk a lyon raumpaunt;   *rampant*
Mony folk he clihte to helle clifte,   *hell's chasm, snatched*
Til the Crosses dunt yaf him a daunt!   *blow; subdued him*
425   Mi dedes are bounden and booked: *bound and recorded*
Alle the werkes that I have wrouht
Weore founden in the Faderes forethouht;
Therfore, Ladi, lakketh me nouht,   *do not find fault in me*
    I dude as me was looked.   *I was destined*

34

430   "Thorw blod and watur, cristenyng was wrouht —   *baptism*
Holy Writ witnesseth hit wel —
And in the welle of worthi thouht,
A mon mai be cristened to soule hele.   *soul's health*
That blod that all the world hath bouht   *[With] That blood*
435   Digne cristenyng He gan me del;   *Sacred; He did deal to me*
At cristenyng Crist foryat me nouht,   *forgot me not*
His blessede blod whon I gan fel.   *When I did feel His blessed blood*
    Maiden, Moder, and Wyve,
Cristes blode yaf me baptem;
440   Bystreke I was with rede streme   *Streaked*

119

Whon His bodi bledde on the beem   *beam*
  Of cipresse and olyve.   *cypress*

35

"As Jhesu seide to Nichodemus:
  'But a barn be twyyes born   *Unless a person; twice*
445 Whon Domusday schal blowen his bemus,   *trumpet blasts*
He may elles liggen loddere forlorn   *lie despisedly forlorn*
Furst of a wombe — ther reuthe remus —   *First [born]; there pity begins*
Siththe in a font — ther synne is schorn.'[1]
I was Cros to monnes quemus —   *for mankind's benefit*
450 I bar the Fruit thow bar biforn   *bore*
   For thi beryng alone.[2]
  But yif I hedde iboren Him eft,   *Unless; a second time*
  From riche reste mon hedde beoreft,   *men would have been bereft*
  In a loren logge ileft   *Left in a forlorn lodging*
455   Ay to grunte and grone.   *Forever*

36

"Thou art icrouned Hevene Quene   *crowned*
Thorw the burthe that thou beere;   *birthed one; bore*
Thi garlond is al of graces grene,   *graces/grasses (pun)*
Helle Emperesse and hevene empere.   *Empress of hell; empyreum*
460 I am a relyk that shineth shene;   *beautifully*
Men wolde wite wher that I were: *wish to know; will be*
At the parlement pleyn wol I bene,   *open to view*
 On Domesday, prestly apere.   *readily appear*
   Whon Jhesu schal seye riht there,
465   'Trewely, uppon the Roode-Tre,
  Mon, I dyede for love of the;
  Mon, what hastou don for Me
   To beon My frendly feere?'   *companion*

---

[1] *Next in a font — there sin is shorn (i.e., washed away)*

[2] *For the sake solely of what you bore (i.e., I did this solely to uphold the outcome of what was your labor)*

37

"At the parlement I shul puiten up pleynyng   *present a bill of complaint*
470 Hou Maydenes Fruit on me gan sterve —   *[About] How; did die*
Spere and spounge, and sharp nayling
Thorw the harde hat the heved gan kerve —   *skull*
I shul crie to that rihtful Kyng,
Uche mon schal have as thei aserve.   *Each; he deserves*
475 Rihtful schul ryse to riche restyng;   *The righteous*
Truyt and tripet to helle shal terve.   *Deceit and treason; fall*
        Mayden, meoke and mylde,
        God hath taken in the His fleschly trene;   *tree branch*
        I bar thi Fruit, leothi and lene;   *slender and lean*
480   Hit is riht the Roode helpe to arene   *arraign*
            Wrecches that wraththe thi Chylde."   *torture*

38

The Queen acordet with the Cros,   *reconciled*
And ayeyn him spak no more speche;
The Queen yaf the Cros a cos,   *kiss*
485 The Ladi of Love love gan seche,   *did seek loving accord*
Theih hire Fruit on him were diht to dros,   *Although; destined to rot*
Whon rendyng ropus gan Him reche.   *tearing ropes; did stretch*
Cristes Cros hath kept us from los,   *damnation*
Maries preyers, and God ur Leche!   *[With]; Physician*
490   The Qween and the Cros acorde;
        The Qween bar furst, the Cros afturward,   *bore (in pregnancy)*
        To fecche folk from helleward,
        On holy stayers to steyen upward,   *stairs to climb*
            And regne with God ur Lorde.

39

495 The clerk that fourmed this figour
Of Maries wo, to wite som,   *teach some [folk]*
He saih himself that harde stour   *saw; torment*
Whon Godes armus weore rent aroum.   *asunder*
The Cros is a cold creatour,   *creature/creator (pun)*
500 And evere yit hath ben def and dom —
Theih this tale beo florisshed with faire flour,

121

The Dispute between Mary and the Cross

This point I preve Apocrafum:[1]

 For witnesse was never foundet

 That nevere Cristes Cros spak;

505 Oure Ladi leide on him no lak; *laid no blame on him*

 Bot to drive the devel abak, *In order to thrust back*

 We speke hou Crist was woundet.

40

In flesshly wede · God gan Him hede *clothes; did clothe Himself*

 Of mylde May; *Maiden*

510 Was bore to blede, · as Cristes Crede *born/borne (pun)*

 Sothly wol say.

On a stokky stede · He rod, we rede, *stocky (i.e., wooden)*

 In red array;

From develes drede, · that Duyk us lede *Duke*

515 At Domesday!

 Whon peple schal parte and pace, *pass on*

 To hevene halle or to helle woode,

 Cristes Cros, and Cristes blode,

 And Marie preiers mylde and goode,

520 Grant us the lyf of grace. Amen.

Explicit disputacio inter Mariam et Crucem secundum Apocrafum.[2]

---

[1] *Although this tale has been flourished with fair rhetorical flowers, / On this point (i.e., the Cross speaking) I admit that it is apocryphal*

[2] *Here ends the disputation between Mary and Cross following Apocrypha*

Notes

Abbreviations:

V Vernon MS (Bodl. MS Eng. poet. a.1). [Base text]
S Simeon MS (BL Addit. MS 22283).
R MS Royal 18 A.x.
M Morris edition (1881). [Diplomatic texts of V and R.]
F Furnivall edition (1901). [Diplomatic text of V.]

The texts of V and S are closely related, and variants between the two tend to be inconsequential. The notes list the variants that affect meaning or meter and omit those that are purely orthographical. The relationship of R to VS is more difficult to determine. R appears to be not simply an abridgement of the longer poem found in VS. Its twenty-eight stanzas represent some mixing up of the stanzas it borrows, and several of its unique passages resemble the poet's style. The following chart outlines the arrangement of stanzas in the two versions:

VS	R	VS	R	VS	R	VS	R
1	x	11	10	21	34	31	
2	1	12	12	22	35	32	
3	2/3	13	13	23	36	33	
4	3/x	14	14	24	37	34	
5	4	15	15	25	38	35	
6	5	16	23	26	39	36	
7	6	17	18	27	x	37	
8	7	18	20	28	40	38	
9	8	19	21	29		39	
10	9	20	33	30		40	

R contains 2½ new stanzas and omits 14½ stanzas found in VS (part of 2, all of 11, 16–17, 19, 22, and 24–32). While the shared stanzas clearly do correspond, most lines in R contain some degree of variation from VS. The notes cite all variants except the merely orthographical, with recourse where necessary to citation of full lines or passages.

The Dispute between Mary and the Cross

Incipit   S: *Here bygynneth a lamentacion that ure lady made to the Cros of hir soone.* R opens with a unique 13-line stanza:

> O litel whyle lesteneth to me
> Ententyfly so have ye blys
> Gode ensaumple here schul ye
> Of noble mater wrought it is
> How Mary spak to the Rode-tre
> Whan her sone was in anguys
> The Cros answeryd that lady fre
> Ful myldely seiye clerkys wys
>   That this tale have made couthe
> Thei have expouned it by sight
> A good ensaumple and a bryght
> But Apocrifum thei holde it right
>   For tre spak never with mouthe.

1   *on.* R: *to the.*

1–8   The innovative meter of this octave reappears in the last stanza (lines 508–15). Internal rhymes create a pattern similar to tail-rhyme verse (*aabaabaabaab*), but with metrically short *a*-lines (two stressed syllables instead of the typical three). M and F printed this stanza as sixteen lines; the scribes write all stanzas as nine lines. George Saintsbury calls it "a very odd creation" (*A History of English Prosody*, vol. 1 [London: Macmillan, 1906], p. 137). On the imagery of fruit and blood, see Fein, p. 106.

2   *Made.* R: *Sche made.*

3   *Heo.* R: *and.*

        seide. F mistakenly printed *seid.*

        the^2. R: *is.*

        Fruit. Christ as the fruit of Mary is a figure found often in devotional literature; in *Dispute* it is played out meaningfully and evoked often. This first reference has a parallel in Philippe de Grève's *Crux de te volo conqueri* (stanza 1; see Holthausen, p. 23).

4   *Is*. R: *Full.*

5   *seo*. R: *gan see.*

7   *Serwe*. R: *Of sorewe.*

      the. R: *hys.*

      fleo. For the verb, see *MED flēn* v.(2) "strip skin from (sth.); peel back." The usage is, however, unusual (because *veines* is subject not object), and it may be influenced by *flen* v.(1), sense 5, "flinch, turn away, give way."

        The graphic image, repeated in line 12, is of Christ's veins, flesh, and bones all coming apart. The visualization of Christ's suffering — and incessant bleeding — is crucial to the poetic conception of the Crucifixion as an anti-birth experience. First formed of Mary's flesh, Christ's human form now deconstructs before Mary's eyes, while it is borne (as in pregnancy) by the Cross. Compare similarly vivid images of Christ bleeding in *Meditation on the Passion*; and of *Three Arrows on Doomsday*, a work influenced by Rolle's writings: "At this smytyng in to the erthe all his vaynes brast, that of all his lyms the blod out stremede" (ed. Horstmann, p. 113); and in Rolle's *Meditation B*, ed. Ogilvie-Thomson, p. 76, lines 281–91, and p. 78, lines 377–85.

9   *Tre*. R; VS: *Cros*. Reading in R adopted for alliteration; compare note to line 66. Lawton also notes the better alliteration of R (p. 154).

      trouthe. R: *treuthe.*

10   *pillori*. The word here and at line 19 is the only recorded instance applied to the Cross; see *MED pillori(e* n., sense (c). Word and image undergo a transformation when the Cross reveals itself to be not merely a pillory for thieves, but a pillar for mankind (stanza 12).

13   *routhe*. R: *reuthe.*

15   *fayre*. R: *gode*. As Lawton notes, the reading in R provides alliteration with *bigyled* (p. 154).

16   *afamed*. R: *famed*. *Dispute* contains the only recorded instance of this word in ME. See *MED afamen* v.

19   *a*. Omitted in R.

     ipiled. The *MED* lists this usage under *pilen* v.(2), sense (a), "To fasten (sb.) to (sth.) with nails," with this passage the only cited example. The word is probably a pun upon this meaning (fitting *pillori* in sense and sound) and "peeled of skin" (fitting the fruit metaphor); see *pilen* v.(1), sense 5(c).

20   *Grete theves thus*. VS: *Grete Jewes thus*; R: *As grete thevys that*. In VS the phrase *grete Jewes* is a synonmyn for "thieves" here and at lines 25 and 27. Here and at line 27 R reads *theves* (R does not contain line 25). Compare, too, the word *theoves* in stanza 4. A scribe has apparently misread or deliberately changed *þeues* to *ieues*. The conservative, often anti-Semitic orthodoxy expressed elsewhere in texts preserved in VS may inform the alteration. Elsewhere, the *Dispute* poet depicts Jews as pitiless, hard-hearted torturers of Christ and scorners of Mary (stanzas 8, 18, and 29), and as potential converts (stanzas 24–27); see notes to lines 98 and 302.

21   *And dyede for*. R: *That deyeden thorough*.

22–26   In R the five-line coda of stanza 3 (lines 35–39) appears here.

24   Line omitted in S.

25   *grete theves*. VS: *grete Jewes*. See note to line 20.

27   *theves*. VS: *Jewes*. In R the word is a genitive plural: *The grete thevys galowes were greyd*. The phrase *grete theves* has developed into a link phrase between stanzas 2 and 3.

     galwes. S: *galles*.

     were. F mistakenly printed *wiere*.

     greid. R; VS: *greithed*. The reading in R is accepted for rhyme; both spellings are attested for the verb *greithen* (*MED*).

28   *robbyng*. R: *robbe*.

     ronnen. SR; V: *ronne*. The reading of SR is accepted for improved meter.

29   *on the*. R: *theron*.

30   *That never nuyyed*. R: *He noyyed never*.

33   *tobursten*. R: *breke*.

           breid. It is difficult to determine which meaning of this word is most appropriate: *MED breid* n.(1), sense 1, "jerk, wrench"; sense 2(d), "an affliction, torment"; or sense 3, "trick, strategem."

34   *nou in a strong stryf*. R: *in stroke and stryfe*.

35–39   In R these lines appear in the preceding stanza (see note to lines 22–26) and the stanza ends with five unique lines:

> The faire fruyte of my flessche
> My leve childe withoute lak
> For Adam Goddis biddyng brak
> The blood ran on my briddes bak
>   Droppynge as dewe on ryssche.

These lines are possibly from the original poem, but they are not obviously superior to the lines in VS, which are retained here. In particular, *The Festivals of the Church* at line 199, "The blood droppyd as dew on ryssche," echoes the last of these lines. Lawton speculates from the presence of these "plausibly original lines" that V and R "were copied from substantially different texts of the poem" and that R's copy "may represent an earlier version in which there were only two speeches on each side" (p. 158). The symmetrical, numerological patterning of VS argues, however, for an original poem of forty stanzas (see Pickering [1978], p. 291).

36   *Fouled*. R: *All tofowled*.

37   *tripet*. R: *treget*.

38   *and ruit*. R: *unrighte* (a word that breaks the rhyme). The R scribe apparently did not know this French word. The meaning "disturbance, disorder" is attested only here; see *MED rut(te* n., sense 2; and *OED ruit*.

40–42   The variant lines in R yield poor sense:

> The jugement have thei joyned
> To bere fooles full of synne
> Yit scholde my sone fro thee be soyned.

43   *uppon.* R: *on.*

44   *teynet.* R: *twyned* (a change in the rhyme). For the verb, rich in meaning, see *MED teinten* v.(1), senses (a), "accused," and (c) "tainted, contaminated," and *teinten* v.(2), "dye, impart color." The past participle spelling found in VS is attested only for the latter verb, but its meaning is blended into the former verb. In the context here, the "taint" is literally blood on the Cross and abstractly treason mixed with truth wrongly accused. Holthausen thought that this word and *feynet* in line 46 break the rhyme. These words, however, are exceptionally fitting in sense; moreover, they rhyme with each other and approximate the first a-rhyme: *enjoynet/ensoynet/teynet/feynet*.

45   *theoves.* S: *the theoves*; R: *a theef.*

fer in fenne. Literally means "far into filth." The usage in *Dispute* is not recorded in the *MED*, but see *fen* n.(2), "dung, excrement, filth" (from OF), and *fen* n.(1), sense 3, "something worthless, trash" (from OE), which may influence the first word.

46   *limes.* R: *feet.* The reading in R provides a word that alliterates, but it changes the visual image of four wounded extremities, which *limes* offers. Since the stanza concludes with the fifth wound in the heart, the reading of VS seems the better one. The line still contains two alliterating words, the poet's norm.

feynet. R: *pyned. Feynet* might mean "restrained," but it appears that the poet chose it to fit with the conceit of Truth tied with treason: the nails "falsify" (feign) His limbs by their foul association with holy flesh. See *MED feinen* v., senses 3 and 8.

49   *That Brid.* VS: *That Fruit*; R: *The brid that* (preferred by Holthausen). The word *brid* is adopted from R because it restores the line's alliteration; compare line 70. The contrast is between the wholeness of Christ's body, born from an

equally whole virgin, and the present tearing of that flesh. Mary views the wound as a sacrilege of her and Christ's own immaculate natures. The rhymes on *born*, *totorn*, and *born* ("borne") reinforce the violence of the contrast.

50   *a theoves*. R: *this*.

      totorn. R: *fortorne*.

51   *thorwout*. R: *thorow*.

      born. VS: *bon*; R: *was borne*. Emendation adopted by M; F emended to *is born*.

52   R reads: *Hys hert now hath a wounde*.

53   *the*. Omitted in R.

54   *deye*. R; VS: *dye*. Both M and F adopted this emendation. The full line in R yields a poorer sense than the line in VS: *That a theefe and a traytour on the schal deye*. Compare lines 256 and 264, and note to line 156.

55   *But*. Omitted in R.

56   *And Vertu falleth in*. R: *Vertue is falle by*.

57   *in*. R: *and*.

58   *Treo*. S: *a tre*.

      hem. R: *do*.

      teye. The verb is rarely used to describe the Crucifixion; see *MED teien* v.

59   *Vertu is*. R: *Now is vertue*.

60   *Crist*. R; VS: *my Sone*. The reading in R restores alliteration; compare Mary's similar reference to her Son at line 406.

61   *Vertu*. R: *Vertue is*.

62   *bereth*. R: *he bereth*.

63   *His*. R: *The*.

65   *dyeth*. R: *thus deieth*.

66   *Cros*. R; VS: *Tre*. The reading in R is accepted for alliteration; compare the similar substitution at line 9.

       ked. VS: *kud*; R: *kyd*. The rhyme indicates the original spelling. All three spellings are attested for the past participle of the verb *kithen* (*MED*).

67   *Sone*. R: *sonys*.

68   *Brid*. R; VS: *Fruit*. The reading in R is adopted for alliteration. The metaphor of Christ as "fruit" is being supplanted by a conception of Christ as a helpless infant, mothered by Mary, and as a delicate flower. The Nativity is recalled in other *planctus Mariae* (Motif 3 in Taylor, p. 10), linking Christ's death with His birth.

       beestes. R: *beeste*.

69   *be*. S: *he*; R: *by*.

       Flour. R: *fruyt*.

70   *With*. R: *And with*.

71   The reference is to the drink offered Christ on the Cross (Matthew 27.34).

73   *fostred*. S: *fostered*; R: *floryssched*.

       fodderes. R: *fodders*; VS: *a fodderes*. Emendation adopted for meter.

76   *I leid*. R: *and leyde*.

77–78   R reads: *And thou Cros haldes hym hiye alofte / Bounde in blody bandes*. Holthausen preferred the variant in R for line 78.

79   *ilolled*. S: *ilulled*; R: *I lulled* (preferred by Holthausen). The idiom in R, *lulled uppe*, is unattested elsewhere in ME (*MED*). The V reading, on the other hand, follows the poet's tendency to play upon words of like sound: Mary's "lulling" in line 76 shifts to Christ's being "ilolled" on the Cross. She lay down her infant gently, an action that has undergone violent alteration in the Cross's holding Christ roughly aloft, leaving him to dangle. Among surviving ME lyrics are many lullabies of Mary that contrast her maternal protection with the foretold Passion; see, for example, the collection printed in Richard Leighton Greene, *The Early English Carols*, second ed. (Oxford: Clarendon, 1977), pp. 85–104.

      thy leyr. VS: *the eyr*; R: *hys leir* (preferred by Holthausen). *Leyr*, the more difficult and interesting variant, also provides better alliteration and rhyme (*eyr* occurs in line 83). The stanza being about where animals rest their heads, Christ is portrayed as uncomfortably accommodated in the Cross's "lair."

80   *gan*. S: *con*. The poet establishes a contrast between Mary maternally wrapping her infant in "cradel bond" and the torturous bonds used on the Cross.

81   *nou on*. R: *uppon*.

82   *ayeyn*. R: *in*.

83   *nestes*. R: *nest*.

      in eyr. VSR: *in the eyr*. The phrase, derived from the biblical saying, modifies *foules* rather than *nestes*.

83–86 Compare Jesus's saying in Matthew 8.20: "The foxes have holes, and the birds of the air nests: but the Son of man hath not where to lay his head" (also Luke 9.58). Richard Rolle includes this passage in both the long and short Prose Meditations on the Passion; see Glasscoe, p. 101; Rolle's *Meditation B*, ed. Ogilvie-Thomson, p. 79, line 431.

84   *Foxes*. R (preferred by Holthausen); VS: *Wolves*. Reading in R adopted because it alliterates and agrees with the biblical source.

85   *in hevene Heir*. S: *in hevene that heyr*; R: *and hevenys eir*.

86   *nou*. Omitted in R.

       holdeth. R (preferred by Holthausen); VS: *leoneth*. The more difficult reading in R is taken for alliteration.

88   *Godes*. R: *My sonys*.

       reste. S: *restyng*.

89   *His*. R: *the*.

90   *His flesch*. R: *the panne is*. F emended to *flesche* to gain a syllable for the meter.

91   *His*. R: *Thys*.

       wyte. F mistakenly printed *wytte*.

       hit. S: *monnus*; omitted in R.

92   *hit*. R: *hym*.

       sleiht. R: *sleithe*.

93   *blody Brid*. R (preferred by Holthausen); VS: *fayre Fruit*. Both versions alliterate, but as Holthausen points out, the quadruple alliteration in R is effective, while VS repeats the fruit figure of line 95 (see also Lawton, p. 154). R is adopted, too, because the bird imagery continues the last stanza's references to fowls and foxes. Compare, also, line 103.

94   *so*. Omitted in R.

       heiht. VSR: *heihth*. Emended for rhyme.

95   *Mi Fruites*. R: *Hys*.

96   *pulte*. R: *putte*.

       streiht. R: *strecche* (a change in rhyme).

Notes

97   *His.* S: *hit.* The line in R is short: *Hys feet to kys.*

98   *keiht.* R: *kecche.* Mary's wish to kiss Christ is common in the *planctus* (Motif 19 in Taylor, p. 11). Allusions to the Jews as hard-hearted villains, torturers of Christ, and pitiless scorners of Mary are also common (Motif 17 in Taylor, p. 11); compare lines 101, 225–26, 230, 234. But note too the three Jews who are softened by compassion (lines 302–42).

99   R reads: *And on me make her mowe amys.*

100   *games.* R: *game.*

101   *me ful.* R: *on me.*

103   *Thou berest my Brid.* R: *My brid thou berist* (preferred by Holthausen).

105   *yaf.* R: *than yaf.*

107   *palmes.* R: *palme.* Two meanings seem to be intertwined: *MED palm(e* n., "palm leaves as an emblem of victory," and *palmes* n. (from Latin), "a branch, spray, or shoot of a vine." The second meaning would augment the vegetative metaphor of Mary and Cross sharing the same "fruit" or "offshoot." This usage prepares for the metaphor of stanza 11, in which Christ the Fruit is a grape of the vine, pressed by the Cross into wine. The word appears in Philippe de Grève's poem: *"Virgo, tibi respondeo, / Tibi, cui totem debeo / Meorum decus palmitum"* (lines 37–39; see Holthausen, p. 24).

108   *thorw.* R: *of.*

109   R reads: *Thy trye fruyt I totere.*

111   *lere.* VS: *lure.* This emendation, adopted by F, is accepted for the rhyme. Both spellings are attested; see *MED lire* n.(1), sense 3(a). The line in R reads: *The worlde to wynne as thou mayst here.*

112   *Blosme.* SR: *blossom.* The line in R reads: *This blossom blomed in thi bour.*

113   *Ac not.* R: *Not all.*

114   *werd*. R; VS: *world*. Reading of R accepted for rhyme.

115   *swelte*. R: *waltereth*.

         swerd. S: *sword*.

116   *feet*. R: *foote*.

         gerd. S: *gord*.

118   *huge*. R: *grete*.

119   *bouh*. S: *bouht*.

119-26   These lines in R contain a great deal of small variation, compared to the VS version:

> He bote a fruyt under a bowe
> Therfore thi fruit spred hys armes
> On tre that is tiyed with tyndes towe
> Hys body is smyte ny the tharmes
> He swelt with a swemely swow
> Hys breest is bored with deethis armes
> And with hys deeth fro deeth us drowe
>   And all hys goode freendys.

Lines 119–20 emphasize the comparison between the forbidden fruit of Paradise and the redemptive Fruit (i.e., Christ on Cross). For this comparison elsewhere in the poem (but not in the R version), see stanza 32. The insertion of *us* in line 125 is also of interest.

120   *hath*. S: *has*.

121   *a Treo*. S: *treo*.

122   *dethes tharmes*. "? Death's worms." This unusual phrase is not cited in the *MED* (*tharm* n.). The basic sense of *tharm* is "entrails, viscera," but see sense 4, "worms," and sense 5, "offspring."

124   *dethes swarmes.* "? Death's swarms." The *MED* glosses *swarmes* in this line as "? A throng of missiles" and also proposes that the word is an error for "*armes.*" Normally the word means "colony of bees" or "throng of people." The inventive quality of the usages of *tharmes* and *swarmes* in this stanza derives from a compressed and somewhat cryptic metaphorical argument in the stanza: Adam bit a fruit, causing Death to attack, culminating in the wounded, exposed Fruit on the Cross being besieged by "worms" and "swarms" (as of bees) but finally emerging victorious against Death. The metaphor posits that Adam's bite presages (or even creates) the wound, by which Life is released to battle Death.

    Although the corresponding stanza 6 in Philippe de Grève's poem mentions Adam's harm being righted and evokes the biblical phrasing of death conquering death, the fructuous metaphor of *Dispute* does not exist there (see Holthausen, pp. 24–25). A closer analogy exists in Love's *Mirror*:

> And this day [Monday] the first man Adam by the frute of the tre forboden, deformede in him that ymage of god, and lost that joyful place, and was dampnet to deth without endyng.
> Bot this day the seconde Adam crist god and man reformed this ymage in his Incarnation, and after by vertue of the blessed fruyt of his body, hangyng on the tre of the crosse restorede man to blisse and life everlastyng. (ed. Sargent, p. 27, lines 26–32)

127–30   Isaiah 25.8; see also Hosea 13.14. Use of this prophecy recurs in *Alle ȝe Mowyn*, stanza 5, and *The Festivals of the Church*, stanza 8.

128   *And.* R: *He.*

129   *on.* R: *in.*

130   *Yaf lyf.* R: *And leveth.*

131   *stipre.* "Post or prop." This usage of the word is the only one attested in ME outside of place-names (*MED stipre* n.). F mistakenly read *scipre* and emended to *stipre.*

131–43   Stanza 11 omitted in R.

133   *me.* F mistakenly read a thorn at the end of this word.

135–41   On the figure of the Cross as a wine press, compare Jacobus de Voragine, *The Golden Legend*, vol. 1, trans. William Granger Ryan (Princeton: Princeton University Press, 1993), p. 295. Jacobus attributes the figure to Dionysius, *On the Celestial Hierarchy*, chapter 7. It also appears in Philippe de Grève's *Crux de te volo conqueri* (stanza 8; see Holthausen, p. 25; Pickering [1978], p. 290). The figure may ultimately derive from Augustine's analogy of Christ and the grape in the press of Isaiah 63.3 (Rubin, pp. 313–14).

136   *in rape*. According to the *MED* (which cites this line), the phrase is idiomatic for "in haste." A perhaps better meaning, from OF, is cited in the *OED*: "stalks of grape clusters, or refuse of grapes from which wine has been expressed." The violence of *rape* n.(2), "forceful seizure," might also be felt in the word as the Cross presses the Grape "with strok and stryf."

142–43   For the account of Jesus and the Samaritan woman, see John 4.7–15. The poet uses the same example to discuss Christ as the water of life in the last stanza of *Whon Grein of Whete Is Cast to Grounde*.

143   *drynke*. F mistakenly printed *drinke*.

144   *doth*. S: *do*.

       to. Omitted in R.

       alegge. The term is one of many legalisms in the debate.

145   *Thi Fruit is*. R: *Fruite*.

146   *On*. R: *I*.

147   *of Godes*. R: *best of*.

147–50   These four lines are omitted in S.

148   *Al is al*. R: *All is*.

       rib and rugge. Idiomatically means "completely," while literally meaning "rib and back." The simile is of Christ's bleeding body as a rich red fruit (e.g., a plum) carved upon a board, oozing juice. It is part of a pattern of food metaphors to connote Christ's eucharistic body (Fruit, Wine, and Lamb). On medieval eucharistic piety, see Bynum, pp. 31–69; Rhodes, pp. 388–419; and Rubin, pp. 288–361.

149   *His bodi.* R: *The bak.*

150   *was.* R: *am a.* The Cross is pillory transformed to pillar, connecting heaven and hell, providing mankind with a pathway — a bridge, with God the Way — heavenward. *Bar* is easily understood to be the preterite of *beren* v.(1), but a second reading is possible: "I was pillar and my crossbar (was) a bridge." This alternate reading brings the Cross's full shape into the symbolism. The figure also appears in the Vernon *Testament of Christ*, line 75: "And to a piler I was ipiht" (ed. Furnivall, p. 643). On the Cross as cosmic, vertical bridge in Anglo-Saxon tradition, see Kaske, pp. 49–50.

151   R reads: *God is the weye, witnesse one worde.*

152   John 14.6: "I am the way, and the truth, and the life."

154   *mihte no mon.* R: *no man cowde.*

156   *deye.* R (preferred by Holthausen); VS: *dye.* Reading of R is adopted for rhyme; compare line 54.

157   R reads: *And Moyses fourmed hys figour.*

157–60   On the sacred lamb, ordained food for the first Passover, see Exodus 12.1–14.

159   *Schulde be sacred.* R: *He sacred so.*

161   R reads: *And chosen cheef in honour.* The sense of R in lines 157–61 is confused.

161–69   Several commentators have cited this memorable figure of the Cross as a charger bearing the Lamb, roasted in the sun. See Gray (1972), p. 69; Bennett, p. 57; and Pearsall, p. 142. Pickering notes the presence of similar imagery in the poet's other works, *The Festivals of the Church*, stanza 10, and *Alle ȝe Mowyn*, stanzas 18–19 ([1978], p. 292; [1997], p. 87).

162   *for.* R: *to.*

163   *Creatour.* R (preferred by Holthausen); VS: *Saveour.* The reading in R, which is slightly harder in sense, is accepted because it both alliterates and eliminates the repetition of a rhyme-word. Holthausen offers a few analogues for this reading (p. 27).

164   *His flesch fedeth.* R; VS: *He fedeth bothe.* The reading in R is accepted because it restores alliteration.

166   *Lomb of Love.* On Christ figured as the Paschal Lamb, see Weber, pp. 95–96, 246 n. 9.

        Rosted ayeyn the sonne. This phrase recurs in the poet's *All ʒe Mowyn Be Blyth and Glade*, line 231. See Pickering (1978), p. 292.

168   *Til feet and hondes.* R: *Whan flessche and veynes.* The image in R repeats one found in the first stanza (line 12). It lacks, however, the vivid similitude of Christ as a Lamb with cloven hooves.

        al toclove. M punctuated this phrase *al-to clove*, with the meaning unchanged (*MED al-to* adv.). Compare *tocloven* in line 325.

169   *With blood I was bironne.* This image recurs in the poet's *All ʒe Mowyn Be Blyth and Glade*, line 233.

170   *in rule this reson.* VS: *in rule hath*; R: *this resoun.* The line in both versions is short; the emendation combines the evidence to lengthen the line.

170–82 This stanza contains much variation between the two versions, which seems to have arisen out of scribal difficulty with the intricate wordplays and a confusion in pronouns. I have emended the mix of *we* and *ye* in VS to a consistent second-person plural form of address — a logical form for Moses's command that does appear in R. For the command, see Exodus 12.8.

171   *Ete your lomb.* R; VS: *We schulde ete ur lomb.*

        in. R: *with.*

172   *vergeous mai make the soule*. VS: *vergeous mai make ur soules*; R: *sous make the sowle*. For Moses's bitter herbs, the poet has substituted "bitter juice" (see *OED verjuice*, sb.: "the acid juice of green or unripe grapes, crabapples, or other unripe fruit"), in order to develop further the imagery of Christ as fruit (stanzas 10–12).

173   *Sore serwe for sinne is your sous*. The two versions read:

        VS: To serwe sore for sunnes ours;
        R: Sorowe for synnes oures.

This line is problematic in both versions because the rhyme-word *ours* is certainly corrupt. The missing word is indicated by sense and soundplay — *sous*, "sauce" — and is supplied in R, line 172. For *sous*, "a medicinal sauce," see *MED sauce* n., sense (b), and *sous(e* n.(1). I have posited also the scribal alteration of *sinne is* (to plural *sinnes*) and *Sore serwe* (a word-skip in R, a misinterpretation of the noun as a verb in VS).

174   *Sour*. R: *That*.

    maketh. R; VS: *schal make*.

    devel. R: *fende*.

175   *Fer*. VS: *For*; R: *And fer. Fer* is adopted from R for sense.

    he fleccheth. R: *fleth*.

176   *ye*. Omitted in VS. The line in VS is awkwardly short; the ampersand in R indicates the loss of a word at this position. Postulating that it was the second-person pronoun agrees with other changes made to the stanza in VS; see notes to lines 171 and 173.

176–77   R reads:

        And bere a staaf and stonde sadde
        Whan flessche the fedith in Goddis hows.

The two versions are significantly variant: a devout person is enjoined either to stand by a staff (VS) or to hold a staff (R). In each instance, the Cross serves as a sign that repels the Devil and protects the eucharistic participant. A similar figure appears in a thirteenth-century lyric: "Thou tak the rode to thi staf / And thenk on him that thereonne yaf / His lif that wes so lef" (ed. Silverstein, *English Lyrics before 1500*, p. 31).

178   *That*. R: *This*.

179   *Stondeth stifli*. R: *Stonde thou styf*. Lines 177 and 179 in R mix the stanza's second-person plural *ye* with the singular *thou*.

180   R reads: *When ye fonge yowre fleissche in take*.

181   *schal no feond*. R: *may the devyll no*.

182   *for*. Omitted in R.

183   *schrine*. S; V: *shrine*; R: *scryne*. The letter *h* in V is misformed. The line in R reads: *When pardoun is schewed with a scryne*.

183–95   The dominant image of this stanza is of a pardon inscribed upon a tablet of either wood or stone (*MED brede* n.[2]) and posted on a pillar. The "writing" is the bloody wounds and bruises on Christ's flesh. A continuing idea of God's flesh as eucharistic "bread" coexists punningly with the main metaphor of a pardon, and the idea of Christ's body as a shrine or reliquary brings in a third, related image that calls upon a different meaning of *brede*, "spread broadly open." The pardon is open to view, as if in an open reliquary, which Jesus's shining body becomes in line 189. The metaphors are thus compressed, merged, and often in flux. By the end of the stanza the idea of Christ as Book supercedes Christ as Pardon. The puns upon *brede* are absent in R (see note to lines 188–92).

      The conceit of *corpus Christi* as a parchment to be read, the wounds as inscriptions, the blood as ink, was well known through the *Testament of Christ*, a version of which appears near *Dispute* in the Vernon MS (ed. Furnivall, pp. 637–57, with two other versions; see especially lines 75–96). For more versions, see Spalding, who traces the figure ultimately to Paul's letter to the Colossians, 2.13–14 (p. xliv). An intermediary source may be Richard Rolle's prose meditation on the Passion; see Rolle's *Meditation B*, ed. Ogilvie-Thomson, p.

75, lines 236–45, and Glasscoe, p. 96. On the significance of the *Testament of Christ* in late medieval piety, see Rubin, pp. 306–08, and Beckwith, pp. 55–63. On the posting of pardons and legal documents, see Aston, pp. 106–09.

184   *Brede on bord with nayl is smite.* VS: *With nayl and brede on bord is smite*; R: *With boke on bord with nayles smyte.* The line in VS makes poor sense until the phrases *with nayl* and *and brede* are inverted, a change based on the line in R. I have omitted *and* (*with* in R). The word *brede* may be read as either a noun "tablet" (hence *boke* in R) or an adverb "(spread) broadly"; see note to lines 183–95.

185   *Rede.* R: *With rede.*

186   *men.* R: *me.* I have translated *pite* ("pight") as "tacked," to follow the figure of a pardon attached to a board, but the carnal sense, "stabbed," is also present.

187   *Ur.* R: *My.* The first-person plural pronouns in this stanza are consistent in VS, but not in R. Compare line 195.

      this. R: *that.*

188–92   R reads, with striking alliteration in the first and third lines:

> The body was bored and on borde bete
> In bright blode oure boke gan schyne
> How woo he was no wight may wyte,
>   Ne rede in hys rode;
> Youre pardoun boke fro top to too.

While the pardon is generally conceived in VS as a piece of writing open to view, it is specifically a book in R. The play upon "bored" (i.e., stabbed) and "board" (for the Cross) appears only in R, line 188. Since *rede* in R, line 191, means "read," its punning nature in VS seems confirmed: "No man may know how woeful Christ was, (bleeding) red upon the Cross," or "No man may know or read (as in a written pardon) how woeful Christ was upon the Cross."

189   *briht.* S: *riht.* F emended to *brihte* to gain a syllable for the meter.

190   *no wight may.* R; VS: *may no man.* R is accepted for its better alliteration (see Lawton, p. 154).

192   *too to.* SR: *to too.* The meaning of *brede* seems still to be either the noun "tablet" or the adverb "broadly," but the phrase *Ur pardoun brede* also invites a third meaning, "bread of pardon," i.e., the eucharistic loaf (see note to lines 183–95). Compare the words of a fifteenth-century carol by James Ryman:

> It semeth white, yet it is rede,
> And it is quik and semeth dede,
> For it is God in fourme of brede;
>   Ete ye it so ye be not ded.
>   (ed. Greene, *The Early English Carols*, p. 194)

193   *with.* R: *full.*

194   *With.* Omitted in R.

195   *Ure.* R: *Youre.* See note to line 187.

196–221 Stanzas 16–17 are omitted in R.

200   *brede.* A fourth meaning for this word emerges: "wooden book-cover" (*MED bred* n.[2], sense [b]). The word is now applied to the Cross instead of Christ's body. On the other usages, see note to stanza 15, lines 183–95. On the figure of Christ as a book, see Woolf (p. 253), who traces it to Revelation 5.1 and Bonaventure.

201   *cleynt.* The first letters *cl* are obscure in V, but confirmed by S. On the verb, see *MED clenchen*, sense 1.(a). F suggested *weynt* as an alternative reading.

209–21 The Cross appears to be summarizing its metaphorical arguments up to this point, recalling the images of wine, a bridge to heaven, the gesture of spread arms, the pardon, and the book. The horizontal axis receives some attention as bridge, directional instruction point, and choir-seat for angels.

210   *wyn.* S: *with.*

214   *sacrynge.* The word denotes Christ's sacrifice, a usage recorded nowhere else in ME. The usual sense is "the consecration of the bread and wine in service of the Mass" (*MED sacring(e* ger.).

215–16 These two lines are omitted in S.

218   *uppon*. S: *up*.

220   *skinne*. VS: *kinne*. The emendation, needed for sense, is homonymic.

223   *the*. Omitted in R.

225   R reads: *To the fikell Iewes withoute othe*.

225–29   The quotation ascribed to Paul appears to be the poet's invention. Compare 1 Romans 2.28–29, on the outward Jew versus the inward Jew. The passage may allude to Isaiah 53, especially verses 5–9.

226   *in*. R: *with*. The repeated description of the Jews as "stone hard" (here and in line 230) refers, in the diction of a *planctus Mariae*, to their lack of compassion, a damning vice. The *planctus* is a genre specifically designed to soften the heart of the Christian believer with intense empathetic feeling, through the medium of the Virgin's maternal loss. In contrast to these Jews' hard-heartedness appears the upcoming tale of the three Jews whose hearts were softened by witnessing Christ's pain and Mary's distress (stanzas 24–27; note to lines 302–42). In the Vernon *Lamentation of Mary to Saint Bernard*, Bernard prays that Mary herself tell the story of her sufferings so that his heart may be softened (lines 105–20; ed. Horstmann, p. 302). Richard Rolle makes a similar appeal in a meditation upon the Passion: "A, modyr of mercy and of compassioun, . . . visite my soule, and set in my hert thy sone with his woundes. Send me a sparcle of compassioun to suple [soften] hit with" (*Meditation B*, ed. Ogilvie-Thomson, p. 78, lines 365–70; see also p. 81, lines 500–05).

227   *Beoten*. R: *Thei bete*.

229   *Meode, or milk medled*. R: *Milk or mede melled*.

230   *harde*. R: *the hard*. On the "hardness" of the Jews, see note to line 226.

231   *eny*. R: *mylk*.

232   R reads: *Or dew that lithe on lily-flour*.

234   *brisseden*. R (preferred by Holthausen); V: *wolden ha broken*; S: *wolden a broken*. The reading in R is adopted as the harder, alliterating reading. See

brisen v., sense 1(a). The line length in VS appears to be corrupt.

235–47   Stanza 19 omitted in R. The prophets' cry for deliverance is generalized and does not derive from any one specific biblical passage.

237   *wildernesses.* S: *wildernesse.* On how medieval theologians viewed the exile in the wilderness as a type for the Passion, see Pezzini, p. 32. This generalized reference to the Hebrews in the wilderness recalls the biblical span of exile, forty years (Deuteronomy 2.7, 8.2, 8.4), and the poet uses the number forty in composing the poem — forty stanzas. The number also has important associations with Christ's Incarnation and Mary's maternity. According to the Vernon *Testament of Christ*, Christ gestated in the womb forty weeks and forty days (line 19; ed. Furnivall, p. 639). Forty days later Mary underwent the ritual for purification (see Introduction to *The Four Leaves of the Truelove*). Furthermore, the author of the Vernon *Testament* emphasizes that the feast of Christ's "newe lawes," that is, Easter with Lent, lasts forty days (lines 197–204). So the epochs of both old and new law (mankind's first and second births) may be represented by the number forty (see note to line 243–47). One may also compare the *Dispute* poet's *Whon Grein of Whete Is Cast to Grounde*, in which Christ's lifespan on earth is put — figuratively, like sprouted wheat — at "ffourti dawes" (line 45).

238   *cromb.* VSR: *cromp.* Emendation is adopted for rhyme; see *MED cromb(e* n. The word is rare, and it generally means either "a crooked staff, hook" or "a piece of land in the bend of a river."

240   *Maydens.* S: *maydenes.*

242   *Thi.* VSR. Holthausen points out that because Mary is speaking to the Cross, the pronoun should be *his* (p. 27). The sense of speaker is not, however, strictly dramatic; if it were, Mary's account of the Incarnation in third-person must also be viewed as strange. More probably, the prophetic words of address to God (lines 236–38) have affected the discourse of this line.

flomb. See *MED flaumen* v., sense 2(b).

243   *barreres. MED barrer* n., sense 1.(a): "A barrier at the approach to the gates of a walled city, castle, or temple"; and sense 3: "A boundary" with the only citation from the Wycliffe Bible.

243   *debate*. "Obstruction"; see *MED debat* n., sense 4(a). Holthausen suggested changing *debate* and *yate* (line 247) to plurals, but no emendation is warranted.

243–47   These lines describe the transition from old to new law, the advent of a "second birth" for Christians. The details of a bloodied passage and a broken gate portray this second birth through a gendered imagery of both childbirth and sexual intercourse. See also stanzas 21 and 35, and Fein, pp. 108–13.

245   *ha*. S: *a*.

249   *with Lomb*. R: *as a lamb so*. F emended *lomb* to *lombe* to gain a syllable for the meter.

251   *For to defoule*. R: *To fowle so*.

252   *Cros*. R: *And Cros*.

253   *To rende my Fruit*. R: *My fruite to foule*.

        feor in fylde. The apparent meaning of this phrase, "far into filth," is difficult; see *MED filth* n., senses 3 and 4, and the examples from the Vernon *Lamentation of Mary to Saint Bernard*. Compare, too, the similar phrase elsewhere, *fer in fenne*, which refers to the thieves (line 45). For better sense, I have taken *feor* to be the comparative "further"; the Virgin compares the Cross to the human torturers who first "defouled" her Son.

254   *Ladi*. R: *The Cros seyde*.

255   *a*. Omitted in R.

255–60   These lines mark the center of the poem (VS only) by recalling how the symbol of the Cross is efficacious as a defense against the devil. An alert, meditative reader might here begin to apprehend that the poem itself is to be taken as a cross-shaped verbal guard against diabolical temptation (compare lines 506–07). Lines 256–57 describe the Christian moment of human redemption not simply as Christ's death, but as an inverted birth experience: on the Cross (Christ's "stepmother"), Christ "yielded the ghost," that is, passed out of the incarnate body that he had received when birthed from Mary.

256   *Til.* R: *Sithe.*

The rhyme-pair *dyede* and *abyde* is an anomaly in the poem, as Holthausen notes (pp. 27–28). Elsewhere *deyed* rhymes with words having the diphthong *ey* (stanzas 5, 12, 21, and 31). Compare note to line 357.

257   *the.* R: *hys.*

258   *I was chose.* R: *Men chose me.*

261   *fende.* R: *defende.*

262   *sawes.* R: *sawe he.*

263   *yates weore keithed.* VS: *yates weore closed*; R: *gate was keithed.* The more difficult alliterating word is adopted from R.

263–65   On the opening of heaven's gates, see Matthew 16.19 and Revelation 21.25, and Rev. 22.14.

264   *deyede.* R: *now he deyede*; VS: *dyede.* Compare emendation to line 54, and see Holthausen (p. 27).

265   *This.* R: *It.*

266   *Aftur.* R: *For.*

267   *the.* Omitted in R.

268   *monkynde.* R: *many folk.*

269   *At.* R: *In the.*

hiye. VS: *his*; R: *hiyest* (preferred by Holthausen). The expression *heigh non* means precisely three o'clock, the time of Jesus's death (Matthew 27.45; *MED non* n.). In VS a scribe has misread yogh as *s*. The phrase can also refer to twelve o'clock noon, but the context indicates the canonical hour nones.

271   *Nou*. R: *All*. John 19.30: "He said: 'It is consummated.' And bowing his head, he gave up the ghost." The phrasing in *Dispute* is close to the gloss given in Love's *Mirror*:

> "Fadere the obedience, that thou hast yiven me I have perfitely and fully done in dede, and yit I am redy to do what so thou bidde me. Bot alle that is writen of me is now fulfillede." (ed. Sargent, p. 180, lines 8–11)

Compare, too, the Vernon *Testament of Christ*, ed. Furnivall, p. 652, line 187; and Rolle's *Meditation B*, ed. Ogilvie-Thomson, p. 82, line 537.

     wel is. R: *well was*.

272   *A*. Omitted in R (preferred by Holthausen). Both versions refer to mankind's collective salvation.

274–86   Stanza 22 omitted in R.

279   *pulte*. S: *put*.

     kelp. See *MED kilp(e* n.: "handle of bucket, kettle, or the like." The meaning here, "claw-like hand," is unique to this text.

280   *hille*. The word refers to Calvary, site of the Crucifixion.

287   *is*. R: *I* (preferred by Holthausen).

287–99   Stanza 23 has been moved in R to follow stanza 15. In R the shepherd similitude comes before the well-developed lamb similitude; in VS it comes afterwards. The logic in VS is better, because the Lamb as victor over the lion is further revealed (in mystical paradox) as Shepherd of the sheepfold. Moreover, an allusion to the shepherds of the Nativity is in development; see note to lines 302–42. On the arrangement of stanzas, see the chart at the beginning of these notes.

288   *That goode*. R: *How riche*.

289   *He is*. R: *a good*. On Christ as Shepherd, see John 10.11–16, Hebrews 13.20, and 1 Peter 2.25.

290   *uche an*. R: *every*.

293   *And with the*. R: *With that*.

296   *That*. R: *How*.

        the. Omitted in R.

297   *breken out of heore*. R: *borsten oute of*.

300–416 Stanzas 24–32 omitted in R.

302–42 Mary's tale of the three Jewish witnesses whose hard hearts are softened by
        Christ's and Mary's suffering is another novel invention of the poet. In
        formality and increasing tension, the three speeches, each one stanza long, may
        be compared to those of the Three Living and the Three Dead in *De tribus
        regibus mortuis*, a poem in a similar stanza (ed. Whiting, pp. 217–23). These
        converted Jews are moved by three levels of suffering: (1) Christ's being nailed
        on the Cross (initial pain and torture); (2) Christ's hanging on the Cross
        (continued pain and torture); and (3) Mary's maternal grieving (affective pain
        and torture). The question is made philosophical: which ordeal was the most
        moving? The affective is given a place of priority, perhaps because Mary is fully
        human, her pain is mortal, and it becomes a more universal way that others may
        access this event.
            One may note some of the narrative curiosities of this passage. Mary is
        made to report upon her own suffering through the voice of the third Jew, and
        this person is made to comment upon the unseemly behavior of other Jews
        toward Mary. Furthermore, Mary's "tale" of the Jews follows a scriptural "tale"
        told by the Cross, about Jesus as Shepherd (stanza 23). Allusions to the Nativity
        as the figure for these post-second-birth events are very strong: at Christ's birth
        there were shepherds and the Three Magi; now mankind may rejoice in God as
        Shepherd and three men of wise heart are converted. I am indebted to Terry
        Shears, who astutely noted the allusion to the Three Magi in a graduate paper.

305   *drouknyng*. Compare *The Debate of the Body and the Soul* (c. 1300): "Als I lay
        in a winteris nyt / In a droukening bifor the day," lines 1–2 (ed. Wright, p.
        334). This version of the body/soul debate appears in all three MSS of *Dispute*
        (see Lawton, p. 158). F printed *dronknyng*.

307 *lumpyng.* This occurrence is the only one recorded in ME. See *MED lumping* ppl. The cold hearts of the compassionate Jews appear to be undergoing a change from those of their compatriots, the Jews "ston-hard in sinnes merk" (line 226). These converts feel sensation in their hearts, a first step toward a softened empathy. The three speeches record a progression in compassionate potential.

316 *His.* S; V: *him.*

318 *threte.* VS: *crepe.* Emendation is adopted for rhyme and alliteration.

320 *teres.* F mistakenly printed *teeres.*

324 *Druiye.* S: *Druyyed.*

325 Christ's extreme dry thirst (John 19.28) is frequently treated in meditations upon the Passion. In *Dispute* Christ is demonstrably wrung dry, his body — called "softur then water, or eny licour" (line 231) — having copiously lost blood, the Cross "pressing" him as a wine press (stanza 11), the sun roasting him (stanza 13). The lesson drawn in the Passion literature is that Christ's thirst was "anely after the luf of man, that he so dere bogth" (*Meditation on the Passion; and of Three Arrows on Doomsday*, ed. Horstmann, p. 113); compare Rolle's *Meditation B*, ed. Ogilivie-Thomson, pp. 80–81, lines 463–75; Love's *Mirror*, ed. Sargent, p. 179, lines 34–41.

332–36 The sword of sorrow that pierces Mary's heart — a sign of her participation in Christ's wounds — derives from Luke 2.35 (Simeon's prophecy) and is a frequent feature of *planctus Mariae* (Motif 10 in Taylor, p. 10). It appears too in the version of *The Testament of Christ* found in MS Reg. 17.C.xvii, ed. Furnivall, p. 650, line 370; in Rolle's *Meditation B*, ed. Ogilvie-Thomson, p. 80, line 452; and in Love's *Mirror*, ed. Sargent, p. 47, lines 26–28, and p. 183, lines 15–20.

333 *knyf.* S: *kniht.*

343 *modres.* S: *moderes.*

345 *al on.* M hyphenated the words, *al-on,* but the primary meaning is "all one" rather than "alone."

350   *flowed*. S: *folwed*.

351   *walt*. The word appears to be used figuratively to mean "was downcast"; see *OED walt* v., sense 2, "To be thrown down, fall over, be upset or overturned."

352   *sorwes two*. That is, the combined sorrow of a father and a mother.

357   *deyde*. VS: *dide*. Elsewhere the word is spelled *dyed* or *deyed*. It normally rhymes with words having the diphthong *ey*, but compare line 256 (and note).

359   *teyde*. Emendation suggested by Holthausen; VS: *soyled*. The MS reading is imperfect in both rhyme and alliteration. A scribe's eye may have skipped down to the next stanza (line 370). Compare *teye* in similar context at line 58, and *teyde* at line 268; at both points the word rhymes with a form of *deye*, "die."

360   *told and darted*. A lexicographer of the *MED* proposes that *darted* be read as parallel with *soyled* in the preceding line, but the syntax would be highly uncharacteristic of the poem; see *darten* v., sense 1.(a.). There appears to be a pun upon Christ's body being "drawn" and abstract Truth being "told." The second verb *darted*, "pierced (as with a dart), punctured," pulls the meaning back toward the first association. The word *told* begins the sound/sense-play upon *telle* (line 363) and *toyled* (line 368). On *told* as meaning "drawn, pulled," see *OED toll* v.[1], sense 3.

368   *trie*. Another fairly rare word drawn from OF.

370   *surded*. See *MED surden* v., a word derived from AN. This line is the only instance of its usage in ME cited in the *MED*.

370–75   Simeon prophesied the child Jesus's future suffering and Mary's "sword" of sorrow (Luke 2.34–35).

371   *Myn*. S: *My*.

372   *bemoyled*. VS: *ben oyled*. Emendation adopted by M and F. See *MED ?bemoiled* ppl. (from OF *moillier*), "bespattered, covered," with no actual usages cited (only this emended line). The earliest instance of *oilen* as a verb is dated in the *MED* about 1425. The MS reading would mean "be anointed"; the emended reading gives better sense in the context.

Notes

378-86   The rupture in nature that occurred during the Passion is recorded in Matthew 27.51-54. The emphasis upon these miracles underscores the event as a metaphysical birth. These signs are also mentioned in the Vernon *Lamentation of Mary to Saint Bernard* (ed. Horstmann, p. 303, lines 125-28), and they occur in other *planctus Mariae* (Motif 32 in Taylor, p. 11).

379   *nihtes*. S: *niht*.

    donne. This usage of *don* as a noun does not appear in the *MED*, but compare *don* adj., sense 2, "dusky, murky, dim."

386   A wordplay upon *kinde* begins here and continues in lines 401-02. Repeated five times (spelled *kende* or *kuynde*), the word changes each time in meaning; see *MED kinde* n., especially senses 6, 7, 12, and 15.

393-403   *Seint Denys*. Dionysius the Aeropagite, who was converted in Athens by Paul (Acts 17.34), and, hence, was a *hethene clerk* during the Passion. In medieval hagiography he was confused with two other holy figures: (1) St. Denis, third-century martyr, bishop of Paris, and patron saint of France; and (2) Dionysius the Pseudo-Areopagite, a mystical theologian, probably a sixth-century Syrian monk, who wrote under the name of Dionysius the Aeropagite (his influence is known in *The Cloud of Unknowing* and related works). For the latter, see Gallacher's edition; and Glasscoe, pp. 165-214, especially pp. 173-76, 180-85. Thus the figure of Dionysius was connected to the early apostles, the conversion of France, and the mystic wisdom ascribed to Pseudo-Dionysius. By tradition he was trained in astrology and was knowledgeable of Christ through an unnatural eclipse witnessed in Athens. For an account of this event, see Jacobus de Voragine, *The Golden Legend*, vol. 2, trans. William Granger Ryan (Princeton: Princeton University Press, 1993), pp. 236-41, especially pp. 237-38.

395   *plais*. VS: *here pris*. For the spelling and astronomical usage, see *MED place* n., sense 2(f). The VS reading is poor in sense and too long.

399   *clerk*. F mistakenly printed *clerke*.

401   Holthausen's proposed emendation of this line, *Al ur kuyndes have lost heore kende*, is unnecessary; see note to line 386.

413-16   Note the parallel to stanzas 10-11.

416   *another.* S: *othur.*

417–18   R reads:

> And I was Cros and kepte that yifte
> That yeve was of Fadres graunt.

422   *lyk a.* R: *as.*

422–24   Note the parallel to lines 278–81. The Cross is explaining how the "dunts" Christ received on the Cross (line 358) enabled the Cross itself to deliver "dunts" to the devil.

423   *he clihte to helle clifte.* R: *he keighte to hell clifte;* VS: *into helle he clihte.* VS lacks the rhyme word, which appears in R.

424   *daunt.* This line represents the only cited usage of this word as a noun, from *daunten* v. (OF *da(u)nter*), "to subdue, defeat" (*MED*). R reads: *Till the dyntes of the Cros gan hym adaunte.*

425   *dedes are bounden.* R: *dede is founde.*

426   *werkes.* R: *werke.*

427   *Weore founden.* R: *It was.*

        Faderes. SR: *Fadres.*

428   *Therfore.* R: *Louely.*

        lakketh. SR: *lak.*

429   *me.* R: *I.*

        looked. R: *loked.* It is unclear whether the verb is from *loken,* "to lock" or (in this context) "to be obligated" (compare line 53), or from *loken,* "to look." I have based my choice of the latter upon a similar impersonal usage cited in the *MED: loken* v.(2), sense 8c(c) *me is no bettre loked,* "I am no better favored, my fortune is no better." The only cited example of the idiom is, however, dated c. 1450.

430   *Thorw.* R: *In.*

         cristenyng. R; VS: *cristendam.*

430–42   This stanza varies between versions in a significant way. In R the Cross claims
         that it was individually baptized with Christ's blood; the pronouns are first-
         person singular. In VS the Cross speaks pastorally about the sacrament,
         explaining how baptism redeems *us*; first-person plural pronouns create a
         distance from the Cross's personal experience. The pronoun *we* in V at line 437
         is rendered *he* in S, attesting to some confusion over the resultant discussion
         of a universal baptism in blood. The more powerful image is certainly that of
         R, and it is more in keeping with the metaphysical nature of the conceits
         elsewhere in the poem. Therefore, much of R has been accepted to emend the
         weaker VS version, which appears to have been altered to conform to orthodox
         teaching.

432   *the.* R; omitted in VS.

         welle. R; VS: *wille.*

         worthi. R; VS: *sothfast.* Reading in R adopted for the alliteration.

433   *to soule hele.* R; VS: *skil* (which Holthausen suggested emending to *be skil* or
         with skil). Both sense and rhyme are improved in the R reading. The Vernon
         MS bears the title "*Salus Anime* or Sowlehele"; see Doyle, p. 3.

434   *all the world hath.* R; VS: *us alle.*

435   *Digne.* R: *A digne.*

         He. R; omitted in VS.

         me. R; VS: *us.*

436   *At cristenyng Crist.* R: *Crist in cristenyng.*

         me. R; VS: *us.*

437   *His blessede.* R: *Hy fressche.*

437   *I.* R; V: *we*; S: *he.*

439   *Cristes blode yaf me.* R; VS: *Thi Fruit hath yiven us.*

440   *Bystreke I was with rede streme.* R; VS: *Cristened we weore in red rem.* F emended VS *red* to *redde* to gain a syllable for the meter. The past participle *bystreke* is apparently rare in ME, the only example of it cited in the *MED* being this line.

441   *His bodi bledde on.* R: *Jhesu bled upon.*

443   *As.* Omitted in R.

443–48   The doctrine of double birth is central to the poet's conception of Mary and the Cross's paired maternity. The biblical passage referenced here is John 3.1–16; see also Romans 6.

446–48   R reads:

> He schulde lye as man lorn
> First bore of wombe where rewthe remys
> Sith with font synne is schorn.

448   *synne.* VS: *synne awey.* Emendation adapted from reading in R.

449   *I.* R: *And I.*

450   *biforn.* R: *aforn.*

451   *alone.* F observed the spacing in V and printed *al one.*

452   *yif.* Omitted in R.

      iboren. R: *born.*

454   *ileft.* S: *ilef.* The line in R reads: *And in a lore logge lefte.*

455   *grunte.* R: *grucche.*

456   *art icrouned.* R: *were crowned.*

457   *Thorw the burthe*. R: *For the birthen*. There appears to be a pun upon "burden" and "birth." Mary's immediate burden is her present suffering of loss at the foot of the Cross.

458   *al of graces*. S: *al of greses*; R: *of gracious*. M glossed "all of green graces."

459   *Helle*. R: *Of hell*. "Of (both) hell and heaven's empyreum (you are) Empress." On Mary as the empress of hell, see numerous examples cited in *MED emperesse* n., sense 2(b), including *Pearl*, lines 441–42: "That emperise al hevenz hatz, / And urthe and helle, in her bayly" (ed. Gordon, p. 16).

    and. R; VS: *in*. Reading of R adopted for sense.

460   *a*. R: *the*.

461   *that*. Omitted in R.

462   *parlement pleyn wol I*. VS: *parlement wol I*; R: *pleyn parlement I schal*. The alliterating word *pleyn* is adopted from R.

463   R reads: *At Domesday prestly to pere*.

464   *Jhesu*. R: *God*.

465   *uppon*. R: *on*.

466   *for love of the*. R; VS: *for the*. The reading in R lengthens a short line.

467–68   The question evokes the traditional Seven Corporal Works of Mercy, derived from Matthew 25.31–45, about which Christ as Judge will inquire on Dooms-day. Compare *The Four Leaves of the Truelove*, stanza 34 (in this volume).

469   *I*. R; omitted in VS. The VS version has no subject for the verbs *puiten up* and *preien* (line 473). The pronoun *I* is restored from R. The substance of the complaint given in lines 470–72 indicates that the speaking Cross intends to deliver its own grievance (against mankind?) on Judgment Day. The bizarre quality of this imagined action accounts, perhaps, for the deletion of a stated agent in VS; compare the treatment of the Cross's baptism in stanza 34.

469 *puiten*. S: *putten*; R: *put*. F read *putten* but the *i* is dotted. On the legal sense of *putten up*, "present (a bill) in court," see *MED putten* v., sense 26.

up. Omitted in R.

470 *Fruit*. R: *sone*.

471 *sharp*. R: *hard*.

472 *hat the heved*. R: *hede the helme*.

gan. R (preferred by Holthausen); VS: *shal*. The past tense makes better sense; *shal* occurs by attraction to the rest of the passage.

473 *I*. R; omitted in VS.

crie to that. VS: *preie to that*; R: *crye*. The word adapted from R is colorful in alliteration and direct speech.

474 R reads: *Ilk man have as the serve*.

475 R reads: *The right schul ryse to ryche reynynge*. R's reading is interesting because the rhyme matches *pleynyng* of line 469.

476 *tripet*. R: *treget*.

terve. R (preferred by Holthausen); VS: *sterve*. Reading of R adopted for alliteration and sense.

477 *Mayden*. R: *Mayde*.

478–81 The crucial reference to Mary as a tree has been misunderstood by a redactor of the R version. It appears that "trene" was read as "treue" and that the succeeding lines were then altered for rhyme:

God took in the hy[s] flessch trewe
I bare thi fruyt lele and newe
It is right the rode to Eve helpe schewe
    Man, woman, and chylde.

Line 480 is a desperate attempt: introducing Eve as counterpoint to Mary, it lacks coherence. On the figure of Mary as a tree, compare the analogues to *Dispute* cited by Yeager, especially *Altercation piteous entre l'arbre verd et l'arbre sec* from Guillaume de Deguilleville's *Pélerinage de l'âme* (Yeager, pp. 55, 59–60, 66), Thomas Hoccleve's *Lament of the Virgin on the Loss of Her Green Apple*, and a fifteenth-century lyric declaration that: "Owre Lorde is the frwte, Oure Lady is the tree, / Blessid be the blossome that sprange, Lady, of the" (ed. Silverstein, *English Lyrics before 1500*, p. 110).

482   *The.* S: *e*, with a space left for the initial thorn; the line appears at the bottom a column, a position that caused the illuminator to overlook the space.

        acordet. R: *thus acorded.*

483   *And.* Omitted in R.

485   *Love love.* R: *love longe love.*

486–89   These four lines are omitted in R.

487   *reche.* For the meaning, see *MED rechen* v.(1), sense 8(c).

491   *furst.* S: *fruit.* This line defines the maternal role of both parties.

494   *God.* Omitted in R.

495   *The clerk that.* R: *A clerk.*

495–507   The claim appears to be (in both versions) that the clerk who *fourmed this figour* witnessed the Crucifixion, as M glossed these lines. The poet's meaning is unclear: Does he claim as source an apocryphal early Christian text, or does he claim to have witnessed the Crucifixion through meditation or mystical contemplation? The poet's need to explain the fantasy of a talking Cross has been labelled naïve by many commentators; see, for example, Yeager, p. 65; Brewer, p. 60; Pearsall, p. 142; Lawton, pp. 155–56; Woolf, pp. 253–54. The poet wants to make an identification between eye-witness truth and imaginative piety; we speak this way, he says, because it is effective *to drive the devel abak.* The Cross may be said to speak because the crafted poem *is* a Cross made up of words, a verbal talisman against diabolical forces (compare lines 255–60), inspired by sacred and true events. A speaking Cross was the model used to illustrate the trope of personification in Geoffrey of Vinsauf's handbook of rhetoric (*Poetria nova*, trans. Margaret F. Nims [Toronto: Pontifical Institute of Mediaeval Studies, 1967], pp. 32–34).

The poet seems, too, to be making a claim for aesthetic truth (see Pickering [1978], p. 298). In "flourishing" his "tale" (line 501), he participates in the organic imagery of Christ as flower and fruit from Mary's tree. If the Flower of Mary's flesh (line 69) blooms more brilliantly upon the Cross (line 108), then the poet's rhetorical "flowers" have merely illustrated this sacred fact. By means of the creative act, the poet imitates the parenting of Mary and the Cross.

496   *wo, to wite.* R: *sorwe to seiye.*

497–98   R reads:

> As he had see in scharp schour
> How Cristes armes were rent and rune.

498   *aroum.* F mistakenly read *aroun.*

499   *cold creatour.* The Cross is a *cold creatour* in two ways: (1) "lifeless creature, i.e., insensient thing created by God," and (2) "dispassionate creator, i.e., of mankind's way to redemption." The second sense follows from the Cross's parental role as defined in line 491.

500   *hath ben.* R: *was.*

501   *Theih this tale beo.* R: *This tale.*

         with. R: *with a.*

502   *This point I preve.* R; VS: *I preve hit on.* The reading in R is both clearer in sense and more alliterative.

503   *For.* Omitted in R.

         foundet. R: *founden.*

504   *nevere.* R: *evere.*

505   R reads: *Ne oure Lady leyde hym no lak*.

506   *to*. R: *forto*.

        drive. R; VS: *pulte*. The reading in R is adopted for alliteration.

507   R reads: *Men speke of Cristes wounden*. After this line R has a unique stanza:

> A clerk fourmed this fantasye
> On Cristes stervyng stok to stere
> That bare the body all blody
> Whan dethes dent gan hym dere
> This Apocrifum is no foly
> In swich a lay dar the naght dere
> That dothe man to seke mercy
> Wikked werkes awey to were
>   In tixte ful well is write
> A lombe hath larged all this glose
> Plente speche therin to prose
> The counseill of the Cros to unclose
>   Of Maryes woo to wite.

This stanza adds another defense to the one offered by the poet in stanza 39. The reasoning is that such *fantasye* will lead men to seek mercy and avoid wickedness. The *lombe* of the tenth line appears to refer to either the clerk-poet or a clerk-reviser, but, either way, the usage is curious. M queried its meaning: "?clerk." Pickering believes this stanza to be authentic (1978), pp. 291, 298.

508–15   On the meter of this octave, see note to lines 1–8. On this heroic vision of Christ as a knight who rides the Cross to triumph, see Woolf, pp. 52–57.

510   *bore*. SR: *born*.

511   *wol*. R: *to*.

512   *a*. Omitted in R.

        we. R: *men*.

517   R reads: *To holy hevene and hell the wode.*

518   *Cristes Cros.* R: *Now Cristes Crosse.*

519   *Marie preiers mylde and.* VS: *Marie preiers that ben ful*; R: *Maries praier mylde and.* The alliterating word *mylde* has been adopted from R.

Colophon *secundum Apocrafum.* S: *et est Apocrafum.*

The Four Leaves of the Truelove

Introduction

The Vertues of Herbs appears in an Oxford manuscript in the vicinity of the alliterative poem edited here. The "virtue" of an herb is its medicinal or otherwise efficacious property, and the word expresses how each God-created substance (mineral, plant, animal) was thought to possess an innate essence or power. The truelove (*Paris quadrifolia*, herb paris) does not appear among the plants listed in this herbal.[1] It is instead featured in an ornate poem, where its special property unfolds over a span encompassing all of Christian history. Ultimately, the "virtue" of truelove is *grace*, the herb becoming an emblem for how people should love God who loves them. This gracious *grasse* offers the cure for spiritual love-longing.

The truelove plant's popular associations permit it to serve as a multivalent emblem: it has, as an organic herb, medicinal potential; it is cruciform in shape; and its four leaves joined at the center create a looped love-knot. To allow these meanings to converge, the poet embeds them in an array of conventional motifs: a pious opening that hints of an amorous *pastourelle*, followed by a love complaint and a sermon. The thread starts as the adventure of a man devoutly absorbed in his orisons, but it is soon diverted to the mournful strains of a young woman desperate in love. The girl's lament is, in turn, wholly subsumed by a bird's speech, delivered to console her. Relegated to the background, the maiden becomes the bird's patient auditor, and both she and the eavesdropping man virtually disappear while the bird sermonizes at length. In the final stanza they rematerialize, the maiden now comforted, and the man concluding his adventure. The poet thus encloses the bird's sermon within two frames, a female listener overheard by a male one.

This structure, both complex and formally patterned, leads the meditant reader to verbal arrangements of increasing sophistication. Through typological allusions that

---

[1]Nor, to my knowledge, does it appear in any English herbal before the Renaissance. The first known instance is in the herbal of John Gerard (1545–1612): *Gerard's Herbal: The History of Plants*, ed. Marcus Woodward (London: Studio Editions, 1994), pp. 101–03; see Plate 1. For the herbal that appears with *Truelove* in MS Bodl. Addit. A 106, see Gösta Brodin, ed. "'Agnus Castus,' a Middle English Herbal Reconstructed from Various Manuscripts," *Essays and Studies on English Language and Literature* 6 (1950), 1–329.

nuance the botanical emblem, the poem conjures the sign of the Cross, with the meditation ultimately centering upon the Passion and Resurrection (stanzas 6–25). The pious turtledove tells the history of God and man as though it were a vast love-knot with alternate tyings, loopings, and retyings.[2] Contrastive ideas — truth/falsehood, love/betrayal — are alternated in a structure of symmetrical oppositions. The emblem signifies the mystic *nodus amicitiae*, "knot of friendship," that binds humanity in kinship to God. Narrative joinings and disjoinings create a metaphorical knot being tied and broken, and, finally, made endlessly circular without break. Blessed souls may return to God and Mary in heaven; the maiden receives comfort; and the narrator ends his adventure in the same place of cyclic natural growth that opened the poem: "In a mornynge of May when medose suld sprynge" (lines 1, 519–20).

With the blooming meadow as a pretext, the poet borrows from a popular belief that the truelove flower brings luck in love. In early spring its fragile blossom rises on a central stalk amidst four equal leaves (Plate 1). Hopeful lovers liked to adorn their hats and clothes with flowering trueloves, taking the flower as romantic token. Seizing a good chance to moralize, preachers used the plant to teach about the font of divine Love: one should seek only God because human love is unstable and fickle. The organic plant signifies corruption — for people wither and die like plants — but, if taken as an emblem of the Divine, the frail cruciform herb signifies God's love revealed on the Cross.[3] The lovesick maiden of *Truelove* receives a variant of this sermon from a talking turtledove, said to be delivered miraculously from Mary. After a long fruitless search for an elusive "trewluf" (herb/lover), the maiden eagerly absorbs the bird's message and finds her health restored.

The vocal dove makes the herb his ruling conceit, comparing its leaves to the Trinity, with the fourth leaf made Mary (by extension, all humanity). When God created humans in his likeness, they willfully disobeyed and left him. Mournful of this separation from his "flowers" and "friends" (lines 102–03), God forged a new union

---

[2]Many of the miniatures in the English Bohun Hours (Oxford, Bodl. Lib. MS Auct. D. 4. 4, c. 1380) are framed in a variety of four-compartmented knots. See Lucy Freeman Sandler, *Gothic Manuscripts 1285–1385* (Oxford: Harvey Miller, 1986), vol. 1, plate 367, and vol. 2, pp. 157–59; and the superb Last Judgment miniature reproduced in L. F. Sandler, "A Note on the Illuminators of the Bohun Manuscripts," *Speculum* 60 (1985), 368.

[3]The moralization is illustrated by a fourteenth-century verse that survives in a handbook for Franciscan preachers: "Trewelove among men that most is of lette, / In hattes, in hedes, in porses is sette. / Trewelove in herbers spryngeth in May, / Bote trew love of herte went is away" (ed. Wenzel, pp. 159–60). On the tradition in ME verse, see Fein (1991). The plant is compared to the Cross in Gerard, p. 101.

Herba Paris.
One Berrie, or herbe Trueloue.

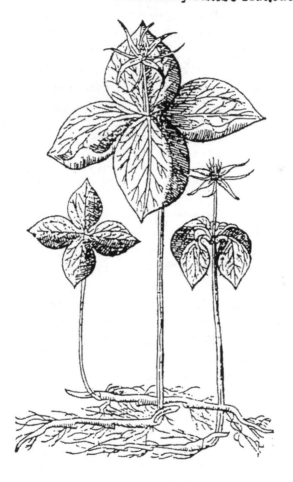

Plate 1. *John Gerarde's Herball* (1597), p. 328 (L.1.5.Med). Woodcut illustration of *One Berrie, or herbe Trueloue*. (Reproduced by permission of the Bodleian Library, University of Oxford).

through Mary, who individually comes to embody the loyalty that mankind could not collectively sustain. The drama culminates in an action by the "second leaf": Christ dies sacrificially in order to allow God's "haly handwarke" to depart from hell and join him in heaven. Hell's gates burst at the climactic center of the poem, and Christ, acting as parent, births his own "bon chylder" into the resurrected life (lines 259–60, 268). God's knotted bond to humanity, forged when he created Adam and Eve, is forever secured when Christ harrows hell.[4]

The remainder of the bird's sermon dwells upon the fate of an individual after death, explained in a tone of concerned warning. Pride and friendships will not avail when the soul finds itself naked and solitary before its Maker. Judicial metaphors create a vivid courtroom scene of final Judgment where even the intercessory pleas of Mary will not help the sinner unrepentant in life. The event on the Cross has divided the fates of men; each individual is now faced with a choice between the hard path to heaven and the smooth one to eternal suffering:

> Bot hard way is to heven and haste to hell.
> In purgatory is payn, whoso passes thare.
> Of mekyll wa may thai wytt, that tharin sal dwell
> Ful lang. (lines 370–77)

Relying upon expiation in purgatory is an undesirable solution, given the painfulness and uncertain duration of that place. The bird warns the maiden not to delay in reforming her life because the deeds she does here will constitute her fate in the next life (lines 374–75). Consequently, "now ware tym to begyn" (line 387).

The bird's 455-line sermon occupies thirty-five stanzas, or seven-eighths of the poem. Modern readers may find the maiden's patience extraordinary. In the final stanza, she is so genuinely thankful that she blesses the "body, bones, and blood" of the miraculous bird (line 509). To be put off by the length of the sermon is, however, to miss its wondrous curative capacity, which is supposed to take place — for both maiden and meditant reader — through a process of absorbing words and designs crafted in poetic sequence. *Truelove* works as a medicine delivered by verbal means, bringing potential health to each fragile, blossom-like soul. The maiden, "syghand and sekand" among the flowers at the opening (line 8), was doomed to wither without a medicinal treatment. The solace she seeks in her secular way is the curative

---

[4]Christ descends and ascends at the poem's midpoint, drawing the vertical trajectory of a "stem." A similar effect marks the Vernon lyric *Maiden Mary and Her Fleur-de-Lys*, lines 65–72, where a mental line drawn by means of the Harrowing (at the center) completes a shaping of the botanical emblem.

herb truelove, or a faithful lover. The bird redirects her to the divine Truelove by means of a sermon-poem shaped like the plant. The sermon thus delivers from Christ as Physician (line 286) the medicine she seeks — an "herbal" cure imbibed as a verbal pill that makes her whole again.

The hope expressed at the end of the exposition is that "we" may win the love of the Truelove (the Trinity and Mary) because, like the maiden, we are edified as to where and how to seek it. The narrator prays God to grant everyone this particular *grace*, a revelatory pun that conflates God's grace with the herbal *grass* (line 515; compare line 66). So in reading this poem of "sowlehele," we swallow the medicine, and each time we reread the poem meditatively, discovering more of its embedded meaning, we increase the dosage and improve its effect.

As a poem of spiritual counsel addressed to a lovelorn woman, *Truelove* is similar to another poem in this volume, Thomas of Hales's *Love Rune*, written generations earlier and addressed to a "young woman dedicated to God," a phrase suggesting an audience removed from secular life. In both poems an advisor steers a young woman away from her yearnings for physical love, arguing that her object will necessarily be false and fleeting, and asks that she turn her affections instead toward God, an infallible Lover. The message of *Truelove* might therefore seem to be monastic, an exhortation to embrace celibacy and take oneself to the convent or cell. *Truelove*'s place in late fourteenth-century alliterative verse situates it, however, in a later tradition of emblematic moral instruction to a pious laity. While the poem does borrow from the longstanding tradition of learned men instructing novitiate women on the religious life, its message is to be understood in a more universal way. The distracted maid is like mankind's fallen soul wandering lost in an Edenic "orchard" (line 4). She resembles the grieving dreamer in *Pearl* more than she does a specific female recipient of paternalistic moral advice. At the same time, in filling a maiden's mind with life-saving "grace," the messenger-bird behaves in shadow resemblance to the archangel Gabriel (who pronounced Mary "full of grace" in the moment marking the Incarnation), just as Thomas of Hales had also made an Annunciatory gesture in giving the "maid of Christ" a message of God's amorous longing.[5]

Truelove borrows, too, from the French-influenced lyric tradition of *chanson d'aventure*, especially the type known as *pastourelle*. Two motifs lead the reader toward certain expectations: a male adventurer spies a solitary maiden, and then he overhears her lament of misfortune in love. In secular verse the set-up often becomes

---

[5]See Introduction to *Love Rune*; and Bernard S. Levy, "The Annunciation in Thomas de Hales' *Love Ron*," *Mediaevalia* 6 (1980), 123–34.

an amorous encounter, as in the lyric *De clerico et puella* of MS Harley 2253,[6] but sometimes the narrator remains, as here, merely an observer of the maiden's beauty and the recorder of an overheard complaint. The man's experience forms the outermost frame, a sensibility whose ordinary perception of things leads the reader into the poetic and meditative experience. In this instance the strolling narrator is absorbed in his own efficacious, health-seeking practice: he is "byddyng" his "owres" (line 4), that is, devoutly saying the prayers prescribed in a book of hours, probably the Hours of Mary [M], or perhaps the Hours of the Cross [C]. The events sequenced in these two offices closely reflect the biblical events appearing in *Truelove*: Creation and Fall of Mankind, Annunciation [M], Visitation [M], Nativity [M], Adoration of Magi [M], Flight out of Egypt [M], Massacre of Innocents [M], Betrayal [C], Christ before Pilate [C], Flagellation [C], Crucifixion [C], Mary and John at Cross, Deposition [C], Entombment [C], Harrowing of Hell, Christ's Appearance to Mary Magdalene, Doubting Thomas, Christ's Appearance to the Apostles, Resurrection, Coronation of Virgin [M], and Last Judgment (Wieck, pp. 39–41, 60, 90). Thus the narrator is not simply witnessing a remarkable maiden/bird dialogue; he is rapt in a state of meditative prayer, and many images associated with specific prayers, as illuminated in a book of hours, unfold before him — and the reader — in the bird's sermon.

Inside the experience of the prayerful narrator exists the setting that becomes the second frame of *Truelove*: a maiden standing beside a tree upon which a turtledove is perched. This tableau possesses emblematic significance reflective of a third literary type, the *planctus*. With another pun operating on the level of revelation, the meditant seems led — as if by grace — to the sight of a "mourning may" during his "May morning" stroll (lines 1, 7). As I have stated, the maiden's grief in the orchard suggests the desolation of humankind in separation from God, an allusion reinforced by the bird's first story of Creation, and, ultimately, when the girl receives comfort, her joy may resemble that of Mary visited by Gabriel, which the bird also depicts in his vignette of the Annunciation. More crucially, however, especially in terms of the meditative focus upon mourning, this preliminary grouping of maiden, tree, and bird provides a detailed shadow-likeness to a sacred image: Mary at the foot of the Cross. Mary's mourning becomes an antidotal model for the "mourning may": Mary mourned her loss deeply but with remarkable stamina and dignity, culminating in stately coronation and reunion (stanzas 17, 24). Her experience, which brackets the

---

[6]The opening of *Truelove* contains several echoes of *Nou Sprinkes the Sprai*, a thirteenth-century *pastourelle*; see the note to line 11 for points of correspondence. On other English *pastourelles*, see Sichert; Reichl; and the list provided in the Select Bibliography (under "secular *chansons d'aventure*").

midpoint Harrowing of Hell, is the anchoring image for numerous English lyric and prose *planctus Mariae*. Its figuration here dignifies the opening strains of lament from a lovesick maiden.

Mary's compassion informs the meditational focus of another alliterative poem in forty thirteen-line stanzas, *The Dispute between Mary and the Cross*. The two poems differ greatly, however, in style: While the *Truelove* poet adopts a tone of pastoral solicitude, the *Dispute* poet seeks startling effects through carnal, often violent imagery. Nonetheless, real correspondences do exist in both external structure and theological argument. The salvific qualities of Mary and Cross are superimposed in both these poems, and in each a doctrine of mankind's second birth through Christian redemption is illustrated in a metaphoric "birthing" of mankind that occurs midpoint. The two forty-stanza poems are quite remarkable in using a woman's form — her procreative capacity to become, mid-body, a point of exit for another body — to make poetry based upon the subjects of incarnation and redemption (Fein [1992], pp. 110–14; see too the Introduction to *Dispute*). In this regard, the number forty possesses great significance. *The Testament of Christ* is a much-copied contemporary poem containing conceits also found in *Dispute* (Christ's body as parchment, his wounds inscribed words of pardon) and *Truelove* (herb truelove as a four-part "rent" of repentance). In this work, which appears near *Dispute* in the Vernon MS, Christ's time in Mary's womb is numbered at forty weeks and forty days. Moreover, forty days was the prescribed space of time under Jewish law for purification of the womb after a woman gave birth, a period that even virginal Mary observed. The author of the very popular *Meditations on the Life of Christ* asks the reader to reenact this period in meditation during the forty days from the Nativity to the Feast of the Purification.[7] Thus forty is the number intrinsically associated with the Incarnation of God in the womb of Mary.

Given the *Truelove* poet's propensity for pun and concrete metaphor, it is not surprising to discover that the careful structuring probably extended even to physical layout. The title *The Four Leaves of the Truelove* references the poem inscribed upon four leaves of parchment, a quarto with eight sides, five stanzas on each half-leaf. Observation of the lines that would have headed or ended individual folios reveals logical transitions at these points. For example, the ending of stanza 5 explains where

---

[7]See the pseudo-Bonaventuran *Meditations on the Life of Christ*, pp. 54–56; Love's *Mirror*, p. 46; and Gail McMurray Gibson, "Blessing from Sun and Moon: Churching as Women's Theater," in *Bodies and Disciplines: Intersections of Literature and History in Fifteenth-Century England*, ed. Barbara A. Hanawalt and David Wallace (Minneapolis: University of Minnesota Press, 1996), pp. 139–54. For other associations of the number forty, see the note to line 237 of *Dispute*.

to "begyn" the search for truelove (line 65), and the opening of stanza 11 — "Now is this ilk second lef . . . (line 131) — would have headed the top of the second leaf. Such a format would have highlighted the symmetries of the poem, and the midpoint would have appeared at the exact middle of four leaves. While neither of the two surviving manuscripts of *Truelove* preserves it in quite this manner, the copy found in Robert Thornton's manuscript (British Library Addit. MS 31042) appears to be based on an exemplar copied just as described. The only other manuscript copy of the poem, Oxford, Bodleian Library Addit. MS A.106, is the composite volume of medical recipes, charms, a lapidary, and an herbal. Here the poem is spread across not eight but seventeen folio sides; it begins midway on a page, averaging two to two and a half stanzas per page. This layout reflects the four-leaf layout in roughly doubled form.

Both manuscripts are from Yorkshire, and they preserve *Truelove* in what is likely its original northern dialect with some midland influence. In its technical features *Truelove* belongs with a small group of surviving verse, dated c. 1380–1400, in the thirteen-line alliterative stanza with northern or north midland affiliations: *The Pistel of Swete Susan*, *De tribus regibus mortuis*, two Saint John poems in a fourteen-line variant stanza, *The Awntyrs off Arthure*, and two plays from York (Pearsall, p. 135; see also Turville-Petre [1974], pp. 3–15; Lawton [1989], pp. 158–61). *Summer Sunday* and *The Dispute between Mary and the Cross* also belong to the style, seeming to represent the early end of the movement, with *Dispute* probably originating in East Anglia. The manuscripts of *Truelove* date much later (c. 1425–50) than its time of composition, which may be ascertained more closely by observing the similarities in structure to *Dispute* and in stanza to *Susan*, poems that appear side by side in the Vernon MS (c. 1385), followed by *The Testament of Christ*, the poem using the truelove as an emblem. These correspondences suggest that *Truelove* is contemporary with the three works gathered in Vernon (c. 1380–85).[8]

As the fifteenth century progressed, the stanzaic alliterative style receded northward, appearing in the Scottish *Rauf Coilyear*, *The Buke of the Howlat*, and *Golagros and Gawane*. When Wynkyn de Worde printed *Truelove* in sixteenth-century London (c. 1510), an appreciation of the stanza had been lost. The printer merged the bob of the ninth line into the tenth or eleventh line of each stanza and set a paragraph sign at the beginning of almost every fourth line, as if the poem was to be read in four-line units. On the frontispiece of de Worde's edition the title *The .iiii. leues of the trueloue* appears ornamentally upon a scroll and beneath it is a woodcut depicting a man and woman in a garden, a tree between them in the background

---

[8]For additional evidence that *Truelove* has a date of composition considerably earlier than the two MSS, see "Note on the Edited Text" (below). There is linguistic evidence that the poem was modernized at least once before the two manuscripts were copied.

Plate 2. *The Four Leaves of the Truelove*, frontispiece woodcut to Wynkyn de Worde imprint, c. 1510 (Huth 102). (Reproduced by permission of the British Library, London.)

(Plate 2). The woman is offering a ring to the man, and a scroll over her head records her words: "Holde this a token yvvys [ywys]." The man responds: "For your sake I shall it take." This woodcut, which is borrowed from a series designed for Stephen Hawes's *The Pastime of Pleasure* (1509), represents the poem's subject in a most superficial way.[9] One wonders whether de Worde's customers would have bought the slim volume as a devotional text or as something by which to celebrate a wedding. Aside from a few printings of *Piers Plowman*, all of them later in date, the Wynkyn de Worde *Truelove* is the only known early print of a medieval alliterative poem (Turville-Petre [1978]; Blake).

Even though *The Four Leaves of the Truelove* had an audience as late as the sixteenth century, it has attracted a small readership in the time since, and even smaller praise. In surveying in 1812 the titles printed by de Word, Thomas Dibdin declared the *Truelove* "wretchedly dull" (Ames, p. 382). The first modern printing occurred in 1901 under a poorly chosen Latinate heading, *The Quatrefoil of Love*, which editor Israel Gollancz, who did not know the de Worde copy, called "a mere suggestion" (p. 112). In completing Gollancz's edition after his death, Magdalene M. Weale kept the title and advanced Dibdin's position, pronouncing the piece to be the work of a moralist "first and foremost" who in his zeal to preach neglected the potential of the fictive frame (pp. xx–xxii). In addition, she found the poem to be antiquated in its subject ("a sublimation of the sex instinct"), lacking in "beauty," and "not too skillfully carried out" (p. xxiii). Led by such unsympathetic and misleading assessments, modern readers have criticized features of the poem that were never intended to be read according to modern notions of proportion, subtlety, or romantic sensibility.[10] The *Truelove* has not deserved these aspersions, which derive from a misunderstanding of what made the poem effective in its own time, place, and culture.

As an alliterative meditation of intricate refinement and serious purpose, *The Four Leaves of the Truelove* has much to tell us about the devotional tastes and reading habits of people for whom literacy was a skill self-consciously cultivated to order to gain personal knowledge of God. Asking that the work be more than merely read, the poet expected his verbal artifact to be mentally embraced and spiritually imbibed as

---

[9]The woodcut is listed as No. 1009 in Edward Hodnett, *English Woodcuts 1480–1535*, second ed. (London: Oxford University Press, 1973), p. 278. It is reproduced from other de Worde printings in Stephen Hawes, *The Pastime of Pleasure*, ed. William Edward Mead, EETS o.s. 173 (1926; rpt. New York: Kraus, 1971), p. 77; and Stephen Hawes, *The Minor Poems*, ed. Florence W. Gluck and Alice B. Morgan (London: Oxford University Press, 1974), plate 14. Besides *The Pastime of Pleasure* (1509, 1517) and *Truelove*, de Worde used it for Hawes's *Comfort of Lovers* (1511), Chaucer's *Troilus and Criseyde* (1517), and *The Squire of Low Degree* (1520?).

[10]In particular, the sermon has been thought too prolix (Sandison, p. 87); too didactic in its neglect of the fictional bird and maiden (Anon., p. 18; Gollancz and Weale, p. xxi); and too blatantly artificial in its working-out of the four-part conceit (Pearsall, p. 186; Lawton [1989], p. 159).

an efficacious "pill" for personal salvation. The user's engagement was to be both contemplative and interactive, mastering the text not just for its content but also for its forms. He or she was to use it to meditate in visualized concepts, from remembered images in books of hours, from patterns and interweavings suggested by sacred emblems, and from the four leaves of the poem in his or her hands.

The restored English title is the poem's proper one, extracted from the sixth stanza and recorded by Wynkyn de Worde. This title unites, by means of the popular plant-name, the dual themes truth and love, and it contains the poet's favorite wordplay on *lufe* ("love") and *lefe* ("leaf" and "belief"). Shortened to *Truelove*, it focuses in on the poet's remarkable effort to make content cohere with a single form articulated in various ways. In this aim the poem may well remind readers of medieval verse of another stanzaic, alliterated poem, the enigmatic masterpiece *Pearl*. If we were to search through surviving Middle English lyrics for the work most likely to have been directly influenced by the shape-making art found in *Pearl*, *The Four Leaves of the Truelove* would certainly be among the leading contenders.

Note on the Edited Text

The poem is clearly older than its manuscripts, some pronunciations being obscured by modernized spellings (e.g., *sorow* instead of *sorwe*; *lady* instead of *lef(e)dy*). The plain style attributed to the *Truelove* (by, for example, Pearsall, p. 185) appears to be a by-product of corruption. While several lines and passages remain deficient in alliteration, careful comparison of the three texts provides ample evidence that the original poem was ornately alliterative and operated on a tighter line than has often survived.

In the long lines of *Truelove*, alliteration tends to be regularly applied in the following patterns: an a-verse possessing three lifts, two of them alliterating, with the lift just before the caesura usually being one of the two alliterating words in the a-verse; a b-verse possessing two lifts, which either alliterate with each other (the aa/bb type of line) or, more typically, alliterate with at least one of the lifts in the a-verse. There is a marked tendency on the part of the poet to integrate the third nonalliterating lift of the a-verse alliteratively into the b-verse. In some particularly expository passages (and especially in wheels), the poet seems to relax the alliteration — or else it has been scribally altered. But even at these places there usually exists an interplay of sound patterns (two or three consonants, with some degree of assonance).

Indeed, sound patterns that go beyond the normal alliterative patterns are an important part of the verbal texture. For example, there is often an alternation of two, sometimes three, initial consonantal or vocalic phonemes interwoven over a series of lines, which may operate only partially within the formal stress patterns. Internal rhymes are frequent. Moreover, the poet paid close attention to echoic medial and end sounds, and he alliterated occasionally upon sounds created by elision of two words, a type of soundplay ignored by scribes as they casually inverted words.

The Gollancz and Gollancz/Weale editions of *The Four Leaves of the Truelove* were both based on the London Thornton MS (T), with a selective listing of the variants from Bodl. Addit. MS A 106 (A) and no consideration of the Wynkyn de Worde print (W), which was unknown to those editors. In each instance the text from T was lightly emended with reference to A. Neither edition included an assessment of the relative merit of each manuscript. When the Gollancz/Weale edition appeared in 1935, reviewers unanimously criticized its textual apparatus. J. P. Oakden found the listing of variants from A to be insufficient for the specialist. He, along with Dorothy Everett, G. V. Smithers, and C. L. Wrenn, called for more editorial consideration of the variants, demonstrating that there were often better readings from A that the editors had omitted. In particular, Wrenn thought that the rhymes ought to have been emended, and he wished for a "more courageous critical text based on the two MSS jointly" (p. 375).

The text offered here expands the work of Gollancz and Gollancz/Weale by its extensive collation of both manuscripts as well as the third witness to the poem. All three copies hold valuable evidence for an editor endeavoring to recover the original text of *Truelove*. In terms simply of alliterative effect, neither A nor T offers a better text than the one that can be achieved by comparison of the variants. Moreover, even though W is more modern than the manuscripts, it often preserves evidence of the best reading. The exemplar of W was a third manuscript that possessed many readings superior in sense or meter to both A and T.

In critically editing *Truelove*, I have found many indications that the poem underwent at least one comprehensive revision between its composition and its copying into the documents that survive. There are numerous errors common to all three texts, a finding that means there was a shared version in the ancestry of the surviving copies, that is, a version at least one remove from the original poem. This shared ancestor represents a revisionary effort to make a demanding meter and older vocabulary more accessible to a new audience. The common errors include several identifiable losses of alliterative words (see, for example, the emendations at lines 40, 44, 213, 482, and 495).

A critical text of *Truelove* has to remain largely the composite product of its two late scribes and printer. Even so, I have restored the poem as far as sound scholarship and editorial practice will allow. Emendations adopted from T or W are spelled in accordance with the A scribe's normal practice. A's few instances of flawed rhyme-words have been emended; for most of these, the expected form is to be found in T or W. For many words, the northern spellings that represent the poet's dialect are easily confirmed by either rhyme or recurrent soundplay; for the most obvious of these, textual consistency has been sought, with cases of emended spelling noted. The comparative edition offered here, based on A but dependent too upon T and W, presents a poem more verbally artful than has been previously recognized. It is my hope that the *Truelove* poet's quietly ornate style can now be better perceived.

Select Bibliography

Manuscripts

Oxford, Bodleian Library Additional MS A 106, fols. 6b–14b. Yorkshire, c. 1425–50. [Base text. A composite MS consisting of six booklets; *Truelove* appears in the first booklet, accompanied by a treatise on the pestilence, a lapidary, an herbal, medical recipes, and three poems.]

London Thornton MS: London, British Library Additional MS 31042, fols. 98a–101b. Yorkshire, c. 1425–50. [One of two miscellanies compiled by Robert Thornton for private or domestic use; Thornton's books preserve several romances and alliterative poems.]

Early Print

London, British Library Huth 102. *The .iiii. Leues of the Trueloue.* Quarto. Printed by Wynkyn de Worde. Fleet Street, London, c. 1510. Listed in: A. W. Pollard and G. R. Redgrave. *Short Title Catalogue of Books Printed in England . . . 1475–1640.* Second ed. Rev. F. S. Ferguson, W. A. Jackson, and K. F. Panzer. Vol. 2. London: Bibliographical Society, 1976. No. 15345. [A slightly modernized version based on a third MS. Two copies survive: London, British Library Huth 102, and San Marino, Huntington Library HEH RB 31382.]

Facsimile

Thompson, John J. *Robert Thornton and the London Thornton Manuscript: British Library MS Additional 31042. Manuscript Studies* 2. Cambridge: D. S. Brewer, 1987. Plates 19b, 20a. [Fols. 98a, 101b.]

Editions

Gollancz, Israel, ed. *"The Quatrefoil of Love*: An Alliterative Religious Lyric." In *An English Miscellany, Presented to Dr. Furnivall*. Ed. N. R. Ker, A. S. Napier, and W. W. Skeat. 1901; rpt. New York: Benjamin Blom, 1969. Pp. 112–32. [London Thornton MS.]

Gollancz, Israel, and Magdalene M. Weale, eds. *The Quatrefoil of Love*. EETS o.s. 195. 1935; rpt. Millwood, N.Y.: Kraus, 1971. [London Thornton MS.]

Textual Commentaries

Everett, Dorothy. *"The Quatrefoil of Love* [review]." *Year's Work in English Studies* 15 (1935), 118–19.

Oakden, J. P. *"The Quatrefoil of Love* [review]." *Modern Language Review* 31 (1936), 209–10.

Smithers, G. V. *"The Quatrefoil of Love* [review]." *Medium Ævum* 6 (1937), 51–57.

Wrenn, C. L. *"The Quatrefoil of Love* [review]." *Review of English Studies* 13 (1937), 374–77.

Related Latin Work

Meditations on the Life of Christ (Meditationes vitae Christi). Trans. Isa Ragusa and Rosalie B. Green. Princeton: Princeton University Press, 1961. Pp. 54–56.

Related Middle English Works

Alliterative poems in thirteen-line stanzas:
> *The Awntyrs off Arthure*. Ed. Robert J. Gates. Philadelphia: University of Pennsylvania Press, 1969.
> *De tribus regibus mortuis*. Ed. Ella Keats Whiting. In *The Poems of John Audelay*. EETS o.s. 184. 1931; rpt. Millwood, N.Y.: Kraus, 1988. Pp. xxiv–xxvii, 217–23, 256–59.

The Dispute Between Mary and the Cross. Printed in this edition. [Forty stanzas; second birth at midpoint; appears in Vernon MS, pt. 3.]

The Pistel of Swete Susan. Ed. Russell A. Peck. In *Heroic Women from the Old Testament in Middle English Verse*. TEAMS Middle English Texts Series. Kalamazoo, Mich.: Medieval Institute Publications, 1991. Pp. 73–108. [Possesses stanza most similar to *Truelove* stanza; appears in Vernon MS, pt. 3.]

Summer Sunday. Ed. Rossell Hope Robbins. In *Historical Poems of the XIVth and XVth Centuries*. New York: Columbia University Press, 1959. Pp. 98–102, 301–03.

York Plays 36 and 45 ("The Death of Christ" and "The Assumption of the Virgin"). Ed. Richard Beadle. In *The York Plays*. London: Edward Arnold, 1982. Pp. 323– 33, 452; 392–99, 460–61.

The Bird with Four Feathers. Printed in this edition. [*Chanson d'aventure* with a bird sermon; structural use of number four.]

Ecce ancilla Domini. Ed. E. K. Chambers and F. Sidgwick. In *Early English Lyrics*. London: Sidgwick & Jackson, 1926. Pp. 112–14. [Annunciation poem in dialogue form; delivered word ties a "knot."]

In a Valley of This Restless Mind. Printed in this edition. [Search for a truelove leads to mystical contact with Christ's body.]

Love, Nicholas. *Mirror of the Blessed Life of Jesus Christ*. Ed. Michael G. Sargent. Garland Medieval Texts 18. New York: Garland, 1992.

Love That God Loveth. Ed. J. Kail. In *Twenty-Six Political and Other Poems*. EETS o.s. 124. London, 1904. Pp. 73–79. [The herb truelove, emblem of Christ's wounds, provides medicine for the soul.]

Lydgate, John. *Purification Marie*. (From *The Lyfe of Oure Lady*, Book VI, lines 1–301.) Ed. W. B. D. D. Turnbull. In *The Vision of Tundale*. Edinburgh: T. G. Stevenson, 1843. Pp. 127–37. [43 rime-royal stanzas on the Virgin's forty-day purification and her offering of a turtledove and a dove, with the birds' meanings explicated.]

Maiden Mary and Her Fleur-de-Lys. Ed. Carleton Brown. In *Religious Lyrics of the XIVth Century*. Second ed. Rev. G. V. Smithers. Oxford: Clarendon, 1957. Pp. 181–85, 280–81. [Vernon lyric with alliteration and botanical emblem.]

The Four Leaves of the Truelove

The Middle English Charters of Christ. Ed. Mary Caroline Spalding. Bryn Mawr College Monograph 15. Bryn Mawr: Bryn Mawr College, 1914. Pp. 63, 65. [An allegorized truelove is the "rent" to enter heaven; earliest version, *The Short Charter*, is Northern; see also *The Testament of Christ*.]

The Middle-English Harrowing of Hell and Gospel of Nicodemus. Ed. William Henry Hulme. EETS e.s. 100. London: Kegan Paul, Trench, Trübner, 1907.

Orison to the Trinity. Ed. Carleton Brown. In *Religious Lyrics of the XIVth Century.* Second ed. Rev. G.V. Smithers. Oxford: Clarendon, 1957. Pp. 121–24, 275. [Northern lyric prayer to Trinity and Mary in 13 stanzas; appears in Vernon MS.]

Pearl. Ed. E. V. Gordon. Oxford: Clarendon, 1953. [Central emblem has multiple, unfolding associations; structure is circular, numerological, framed, and a diptych; style is alliterative and stanzaic.]

Secular *chansons d'aventure* with a maiden's lament:
  De clerico et puella. Ed. G. L. Brook. In *The Harley Lyrics.* Fourth ed. Manchester: Manchester University Press, 1968. Pp. 62–63.
  I Met in a Morning a May in a Meadow. Ed. A. Brandl and O. Zippel. In *Middle English Literature.* New York: Chelsea, 1949. P. 128.
  The Meeting in the Wood. Ed. G. L. Brook. In *The Harley Lyrics.* Fourth ed. Manchester: Manchester University Press, 1968. Pp. 39–40.
  The Murning Maidin. Ed. G. Gregory Smith. In *Specimens of Middle Scots.* Edinburgh: William Blackwood and Sons, 1902. Pp. 64–69.
  Nou Sprinkes the Sprai. Ed. Carleton Brown. In *English Lyrics of the XIIIth Century.* Oxford: Clarendon, 1932. Pp. 119–20.

The Sweetness of Jesus. Ed. Carleton Brown. In *Religious Lyrics of the XIVth Century.* Second ed. Rev. G. V. Smithers. Oxford: Clarendon, 1957. Pp. 61–65, 262–63. [Northern love-song to Jesus, who asks nothing "Bot a trewluf for His travai."]

The Testament of Christ. Ed. F. J. Furnivall. In *The Minor Poems of the Vernon Manuscript.* Part 2. EETS o.s. 117. 1901; rpt. New York: Greenwood, 1969. Pp. 637–57. [Follows *The Pistel of Swete Susan* in Vernon MS; see also *The Middle English Charters of Christ*.]

Introduction

William of Nassington. *On the Trinity.* Ed. George G. Perry. In *Religious Pieces in Verse and Prose.* EETS o.s. 26. 1905; rpt. New York: Greenwood, 1969. Pp. 63–75. [Didactic poem on the Trinity, with an account of Christ's life and the Last Judgment.]

Criticism of *The Four Leaves of the Truelove*

Ames, Joseph. *Typological Antiquities of the History of Printing in England, Scotland, and Ireland.* Ed. Thomas F. Dibdin. Rev. William Herbert. Vol. 2. 1812; rpt. London: Bulmer, 1969. P. 382.

Anon. *"The Quatrefoil of Love* [review]." *Notes & Queries* 169 (1935), 18.

Bennett, J. A. W. *Middle English Literature.* Ed. Douglas Gray. Oxford: Clarendon, 1986. Pp. 49–50.

Blake, N. F. "Wynkyn de Worde and *The Quatrefoil of Love." Archiv für das Studium der Neuren Sprachen und Literaturen* 206 (1969), 189–200.

Davidoff, Judith M. *Beginning Well: Framing Fictions in Late Middle English Poetry.* Rutherford, N. J.: Fairleigh Dickinson University Press, 1988. Pp. 92, 190–92.

Fein, Susanna Greer. "Why Did Absolon Put a 'Trewlove' under His Tongue? Herb Paris as a Healing 'Grace' in Middle English Literature." *Chaucer Review* 25 (1991), 302–17.

——. "Form and Continuity in the Alliterative Tradition: Cruciform Design and Double Birth in Two Stanzaic Poems." *Modern Language Quarterly* 53 (1992), 100–25.
Lawton, David. "The Diversity of Middle English Alliterative Poetry." *Leeds Studies in English* 20 (1989), 159–62.

Pearsall, Derek. *Old English and Middle English Poetry.* London: Routledge & Kegan Paul, 1977. Pp. 185–86, 299.

Phillips, Helen. *"The Quatrefoil of Love."* In *Langland, the Mystics, and the Medieval English Religious Tradition: Essays in Honour of S. S. Hussey.* Ed. Helen Phillips. Woodbridge, Suffolk: Boydell and Brewer, 1990. Pp. 243–58.

Raymo, Robert R. "Works of Religious and Philosophical Instruction." In *A Manual of the Writings in Middle English, 1050–1500*. Ed. Albert E. Hartung. Vol. 7. New Haven: Connecticut Academy of Arts and Sciences, 1986. Pp. 2334, 2541–42.

Sandison, Helen E. *The "Chanson d'Aventure" in Middle English*. Bryn Mawr College Monographs 12. Bryn Mawr: Bryn Mawr College, 1913. Pp. 83, 86–87.

Related Studies

Barratt, Alexandra. "The Prymer and Its Influence on Fifteenth-Century Passion Lyrics." *Medium Ævum* 44 (1975), 264–79.

Duggan, Hoyt N. "The Shape of the B-Verse in Middle English Alliterative Tradition." *Speculum* 61 (1986), 564–92.

Friedman, John Block. *Northern English Books, Owners, and Makers in the Late Middle Ages*. Syracuse: Syracuse University Press, 1995. Pp. 67–72.

Harwood, Britton J. "*Pearl* as Diptych." In *Text and Matter: New Critical Perspectives on the Pearl-Poet*. Ed. Robert J. Blanch, Miriam Youngerman Miller, and Julian N. Wasserman. New York: Whitson, 1991. Pp. 61–78.

Keiser, George. "The Progress of Purgatory: Visions of the Afterlife in Later Middle English Literature." In *Zeit, Tod und Ewigkeit in der renaissance Literatur*. Ed. James Hogg. Salzburg: Institut für Anglistik und Amerikanistik, Universität Salzburg, 1987. Pp. 111–59.

Lawton, David, ed. *Middle English Alliterative Poetry and Its Literary Background: Seven Essays*. Cambridge: D. S. Brewer, 1982.

Phillips, Helen. "The Ghost's Baptism in *The Awntyrs off Arthure*." *Medium Ævum* 58 (1989), 49–58. [*Truelove* cited, p. 55.]

Reichl, Karl. "Popular Poetry and Courtly Lyric: The Middle English Pastourelle." *REAL: The Yearbook in Research in English and American Literature* 5 (1987), 33–61.

Sichert, Margit. *Die mittelenglische Pastourelle*. Tubingen: Max Niemeyer, 1991.

Turville-Petre, Thorlac. "'Summer Sunday,' 'De Tribus Regibus Mortuis,' and 'The Awntyrs off Arthure': Three Poems in the Thirteen-Line Stanza." *Review of English Studies*, n.s. 25 (1974), 3–15.

―――. *The Alliterative Revival.* Cambridge: D. S. Brewer, Rowman & Littlefield, 1977. Pp. 35, 44, 62–63.

Wenzel, Siegfried. *Verses in Sermons: "Fasciculus Morum" and Its Middle English Poems.* Cambridge, Mass.: Mediaeval Academy of America, 1978. Pp. 159–60.

Wieck, Roger S. *The Book of Hours in Medieval Art and Life.* With essays by Lawrence R. Poos, Virginia Reinberg, and John Plummer. London: Sotheby's Publications, 1988.

Williams, D. J. "Alliterative Poetry in the Fourteenth and Fifteenth Centuries." In *The Middle Ages.* Ed. W. F. Bolton. London: Barrie & Jenkins, 1970. Pp. 116, 128.

The Four Leaves of the Truelove

1

In a mornynge of May when medose suld sprynge		*meadows do sprout*
Blomes and blossomes of bryght colours,		*Blooms*
Als I went by a well apon my playnge,		*to amuse myself*
Thurght a mery orchard, byddyng myn owres, [1]		
5	The birdes on the boghes began for to syng,	*boughs*
	And bowes to burjun and belde to the boures;	*burgeon; flourish into leafy bowers*
	Was I war of a may that made mournyng,	*I was aware of a maiden*
	Syghand and sekand emange the fayre floures	*Sighing and searching*
	So swyte.	*sweetly*
10	Scho made mournyng enogh;	
	Hyre wypyng dyd me wogh!	*Her weeping saddened me*
	To a derne I me drogh;	*private place; drew*
	Hir wyll wald I wyte.	*I wanted to learn of her longing*

2

	Stilly I stalked and stode in that stede,	*Quietly; place*
15	For I wald wyte of hir wyll and of hir wyld thoght:	*know; disordered*
	Scho kest of hir kerchyfes, hir kell of hir hede; [2]	
	Wrange scho hir handes and wrothly scho wroght!	*sorrowfully*
	Scho sayd: "Myld Mary, right thou me red —	*advise me correctly*
	Of al the well of this warld, iwys I wald noghte! [3]	
20	Send me som solace, or son be I ded,	*soon; dead*
	Som syght of that selcouthe that I hafe lang soghte	*marvel; long*
	With care."	
	Than spake a turtyll on a tre,	*turtledove*
	Wyth fayre nottes and fre:	*notes; noble*

---

[1] *Through a pleasant garden, saying my hours (i.e., prayers recited at the same time each day)*

[2] *She cast off her kerchief, her netted headdress from her head*

[3] *Of all the fortune in this world, indeed I enjoy none!*

25   "Bryght byrd for thi bewte,   *girl; beauty*
        Whi sythes thou so sare?"   *sigh; grievously*

3

     "Thow fayr foule, fayle noghte thi speche nor thi spell!
     Thy carpyng is comforth to herkyn and here;[1]
     All my wyll and my wytt wald I the tell,   *longing; thought; you*
30   My wa and my wanderyng, wald thou com nere."   *distress; if you would*
     Lufly he lyghted, wald he noghte dwell   *Lovingly he perched; hesitate*
     To comforth that comly and cover hir chere.   *lovely [girl]; restore her happiness*
     Scho blyssed his body with buke and with bell,   *completely*
     And lufed owr Lady had send hir that fere   *who had given; companion*
35   So free: *generously*
     "When that I was sary,   *When I was sorrowful*
     Besoght I owr Lady;
     Scho has sent me company;
     Blyssed mot scho bee!   *may*

4

40   "Fayr foule full of lufe, so myld and so mete,   *bird; proper*
     To move of a mater now may I begyn: *To broach a subject*
     A trewluf hafe I soght be way and be strete   *everywhere*
     In many fayre orchardes thar floures ar in;   *in which are flowers*
     So fayr as I hafe soght, fand I nane fete;   *far; found; fitting*
45   Fele hafe I fonden of mare and of myn.   *Many; more; less*
     Bryght bird of thi ble, my bale may thou bete,   *countenance; sorrow; relieve*
     Wald thou me wysse wysely a trewluf to wyn   *advise wisely*
        With ryght.   *In the right way*
     When I wen rathest   *think most certainly*
50   For to fynd lufe beste,   *[That I shall] find love*
     So fayntely it is feste,   *feebly; fastened*
     It fares al of flighte!"   *goes flying away*

---

[1] *Fair bird, fail not [in] your words and instruction! / Your speech is [a] comfort to hearken and hear*

The Four Leaves of the Truelove

5

    "The wytt of a woman is wonder to here!   *hear*
    Is al thi sary syghinge to seke a lufe trew?   *painful*
55   Al this syd may thou seke and never nan be nere   *lifetime*
    Bot if thou had counsell of an that I knewe.   *Unless; one*
    If thou be sett to seke it, sall I the lere   *determined. teach you*
    Whare it is spryngand and evermare newe,   *growing; fresh*
    Withowt any fadynge, full fayr and full clere,
60   Or castyng of colour, or chanuyng of hewe,   *graying*
          So yare.   *So hardily [growing]*
       Hardely dare I say   *Assuredly*
       Thare is no luf that lastes ay   *forever*
       Withowtyn treson and tray   *deceit*
65   Bot it begyn thare.   *Unless*

6

    "Whar thou fyndes grewand a trewlufe grysse   *growing; grass*
    With four lefes is it sett ful lufly abowte.   *beautifully about [a center]*
    The fyrst lef may we lykyn to the Kyng of Blys   *leaf; liken*
    That weldes this wyld world within and withowte.[1]
70   He wroght heven with His hand and al paradyse   *made*
    And this mery medyllerth withowtyn any dowt.   *middle-earth; doubt*
    All the welth of this world hally is Hys,   *wholly*
    In wham us aw for to lefe, lufe Hym, and lowte   *ought to believe; bow down*
          Ful well.
75   Hald this lefe in thi mynd   *leaf (pun: belief)*
       To we may His felawes fynd —   *Until; fellows*
       That trew luf and that kynd   *gracious [love]*
       That never sall kelle.   *diminish*

7

    "The second lefe of the lufe I lykyn to God Son,
80   That to the fyrst lefe is felawe and fere;   *companion*
    The third to the Holy Gost, togeder thay won,   *dwell*
    All halesom in a Godhede and Persons sere!   *sound; separate*
    Welder of water, of son, and of mon,   *Ruler; sun; moon*

---

[1] *Who rules this natural world both within and without (i.e., spiritually and physically)*

Thase thre lefes ar of price withowtyn any pere,   *value; peer*
85 When that semly Syre is sett in Hys tron,   *stately; throne*
Comly of colour and curtas of chere   *appearance; courteous; face*
    For grace.
    Al this world He began
    With wyndes and waters wan,   *dark-hued*
90   And syne made He man   *afterward*
    Efter Hys awn face.   *In His own likeness*

8

"Fyrst made He Adam and syn mad He Eve;   *then made*
Putt tham in paradyse in gret degré;   *in high estate*
Forbed He tham nothyng, hym and hys wyfe,   *He forbade them nothing*
95 Bott a gren apyll that grewed on a tree.   *Except; grew*
Than sary Sathanas soght tham belyfe   *vile; quickly*
For to waken owr wa. Weryd mygh he be!   *woe; Accursed*
Toke thai that apill to stire mekyll stryfe;   *stir much strife*
The foule fend was fayn that syght for to se   *pleased*
100   For tene.   *spite*
    The first lefe was full wa   *very woeful*
    When Hys flours fell hym fra;   *flowers; from him*
    Hys frendes suld tyll hell ga   *had to enter hell*
    For an appill gren.   *Because of*

9

105 "Than began the fyrst lefe to morn for us all   *mourn*
For his lufly handwarke that was forlorn.   *lost*
Gabriell, that aungell, on hym gon He call;   *did*
Frurth com that comly and kneled Hym beforn: *Forward; fair [angel]*
'Unto mayden Mary my message thou sall;   *you shall [take]*
110 Bere hir blythe bodword: Of hire be I born.'   *a glad message*
Thus He sent Hys der son owt of Hys hye hall   *[Gabriel] (see note)*
Unto that myld mayden on a mery morn,   *pleasant morning*
    Hir grette.   *In order to greet her*
    Gabriell, that fayre face,   *fair creature*
115   Sayd, 'Mary, full of grace,
    Pereles in ilka place,   *Peerless; every*
    With myrth ert thou mette.   *joined [with God]*

10

'Thow sall consave a knaw-child comly and clere;   *conceive; boy-child*
All the was of this world in the sall be bett.'   *woes; in you shall be remedied*
120 'That ware a mekyll mervayle I mot a cheld bere;   *great miracle; might*
Was I never mayryed, ne with man mett.'   *married*
'Behald to thi cosyn: consaved has toyere   *cousin; this year*
Elyezabeth in hir held, that lang has ben lett.'   *old age; barren*
'Lord, Thi handmayden,' says Mary, 'is here.
125 Full haly in Thi service is my harte sette   *wholly*
         So still.'   *meekly*
     Blessyd be that swete wyght,   *creature*
     That God Son in lyght,   *In whom God's Son alighted*
     Becom a man full of myghte   *Became*
130 With Hys Fader wyll.   *By*

11

"Now is this ilk second lef, for owr luf maste,   *same; love above all*
Lyght in that Lady that Gabriell grette;   *Alighted in*
Withowt any treson, so trew for to traste,   *trust*
With myrth in a mayden is God and man mette.
135 Thys is the Fader and the Son and the Holy Gaste —
Thre lefes of lufe withowtyn any lette;   *break [in the design]*
The fourte is a mayden chosen for chaste.   *chastity*
Swylke another trewluf was never in land sett   *rooted in ground*
         For bute.   *remedy*
140   Thare foure lefes may never fall,   *These*
     Bot evermare thai springe sall,   *sprout*
     So gently thai joyn all
     On a ryche rute.   *strong root*

12

"Now has thre lufly lefes a fourte fela tan —   *fellow taken*
145 For luf in owre Lady is owre Lord lyght.
Joseph hir wedyd and with hir gon gane;   *did go*
In the borgh of Bethleem beldyd that bryght;   *town; dwelt; beauty*
Betwyx an oxe and an asse, pride was thar nan:
A blyssed barne was thar born apon a Yolenyghte.   *child*
150 Thare rase a starn schaply schewed and schan;   *rose a star; shone*
Thre kynges of Colan tharof caght a syght   *Cologne; caught*

And soght.   *sought [it]*
Thai offerd Him, as thai wold,   *wished*
Myr, rekyls, and gold;   *Myrrh; incense*
155 He thanked tham seven-fold;
To blysse He tham broght.

13

"Unhappy Herode thase tythandes hard tell: *Ill-fated; heard*
A knaw-child was born, that kynge suld bee. *boy-child; should*
Gart he make messages, and sent he full snell[1]
160 To slee all knafe-chylder in that contré.
Left he nan in wharte, bot all gon he whell; *alive; he did kill*
Thai sputt tham on spere-poyntes — gret pyté to se! *impaled*
Joseph, with his wedyd wyfe, wald he noght dwell, *tarry*
Bot led hir into Egype with hir lefes thre *(i.e., the Trinity in her womb)*
165 To safe.   *save*
Childer gon thar ded take,   *did receive their death*
For this same trewluf sake;
The mare myrth may thai make —   *more gladness*
Hymself wald tham hafe.   *God Himself would receive them*

14

170 "Yitte wald He do mare for His frendes dere,
His awn haly handwarke, to hell wald He gan.
To sette us ensample, His lawe for to lere, *provide; example; learn*
Saynte John Hym baptyste in flume Jordane. *baptized; river*
For thirty penys was He sald thurght a fals fere *sold; false friend*
175 Unto fell famen wald fayne Hym hafe slane.[2]
All He sufferd for owr sake — Hymself was clere. *All [this]; innocent*
Thurght a kysse thai Hym knew and tytte was He tan *quickly; seized*
  Alswa.   *In this manner*
It was gret sorow for to see
180 When He suld blynke of His ble, *grow pale in complexion*
The second lefe of the thre;
The fourte was wa.   *fourth was [full of] woe*

---

[1] *He ordered messages to be made, and he sent [them] immediately*

[2] *To [His] wicked enemies [who] wanted to see Him slain*

The Four Leaves of the Truelove

15

"Pylate was justes and spake apon hye,   *judge*
For to dem Jhesu that Judas had sald: *sentence*
185 'Leve, lordynges, the trewth for to trie;   *Refrain; from putting on trial*
That semely is sakeles, say what ye wald.'   *fair one is innocent*
The Jeuys apon Jhesu began for to cry: *Jews*
'He cald Hymself a kyng. Swylk bourdes be bald! *Such jests are bold*
If thou wyll not dem Hym today for to dye,   *condemn*
190 Ryght before Emperowre this tale sall be tald *Directly; accusation*
     For dred.'   *Because of [our] fear*
   A drery dom gafe he thare: *dire judgment gave*
   'Sais! I can say na mare;   *Cease; nothing else*
   I red ye take Hym yare   *command; without delay*
195 And forth ye Hym led.'

16

"Allas! for that fourte lefe was leved allane,   *left*
When hir fayr felischipe was taken and torn,   *fellowship*
Betyn with scharpe scourges body and bane,   *Beaten; bone*
Syne spred on a Crosse, crowned with a thorn;   *Afterward*
200 Thurght Hys handes and fett hard nales go gan; *feet hard nails did go*
A bryght spere to Hys hart brathely was born.   *violently; thrust*
He bled His blod for our luf; lyfe leved Hym nan. *[but] life never left Him*
Attire and aysell thai served Hym in scorn   *Gall; vinegar*
     With gall.   *Maliciously*
205   Grett grefe was to se   *Very grievous [it]*
   When He was naled on the tre;
   The second lef of the thre
   Suld falow and falle.   *wither*

17

"The fourte lefe of the lufe alanly scho stode;   *alone*
210 Wrange scho hir handes and wepyd for wa,   *Wrung*
With a mournande chere and a myld mode.   *compassionate sorrow*
The Son blenked of His ble and wex al bla; *paled in visage; lead-colored*
Be Hys blank sydes ran the red blode.   *Along; white*
The hard roche gon ryfe the temple in twa.   *rock; split*
215 Than swouned the fourte lefe and to the grond yode. *swooned; fell*
Allas for that trewlufe, that it suld twyn swa   *break apart*

So yare.   *completely*
Scho saw hir der Son dye,
Bot Sante John stode hir by
220 And comforthed that Lady,
Was casten in care.   *sorrow*

18

"Yitt cuth that noble Kyng, was naled on a tre, *quoth; [who]*
Unto His myld Moder, was mournande that tyde: *[who]; hour*
'Leve thi wepynge, woman, and mourne noghte for me;
225 Take John to thi son, that standes be thi syde.
John, take Mary to thi moder, for to myrth the, *comfort you*
To kepe and to comforth, your blys to abyde.' *await*
The hate blod of His hert dyd Longeus to see, *hot; caused; Longinus*
That soght be a spere-schafte His woundes wyd *examined*
230 That day.
Itt was gret sorow for to see
When He was taken of the tre; *from*
The second lef of the thre
  Was closed in clay. *entombed*

19

235 "When He was ded on the Rod and delved so yare, *buried so thoroughly*
All the welth of this world in thre lefes lay.
The fourte for wa falowed and syghed full sare; *withered*
Al the treuth of this world was in a trew may. *maiden*
If His manhed war marde, His myghte was the mare: *humanness; greater*
240 Upon His haly handwarke His hart was ay. *was [set] always*
The saule with the godhed to hell gon it fare; *godhead; did it go*
The body and the manhed abade the third day *awaited*
  Ful yare. *eagerly*
That He had with His hand wroght, *Those whom; made*
245 And syne with His blod boght, *then*
Till thai war owt of bale broght, *torment*
  Hym langed full sare. *He pined deeply*

20

"Than sayd sary Sathanas, his sorow was sad, *vile; profound*
For syght of that selcouthe he wox unfayn: *wonder; grew displeased*

187

250 'Us bowes som bodword — I trow it be bad!   [To] Us comes some message
What art thou, fayr face?' fast gon Hym frayn.   quickly did ask of Him
'Kyng of Joy is my name, thi gystes to glad!   guests to make glad
Lat me in for thar lufe — thar thou noghte layn!'   you need not hide
'Wend thi way with thi myrth! Thou makes us al mad!   Go away
255 What suld thou do in this pytt? Thou sees her bot payn   here only
    So fast.'   binding
    When thai hard the Kyng spek,   heard
    Al the gattes gon thai steke,   did they bolt [with bars]
    Bot son gon the barres breke   bars broke
260   And al the bandes brast.   hinges burst

21

"For Hys haly handwark heryed He hell,   harrowed
Al broghte He out of bale that ever had ben His.   delivered all
Tharof David, His derlyng, mad myrth imell;   rejoiced in the midst
He toke a harp in hys hand and well hedyd iwys;   heeded [Christ's presence]
265 And al Hys retenew, owt gon He tell,   He did separate out
And of His gret mercy forgafe tham thar mys.   sins
'I was sald for your sake and sufferd wondes snell,   wounds painful
And al My bon chylder ar boght unto blys   good children
    On Rod.'   By means of the Cross
270   The soth is noghte for to layn: truth; hide
    When thai war broght out of payn,
    Unto the blyssed body agayn
    The holy gost yode.   (i.e., Christ's soul) entered

22

"The fourte lef of that lufe falow is for wa   withered; from grief
275 When scho was lefed moder, mayden, and wyf.   left alone [as]
The fyrst lef full wyghte, His will was swa,   very strong
Be assent of the third lef, was thar no stryfe.
Raysed Thai the second lef betwen Tham twa,
Thurght grace of the godhed, fro ded unto lyf.
280 He toke a crose in His hand and furth gon He ga;   He = Christ
With His flech and His fell and His wondes fyfe,   skin (i.e., his whole body)
    He yode.   returned
    When He was resyn agayn,
    He mett Mary Mawdelayn;

285   No ferly yf scho war fayn!   *No wonder she was joyful*
            He was hir lech gode.   *physician*

23

            "Furth went the Mawdelayn with myrth and with mod.   *vigor (devotion)*
            Scho tald this tithandes to Thomas of Ynde,   *tidings*
            How Crist is resyn all hale, that bled His hart blod: *whole*
290   'Trew now this, Thomas; thou sal it soth fynd!'   *Believe; true*
            Than spake Thomas, in sted thar he stod: *in the place where*
            'Women ar carpand. It comes thaim of kynd.'   *prone to chatter; naturally*
            Wald he never trew it or Criste Hymselfe yode,   *believe it before; came*
            Apperyd to the Apostels, as clarkes has in mynd,   *writers have recorded*
295   In hye.   *haste*
               He pute his hand in Hys syd;
               And al He blyssed in that tyde   *time*
               That trewyd in His wondes wyd
               And saw tham never with eye.

24

300   "Furth went that Semely, the soth for to say;   *Fair One*
            He soght His dyssyples, taght thaim the treuth trew,   *disciples*
            And syne to that Lady that He lufed ay,   *always*
            Al hall of His hurte in hyd and in hew.   *whole; skin and complexion*
            Scho was stable and stell and faled never fay.   *steadfast; meek; faith*
305   Thase foure lefes of lufe springes all new!
            Oure Lord stegh intil heven on Halow Thursday;   *ascended*
            Syn folowyd His Moder with gamen and glew   *delight and rejoicing*
               Ful even.   *Straightaway*
               Befor hir Son scho kneled down,
310   With full gode devocoun;
               Apon hir hed He sett a crown
               And mad hir Quen of Heven.

25

            "The fourte lef of that lufe, blyssed mot scho be!   *blessed may*
            Scho may hafe joy in hir hart of hir gentil Chyld.
315   Apon His Fader ryght hand, hir Son may scho see,
            And the hend Holy Gost unto tham both bylde.   *gracious; dwells*
            Now ar thay same in a God and Persons Thre,   *together*

And scho is Madyn of myght and Moder full myld.	*miraculous power*
Swylk another Trewfull grew never on tree!	*Such (see note)*
320 Whoso lufys that Lufe sall never be begyld	*deceived*
So hend.	*noble (modifies Love)*
Bot well is that ilka wyght	*fortunate; same creature*
That may be sykere of that syght;	*assured*
Whar ever is day and never nyght,	*always*
325 And joy withowtyn end!	

26

"Thus hase this fayr Trewfull mad us al fre;	
Owre bodyes owt of bondage He boghte on the Rode.	*Our; Cross*
He commandes us for to kepe (and gyftys us posté)	*gives us the ability*
Owr saules owt of syn, for owr awn gode.	
330 Mekyll sorow wald we hafe myght we owre saules se	*Much; our [own] souls see*
When thay ar sonkyn in syn, as farcost in flode.	*ship in the sea*
Than byde we in bondage, in bale for to be,	*remain; torment*
That He has boghte haly with His hert blod	*Whom; wholly*
To blys.	*For [heaven's] bliss*
335 Aske mercy whyls we may;	
Byd owr Lady for us pray,	
Or we be closyd in clay;	*Before; buried*
Of myrth may we mys.	*[Or else] We may miss [heaven's] mirth*

27

"Blyssyd be that Trewluf so meke and so myld,	
340 Syker and stedfast and stabyll in faye.	*Unfailing; faith*
When we hafe wrethed thre with owr warkes wild,[1]	
The fourte is gracyos and gode for to helpe ay.	
Than kneles that Lady down befor hir dere Chyld,	
And sare wepes for owr sayke with hir eyn gray.	*sake; eyes*
345 Scho is ever grett of grace (els whar we begyld),	*or else we would be beguiled*
For scho wynnes with hir wepyng many fayre pray	*prey*
To kepe.	*save*
Sen scho is well of owr wele,	*Since; source of our prosperity*

---

[1] *When we have angered [these] three with our wayward deeds*

	And al owr cares wyll scho kele,	*assuage*
350	Allas, why gare we hir knele	*do we cause her to kneel*
	And for owre warkes wepe?	*weep for our deeds*

28

	"Nis no wyght in this werld so dern nor so dere,	*trusted; beloved*
	No kyng ne no caysor, yf thai ber crown,	*ruler; bear*
	Ne nan so fayr lady of colour so clere,	
355	Bot comes dredfull Dede and drawes tham down.	*Death*
	Us lyst never lefe it for preste ne for freere,	
	Or we fele that we fall, with swelt and with swown.[1]	
	Bot when owr bare body is broght on a bere,	*bier*
	Than fayles al felychepe in feld and in town	*fellowship everywhere*
360	Bot fone.	*few*
	In a cloth ar we knytte,	*wrapped*
	And syen putte in a pytt;	*then; grave*
	Of al this warld ar we whytt;	*deprived*
	Forgyttyn ar we son.	*Forgotten; soon*

29

365	"For that catyfe cors is full lytyll care,	
	Ware we sykere of owr saules ware we suld dwell;[2]	
	Bot now no wyght in this warld so wys is of lare,	*knowledge*
	Ne no clarke in his conyng tharof can tell,	*wisdom; foretell*
	How fell ne how fayr us falles for to fare;[3]	
370	Bot hard way is to heven and haste to hell.	*hasty*
	In purgatory is payn, whoso passes thare.	*whoever*
	Of mekyll wa may thai wytt, that tharin sal dwell	*much woe; learn, who*
	Full lang.	
	That we do ar we fare,	*What we do before we go*

---

[1] *We prefer not to believe it (that we will die) despite [warnings of] priest or friar, / Before we feel ourselves fall, with illness and swooning*

[2] *But about that wretched body we would worry very little / If we were sure, concerning our souls, where we shall dwell*

[3] *How cruelly nor how favorably (with pun: How much nor how far) it is allotted us to travel [after death]*

375	Befor us fynd we thare;
	We may be syker of no mare
	When paynes are so strang.

Awaiting us we shall find there
certain

30

	"When gret fyres grym ar graythed in owr gate,
	Thar is no glasyng by, bot in bus us glyd;
380	When we ar putt in that payn, so hard and so hate;
	We seke efter socoure on everilka syd;
	We cry efter kynred; thai com al to late!
	When we hafe frayst of that fare, feld is owre prid.[1]
	Than of al owre sorow, no certan we wate,
385	Bot trest in a Trewlufe, His mercy to abyd[2]
	With dred.
	Bot now ware tym to begyn
	That Trewlufe for to wyn,
	That al owr bales may blyn
390	When we hafe most ned.

prepared in our path
slipping past; in must we glide
hot
succour; every side
kindred

it is time

Who; woes; cease

31

	"Of al the days we hafe to dred, yitt aw us to knaw,
	When we umbethynk us of ane, full sare may we gryse![3]
	When that brym Lord above His bemes sall blaw,
	And the Hy Justyse sall sytt in His gret syse,
395	And al the folke of this warld sall rys on a raw,
	Than the whike may whake when the whelled upryse![4]
	We may schrynk for no scham owre synnes fore to schaw;
	Thar may no gold ne no fee make owre maynpryse,
	Ne kyn.
400	Than is al owre prid gane,
	Owre robes and owre rych pane,

yet ought we

stern; trumpets
i.e., Christ; court (assize)
arise; row

not hold back
bail (see note)

fur-trimmed cloak

---

[1] *When we have experienced that event, our pride is overcome*

[2] *Then concerning all our sorrow, we may count on nothing certain, / Except trust in a Truelove, hoping for His mercy*

[3] *Whenever we call to mind one (i.e., Doomsday), very fearfully we may tremble!*

[4] *Then the living may quake when the dead (lit., quelled ones) arise*

Al bot owre crysom alane,   *christening robe*
    That we ware cristened in.

32

"When we ar cald to that courte, behoves us to here;   *we must respond*
405 Al sall be thar seyn, both bondmen and free;   *seen*
The saule and the body, that lang has ben sere,   *separate*
Tham behoves to be sam at that sembelee;   *together; assembly*
And ilke saule sall be sent to fett his awn fere,   *each; fetch; body*
Then Criste wyll us geder — a gret Lord is He! —   *gather*
410 With owre flesch and owr fell, als we in warld were,   *skin*
And never sal sonder efter that day be   *separate*
    To knaw.   *Known*
    Our warkes ar wretyn and scord   *recorded*
    In a rowle of record   *roll*
415   Befor that ilke gret Lord,
    Full schaply to schaw.   *duly*

33

"We sall seke theder in symple atyre,   *thither; attire*
Tremland and schakand, as lefe on a tree;   *Trembling and quaking*
When al the warld is umbsett with water and fire,   *surrounded*
420 Thar may no wrynke ne no wyll wis us to fle;   *trick nor wile enable*
When Criste is greved so sare, He is a grym Syre!   *aggrieved; fierce*
So many synfull saulles as He thar sall see,
Dare noghte His Moder, yf scho myght desyre,   *even though she*
Speke to hir dere Son — so dredfull is He
425   That day!
    Al the halowes of heven   *saints*
    Sall be still of thar steven;   *cease speaking*
    Dare thay noghte a word neven,   *say*
     For no man to pray.

34

430 "The warkes of mercy He rakynys all seven: *reckons*
'When I was hungré, how hafe ye me fed?
When I was thrysty, ye hard noght my steven?   *thirsty; heard; petition*
When I was naked, how hafe ye me cled?   *clad*
Or when I was houseles, herberd me even?   *sheltered; properly*

193

435   Or vysett in seknes, or soght to my bed?   *visit; came*
        Or comforth in preson? That wald I here neven.   *comfort [me]; spoken*
        Or broghte me to beryall when Ded me by-sted?' *burial; Death; overcame*
            Thai say:
            'Lord, whare say we The   *saw*
440   Ever in swylke a degré?'   *such a condition*
            'The leste, in the name of me   *least*
            That to yow myght pray.'

35

        "He wil schew us His woundes blody and bare,   *exposed*
        As He has sufferd for owre sake, wytter and wyd. *manifest and large*
445   Kynges and kasors before Hym bus fare;   *must go*
        Byschoppes and barons and all bus abyd;   *must await [judgment]*
        Erles and emperours, nane wyll He spare;
        Prestes ne prelates nor persons of pride;   *parsons*
        Thar justes and juellars of lawe or of lare,[1]
450   That now ar full ryall to ryn and to ryd   *dignified; run*
            In land.
            Thar dome sall thai take thare,   *judgment*
            Ryght as thai demed are,   *Just as; judged*
            When thay ware of myghtes mare,   *held jurisdiction*
455   And domes had in hand.

36

        "Rych ladyes ar arayed in robes full yare —   *elaborate*
        Reveres and rybanes on gownes and gyd,   *Lapels; ribbons; mantle*
        Bendes and botonys, fylettes and fare,   *Sashes; fillets. trappings*
        Gold on thar garlandes, perry and pride,   *coronets; jewels; finery*
460   Kelles and kerchyffes cowched on thar hare — *Headdresses· arranged*
        So schaply and schynand, to schew by thar syd.
        Al that welth is away; myrth mekyll mare![2]
        Bot if we wyn that Trewlufe, unglad may we glyd *Unless; glide [into hell]*
            For sorow.

---

[1] *These justices and jewellers (i.e., appraisors) of law and of learning*

[2] *So elegant and attractive, as displayed on their sides. / All that wealth disappears· heavenly mirth [is] much more!*

465 Betym is best to begyn;   *Right now; best [time]*

     If we be fon full of syn,   *found*

     Thare no kyth ne no kyn   *friends*

       Fra bale may us borow.   *rescue*

37

     "Be lordes and be ladyes noghte anely say I,

470 Bot alswa be other I fynde full fele:

     Thar galiard gedlynges kythes gentrye,

     With dengyouse damesels, thar may men dele,

     With purfels and pelours and hedes full hye —

     Hir cors is in mydward of hir catele.[1]

475 If men carpe of hir kyn, away wil scho wry;   *talk about; turn*

     Hir fader and hir moder fayn wald scho hele   *eagerly; conceal*

       And hyde.

       Bot when that day sall begyn,

       Sall no man scham with his kyn,   *be ashamed of*

480   Bot al sall scham with thare syn,

       And with thar saule pride.   *soul's*

38

     "The dom of that Trewlufe full dere may we dred; *grievously*

     For than is al the tym past of mercy to crafe.   *crave*

     When ilka ane sall be demed efter his awn ded,

485 Than may not owreself stert and send furth oure knafe.[2]

     He rekyns be resoun, als clarkes can red,   *justly; relate*

     And settes on His ryght hand the saules He wil safe.

     Thase wafull wreches that wil noghte sped,   *prosper*

     Thar sang is of sorow and swa sall thai hafe   *song; such*

490   For ay!   *Forever*

       Than wil oure Lady wepe sare,

       For sorow scho sal se thare,

---

[1] *My remarks do not refer solely to lords and ladies / But also to other [folk] that I find in great number: / These gaily dressed low-born fellows display [fashions of the] nobility / With haughty ladies, with whom men may meddle, / With embroidered borders and fur trims and very high headdresses — / Her body is in the middle of her property*

[2] *When each one shall be judged according to his own deed (pun: after his death), / Then may we not remove ourselves and send forth our servant*

When scho may helpe no mare.
Gret dole sal be that day!

39

495	"Bot now is space for to speke, whoso wil sped,	*be fortunate*
	And for to seke socours, and folys to flee,	*assistance; sinfulness*
	And noghte apon Domesday, when we hafe most ned;	*not*
	For now is mekyll mercy, and than sall nane be.	
	When oure dere Lady dare noghte, for dred,	
500	Speke to hir der Son, so dredfull is He,	
	How may we axe mercy fore our mysded	
	That wyll noghte folow tharto when it is fre	
	And yare?	*available*
	Thare is no way bot twa:	*only two ways*
505	Unto wele or to wa;	
	Wheder-swa sall we ga,	*Whichever way*
	We dwell fore evermare."	

40

	Thus this trew turtyll teches hys may.	*turtledove; maiden*
	Scho blyssed his body, his bane, and his blod.	*bones*
510	Unto this ilk fourte lefe red I we pray,	*I advise that*
	That scho may do oure message with a myld mode,[1]	
	And speke fore oure lufe before the last day	*for the sake of*
	Unto thase ilk thre lefes, gracyous and gode,	
	The lufe of thase foure lefes that we wyn may.	
515	That grace grante gret God, that died on a Rod,[2]	
	That Kynge.	
	This hard I in a walay	*heard; lament*
	Als I went on my way	
	In a mornynge of May	
520	When medouse suld sprynge.	

---

[1] *That she will intercede compassionately on our behalf*

[2] *May God, who died on a Cross, grant that grace (pun: truelove grass)*

Notes

Abbreviations:

A   Bodleian Addit. MS A 106. [Base text.]
T   London Thornton MS (BL Addit. MS 31042).
W   Wynkyn de Worde imprint (BL Huth 102).
G   Gollancz edition (1901). [Based on T.]
GW   Gollancz and Weale edition (1935). [Based on T.]

There are three extant copies of the poem, each of them complete in forty stanzas. Two of these, A and W, have received scant scholarly attention. My editorial procedure has been to adopt A as the base text with consideration of all variants in T and W, especially where they appear to restore sense, preserve a more difficult word, or supply an alliterative stave. A comparative edition of all three copies leads, in this instance, to a better text. The notes record meaningful variants and exclude only minor differences in orthography or verbal inflexion, physical losses supplied by T, and overt modernizations in W.

1   *suld*. A: *schuld*; T: *sall*; W: *can*. The verb *suld* denotes necessity, "must needs," and *sprynge* is used transitively, as in *Otuel* (c. 1330): "A yong knight, that sprong furst berd" (line 1445). The northern spelling *suld* is adopted in accord with the form that predominates in both A and T. The word often supports alliteration upon *s* (as in lines 255 and 366). Instances where the midland spelling *schuld* might support alliteration on *sch-* are all dubious (see notes to lines 158 and 443). The poet ends the poem with this opening line; see lines 519–20.

2   *Blomes*. W: *Braunches*.

3   *well*. A well, fountain, or spring is a convention of the garden setting. In addition, the details of well, maiden, tree, and bird foreshadow the central drama of the poem: the lamenting maiden is a type for Mary mourning the death of Christ; the bird on tree is like Christ on Cross. The well is one of many symbols associated with Mary (and her weeping); compare lines 346–48.

3 *apon*. A: *of*; TW: *on*. The A reading is probably an error caused by attraction to the preceding line. The emendation is based on evidence elsewhere that the poet uses *apon* as an equivalent for *on* to lengthen short half-lines (e.g., lines 149, 183, 187, 497). In line 183 he may have intended it to supply *p*-alliteration, as here.

4 *byddyng*. T: *bedend*; W: *sayenge*. The *MED* cites the reading of T under the verb *beden*, "offer, present," which is influenced somewhat by *bidden*, "to pray." The spelling in A indicates the latter verb.

 owres. The narrator is engaged in a private, semi-liturgical devotional practice that imitates the regular office for the seven canonical hours (matins, prime, tierce, sext, none, vespers, and compline). He is reciting specific prayers, probably from a book of hours, which would have followed a standard sequence of event and image for the Hours of Mary or the Hours of the Cross. The sequence presented in stanzas 9–24 is evocative of such prayer regimens.

5 *on the boghes*. A: *on the boght* (scribal error); T: *one bewes*; W: *full bysely*. *Bewes* in T is a rare spelling of *boghes*, the reading apparently intended by the A scribe.

6 *burjun*. A: *brujun* (scribal error); T: *burgeon*; W: *borgeon*.

 belde to the boures. A: *belde to thare bores*; T: *belde to the bo* . . . ; W: *borde to the browes*; G and GW emend: *belde to the boures*. The spellings of *boures* is emended for the rhyme. The verb is more likely *belden*, "to flourish," than *bilden*, "to construct," but the two ME words overlap in meaning. Oakden first proposed the former verb (p. 209); GW adopt the latter (p. 19). In A *thare* probably means "their" (referring to the boughs), but it is also frequently the northern form for the demonstrative adj. "these," preserved only in A (see note to line 140). Spelling *boures* has been adopted for rhyme.

7 *may that made mournyng*. Mourning maidens and May mornings (line 1) are commonplaces in lyric *chansons d'aventure*, but the turn of phrase to punningly unite them seems to be unique to this poem.

8 *Syghand and sekand*. T: *sekand and syghande*; W: *She sate and syghed*. The word order of A is superior, as Smithers noted (pp. 52, 54), because it depicts the maiden "seeking" a plant among the flowers. It also does not rule out another

definition for *sekand*, "sickening, pining with yearning" (GW, p. 20; ME *siccen*). The word's primary meaning is "seeking"; its secondary one points to the maiden's withering health in the midst of blossoming nature.

8   *the fayre*. W; AT: *thase*. Alliteration in the b-verse appears in W (adopted here), but not in AT.

9   *swyte*. The adverb refers back to the maiden, to whom the narrator is sympathetically attracted.

11   *me*. A (adopted by G and GW); omitted in T; W: *my herte*.

    wogh. T; A: *rogh*; W: *woo*. A's reading *me* conforms to the ME idiom *to do (one) wough* (*OED wough* sb.[2], sense 2.a.), "to do someone harm." The spelling with *r* in A appears to be an error.

    Echoes of a secular lyric, *Nou Sprinkes the Sprai*, pervade the first two stanzas of *Truelove*. There, a narrator out upon his "pleyinge" (line 5) overhears a maiden singing a love-lament; drawn by an erotic pleasure in discovering a pretty girl with a sweet voice (and callously ignoring her pain), the narrator recounts that "thider I drogh; / I fonde hire in an herber swot / under a bogh / with joie inogh" (lines 12–15). After lamenting that her own "lovve trew / he chaunges a newe," the maiden then adds — indicating her own degree of pragmatic inconstancy — that "yiif I mai, it shal him rewe / bi this dai" (lines 21–24). Thus the brief lyric song ends, strongly intimating that the narrator will find a way to console the maiden, and that "lovve trew" means little more than the sentiment of the moment. The secular lyric provides a perfect counterpoint to the moralizations of the *Truelove* poet. Here the narrator is piously occupied in prayer, and the maiden's lament arouses his compassion, not his lust.

12   *To a derne*. W; A: *under a bogh*; T: *under a tree*. W preserves the more difficult word, and the alliteration. The error in A and T, which both position the hiding narrator under a tree, appears to have been caused by a scribe either misconstruing or deliberately changing *derne* (to *under*). On *derne* as a noun, see *MED derne* adj., sense 6, and *OED dern* a. & sb., sense B.3., where W is cited.

13   *wyll*. The word probably means "desire, longing" (OE *willa*), but it could be here and at line 15 the rarer word meaning "distraction, bewilderment" derived

from the adj. *will* (ON *villr*). See *OED will* sb.[2]

13   *wyte*. A: *wytte*; T: *wete*. Spelling adopted for rhyme.

14   Line omitted in A, supplied by T and W.

16   *Scho kest of*. T: *Rafe scho*; W: *Then cast she*. Smithers (p. 52) and Oakden (p. 209) both noted that the reading in A is superior to that in T.

17   *hir*. AW (adopted by G and GW); omitted in T.

18   *right thou*. TW; A: *I aught to*, an apparent scribal misreading of *R*; compare a similar misreading at line 190.

19   *Of*. T: *For of*.

      iwys. A (adopted by G and GW); omitted in TW.

21   *Som*. T; A: *priven*; W: *A*. The reading in A is puzzling.

      hafe. T; A: *have*. W's b-verse: *I have it longe sought*. One can deduce that the poet's dialect used unvoiced [f] rather than voiced [v] in the words *hafe*, *lufe* ("love"), and *lefe* ("leaf" and "belief"). Most of the time the scribes of A and T preserve these spellings. In the relatively few instances where they have not, I have emended. *Haue* is emended to *hafe* four times (lines 431, 433, 489, and 497); seven more times the spelling *hafe* is retained in T and adopted from there (lines 44, 45, 314, 330, 341, 390, and 391). On this spelling, note the rhyme-words in stanza 38, and compare note to line 136.

23   *Than*. TW; A: *fortan*.

      turtyll. A standard item in medieval bestiaries, the turtledove was renowned for its affectionate nature and constancy. The ME bestiary in MS Arundel 292 glosses some meanings and associations of the bird in *Truelove*: devoted to her mate, she "holdeth luve al hire lif time" (line 696); like her, one should be faithful to Christ, the soul's spouse, who will judge all on Doomsday and take only his beloved to heaven (ed. Richard Morris, *An Old English Miscellany*, EETS o.s. 49 [1872; rpt. New York: Greenwood, 1969], pp. 22–23). The bird also figures in the story of Mary's purification forty days after the Nativity;

John Lydgate explicated several of its meanings in *The Lyfe of Oure Lady* (contemplation, sorrow for sins ["with waymentyng"], love of eternal life, constancy to mate, etc.; see Lydgate's *Purification Marie*, ed. Turnbull, pp. 129–36). See also T. H. White, trans., *The Bestiary, A Book of Beasts* (New York: G. P. Putnam's Sons, 1954), pp. 145–46; and Louis Charbonneau-Lassay, *The Bestiary of Christ*, trans. D. M. Dooling (New York: Penguin, 1991), pp. 229–37.

23   a^2. The article appears in all three texts, but may be scribal.

24   *Wyth*. TW; A: *Of ryth*, an apparent scribal misreading of *W*.

25   *Bryght byrd for thi bewte*. A: *..rd for thi bowte*; T: *Thou birde for thi beaute*; W: *Bryght byrde of bewte*. W preserves an alliterating word, *bryght*, with echoes of *syght* and *soghte* in line 21.

26   *sythes*. T: *syghys*; W: *syghest*.

27   *Thow fayr foule, fayle noghte thi speche nor thi spell*. The texts read:

        A: Thow fayr feule, fayle noghte thi speche and thi spell;
        T: A thou faire foule faile noghte thi speche and thi spelle;
        W: O fayre foule spare not thy speche nor thy spell.

The alliterating word *spare* in W is interesting, but less so than *fayle* in AT, which anticipates the *f/l* soundplay throughout the poem; see note to line 40. W's *nor* is, however, better than *and*; given secondary stress in the b-verse, it alliterates with *noght*.

28   *here*. A (adopted by G); T: *to ...*; GW emend: *to here*.

29   *All my wyll and my wytt wald I the tell*. The texts read:

        A: All my wyll and my thoght wold I the tell;
        T: All my hert and my thoughte walde I the telle (G adopts *wyll*);
        W: All my wyll and my thoght wolde I the tell.

Of the a-verse variants *wyll* and *hert*, *wyll* is more likely correct, for it picks up the consonantal *-ll*s in the line and it alliterates with *wald* in the b-verse. *Thoght* is taken to be a gloss for *wytt*, the obvious *w*-word that would pair with *wyll*. Compare line 53, where the maiden's distracted speech is called *wytt*, but also line 15, where the narrator seeks to know the maiden's *wyll* and *thoght* (a rhyme-word). For *wald*, the midland spelling with *o* is unusual in A; here and at lines 30, 31, 47, and 170 the spelling *wald* in T has been adopted. Compare line 186 and note to line 153.

30   *wanderyng*. T: *wandrethe*; W: *wandrynge*.

31   *Lufly he lyghted*. T: *Than lufly he lyghtede*; W: *Then he lyghted lovely*.

31–32   *dwell / To comforth*. "hesitate to console." For this sense of the verb *dwellen*, see *MED*, sense 1(a).

33   *with buke and with bell*. "completely." For this idiom see *MED belle* n.(1), sense 9(c).

34   *And lufed owr Lady had send hir that fere*. The texts read:

> A: And loved that lady had send hir that fere;
> T: And lovede that lady that sente hir that fere;
> W: And loved our lady that sente her that fere.

The spelling *loved* has been emended here and at line 302. *Luf(e)* and *Trewluf(e)* always appear in A spelled with *f*; the verb *lufys* appears at line 320. A mix-up of *that* and *our*, both normal abbreviations, is a plausible error; the reading *owr* in W is better. The word *Lady* was probably pronounced "lɛf(e)di," supplying another echoing *f*; compare note to line 302. *Send* is probably not the original word. It may have replaced *lend* ("lent"), *fand* ("found"), or *fett* ("brought"), any of which fits the alliterative pattern and the form of *send*.

35   *free*. GW define this word as an adjective (p. 40), but the syntax and its position within the bob make it more likely to be an adverb.

36   *that*. Omitted in TW.

40   *Fayr*. AT: *Thu fayr*; W: *O fayre*. The variant words that open the line slow down the a-verse and are likely to be scribal.

40   *foule full of lufe*. The poet plays upon the sounds [l] and [f] in alliterative interplay, a recurring sound effect drawn from the emblematic *trewlufe*. Verbal play upon *lufe* and *full* may have been something of a fashion in the North. One of the six booklets that make up MS A is signed "Charke Plena amoris." According to William Dunn Macray, "*Plenus-Amoris*, or *Fullalove*, seems to have been a name of a family of scribes" (*Annals of the Bodleian Library*, Oxford [Oxford: Clarendon, 1890], p. 21). This intriguing surname or rhetorical tag crops up in many northern scribal signatures; in English it becomes the palindrome "FULALUF." See also Falconer Madan, *A Summary Catalogue of Western Manuscripts in the Bodleian Library at Oxford*, vol. 5 (Oxford, 1905), p. 541; Thomas J. Heffernan, "The Use of the Phrase *Plenus amoris* in Scribal Colophons," *Notes and Queries* 28 (1981), 493–94; and Friedman, pp. 67–72.

    so mete. AT: *so swete*; W: *swete*. This adjective completes the alliterative phrase and well suits the moral turtledove. See *MED mete* adj., sense 1.

41   *move of*. W: *medle on*. *Move* ("mufe") participates in the soundplay on *lufe*.

    may I. T: *walde I*; W: *we may*. As Smithers noted (pp. 52–53), T has lost the stave alliterating on *m*.

42   *trewluf*. A: *trewful luf*, with *ful* deleted. The maiden is searching for an herb reputed to cure love-longing. There is also a pun upon the abstract object of her search, i.e., "true love." On the scribe's correction of *trewful* to *trewluf*, compare line 319 (and note).

44   *So fayr as I hafe soght, fand I nane fete*. The texts read:

        A: Als fayr as I have soght fand I none yitte;
        T: Als ferre als I hafe soughte I fande nane yitt;
        W: So ferre as I have sought sawe I none yet.

The word *yitte* cannot be the correct rhyme-word. Alliteration, rhyme, and sense indicate a rarer word: *fete* (from OF *fait*), "suitable, fitting, worthy"; see *MED fet* adj. W's reading *So* restores alliteration to the a-verse. The spelling *fayr* for "far" is not attested elsewhere, but the phrase identifies the sense (*MED fer* adv. 7[b]). The meaning "fairly, carefully" is also possible but less likely; compare the probable pun on *fayr* ("favorably, far") at line 369. For *nane*, the rhymes at lines 148 and 202 indicate the original northern spelling; the few other instances in A spelled *non(e)* have been emended (lines 161 and 354).

45 *hafe I fonden.* A (adopted by G and GW); T: *hafe funden*; W: *I have founde.*

46 *bale.* T: *balis*; W: *sorowe.*

   bete. TW; A: *bute.* Emendation is adopted for rhyme.

48 *ryght.* W; A: *ryg..*; T: *reghte.*

51 *fayntely.* W: *feble.* The *MED* queries the meaning "rarely" for *feintli* adv. 3(c), citing only this occurrence. The attested meaning "feebly" seems suitable, however, and is supported by the reading in W and by GW (p. 40).

52 *of.* TW: *on.*

53 *a woman.* W: *wymen* (extending the attitude toward all women).

   wonder. This word is formally a noun (genitive use), not the adjective "wondrous," as glossed by GW (p. 48); see Smithers, p. 56.

54 *sary.* T: *sare*; W: *sory.*

   a. Omitted in T.

55 *Al this syd may thou seke and never nan be nere.* So A. The other texts read:

    T: Alle thi sythe may thou sighe and never mare be nere;
    W: All thy lyfe dayes may thou seke and never none be nere.

   W offers a gloss of *syd*, "life days." The AW reading *seke*, "seek," puns on *sike*, "sigh"; T's reading glosses the original word (compare note to line 8). Smithers preferred the reading in A (p. 53). The AT reading *nan* is also better than T's *mare.*

56 *knewe.* The rhyme required the poet to use the past tense, when the present tense would seem better to suit the context. Perhaps the meaning "have known" was intended. GW comment on the difficulty of the preterite *had* (instead of present *has*) in the line (p. 21), but the verb is the subjunctive "(were) to have," expressing a hypothetical situation.

57 *If thou be sett to seke it, sall I the lere.* The texts read:

A: If thou be sett to seke yitte, sall I ye lere;
T: If thou be sett for to seke yit sal I the lere;
W: Yf thou be set to seke truelove I shall the lere.

My emendation of *yitte* to *it* follows W, which glosses *yit(te)* in AT as "truelove," that is, "it," rather than "yet, still," as glossed by GW. The word alliterates with *I* in the b-verse. Northern spelling *sall* appears consistently in AT; the few appearances of the midland form *schal(l)* are not supported by alliteration (compare note to line 1). A's *ye* is one of several confusions between thorn and yogh that afflicts both MSS; compare line 441, and see also lines 194, 375, 503 for confusion between *yare* and *thare*. In addition, both scribes sometimes interchange *y* for thorn (*þ*).

In T this line appears after line 60; both rhyme and meaning indicate that the order of AW is correct. The error in T was caused by the phrase *if thou* repeated at lines 56 and 57; when the scribe (perhaps Thornton) discovered the loss of the line, he copied it at the end of the octave. Smithers criticized G and GW for failing to note the error (p. 53).

58   *spryngand and.* A (adopted by G and GW); T: *spryngande*; W: *spryngynge*. The error in T is easy to explain: having written *-and*, the scribe left out the ampersand.

    evermare. ATW: *evermore.* The word *mare*, and once *evermare* (line 507), is so frequently a rhyme-word that the original northern spelling with the vowel *a* is confirmed. The spelling is likewise changed at lines 141 and 170.

59   *Withowt any fadynge.* T: *withowtten diffadynge*; W: *Without ony fautynge.*

60   *castyng of colour.* "turning pale." This line in *Truelove* is the only example of this phrase cited in the *MED* (*casting* ger. 1c). It is, however, used to describe the condition of death in a ME *Life of Saint John the Evangelist*: "A while ye sall be faire als floures, / Bot forever ye sall cast colours" (lines 237–38; ed. Carl Horstmann, *Altenglische Legenden, neue Folge* [Heilbronn: Henninger, 1881], p. 37).

    chanuyng. TW: *changynge.* A preserves a rare word, unrecorded elsewhere in ME and altered in T and W to a more familiar word. The *MED* records only two instances of derivatives of OF *canüer*, "turn gray." The full line delivers a strongly hued image of decay: "turning pale and graying."

The Four Leaves of the Truelove

63   *luf*. AW (adopted by G and GW); T: *lyfe*.

65   *Bot*. TW: *Bot if*.

66   *grysse*. T; AW: *gresse*. The plant popularly called truelove in medieval England
        is herb paris, defined in the *OED* as follows: "A dictyogenous plant found in
        moist woods, bearing a single greenish flower at the top of the stem, and just
        beneath it four large ovate leaves in the form of a cross." Its etymology is
        obscure but may derive from the genitive form of Latin *pars*, "equal. a mate,
        a pair," because its leaves are quite uniform in shape and size. John Gerard,
        the author of a popular Elizabethan herbal (1597), implies that the plant was
        commonly likened to either a Cross or a love-knot:

>   Herb Paris riseth up with one smal tender stalke two hands high; at the very top
>   whereof come forth foure leaves directly set one against another in manner of a
>   Burgundian Crosse or True-love knot: for which cause among the Antients it hath
>   been called Herbe True-love. (Marcus Woodward, ed., *Gerard's Herbal: The History
>   of Plants* [rpt. London: Senate, 1994], p. 101)

Trueloves frequently appear in medieval romances as an ornamental design
woven into tapestries or costumes, or as a truelove knot, as in *Sir Degrevant,
Awntyrs off Arthure, Sir Gawain and the Green Knight, Rauf Coilyear, The Court
of Love*, and *Emare* (Sandison, p. 86). An illustration of the herb can be found
in Strasburger's *Text-Book of Botany*, 5th ed. (Macmillan: London, 1921), p.
727. GW incorrectly identified the plant as the four-leaf clover (pp. xxiv, 20).

67   *With four lefes is it sett ful lufly abowte*. The texts read:

>   A: With four (iiij) lefes is it sett fully abowte;
>   T: With foure (iiij) es it sett full lovely aboute;
>   W: That with four (.iiij.) leves fully is set aboute.

Lufly has been adopted from T, the only text to preserve the characteristic *f/l*
soundplay in the b-verse. G emends T by inserting *lef* (a misreading of A) after
foure. Roman numerals appear often in the texts in place of cardinal or ordinal
numbers; I have substituted the appropriate spelled-out words at lines 137, 140,
144, 155, 196, 209, 237, 274, 277, 278, 305, 313, 341, 342, 513, 514.

The English tradition of moralization upon the plant's four leaves is
summarized by Fein (1991), pp. 302–10. The most important analogue exists
in *The Long Charter of Christ*, both A- and B-Text (ed. Spalding, pp. 30,
63–65). While the *Short Charter*, which is earlier and northern in origin, has

Christ asking mankind only for "trew luf" to pay his "rent" (the plant metaphor appears to be absent), the more Southern *Long Charter* develops "truelove" into an exemplum where the four parts are expounded as shrift, repentance, not sinning, and fear of God (Vernon).

68   *to*. AW (adopted by G); T: *unto*.

        Kyng. A substitution of *Lord* would create aa/ax alliteration, but *Kyng* may be chosen for assonance (with *Blys*). *Kyng* is the more typical term used for God in the poem.

69   *this wyld*. T: *alle this*; W: *all the*. It is possible that the original reading was the more common phrase *wyde world*, especially in light of the readings in T and W. There is no necessity, however, to emend the line as it stands in A.

70–71   *Heven*, *paradyse*, and *medyllerth* refer to different parts of God's creation. *Heven* denotes the natural heavenly spheres surrounding the firmament; *paradyse* denotes the heavenly paradise, abode of God and angels; and *medyllerth* denotes the earth, situated between heaven and hell.

71   *And this*. TW; A: *And all this*, an apparent scribal error caused by attraction to *al(l)* in either line 70 or line 72.

72   *hally*. TW; A: *fully*. The reading in A has lost the alliteration upon *h*. The original phrase was perhaps *ful haly*; compare the emendation to line 67 and the phrase *full haly* at line 125.

73   *for*. T; omitted in AW.

        lufe Hym, and. T; A: *and love hym and* (adopted by G); W: *and lowe for to*. Compare analogous phrasing in *York Play* 45 (ed. Beadle, p. 392), in which Thomas the apostle speaks: "Itt leres me full lely to love hym and lowte hym" (line 8).

75   *lefe*. A pun on "leaf" and "belief" is evident here, having been prepared for by the usages in lines 67, 68, and 73. The word is omitted in W.

        thi. A (adopted by G); T: *your*; omitted in W. GW's argument in favor of the reading in T is strained: "the author here suddenly ceases to speak in the person of the turtle-dove to the girl and is now, in his double role as cleric and author, addressing a wider audience, viz. all the readers of his poem" (p. 22). The reading in A maintains the narrative fiction of bird speaking to maiden. There are signs elsewhere, however, that the poem was adapted to stress its didactic effectiveness (see note to line 510).

76   *To*. A (adopted by G); TW: *Till*.

       may. TW; omitted in A (and by G and GW); the word *may* adds to the alternating alliterative effect on *m*, *f*, and *l*.

77   *That trew luf and that kynd*. T: *Of that trewlufe and that kynde*; W: *The true love and kynde*. GW mistakenly glossed *kynd* as the noun "kind, family, race," and attributed the poor sense to the poet's need for a rhyme (p. 22). As Smithers noted, *kynd* is an adjective, as is *trew*: "that steadfast and that gracious love" (p. 54). My editorial word-split between *trew* and *luf* emphasizes this sense, although, of course, the pun on *trewluf* is also present, allowing a reading of *kynd* as a substantive, "gracious one."

78   *never*. TW: *never more*.

79   *The second lefe of the lufe I lykyn to God Son*. The texts read:

       A: By this ilke second lefe, I lykyn God Son;
       T: Now bi this ilk seconde lefe I liken goddis sone;
       W: The seconde lefe of the truelove I lyken to goddes sone.

       Alliterating regularly on *l* and *s*, the line in W is best. It is adopted here, adjusted to spellings typical of A. For line length, W's *truelove* is shorthanded to *lufe*, a usage of the poet that may help to explain the variants. There is evidence that the many repetitions of *ilke* in A and T are scribal (see notes to lines 80 and 510). The phrase in AT, *liken bi*, is not listed in the *MED*; the usual construction is made with *(un)to*, as in lines 68 and 81. Numerous examples of the northern genitive form *God* are listed in the *MED* (see *God* n.[1] 4a[a]). Although only A records the form here, both MSS preserve it at line 128.

80   *That to the*. W; AT: *Unto this ilk*. The repetition of *ilk* here and in the last stanza does not appear in W. The repetition seems overly didactic and probably scribal, as if adopted for use with a diagram. In this line, moreover, it detracts from the alliterative meter. Compare note to line 510.

81   *to*. AW (adopted by G); T: *unto*.

       thay won. AW (adopted by G and GW); T: *are done*.

82   *All halesom in a Godhede and Persons sere!* The texts read:

       A: Thase thre ar sam in a God and Persons sere;
       W: All hole in a godhede and persones thre.

Repetition at line 84 suggests the corrupt nature of A's *Thase thre*. W has an alliterating a-verse, but it lacks the word *sam*, which connects the half-lines. The line adopted here blends *hole* and *sam*, making northern *halesom*, "sound, healthy," a word fitting the context and medicinal metaphor; see *OED halesome* a. and *wholesome* a., sense 3, and *MED holsom* adj.

T omits these two lines and inserts new ones after line 86: *Es no thynge in this werlde lyke to hym one / His gladenesse and his gudnesse comforthes vs here.* The cause for omission can be detected in the identical opening of line 84, *Thase thre*, in an exemplar that matched A. A scribe skipped these two lines; a subsequent copyist (perhaps Thornton) fashioned new lines at the end of the octave.

84   *ar*. T; omitted in AW. The verb is needed to provide a vocalic lift, which alliterates with the *o* in *withowtyn*.

85   *When that semly Syre is sett in Hys tron*. The texts read:

       A: When that comly kyng is sett in hys tron;
       T: When that semly kynge es sett on his trone;
       W: Whan the comly kynge is set in his trone.

T's reading *semly* is adopted because A's repetition of *comly* (see line 86) is probably an error; it provides alliteration with *sett*. *Kyng* is a shared error; what is indicated is a name for God beginning with *s*. *Syre* appears later in the poem at line 421 and fits the context of God as Creator.

86   *and curtas of chere*. T: *curtase and clere*.

87   *For*. T: *off*; W: *with*.

89   *wyndes and waters.* T: *wynde and with water*; G and GW emend: *wynde and water.*

90   *And syne made He.* T: *And sythen he makede*; W: *Then he marked man* Everett preferred the reading in A because it provides a stanza link to line 92 (p. 119); stanza linking is not, however, a feature of the poem.

92   *syn.* T: *sythen.* The line modulates in a very interesting way the sounds [m], [d], [h], and initial vowels. The line in W, *Fyrst he made Adam and then he made Eve*, is less artful.

93   *Putt.* T: *putt he*; W: *He put.*

94   *Forbed He tham nothyng.* W: *Forbyddynge nothynge to.*

        hym and hys wyfe. AW; T: *als I bileve.* The weak tag found in T is a scribal attempt to improve the rhyme with *Eve* (line 92).

96   *Than.* T: *Bot than.*

97   *Weryd.* T: *ther weryede*; W: *cursed.*

98   *thai.* T: *tham.*

        that apill. The phrase provides an example of elided alliteration, upon *t*, in an *axa/bb* line.

101   *full.* T; omitted in AW. The reading in T is adopted because it improves the meter. Lines in the wheel typically have six or seven syllables. *Full* not only helps the line in length, but accords well with the alliteration on *f*, the recurrence of words ending in *-ll*, and the common *f/l* soundplay (note to line 27).

103   *tyll.* TW: *to.*

104   *an appill.* T: *a nappill.*

105   *morn.* The line lacks alliteration, although the *l* is to be picked up in the next line. *Morn* may be a substitute for an original word *greve*. Even so, *morn* here

echoes one of the stanza's rhymes (line 112), and there is a link between "mourn" and "morning," as in stanza 1.

106   *For his lufly handwarke that was forlorn*. The texts read:

> A: For lufe of hys handwarke that than was lorn;
> T: For his lufly handwerke that he hade lorne;
> W: For his holy handy werke that was forlorne.

A's a-verse is probably a gloss of T's a-verse, which best retains the alliterative soundplay on *l, f, h,* and *w;* W's b-verse resembles A's, but again excels it in alliteration. Everett preferred the a-verse in A over T because it accentuates the theme of love (p. 119), but T's meaning, "beloved handiwork," is similar.

107   *aungell*. Apparently the *g* is hard, as in OE; see *OED angel*, which explains that the *g* softened under the influence of French from the thirteenth century onwards. The line in W is short and corrupt: *Gabryell to hym he dyd call*.

108   *comly*. T: *semely*. As Smithers noted (p. 53), the A reading preserves the alliterating stave.

109   *Unto*. A (adopted by G); T: *Goo to*; W: *He sayd to*.

my message. A (adopted by G); T: *my messagere*; W: *on message*.

sall. T; A: *schall*; W: *shall*. The northern form found in T is typical of both MSS; see note to line 57.

110   *Bere hir blythe bodword: Of hire be I born*. The texts read:

> A: Bere hir bodword of hire I wyll be born;
> T: And bere hir blythe bodworde of hir will I be borne;
> W: To bere her gladde tydynges of her I wyll be borne.

T's reading *blythe* is adopted to lengthen the a-verse and add alliteration; W supports the likelihood that an adjective has been lost. The texts' metrically odd b-verses seem to gloss a more difficult, better reading that simplifies the verb to *be*, which would express God's divine intention as both of the future and outside time. God's intent and actions here may be compared to a passage in Nicholas Love's *Mirror*:

211

The Four Leaves of the Truelove

> When the plente of tyme of grace was come in the which the hie Trinite ordeynet to save mankynd that was dampnet thorh the synne of Adam, for the grete charite that he hade to mankynd, spiryng him his grete mercy, . . . [t]he fadere of heven called to him the archangel Gabriel and seid to him in this manere:
>
> Go to oure dere doghter Marie the spouse of Joseph the which is most cnere to us of alle creatures in erthe, and sey to hire that my blessed son hath coveyted hire shape and hire bewtye and chosen hire to his modere and therfore pray hir that she receyve him gladly. For by hir I have ordeynet the hele and the savacion of al mankynd, and I wole foryete and foryive the wrong that hath be done to me of him here before. (ed. Sargent, p. 21, lines 15–18, 21–29)

The word *bodword*, chiefly northern or north midland, means "promise, pledge" as well as "message." News-bearing represents a verbal counterpart to the theme of good versus sinful deeds. Other examples of *bodword* in the poem are God's forbidding the fruit in Eden, the Jews' accusations against Jesus, Christ's tidings brought to hell, Mary Magdalene's message of the Resurrection to the apostles, the unheard pleas for mercy from the damned souls, the repentant sinners' prayers to Mary, her acts of intercession, and, especially, the poem itself as a speech-act by bird to maiden and as a message to a meditant reader.

111   *son*. The syntax of the bob (which always connects it to the octave) seems to require that *son* refer to Gabriel. For scriptural authority in calling an angel a son of God, see Job 1.6. The alternate reading is, however, interesting: God acting as Father sending Son (Christ) from His dwelling to live in Mary and on earth. Stanzas 10–21 expound the scriptural events in terms of many separate-but-joined powers and actions of the Persons of the Trinity, and line 273 closes stanza 21 with another ambiguous reading.

112   *on*. T: *in*.

      mery morn. Note the echo of the opening stanza, the theme of mourning being transformed in this stanza to the good news of Gabriel's Annunciation, and the wordplay on the name of Mary, who will shortly become the new "mourning may."

113   *Hir*. TW: *and hir*. Smithers preferred the more compact bob of A to that of T (p. 53).

114   *face*. For the meaning "person, personage," see *MED face* n., sense 3.(d), which cites this passage among several other examples. W glosses the line: *Gabryell with the fayre face*.

115   *Sayd*. T: *Haylsede*; G emends T: *Hayl sede*.

       full of grace. These words by tradition mark the moment of conception through Mary's ear: "At that worde knot was knitte," according to the lyric *Ecce ancilla Domini* (ed. Chambers and Sidgwick, p. 114). The Incarnation "knits" man and God: "For this day was mankynd sovereynly wirchiped in that he was oned and knyt to the godhede in Crist without departyng" (Nicholas Love, *Mirror*, p. 27). God conceived as Trinity was also figured as a "knot," as in Dante's vision at the end of *The Divine Comedy* ("*La forma universal di questo nodo / credo ch'i' vidi*," *Paradiso* 33.91–92). So, to extend the truelove knot metaphor, the knot of the Trinity is knit to humankind in the Incarnation, tied as a knot by the words uttered here. It should also noted that Mary's becoming filled with grace parallels the ending of the poem, which gives "grace" to both maiden and reader (see note to line 515).

116   *Pereles in ilka*. T: *Sayde pereles in alle*; W: *Pyerles in every*.

119   *All*. T: *and all*.

       was. A: *wos*, written over a deletion of the word *bale*; TW: *bale*. The northern spelling *wa*, appearing everywhere in the poem (often in rhyme position), was used for the plural *was*, which misled a scribe into writing *bale* (a plausible misreading of the letters; see note to line 444). Scribe A caught the error and supplied the obvious correction.

       sall be bett. W: *it shall be let*.

120   *I mot a cheld*. A: *I suld a cheld* (adopted by G); T: *that I a childe solde*; W: *and I a chylde sholde*. Emending *suld* to *mot* is indicated by the *m*-alliteration of lines 120–21. The subjunctive form fits the context and gives consonance with the rhyme-words; compare the word at lines 38 and 313.

121   *ne with man mett*. T; A: *with no man yitte*. The reading in T is adopted because it provides better rhyme and alliteration. The word *mette* appears in stanzas 9 and 11 (lines 117, 134) in reference to the Incarnation, where it euphemistically

refers to the conception of God in the Virgin. The usage here, though more carnal, is similar.

123   *held*. W: *age*. The spelling with *h* for the word *eld* is not recorded in the *MED* and is curiously unnecessary here for the alliteration with *Elyezabeth*. Thus one needs to note that there is a similar word meaning "grace, favor" (*MED held[e]* n.[2]). As GW point out, however, the meaning "eld" has scriptural basis; the word "corresponds to the Wyclifite *elde*, *eelde*, in the same context. Compare the Vulgate: 'in senectute sua'" (p. 23).

        lett. W: *led*. The meaning here, "barren," is not recorded in the *MED* (*letten* v.).

124   The line in W reads: *O lorde I am thy mayde sayd Mary so dere*. Elsewhere in the stanza the W reviser adds the phrases *she sayd* (line 120) and *he sayd* (line 122) to distinguish speakers.

128   *in lyght*. This is the usual idiom to describe the Incarnation of Christ; see *MED lighten* v.(2), sense 4a(a) for many examples. Compare line 132.

129   *Becom a*. TW: *Become*.

131   *is this ilk*. A (adopted by G); T: *this ilk*; W: *is the*. The phrase may add through elision to the *s*-alliteration of the a-verse. It also gives emphasis to the second leaf at the point where the text would have commenced on a second folio (on the original lay-out, see the Introduction). On the word *ilk* elsewhere in MSS A and T (but not in W), see notes to lines 80 and 510.

        owr. AW (adopted by G and GW); omitted in T.

132   *that Lady*. A (adopted by G and GW); T: *a mayden*; W: *the lady*. A and W preserve the alliterating word. T's error was apparently caused by the phrase *in a mayden* appearing at the same position in line 134.

133   *so*. Omitted in W.

        traste. A: *treste*; T: *trayste*; W: *tryste*. This spelling (emended for rhyme) as well as the two MS readings are attested for the northern verb *traisten*, cognate with *trusten*. See *OED traist* v. and *trest* v.

135   *Thys.* T: *It.*

        Gaste. T; AW: *goste.*

136   *lefes of lufe.* AT: *leves of lufe*; W: *lefes of love.* The spelling of the plural *lefes*,
        "leaves," varies in A, appearing with *f* six times and with *v* four times (here and
        lines 140, 144, and 164). These spellings have been made uniform because the
        soundplay upon [l] and [f] is important and pervasive (note to line 40). *Lef(e)*,
        meaning "leaf" or "belief," is always spelled with *f*. *Leve*, meaning "leave,
        cease," is, however, typically spelled with a *v* (lines 185 and 224).

        withowtyn any lette. This phrase is a formulaic tag meaning "truly, indeed," but
        the literal meaning is also appropriate, "without physical hindrance, without
        a break (in the design)." See *MED lette* n. (b).

137   *a.* T: *the.*

        for chaste. Chaste is probably a noun, not an adjective (as cited by GW [p. 23]
        and the *MED*), meaning "chasteness, faithfullness." The *MED* lists this noun
        (derived from OF), but with a query and only two examples (*chaste* n.[3]). For
        the possibility that it is an adjective used as a noun, see M. Y. Offord's
        discussion of a similar phrase (*for slepeles*) in *The Parlement of the Thre Ages*,
        EETS e.s. 246 (Oxford: Oxford University Press, 1967), pp. 42–43 n. 101; and
        M. L. Samuels, "Middle English 'wery forwandred': A Rejoinder," *English
        Studies* 36 (1955), 310–13.

138   *another.* TW; A: *ane other.*

139   *bute.* A: *butte*; TW: *bote.*

140   *Thare.* A: *There*; T: *Thies* followed by deleted *thre*; W: *The.* The word *there/thare*
        is a northern form meaning "these" with an obscure etymology; see *MED thir(e*
        adj. and *OED thir* dem. pron. & adj. Its earliest recorded appearance is in
        Cursor Mundi and other northern texts. Thornton has changed the word
        everywhere except at line 456 and possibly 341 (where he may have interpreted
        it to mean "there"); he typically substitutes the more familiar plural form,
        spelled *theis* or *thase.* W often has *the* where the MSS have a demonstrative
        adjective. The spelling *thar(e)* (or an abbreviation that omits the vowel) is the
        usual form in A for the words meaning "these" and "there."

141   *evermare.* AT: *evermore*; W: *ever*. See note to line 58.

        sall. T; A: *schall*; W: *shall*. On the emended spelling, see note to line 57.

142   *joyn.* TW; A: *grewyn* (adopted by G). The word in T has the support of W and restores the alliteration. The poet alliterates words beginning in *j* with words beginning in vowels, *h*, and soft *g*.

144   *Now has thre lufly lefes a fourte fela tan.* The texts read:

        A: Now has thar iij lefes a fourte fela tan;
        T: Now all thies foure lovely leues a frende to tham hase tane;
        W: Now hathe the thyrde lefe a swete felowe taken.

        The adjective *lufly* has been adopted from T to restore alliteration in the a-verse. Evidence for *thre* appears in all three texts, even though scribes of T and W both read *iij* incorrectly. The meanings of T and W are also variant: in T, the four leaves have taken Joseph as their friend; in W, the Holy Ghost alone has joined with Mary.

148   *an oxe and an asse.* TW; A: *a oxe and a asse*. The reading of T and W provides alliteration on *n* with *nan* at the end of the line and anticipates the secondary play on *n*-sounds in the next three lines. The exemplar of A probably had *a noxe and a nasse*, which the A scribe tried to correct; compare the difference between A and T at line 104 (*an appill*).

149   *barne.* T; AW: *chyld*. Emendation adopted from T for alliteration.

        a. T; A: *the*; omitted in W.

150   *stam.* T: *sterne*; W: *sterre*. A northern word; see MED *stern* n.(1) and *OED stern* sb[2].

        schaply schewed. T: *hastily that schynede*; W: *stabely shewed*.

151   *caght.* ATW: *had*. Alliteration and the pararhyming play upon *syght* and *soght* indicate the word for which *had* has substituted.

        a. AW (adopted by G and GW); T: *thay*.

153   *Him*. A (adopted by G); TW: to hym.

         wold. Almost everywhere else this word has the northern spelling *wald* (see note to line 29). While the midland spelling is used for the rhyme here, *wald* supplies the rhyme at line 186.

155   *seven-fold*. T: *fele folde*; W: *many folde*. It is difficult to determine whether the reading in W is a gloss of T or a mistake for the roman numeral *vij* found in A. Alliteration is weak in all three versions of the wheel.

157   *Unhappy*. W; AT: *Unsely* ("proud"). W preserves the alliterating word.

         thase tythandes. T: *this tythynges*; W: *the tydynges*. The MSS disagree internally as to whether *tythandes* is to be construed as singular or plural. Here A gives it the plural demonstrative adjective *thase*, while T assigns it *this*. At line 288 A reads *this tithandes* and T reads *thies tythynges*. Both constructions are attested (*OED tidings* sb.).

158   *A*. TW: *that a*.

         knaw-child. A (adopted by G and GW); TW: *childe*. A preserves alliteration on *k*. W's agreement with T is unimportant because it is congruent with a six-teenth-century modernization; W prints *childe* at line 118 and *male children* at line 160. The alliterative stresses fall upon k*naw*-ch*ild* and b*orn* (a-verse) and k*ynge* and b*ee* (b-verse). *Suld* provides consonance with *child* but does not play a role in the alliterative meter, an observation that supports the originality of northern *suld* over midland *schuld*.

159   *messages*. T: *message*; W: *messagers*.

         sent he. T; A: *sent*; W: *sende them*. The word omitted in A is either *he* or *them*; I have adopted the reading in T. Note the similar error at line 262.

160   *To slee all knafe-chylder in that contré*. The texts read:

         A: To seke knafe chylder in that contre
         T: To seke that knave childe in that cite;
         W: To slee all male chyldren in that countre.

160   W's variant *slee all* is adopted because it is the more vivid phrase, and it continues a play upon the sounds *s* and *l* found in line 159. If an original word beginning with *k* has been lost, it was probably *kell*, "kill." G and GW emend T by adopting *knafe-chylder* from A.

161   *Left he nan in wharte.* T: *Lefte he nane in qwarte*; W: *They lefte none alyve.* *Wharte* means "alive, unharmed"; for the idiom, see *MED quert(e)* n. 1(b). The spelling *wh-* for *qu-* is a form frequently used by northern scribes of the fourteenth and fifteenth centuries. While the reading in W is clearly a modernization, it is interesting for the alliteration on *l*. *Left* may be a substitute for an original verb beginning with *wh/qu*.

162   *Thai sputt tham on spere-poyntes — gret pyté to se.* The texts read:

        A: Thai putt tham on speres gret dole it was to se;
        T: Thay spetide tham one speris grete dole for to see;
        W: They spytted them on spere poyntes grete pyte was to se.

The emended verb *sputt* is derived from A's *putt* and the verb found in TW. W's *spere-poyntes* gives the sharpest effect, both visceral and alliterative. The emended b-verse blends the variants of T and W. W's *pyte* is obviously better than AT's *dole*. An alternate possibility for the b-verse — *was pyte to se* — would effectively echo the *sp* and *t* sounds of the a-verse, but it seems unwise to omit the word *gret* found in all three texts.

164   *Bot.* T: *he.*

166   *Childer gon.* A: *There childer gon*; T: *Thase childre gane*; W: *The chyldren coude.* Omitting the article, which is different in each text, makes the line more effective.

167   *this.* A: *that* corrected to *this*; T: *that*; W: *the.*

        same. T; omitted in AW.

168   *myrth.* A: yogh corrected to *r.*

170   *mare.* T; AW: *more.* See note to line 58.

171   *His awn.* TW: *For his.*

172   *lawe*. T: *lay*.

173   *Hym baptyste*. A (adopted by G); T: *Baptiste hym*; W: *crystened hym*.

175   *fell famen*. T: *fele famen*; W: *the Jewes*.

       wald fayne Hym hafe slane. AW: *that wald Hym hafe slane*; T: *that fayne walde
       hym* .... T preserves the alliterating word, but its syntactic position is atypical
       of the poet's half-verse style. Transposition and removal of a scribal explanato-
       ry *that* solves the problem and tightens the line.

176   *sake*. T: *syn*.

177   *thai Hym knew*. T; A: *thai knew*; W: *was he knowen*. T supplies the word lacking
       in A.

       tytte. T; AW: *son*. The word in T preserves alliteration and is the more difficult
       variant. The reading in A and W is a gloss of *tytte*.

178   *Alswa*. ATW: *Also*. Both MSS read *also*, but the attested northern spelling *wa*
       for the rhyme-word elsewhere in the poem reveals this was probably the
       original spelling. The word has the same meaning as *swa*, "in the way or
       manner described" (distinct from *so*, "to such an extent"). See the note to lines
       216–17, and compare *alswa* (spelling preserved in T) at line 470.

179   *sorow*. AT: *dole*; W: *pyte*. *Sorow* alliterates with *see* and picks up the *w*'s in
       alswa and *wa*. Always spelled *sorow* or *sorowe* in ATW, the word may have
       been pronounced *sorwe*; it appears typically amidst *s* and *w* sounds (lines 248,
       330, 384, 464, 489, 492). On the formula of the wheel, see note to lines
       179–82.

179–82 The wheel follows a formula used again by the poet in stanzas 16 and 18, in
       which the first line expresses grief (lines 179, 205, and 231), and the third
       repeats "The second lefe of the thre" (lines 181, 207, and 233). The poet has
       created a temporary refrain upon mourning. The scribes recognized the refrain
       to the extent that they substituted the same noun in its first line: *dole* in T; *pyte*
       in W; *dole* twice, *reuth* once in A. It is inconceivable, however, that the poet
       did not use an alliterating noun, the obvious choices being *grefe* or *sorow*. I
       have followed the slight differences found in A and the contextual soundplays

to choose *sorrow* for stanzas 14 and 18, *grefe* for stanza 16; see notes to lines 179, 205, and 231.

182   *wa*. ATW: *wo*. This original northern spelling is well attested in both MSS by the numerous uses of the word in a rhyming position. Compare line 101.

183   *spake*. W; AT: *satt*. The reading in W helps the sense of the passage because the phrase *He sayde* in line 185 is probably a scribal addition. The *p* in *apon* may support alliteration on *p*. The word *justes*, pronounced with an initial vowel phoneme, alliterates with *hye*; for other signs of *j/h* alliteration, see lines 146, 163, and 314.

185   *Leve*. AT: *He sayde leve*; W: *He sayd loke*. The explanatory phrase is probably scribal; compare note to lines 124 and 183. On the spelling of *leve*, see note to line 136.

        the. T: *a*; omitted in W.

188   *He cald Hymself a kyng. Swylk bourdes be bald*. The texts read:

> A: He says hymself he is a kyng swylk wordes ar bald;
> T: He said hymselfe he es a lynge slyk wordis are . . .;
> W: He calleth hymselfe a kyng suche bourdes be to bolde.

Line 188 is a striking instance of A and T being in virtual agreement but demonstrably more corrupt than W. W preserves three alliterating words lost in AT:

(1) The verb *callen* in the a-verse: The preterite form (as in T) is indicated by the b-rhymes, with which it rhymes internally (for the form compare line 404). When *sayen* replaced the original verb *callen* in AT, the words *he is* were added for clarity. This phrasing of the accusation with the verb *callen* occurs twice in *York Play* 36 (lines 58, 75, and compare line 112). G adopted the a-verse of A.

(2) The noun *bourdes*, from OF *borde, bourde*, "jests, witty remarks": A scribal confusion between *b* and *w* is a plausible error; compare notes to lines 119 and 444.

(3) The verb *be*: Compared to *ar*, its effect is better.

189   *If*. W; A: *& if*; T: *and if*. The ampersand found in A, expanded in T, probably replaced an original, misread yogh.

189 *today.* W; AT: *this day.* W preserves an interesting wordplay in the b-verse. Analogous lines appear in *York Play* 36 (ed. Beadle, p. 324): "And cursedly he called hym a kyng. / To deme hym to dede it is diewe" (lines 58–59).

190 *Ryght before.* T; AW: *Lowd before the*; G and GW emend: *Ryghte before the.* The reading in T is adopted because it possesses alliteration on *r*, absent in AW. The second stave is apparently formed by elision, *before* preceding *Emperowre.* *Ryght* may be a substitute for a harder alliterative word, such as *roydly* (*MED roid(e* adj., sense 1.[c], "of an outcry: furious, vehement," and *roidli* adv. "boldly, brazenly"), or *rathe* (*MED rathe* adv., "immediately"; compare line 49).

191 *dred.* TW; A: *dr* . . .

193 *Sais! I can say.* T: *I kane say yow*; W: *And sayd that he coude say. Sais* is interpreted here to be the imperative plural "cease." W understands the word as "says," but T is ambiguous, with Pilate making a statement to cut off the accusers' voices. The verb "says" is elsewhere spelled *says* (line 124 and note to line 188). The spellings *seesen*, *seisse*, and *seas(s)e* are attested for *cesen* (*MED*). To read the word as "cease" avoids the redundancy of *say* appearing twice and shows Pilate's position of authority as judge.

194 *red.* W; AT: *red that.* The alliteration upon *y* is more apparent in the compact line of W.

  yare. A (adopted by G and GW); T: *thare*; W: *there.* The error, common to both MSS, reflects the confusion between thorn and yogh that may derive from a common exemplar. Compare note to line 57.

196 *leved.* ATW: *left.* The emended spelling is based upon evidence elsewhere that this word was pronounced with two syllables (lines 202 and 275) and note to line 136).

  allane. T: *than allan.*

198 *scharpe.* Omitted in T.

  body. TW; A: *& body.* The ampersand in A is an obvious error.

199 *Syne.* T: *Sythyn*; W: *Syth.*

199 a^2. A (adopted by G); omitted in TW.

200 *hys handes and fett hard nales*. T: *his handis and his fete the nayles*; W: *his handes and fete herte. nayles*. The reading in W indicates an alliterating word before *nales*. *Herte* makes little sense except as an altered form of *hard*.

201 *bryght*. T: *bygg*.

   to. T: *till*.

   brathely. T; A: *baldly*; W: *sharpely*. As the more difficult word, the reading in T is accepted. Most of the examples of this fairly rare word appear in alliterative verse (*MED broth(e)li* adv.).

202 *bled*. ATW: *sched*. Emendation is indicated by alliteration and the form of the substituting word. Compare the many collocations of *bled* and *blod* cited in the *MED* under *bleden* v., and the similar emendation at line 289.

   lyfe leved. W; A: *lyfe left*; T: *leved he*. The meaning of T's reading is quite different: "he was left with none (i.e., blood)." The error in T can be seen to derive from the omission of *lyf* after *luf* because of the similarity of the two words.

   nan. T; AW: *non*. Spelling adopted for rhyme.

203 *served*. A: *bed*; T: *bedde*; W: *gave*. One expects *s*-alliteration here. The reading in A is paleographically almost identical to *ved* and the preceding word *thai* is written as an abbreviation. It is possible that an abbreviated *ser* has dropped out. The reading in W supports the presence of an original *v* in place of *b*.

   in. TW: *for*. The variants are semantically equivalent.

204 *gall*. A (adopted by G and GW); T: *alle*; W: *gyle*. In accepting the reading of A over T's meaningless tag, GW observe that it merely repeats the sense of *attire*, "gall," in line 203 (pp. 24–25). On the contrary, *gall* has a fuller semantic range (here meaning "maliciously"), and a play upon the two meanings of *gall* is present. The biblical reference is to Matthew 27.34.

205 *Grett grefe was.* A: *Grett reuth was* (adopted by G); T: *It was gret dole for*; W:
It was grete pyte for. While *sorrow* would also supply alliteration, *grefe* is better
in this context of *g*-alliteration. Compare *greved* at line 421, and *Pearl*, "The
adubbemente of tho downez dere / Garten my goste al greffe foryete" (line 86).
Grefe creates an interesting internal rhyme with *lefe* in the wheel's third line.
On the formula of the wheel, see note to lines 179–82. The formula is varied
(in A only) by omission of the words *It was* and *for*; the variation adds an
interest not found in the rote sameness of T and W.

206 *the.* TW: *a.*

207–08 W reads: *The seconde lefe sycurly / Dyed for us all.*

208 *Suld.* T; A: *Schuld*; omitted in W. The northern spelling found in T, character-
istic of both MSS, is adopted; see note to line 1.

 falow. T; A: *fayd*; omitted in W. The reading of T, with the characteristic
repetition of *f* and *l* sounds, is superior to the formulaic *fayd and falle* of A
(which Oakden preferred *because* it is a tag phrase [p. 209]).

209 *the lufe.* T: *that trewlufe*; W: *the loke.* This syncopated form of *trewlufe* is usually
expanded in T as if to avoid confusion, but it appears to be the poet's way to
generalize the symbol. The same difference exists between the MSS at lines 274
and 313.

210 *Wrange scho.* A (adopted by G and GW); T: *scho wrange*; W: *Wryngynge.*

 wepyd. T: *wepe than*; W: *wepynge.* Note the echo in this line to line 17; a
description of the mournful Virgin has supplanted the secular lovelorn maiden
of the opening stanzas.

211 *a myld mode.* T: *with a drery mode. Myld mode* is a formula for Mary's compas-
sionate bearing, but *mode* also bears the meaning "grief, sorrow, distress"
(*MED mode* n., 6[c]). Compare the same phrase at line 511, where the context
has shifted to Mary's compassion for mankind.

212 *wex al.* T: *wexe than all*; W: *wexed wonder.*

213 *Be.* W: *Downe by.*

213   *blank*. ATW: *whyt*. The loss of a *bl*-word is obvious in the context of the preceding line and the word *blode* in the b-verse, which holds the position that often reinforces the alliteration of the a-verse. The word *whyt* has a French-derived alliterating synonym of greater difficulty. See *MED blaunk* adj. and *OED blanch* a.

215   *the*[1]. T: *that*. This line lacking in alliteration appears in all three texts.

216–17   *that it suld twyn swa / So yare*. "that it should break apart in such a way, so completely." The distinction between *swa* (*OED so* adv., significations grouped under I) and *so* (*OED so* adv., signfications grouped under III) is maintained in both MSS. Only *swa* appears in a rhyming position. This distincion holds as well for *alswa* (same meaning as *swa*) and affects editorial decisions at lines 178 (note) and 470.

219   *Bot*. A (adopted by G and GW); T: *And*; omitted in W.

       stode hir by. W; A: *was hir by* (adopted by G); T: *was by*.

221   *Was*. T; AW: *That was*. The repetition of *that* is likely to be scribal.

222   *Yitt*. AW (adopted by G); T: *than*.

       cuth. ATW: *spake*. Alliteration reveals the original word to have been a form of *quoth* pronounced with an initial hard *c*. See *MED quethen* v. — listing northern spellings *cothe, cod, kod*, and *cuth* — and *OED quoth* v.

       a. T: *that*; W: *the*.

223   *Unto*. T: *Until*; W: *To*.

       myld Moder. T: *modir dere*; W: *moder so mylde*. The readings in A and W preserve the alliterative adjective *myld*.

226   *to thi moder, for to myrth the*. W; A: *to thi moder Mary to the*. T: *thi moder now to the*; G emends: *thi moder now moder to the*; GW emend: *mi moder now moder to the*. The sense of the line — a problem in both MSS — is clarified by W, which was unknown to previous editors. The biblical reference is to John 19.26–27.

227   *to abyde.* TW: *for to byde.*

228   *hert.* T; A: *syd*; W: *sydes. Hert* offers the better alliterative a-verse. Even though the line has poor alliteration in itself, *blode* carries on the alliteration of the preceding line, and *see* begins *s*-alliteration in the next line. The variants in A and W can be explained as scribes supplying the usual tradition of blind Longinus, which told of his piercing the side of Christ and regaining eyesight when touched by drops of Christ's blood. The story is based upon John 19.34 and the apocryphal Gospel of Nicodemus, and it influenced the Holy Grail legend of Arthurian romance. See the ME *Harrowing of Hell* (ed. Hulme, pp. lxviii–lxix) and *York Play* 36 (ed. Beadle, p. 330).

228–29   These lines are out of place in T, where they are copied as the first two lines of the stanza (before line 222); G and GW emended by following the line order of A. That the arrangement of lines in A (and W) is better than in T can be seen by the syntax of the bob *That day*, which follows more logically upon line 229 than line 227. Such an error would match the pattern found in other cases of T's rearranged lines, in which omitted lines are inserted later in the octave. See notes to lines 57 and 513–15.

229   *soght be a spere-schafte.* AW: *soght be a spere-schafte fra*; T: *rane by the spere-schafte fra.* The reading in AW preserves alliteration, as Oakden noted (p. 210). However, the preposition *fra*, found in all three texts, makes sense only in T, "the blood ran down the spere from his wounds." In the other versions, Longinus's spear "seeks" or explores the wounds, the direct object of *soght.*

231   *sorow.* AT: *dole*; W: *pyte.* On the formula of the wheel, see note to lines 179–82.

235   *ded on.* T; A: *on*; W: *take of.*

236   *lay.* T: *it lay.*

237   *The fourte for wa falowed and syghed full sare.* The texts read:

         A: The fourte fela for wa syghed full sare;
         T: The ferthe lefe than falowede and syghede full sare;
         W: The fourth for woo fell and syghed full sare.

The poet seems to prefer the pattern in TW (*axa/bb*) over the pattern in A (*aax/bb*). A and W point to the probability that *for wa* provided both a stave and soundplay with either *felawe* or *falowed*. The emendation adopted here relies on clues from all three texts; compare, too, line 274. G emends T by substituting *fela* for *lefe*.

238   *Al the treuth of this world was in a trew may.* T's line begins with the word *And* but otherwise agrees with A. W reads: *With truth of the worlde was with the true maye.* The elements of the opening situation have been recombined, the maiden's wayward distress (lines 16–22) transforming to Mary's stable faith. The phrase *of this world* repeats line 236; it and *treuth* may have replaced an original phrase, both alliterative and suitable in context: *mirth of this mold*; see *MED mold(e* n., sense 3(b).

239   *If.* T: *thof*; W: *Thoughe.* This usage of *if* ("even if, though") probably reflects the poet's usage (see also lines 353 and 423).

        marde. ATW: *ded.* The word *ded* disrupts the meter; *marde*, past participle of *mar*, "hinder, stop, interrupt," gives a more nuanced meaning that fits the subject and provides soundplay with the rhyme-word *mare.* Compare Liffe's accusation of Death's boasting, concerning Christ's death, in the northern alliterative poem *Death and Liffe*: "How thou hast wasted this world sith wights were first, / Ever murthered and marde, thou makes thy avant" (lines 365–66; ed. Joseph M. P. Donatelli [Cambridge, Mass.: Medieval Academy of America, 1989], p. 50).

        myghte. T: *myghtis*; G emends: *myghtie.*

241   *it.* T: *thay*; omitted in W.

242   *and.* T: *with.*

243   *Ful yare.* "very readily, eagerly." This sense for *yare* is not cited in the *OED* (*yare*), but it is easily construed from the adjective *yare*, "ready, prepared."

244   *hand.* TW: *handis.*

245   *syne.* T: *sythen*; W: *sayth.*

246   *bale.* T: *balis.*

248   *sary.* AW (adopted by G and GW); T: *that sary.*

        was. W; A: *wex* (by attraction to next line); T: *was full.*

249   *syght.* A (adopted by G and GW); T: *light*; W: *the syght.*

        wox unfayn. T: *wexe al unfayne*; W: *was nothynge fayne.* The *x* followed by a
        vowel creates the line's third *s*-alliterating stave.

250   *bowes.* ATW: *comes.* Form and alliteration strongly indicate this word has been
        supplanted by *comes*, a synonym that could be very similar in appearance.

        trow. T: *hope.* This word may also be a substitution, and, if so, for a word
        beginning with *w* (*wot*, "think," or *wen*, "expect").

251   *What art thou, fayr face?' fast gon Hym frayn.* The texts read:

            A: What art thou with thi fayr face gun he Hym frayn;
            T: What art thou with thi fare faste gon he frayne;
            W: What art thou with thy fayre face thus dyd hym frayne.

        The differing interpretations are of interest. In A and W Satan asks Christ who
        he is, having such a fair countenance. In T Satan asks Christ who he is and
        what is his business (*fare*) in hell.

253   *thar thou noghte layn.* A (adopted by G); T: *now thare the noghte layne*; W: *thou
        sholde not layne.*

254   *thi way.* TW: *away.*

        us. T: *me.*

        al. The word is probably an adjective, "us all," rather than an adverb, "entirely
        mad." Compare line 326, *mad us al fre.*

257   *Kyng.* A: *Kynlg* (scribal error).

259–60   *barres . . . bandes*. T: *bandis . . . barres*. The action can be visualized as follows: The fiends frantically bolt the doors with bars, the bars crack and break, and the doors burst from the hinges. The verbs accompanying the respective nouns — *barres breke* and *bandes brast* — seem to suit them and argue somewhat in favor of the word order found in A and W and against the T version. Compare, however, the same scene in different versions of the ME *Harrowing of Hell* (ed. Hulme, pp. 110–11); two MSS read *bandes al brast* where the other two read *barres tobrast*.

262   *Al*. W; AT: *& al*. The ampersand of A and T is a scribal addition.

         He. T; A: *he* written after deleted *th*; W: *them*.

263   *Tharof David, His derlyng, mad myrth imell*. The texts read:

         A: David, His derlyng, mad myrth tharof imell;
         T: Davyd his derlynge made myrthe ther emelle;
         W: Davyd his derlynge made myrthe them amonge.

Scansion of this line in all three texts suggests four lifts in the a-verse, a real peculiarity: *aabb/xb*. The emended version scans more regularly, *axa/bb*, with a secondary vocalic alliteration in *His* and *imell*. The source for David's epithet is 1 Samuel 13.14. The definition of *imell* is uncertain: (1) "concerning this, about this" (the *MED*'s meaning, but redundant with *tharof*); (2) "in the midst" (N. Davis, ed., *Sir Gawain and the Green Knight* [line 1451], p. 198); or (3) "altogether, utterly" (the *MED*'s meaning for the word in *Gawain*).

264   *a*. TW: *an*.

         and well hedyd. T: *and weldide it*; W: *he harped*. For the verb, see *MED heden* v.(2), sense (d), "to heed, comply." The sense "headed up, took the lead" is rare before the seventeenth century and is cited only in transitive use; see *OED head* v., sense III.9, and the example from *The Pistel of Swete Susan*, line 188. Alternatively, *hedyd* is a mistake for *he dyd*, "he played [the harp]," as the line is understood in both T and W. The variants attest to scribal difficulty over the line.

265   *retenew*. An adjective seems missing from the a-verse. Possibilities include *ryche*, *royall*, or *trew*.

265   *owt gon He tell*. For the idiom *tellen out*, "separate out by counting," see *OED tell* v., senses under II, especially 23a, and *MED tellen* v., sense 17(b).

266   *of*. T: *for*.

267   *snell*. T: *felle*; W: *wyde*. The reading in A may be better than that in T because it adds alliteration on *s* (although a fourth alliterating stave is not metrically necessary). A confusion between calligraphic *s* and *f* is not unusual; it helps to account for variant readings at lines 340, 384, 408, and 481.

268   *bon*. T; AW: *gud*. The reading in T is adopted because it alliterates and is the more difficult word. *Gud* is likely to be a gloss upon its rare French-derived synonym.

           boght. TW: *broghte*. With *broght(e)* occurring elsewhere in the stanza twice, *boght* is the stronger reading. It adds consonantal repetition, and it completes the metaphor couching the redemption of mankind in terms of a commercial transaction: *I was sald . . . My bon chylder ar boght*. Compare similar language at lines 245 and 333.

272   *blyssed*. Omitted in T.

273   *holy gost*. As GW note, "The reference is not to the Holy Ghost, . . . but to the soul of Christ, which . . . now returned to the body to raise it to life" (p. 26). Nonetheless, the poet may be inviting some ambiguity; compare line 111 and note.

274   *lufe*. TW: *trewlufe*.

           falow is. T: *falowede*; W: *was folden*.

274–79   These lines summarize the persons of the Truelove, with the wordplay upon *lef* and *luf* ending on *lyf* in the sixth line. The titles given to Mary underscore her familial relationship to the Trinity: Mother of Christ, Maiden-Daughter of the Father, Wife of the Holy Ghost. The miracle of the Annunciation attains its end in the Harrowing. See Nicholas Love, *Mirror*, where the kinships willingly adopted by Mary are seen as necessary to man's reconciliation to God:

        This day [Feast of the Annunciation] was chosen of the fadere of heven in to his dere douhter and of the Son in to his mylde modere, and of the holi gost in to his speciale spouse. This day is also a special solempnite of alle the blessed sprites of heven for this day was begunne the restoryng of hire company and felaschipe that felle done by synne of Lucifere. (ed. Sargent, p. 27, lines 8–11)

Mary's tie of dutiful kinship to God begins the process by which all humans can return to God as Father.

275   *lefed moder, mayden.* W: *lefte mayde moder.*

276   *wyghte.* ATW: *of myghte.* "Strong, powerful"; see *OED wight* a. The error in all three texts ruins the alliteration of the a-verse. The original can be discerned not only from the form *myght* but also from the play on *w* existing in the b-verse and *wyf* (line 275).

278   *Raysed Thai.* W: *They reysed up.* The word *raysed*, from all three texts, is suspect. The b-verse suggests a word beginning with *tw*, such as *twyght*, "pulled or plucked up"; see *OED twitch* v.[1].

        betwen. T: *bytwixe.*

279   *grace.* T; A: *the myghtht*; W: *myght.* Alliteration is problematic in much of this stanza; the original of this line may have been: *Thurght grace of the godhed, He growed unto lyf.*

280   *a.* T: *the.* The a-verse is deficient in alliteration.

284   *mett Mary.* W; A: *mete with Mary*; T: *mett with the.* The version in A is hypermetric. The choice is between either W, adopted here, or T, which omits *Mary.* The scriptural authority for this episode is Mark 16.9.

286   *lech.* The word is part of the medicinal metaphor that informs the poem. See note to line 515.

        gode. A: *ful gu* . .; TW: *gude.* Spelling is adopted for rhyme. The poet normally closes the wheel with a five-syllable line. When an intensifying adverb, such as *ful*, occurs in one version only, it may be an instance of scribal emphasis. T contains the adverb *ful* more often than does A (see notes to lines 101, 248, and 375), while A, in general, presents more compact readings. This line provides an exception to this tendency.

287   *went*. T: *yode*.

           the. W: *Mari*.

           and with. T: *in hir*.

287–99   The poet's account of the events of Christ's resurrection draws upon, and conflates for dramatic purpose, three separate biblical passages: Mark 16.11, in which Mary Magdalene tells the disciples of the event; John 20.25, in which Thomas doubted the other apostles; and Luke 24.10–11, in which the apostles would not believe the three women (see GW, p. 26). In the poet's narrative Thomas becomes the spokesman for all the disciples and Mary for all the women. For other ME treatments of Thomas's doubt, see *York Play* 45 (ed. Beadle, pp. 392–94); C. W. Marx, "The Virtues of Skepticism: A Medieval Interpretation of Thomas's Doubt," *Neophilologus* 71 (1987), 296–304; and Lawton (1989), 160–61.

288   *this tithandes*. T: *thies tythynges*; W: *the tydynges*. See note to line 157.

           Thomas of Ynde. St. Thomas the Apostle, who according to medieval tradition preached in India.

289   *How Crist is resyn all hale, that bled His hart blod*. The texts read:

        A: Crist is resyn agayn that sched his hart blod;
        T: Criste es resyn alle hale that schede his hert blode;
        W: How Cryst was rysen agayne that sched his hert blode.

The combined evidence of T and W helps to restore alliteration on *h* in the a-verse, and the phrase in T (*alle hale*) continues the medical metaphor of line 286. On the emendation of *sched* to *bled*, see note to line 202.

290   *Trew now*. T; A: *Trew thou now*, with *thou* interlined; W: *Trave* (= *traw*? The reading is uncertain because the top of the word has been cut off by the binder). The a-verse is more effective without the word added for emphasis by the A scribe.

231

291   *Than.* T: *And than.*

292   *carpand.* A (adopted by G and GW); T: *of carpynge*; W: *be talkynge.*

293   *trew.* T: *leve*; W: *byleve.* With some straining, one can find vocalic alliteration in this line: he/*trew*/it//*Hymselfe*/yode. None of the variants helps. The shift in this stanza (more apparent in A) from the verb *lefe* to the verb *trew* for "believe" may mark an emphasis on the theme of truth in stanzas 23–26.

        or. T: *that*; W: *tyll.*

294   *Apperyd.* A (adopted by G); T: *or he appered*; W: *And apered.*

        as clarkes has in mynd. For the idiom see *MED mind(e)* n.(1), sense 5. A different word, such as *prestes*, could, however, bring alliteration to the b-verse, and might be more specific to the subject of belief.

298   *trewyd.* T: *levede*; W: *byleved.*

300   *Furth went.* The weak opening of this stanza echoes line 287, the beginning of the preceding stanza. There is probably the loss of an *s*-word.

        the soth for to say. T: *a soth for to say.* GW point out the important difference between this version, which expresses Christ's purpose, and the reading in T, which is a mere metrical tag (p. 27).

301   *He soght.* T: *he yode to*; W: *To seke.*

        dyssyples. W; A: *dyciplys*; T: *discypills.* The reading is the same in all three texts, but the spelling in W is adopted because it best highlights the alliteration with *soght.*

        taght thaim the treuth. T: *and taghte tham trewthe*; W: *that ever were.*

302   *And syne to.* T: *And sythen to*; W: *Sayth to.* There may be the loss of an *l*-word here. Perhaps *syne to* has replaced *layted*, "search for, seke," a form similar to the variant in W; see *OED lait* v.[2] and *MED leiten* v.(2).

        that Lady that He lufed ay. Perhaps the poet's pronunciation of *Lady* was "lef(e)di." If so, there is here a play upon the aural likeness to *lufed aye.* Similar, if less dramatic, soundplays would also occur in lines 34 and 145.

303   *hurte*. TW: *hurtes*.

304   The quiet constancy of Mary stands in direct contrast to several derogatory comments about the nature of women; compare, for example, the bird to the maiden (stanza 5), Thomas to Mary Magdalene (stanza 23), and the depiction of proud ladies (stanzas 36–37).

307   *Syn*. T: *sythen*; W: *Then*.

     with gamen and glew. Adopted by G and GW; A: *with gamen and with glew*; T: *gamen . . . glew . . .*; W: *myrthes ynowe*. The a-verse has clearly lost alliteration.

308   *even*. TW; A: *ev . . .*

310   *gode*. AT: *gud*; W: *good*. The word elsewhere rhymes with *yode*, *rod(e)* ("rood"), *flode*, *blod*, and *mode* (lines 286, 329, 513). The spelling in A, consistently *gud*, has been emended throughout to *gode*.

312   Mary's ascension to heaven marks another moment of transcendent reunion: "when she was endlesly thorh plente of Charite knyt to hire blesed son Jesu and he to hire" (Love, *Mirror*, ed. Sargent, p. 29, lines 18–20); compare notes to lines 115 and 274–79.

313   *lufe*. TW: *trewlufe*.

314   The alliterative pattern suggests that *j* (which is vocalic) alliterates with *h*: *hafe/joy/hart//gentil/Chyld*. The sounds are also paired in lines 146, 163, and 183 (see note).

316   *bylde*. W; A: *belde*; T: *b . . . .* Spelling emended for rhyme. For the verb, see *MED bilden* v., "to dwell, settle, live." The verb appears with the Holy Ghost in the context of the Annunciation in *Ecce ancilla Domini*: "Tho holy goste will in thee bildon" (ed. Chambers and Sidgwick, p. 113).

317   *same*. T: *samen*; W: *hole*.

     and. T: *thase*.

     Thre. ATW. An editorial error committed by GW has caused confusion about this line in the MSS. GW omitted the word *thre*, which appears in both MSS (as *iij* in T). Smithers noted the error and pointed out that G had printed the proper rhyme-word (p. 53). Wrenn checked A only, noted that it had the proper word, and criticized GW for not giving "greater attention to the Oxford text" (p. 376). Later, in an analysis of W, N. F. Blake wrote:

> In one instance WW has a rhyme which may represent the original one not found in either of the extant manuscripts. At line 317 *thre* . . . is missing in both B.M. and Bod. But as the reviser has a line of his own very much like this one at line 82 and as he was attentive to the rhyme, we cannot be certain that this rhyme is original, though it seems probable. (p. 196)

Blake failed to determine that line 82 appears in A and that both A and T have the rhyme-word *thre* needed at line 317.

319   *Trewfull.* TW: *trewlufe.* This curious word recurs at line 326, and at line 339 scribe A wrote *trewfull* but corrected it to *trewlufe.* Possibly scribe A was mistaken here too and failed to correct himself. It is also possible, however, that this new word represents an authorial play upon ideas and sounds, analogous to the wordplay in *ful lufly* (line 67); for this reason the unique readings in A are retained. *Trewfull* would here mean "truthful one" (i.e., Christ). Truth has become a dominant theme throughout the depiction of Christ's Resurrection (compare note to line 293 and Christ's role teaching *the treuth trew* [line 301]). At line 326 the word may also contain a triple pun: "truthful one," "tree-full" (that is, the Cross bearing its burden), and "trefoil" (the Trinity). GW suggest the last meaning (see their notes to lines 42, 81, and 319). For a similar wordplay in other alliterative poems, compare *Awntyrs* 510: "Trifeled withe tranes [var.: trayfoyles, "trefoils"] and true-loves bitwene," and *Plant-Names* 49: "Tomesyn with trefoyles and trewlovys feyre."

320   *lufys that.* T: *leves in ther;* W: *trysteth on that.*

       be begyld. T; AW: *be gyled.* The spelling found in T (*bigyled*) has been emended for rhyme; compare line 345.

322   *ilka.* T: *ilk;* omitted in W.

324   *Whar.* T: *ther.*

325   *joy.* TW; A: *day.* The reading in T and W preserves the vocalic alliteration. The error in A appears to derive from the occurrence of *day* in the preceding line.

326   *hase.* T; A: *iase* (scribal error); W: *hathe.*

326   *Trewfull.* TW: *trewlufe.* See note to line 319.

327   *bodyes.* ATW: *saules.* Alliteration indicates that the original word was *bodyes.* The change in meaning would seem to be insignificant, since bodies and souls both suffer death, and the argument is extended to souls in line 329. This error shared by all three texts shows an earlier reviser of the poem editing out alliteration for "improved" doctrine. The stanzas with the worst alliteration tend to be those that use the theology of the Trinity and Mary to explicate divine events. From a metrical point of view, one can suspect tampering at those points.

      bondage. TW; A: *bondag, dag* written over deleted *ga.*

328   *gyftys.* T: *giffes*; W: *gave.*

329   *owr awn gode.* A: *owr awn gud*; T: *our awen goode*; W: *ony worldes good.* Spelling of *gode* is emended for rhyme; compare note to line 310.

332   *Than.* T: *For than.*

333   *haly with His.* W: *with his holy.*

      hert blod. W; A: *awn blod*; T: *hert* . . . . The reading in TW preserves the better word for alliteration.

336   *Byd.* T: *Bot*; W: *And byd.*

339   *Blyssyd.* The original word may have been *Belufyd.*

      Trewluf. TW; A: *trewluf,* originally *trewfull,* but scribe deleted *full* and wrote *luf* above it. If scribe A's copying of *trewfull* at lines 319 and 326 is correct, the poet's return here to the word *truelove* is appropriate, for now the reference is to the foursome of Mary and the Trinity, and to the four-leaved herb paris that carries the conceit.

340   *in faye.* T: *at assaye.* On this variant, see note to line 267.

341   *wrethed.* TW; A: *grevyd.* T and W preserve the alliterating word.

341   *thre*. W; AT: *thar thre lefes*; G reads T: *the thre lefes*. The length of the line in A and T, beside the compact line in W, suggests that an earlier scribe added superfluous words to make the conceit more explicit.

342   *gode*. AT: *gud*; W: *good*. See note to line 310.

        for. W: *us*, an interesting variant that seems to add vocalic alliteration.

342–47 On the conception of Mary as queen and mediator, see GW's note, which lists several other significant instances in ME, including *Pearl*, lines 441–42 (pp. 28–29). To this list may be added *The Dispute between Mary and the Cross*, lines 456–59 (edited in this volume).

344   *And sare wepes*. W: *Sore wepynge*. *Wepes* might be a substitute for a synonym beginning with *s*, such as *sobbes* or *sorows*.

        gray. The eye color is probably what we would call light blue. "Gray" is the standard color for beautiful eyes in ME literature. *Eyn* seems to alliterate with *owr* in the a-verse, even though *owr* may not receive primary stress.

345   *grett*. ATW: *full*. The loss of this synonym is indicated by the alliteration.

        els whar we. A (adopted by G and GW); T: *and ells were we*; W: *alas we were*.

346   *For*. Omitted in TW.

        pray. The context requires the definition "prey." The *MED*, however, cites no examples of the Virgin Mary winning prey, and only one of Christ. The predatory term is more commonly used of the devil, as one might expect. See *MED prei(e)* n.(2), sense 3(c). Another noun *preie* (a back formation from the verb *preien*), meaning a "request" or "a prayer," does not suit the context.

350   *knele*. TW; A: *knell*. Spelling emended for rhyme.

352   *Nis no wyght in this werld so dern nor so dere*. The texts read:

        A: Thar is no wyght in this werld so dern nor so dere;
        T: Now es no wighte in this werlde so dewe ne so dere;
        W: There is none in this worlde so doughtye nor so dere.

The emended opening of the stanza effectively begins the negatives and *n*-alliteration carried on (secondarily) in the next two lines. The definition of *dern* wanted here, "trusted, discreet," is rare, but compare a line from *Cursor Mundi*, "This Moyses was ful dern and dere to Drightin" (line 6509). See *MED derne* adj., sense 4(a). G adopted the reading *dern* from A; GW define the reading in T, *dewe*, as "proper, true" (p. 29).

353 *ne no.* T; A: *ne*; W: *nor*. The reading in T is adopted for improved meter.

   yf. T: *thof*; W: *thoughe*. Compare notes to lines 239 and 423.

354 *Ne nan so.* T; A: *Ne no*; W: *Nor no.*

355 *Dede.* T; AW: *deth.* The spelling in T is adopted because *ded(e)* is the northern form used everywhere else in the poem (lines 166, 279, 437, and 484 [a rhyme-word; see note]).

356 *Us lyst.* A (adopted by G and GW); T: *liste us*; W: *Yet lyst us.*

   preste. TW; A: *peste* (mark for *r* omitted).

357 *fele.* TW; A: *fell.* Compare the emended spelling at line 350.

   with swelt and with swown. A: *with swelt or with swone*; T: *we swelte and we swoun*; W: *with swelte and with swowne. And* has been adopted from TW and the spelling of *swown* adopted from W. The noun *swelt*, rare in surviving ME, appears to be a medical term (*MED swelt(e* n.).

360 *fone.* "few," a northern word. On the etymology, see *MED fon* num. The word does not appear in W, in which the bob has been embellished and added to line 362: *Syth put in a pyt and erth upon us done.*

362 *syen.* T: *sythen*; W: *Syth.*

   pytt. T; A: *pyte*; W: *pyt.* T's spelling yields better rhyme.

363 *whytt.* ATW: *qwytt.* The spelling is emended in accord with the northern *wh-*

found for *qw-* elsewhere in A; compare notes to lines 161 and 396. The emended word appears to add *w*-alliteration; compare lines 49 and 502, where *when* appears to alliterate with *w*-words.

365   *For.* W; AT: *Bot for. Bot* recurs in line 367, which would have been copied below this line. Many line-opening conjunctive words appear to be explanatory connectors that could be scribal in origin. Lines often read better without them.

366   *Ware we.* AW: *And we ware*; T: *And we be.* The word *And* (= "if") is again explanatory and probably scribal, added after these two words were inverted. The meter of the line does not require, but does point to, this emendation.

        saules. W; A: *sales* (an aberrant spelling); T: *saule.*

        we suld. A: *we schuld*; T: *that we sall*; W: *they sholde.* The northern spelling *suld*, characteristic of both MSS, is adopted; see note to line 1.

368   *Ne.* Omitted in T; W: *Nor.*

        in. T: *bi.*

        tharof. TW: *that tharof.*

369   *How fell ne how fayr.* T: *how felle wayes ne how ferre*; W: *How ferre and how fele.* The spellings in A suggest the presence of a pun ("cruelly/favorably" and "much/far"), while only the "much/far" interpretation appears in TW. See *MED fallen* v., sense 34a(c), for the idiom *faire falles him*, "he comes (to something) by luck or good fortune." On the spelling *fayr* for "far" (and another possible pun), compare note to line 44. GW translate the phrase in T as: "what hard ways nor how far" (p. 29) As they point out, the sense of contrast and the singular *way* found in A (lines 369–70) are more faithful to the biblical reference Matthew 7.13–14.

        fare. TW; A: *fayre.* Spelling *fare* (which is typical elsewhere in A) is adopted for rhyme; compare line 374.

370   *way is.* T: *wayes are*; W: *wayes is.*

371   *passes*. AT: *comes*; W: *cometh*. The reading in ATW is a weak substitution for a verb probably beginning with *p*. This word is the likeliest candidate.

372   *may*. T; A: *sal*; W: *shall*. The interplay of *m* and *w* in the a-verse is typical of the style of the poem, making the variant in T the better choice.

374   *fare*. TW; A: *fayre*. See note to line 369.

375   *thare*. T: *full yare*; W: *there*. On the thorn/yogh confusion, see note to line 57.

377   *paynes*. The original word may have been the relatively rare northern word *stanges*, "stings, pains," which would offer soundplay with *strang* and *lang*, as well as alliteration. See *MED stang* n.(2), sense (c).

      are so. W: *be full*.

378   *gret fyres grym*. W; AT: *gret fyres and grym*.

      ar graythed. T; A: *ar geder*; W: *be made*. The frequent alliterative collocation of *greithen* and *gate* strengthens the likelihood that the reading in T is the original one. See *MED greithen* v., senses 1a and 5.

      gate. TW; A: *gayte*. Spelling emended for rhyme.

379   *Thar is*. T; A: *Is thar*; W: *Then is there*. The lift on *is*, linking it to the vocalic alliteration of the b-verse, works best in the word order of T.

      glasyng by. T; A: *gladynge*; W: *glosynge*. The meaning of the word found in T, "slipping by, missing the mark," is especially appropriate for the context, and W's reading lends support to its adoption. See *MED glacen* v. and *glacinge* ger. The reading in A has a weaker meaning, "rejoicing," and is plausibly a misreading of *glasynge*.

      bus. "must." The word is a northern and north midland form of *bihoves*. See *MED bihoven* v.

382   *cry efter*. T: *calle on oure*.

      kynred. A (adopted by G); T: *kynredyn*; W: *kynne folke*.

383   *frayst of that fare, feld.* T; A: *of that fayr felled*; W: *felte the fyer fayled.*

384   *of.* W (adopted by GW, who were unaware of W); AT: *is.* The cause for confusion is easily discerned in the physical similarity between *es* and *of* (see note to line 267). The alliterative pattern of the a-verse is vocalic: a*l/owre/* s*orow.*

        no certan. T: *na certayne ende. Certan* continues the alliteration on *s*

        wate. The verb is the subjunctive first-person plural of *wait*, not the present first-person plural of *wit*, as glossed by GW (p. 47). The meaning is "may count on, expect."

385   *trest.* Syntactically parallel to *wate*, this verb is also the subjunctive, not the infinitive or noun, as suggested by GW (p. xiii).

        mercy. The original word may have been *treuth.*

391   *we hafe to.* TW: *that we hafe.*

392   *umbethynk.* T: *umthynke*; W: *remembre.*

393   *When that brym Lord above His bemes sall blaw.* The texts read:

        A: That gret lord and brym when his bemes sall blaw;
        T: That gret lorde and that grym when his bemys sall blawe;
        W: Whan the grete lorde above his bemes shall blowe.

        The b-verse in AT violates the metrical rules for the number of dips between lifts (Duggan, pp. 570, 578 n. 29). By repositioning *when*, W provides a metrical reading; it also supplies the alliterating word *above*. The second alliterating word in the a-verse is to be found in A, *brym*. The variants can be explained as attempts, first, to gloss *brym* (AW), and, then, to correct alliteration in the a-verse (T).

394   *And the Hy Justyse sall sytt in His gret syse.* The texts read:

        A: And that Hy Justyse sall syte in His syse;
        T: And the hey justys sall sytt apon a ful gret sysse;
        W: And hye Justyse shall syt in his trone.

Adoption of *gret* from T improves the length of the b-verse. On the emended spelling *sytt*, compare notes to lines 284 and 362.

Here begins an extended metaphor of the Last Judgment as a legal courtroom proceeding; the analogy continues through stanza 35. GW cite several ME analogues to this very common medieval conception (p. 30).

395   *folke.* This word looks to be a substitute for a word beginning with *r, w,* or *wr.* The original word could have been *wyghtes,* "creatures" (see note to line 488), or *rynks,* "men, warriors" (*OED rink* sb.¹). A medieval reviser has preferred a more homely term.

396   *Than.* AT; omitted in W.

       whelled. ATW: *ded.* The word found in the texts must have been substituted for the synonym beginning in *wh* (*qu*) used by the poet at line 161.

       upryse. TW: *sal up rysse.*

397   *schrynk.* ATW: *lett.* The word in the texts has the appropriate meaning, "refrain (from), hinder," but it lacks alliteration. The standard alliterative phrase is *schrynkes for schame,* "draws back in shame"; compare *Death and Liffe,* line 400; and *Golagras and Gawain,* line 1077.

       scham. T: *chance.* A and W preserve the alliterating word. Smithers criticized GW for failing to adopt the superior reading from A (p. 53).

       schaw. AT: *schewe;* W: *showe.* Compare line 416. The northern spelling is indicated by the rhyme.

398   *maynpryse.* This legal term refers to the release of a prisoner by somebody's undertaking to act as surety for his appearance at court. The reference to a fee implies the payment of bail as part of the *maynpryse.* The legal language is, of course, a figurative way to say that there is no release from the final reckoning. On the inability of kinfolk to help souls in this plight (in this and the last stanza) compare the general theme of kinship in the poem (note to line 274–79).

402   *owre.* TW: *a.* On the evidence of T and W, this word may be an error, caused by attraction to the word in the two preceding lines. There is, however, no need to emend.

402   *crysom*. Probably "christening robe," but the meaning is uncertain. The term usually refers simply to the cloth wrapped about the head of a newly baptized infant, but the context implies a garment of some sort. See *MED crisme* n., sense 2(a), where this line is cited.

alane. AW (adopted by GW); T: *onane*.

404   *ar*. W: *be*, an interesting reading because it may add a secondary alliteration upon *b*. *Ar* is worth retaining, however, for its support of *h*/vowel alliteration in the b-verse.

courte. AW (adopted by G); T: *count*. Both readings fit the context, but A and W more directly conform to the courtroom metaphor.

behoves us. T; A: *us behoves*; W: *us behoveth*. Duggan's note that the b-verse in T is unmetrical is in error; he probably meant the b-verse of line 405 (p. 578 n. 29), which is suitable in A. The b-verse of A in this line is, however, unmetrical, which is why T has been adopted.

405–06   T has two variant lines:

Ther all sall be soyttures bothe the bonde and the free
The saulles and the bodyes that lange hafe bene sere.

GW read *hase* for *hafe*. *Soyttures*, "petitioners," is another legal term; see *MED sutour* n., senses 2 and 3.

407   *Tham behoves to be sam at that sembelee*. The texts read:

A: Behoves to be sam at that sembelee;
T: Tham [behov]es samen come unto that semelye;
W: Behoveth to be present at the semble.

T's word *tham* has been adopted to improve the line found in A; it adds to the *th*/*m* consonance. The alliterative pattern is formally *aab*/*xb*: *behoves*/*be*/*sam*//*that*/*sembelee*. It is fascinating to note how in lines 405–08 a continuous interplay of the sounds [b] and [s] reinforces the subject of bodies and souls.

408   *And ilke*. T: *ilk a*; W: *Every*.

408   *sall*. T; A: *sale* (an aberrant spelling); W: *shall*.

    to. T: *at*.

    fett. T; A: *seche*; W: *seke after*. The reading in T is adopted because: (1) it is the harder reading; (2) it better suits the context (fetching the bodies, not searching for them, describes the souls' task); and (3) the error is attributable to the common confusion between *s* and *f*, more often found in A than in T (see note to line 267).

409   *Then*. ATW: *Whan*. Emended for sense.

411   *And never sal sonder efter that day be*. The other texts read:

        T: And nevere sall sonderyng fra that day be;
        W: Never more to sonder after that daye be.

413   *and*. A (adopted by G and GW); T: *in*.

    scord. This verb apears to have been rare in the fourteenth century. See *MED scoren* v., sense (d), and *OED score* v., sense 13.

414   *rowle of record*. "document recording the official list, or material points, of a cause of law"; see *OED roll* sb.[1], senses 2 and 3; *MED rolle* n., sense 1b). According to GW, "The phrase continues the conception of the Last Judgment as a trial of law, the 'roll' being the legal equivalent of 'the books' in Revelation xx. 12" (p. 31).

415   *that ilke*. W: *the*. On the word *ilke* elsewhere, see note to line 510.

416   *schaply*. AT; W: *scharply*; G and GW misread T and print *scharply*.

    schaw. T; A: *schew*; W: *showe*. The spelling of T has been adopted for the rhyme. Compare note to line 397.

418   *Tremland*. T; A: *tremband*; W: *Tremblynge*. The northern variant spelling of T is adopted on the chance that the poet wanted the initial consonants of both syllables heard for alliteration, that is, both *tr* and *l*.

    schakand. T: *qwakande*; W: *quakynge*.

418   *on a.* AW; T: *appon.*

419   *When al the warld is umbsett with water and fire.* The texts read:

> A: When al is unbesett with with water and fire;
> T: When alle umbsett with water and with fyre;
> W: Whan all the world is set with water and fyre.

Again, the best line derives from combined evidence because none of the surviving texts exhibits a fully alliterating line. T's *umbsett* is emended by G to *is umbsett*, by GW to *is unbesett.* GW cite two other English representations of the world's ending in water and fire: *Cursor Mundi* and the OE *Be Domes Dæge* (p. 31).

420   *fle.* T: *flye.*

421   *greved.* TW; A: *grewed* (probably to be read *grevved*).

422   *synfull saulles.* AW: *synfull wreches*; T: *a synfull wreche.* Alliteration is lost; the word *saulles* restores it and fits with the play upon *ll* in the line. The error may have originated as an omission after *synfull.*

     He. AW (adopted by G and GW); T: *we.*

     thar sall. T: *sall ther.*

423   *Dare.* TW: *than dare.*

     yf. T: *thofe.* The usage in W, when it was probably archaic, helps to confirm *yf* = "though" in the poet's usage; compare lines 239 and 353.

     myght desyre. AW: *wald desyre*; T: *wold gyff hyre.* The auxiliary verb is changed to the form that alliterates; the error is common throughout the three texts. The reading in T is odd even in the context of the legal metaphor. Translating the phrase in T to mean "though she would give payment," GW remark that:

> The idea may be that Mary would be willing to repay her faithful servitors by pleading for them at the Last Judgement, but, as the sentence stands, it seems to mean that Mary would be willing to bribe the Judge to have mercy on sinners. (p. 31)

424   *to*. T: *till*.

429   *For*. A (adopted by G and GW); T: *Fo*.

430   *The*. T: *Than the*.

      warkes of mercy. That is, the Seven Corporal Works of Mercy (as distinguished from the Seven Spiritual Works of Mercy). The classification is medieval, but based upon Christ's words to his disciples at the Last Supper (Matthew 25.42–45), of which this stanza is a paraphrase. GW refer to two depictions of the motif in medieval art: Van der Weyden's triptych in the Madrid Museum and the illuminated *Biblia sacra* (pp. 31–32). For a collection of ME references, see *MED merci* n. 5(g).

      He rakynys all seven. T; A: *he sall rakyn tham seven*; W: *he wyll reken them seven*. The b-verses in A and W are unmetrical, according to the rules extracted by Duggan (p. 570). In this line it appears that *war-* alliterates with *r-*, and the second syllable of *mercy* alliterates with *seven*, in the pattern *axb/ab*.

431   *When*. T: *When that*.

432   *was thrysty*. T: *askede yow a drynk*.

      hard. T: *ne harde*.

433   *When*. T: *and when*.

434   *me*. TW: *ye me*.

      even. AW (adopted by G and GW); T: *never*. See note to line 436.

435   *vysett*. TW: *vesett me*.

436   *comforth*. TW: *comforthede me*.

      wald I here neven. A (adopted by G and GW); T: *wolde ye here never*; W: *worde I here meven*. T loses the rhyme words (*even/neven*) in line 434 and this line by substituting phrases of negative accusation that conform to the biblical reference, but these insertions do not fit the pattern of the stanza, which is interrogatory in the fashion of a legal proceeding.

437   *beryall*. TW: *berying*.

me by-sted. T; AW: *had me sted*. The reading in T provides alliteration.

439   *whare*. TW: *when*.

440   *Ever*. AW (adopted by G and GW); T: *Everer*.

441   *The*. TW; A: *ye*. A's reading is clearly incorrect and again exemplifies the confusion between thorn and yogh (see note to line 57).

443   *wil schew*. W; A: *sal schew*; T: *schall schew*. The reading in W preserves alliteration; A is a misreading. Thornton (or a predecessor) has tried to supply alliteration by writing the midland spelling *schall*, but this spelling is uncharacteristic of both MSS. Moreover, both *sall* and *suld* are used by the poet to alliterate with *s*; see notes to line 1 and 57.

us His. W; A: *us*; T: *his*. W preserves the best reading for this line, and, as a combination of the evidence in A and T, it has a degree of likelihood. Both pronouns are probably original, with the error in each case caused by the need to copy two short but similar words.

444   *wytter*. T; AW: *bytter*. The reading in T is the rarer, as well as the alliterating, word and is more likely original than the reading in A and W. A hastily formed *w* could have been mistaken for a *b*. For similar errors see notes to lines 119 and 188.

445   *bus*. T: *than sall*; W: *must*.

446   *abyd*. T: *habyde*. Compare line 4.

447   *nane*. AW (adopted by G and GW); T: *for nane*.

448   *ne prelates nor persons.* T: *and persones and prelatis*; W: *nor prelates or persones*; G emends *persones: parsones.* The inverted word order of T helps to confirm that *persons* is to be defined "parsons." The line depicts ecclesiastics of various rank.

449   *Thar.* T: *Thies*; omitted in W.

        juellars. T; A: *the domes men*; W: *juges*; G and GW: *mellarse* (a misreading of T). The readings of A and W are glosses of the more difficult word in T, "jewellers," which is understood specifically as "appraisors, evaluators of worth." The contrast is between those who hold judgmental power over earthly things (judges and jewelers) and the power of God as the ultimate judge over them.

        or. TW: *and.* The reading in A does not significantly differ in meaning from that of the variant.

452   *Thar.* TW; A: *The.* The reading in TW is adopted because it enhances the play upon the rhyme-sound *-ar.*

456   *Rych ladyes ar arayed in robes full yare.* The texts read:

        A: There rych lades has robes full yare;
        T: Thire ladyes are arayede in robys ful yare;
        W: Ryche ladyes that hath robes full yare.

        The superfluous word *there* breaks the crisp style of the alliterating lists in stanzas 35–36; it is most certainly scribal. While T has lost the alliterating word *rych*, it is the only text to preserve *arayed ar* along with the characteristic echoes in *ar*, continued from the preceding wheel and in the stanza's rhyme-words. The word *yare* is more likely an adjective modifying *robes* ("elaborate") than an adverb; this meaning, not in the *OED*, is easily construed from the word's semantic range. For other medieval critiques of female extravagance, see *Knight of La Tour-Landry* (chap. 47–49, 53) and *Cursor* (p. 1550).

457   *Reveres and rybanes on gownes and gyd.* The texts read:

        A: Reveres and rybane gown and gyd;
        T: Revers and rebanes with gownne and with gyde;
        W: Ryches and rubyes with gownes full wyde.

Reveres, "parts of garments turned back so as to exhibit the under-surface," is a French-derived word of rare usage; see *MED revers(e* n. The plurals *rybanes* and *gownes* are adopted from T and W, respectively, because they better fit the context with line 458. The preposition *on* also fits the sense better than does *with*.

458   *botonys*. T; AW: *meroures*. T preserves the alliterating word.

459   *perry*. TW; A: *perly*. The word *perry* for "jewels" is standard in alliterative collocations; the word can also mean "pearl," which helps to explain the reading in A.

460   *cowched on*. T: *at covere*; W: *that coucheth on*. Both T and W agree on an added word *that*. In W, however, which keeps the word *on*, the word *that* may be an addition by the reviser to clarify the syntax. It is not necessary for sense.

461   *schynand*. T; A: *semand*; W: *shynynge*. W corroborates the word in T, which provides better alliteration than does the word in A. A's *sem* could plausibly have derived from a misread *scin*.

        syd. T: *hyde*. The variant in T, meaning "skin," is of interest and preserves the rhyme, but it is somewhat inferior to *syd*, since the stanza concerns the ladies' external adornment. Moreover, *syd* contributes to the line's alliteration upon *s*.

462   *myrth*. TW: *and myrthe*.

463   *unglad*. AW (adopted by G and GW); T: *ungladly*.

465   *to begyn*. T: *that we blyn*. Both variants are attractive. T has a stronger sense of apocalyptic warning: "We had better stop now!" A is more gentle (and attuned to the pastoral spirit of the poem): "Let's begin to amend."

467   *Thare no*. T: *ther es no*; W: *For then is nother*. The verb *es* inserted between these words (found in both T and W) may represent the original reading, but it is not needed for sense or meter.

469   *Be*. "concerning"; GW are incorrect in glossing *be* as "against," as Smithers pointed out (p. 55).

469   *ladyes*. W; A: *lades*; T: *ladys*. Compare line 456.

          noghte anely say I. A: *noghte anely I say*; T: *not alle tell I*; W: *all I will not saye*. GW cite the "better effect" of the reading *anely* in A, versus *alle* in T (p. 34), but they do not adopt it. Emendation of *I say* to *say I* is needed for rhyme.

470   *alswa*. T; A: *also*. The spelling of T is adopted because of evidence elsewhere that the poet differentiated the words *so* and *swa*. See notes to lines 178 and 216–17.

          fele. T; A: *fell*; W: *wele*.

471   *Thar galiard gedlynges kythes gentrye*. The texts read:

          A: This kaliard godlyng kythes gentrye;
          T: Thies galiard gedlynges that kythes gentry;
          W: The galande gedlynge that kithes gentry.

          The reading in T has the better attested forms for *gaillard* adj. and *gadeling* n. (*MED*), and the plural number is better suited to the context. The demonstrative adjective has been emended to the northern plural form that is always used in A.

472   *dengyouse*. T: *denyus*; W: *daynty*.

          thar. "with whom" (literally "where"). The suggestion is that these proud ladies have low moral standards.

          may. T: *many*.

473   *purfels and pelours*. T: *purfelle and peloure*; W: *purfels and perles*.

          hye. TW; A: *hey*. The spelling of T is adopted for the rhyme. Compare line 183.

474   *Hir*. TW; A: *his*. The sense requires this reading from TW; *hir* and the omission of *in* in A are apparently scribal errors. The poet has shifted from a generalized target (*gedlynges* and *damesels*) to a satiric depiction of one such overproud person.

          in. T; omitted in A; W: *the*.

474 *of*. AW (adopted by G and GW); T: *in*.

475–77 On the kinship motif connecting this proud damsel with the maiden who opens the poem, see Fein (1992), p. 122.

477 *hyde*. T; A: *hyed*.

479 *Sall no man scham*. T: *Than schames nane*; W: *No man shall schame*.

   his. TW: *thair*. The reading in A is grammatically better than the variant, but it is interesting that both T and W agree in the reading *thair*. It possibly derives from the same word in the next line.

480 *sall*. T: *may tham*. The repetitions of *sall* prepare for the alliterative linkage of *syn* and *saule*. It is unlikely that *sall* here and in line 479 was originally *schall* (midland form) to alliterate with *scham*; compare notes to lines 57 and 443.

481 *saule*. A: *soule*; T: *full*; W: *foule*. The reading in A echoes the alliteration on *s* (but the spelling with *ou* is unusual). Here the confusion between *s* and *f* appears to have caused the variants in T and W; see note to line 267.

482 *dere*. AT: *sare*; W: *sore*. The reading in ATW looks to be a substitute for a word alliterating on *d*; the obvious choice is *dere*, a similar-looking word. See *MED dere* adv.

483 *al the tym past*; T: *tym paste*. The line in all texts has lost alliteration. An original for *past* may have been *myst* (compare line 338), but this conjectural emendation still would not restore the line's full alliteration.

   crafe. ATW: *crave*. For the rhyme-word spelling with *f*, which appears in *knafe* (line 485), see note to line 21.

484 *ilka ane*. A: *ilka man*; T: *ilk man*; W: *every man*. The original phrase probably did not contain *man*, but was something more akin to the northern form *ilkane*, which would accentuate the vocalic alliteration. See *OED ilkane, ilkone* pron.

   efter his awn ded. The phrase is a pun. For *ded*, "death," see note to line 355; for *ded*, "deeds," compare *mysded*, "misdeeds," line 501 (spelling confirmed by rhyme).

485 *may.* T: *may we.*

   stert. T: *sytt.*

486 *clarkes can.* W; A: *clarkes* (adopted by G and GW); T: *theis clerkes.* The half-line in A is deficient in meter and length; the word *can* in W improves the half-line metrically and echoes the secondary alliteration upon *c.*

487 *And settes on His ryght hand the saules He wil safe.* The texts read:

> A: And settes on His ryght hand thase that he wil have;
> T: He settis one his ryght hande that he will save;
> W: He setteth on his ryght hande the soules that he wyll save.

In T the word *sytt* is deleted after *He.* Only W preserves the b-verse alliterating word *soules.* The rhyme-word *hafe,* found in A and repeated at line 489, is less likely to be original than *safe,* found in TW. For the spelling with *f,* see note to line 21.

488 *wafull wreches.* T: *wafull wyghtis*; W: *synfull wretches.*

   wil. ATW: *may.* Emendation is made for alliteration.

   sped. T: *ther spede.*

489 *Thar sang is of sorow and swa sall thai hafe.* From T. The other texts read:

> A: Sal stand on His left hand and wa sal have;
> W: Shall stande on his lefte hande awaye for to have;
> G/GW emend: Sal stand on His left-hande and wa sall thay have.

The reading in T, adopted here, is the more difficult and vivid line. GW preferred A, observing that T "departs from the Biblical account [Matthew 25.33] and spoils the picture" of the damned divided from the saved (p. 35). But the reading in A lacks alliteration, while that in T preserves it. The wailing lost souls provide counterpoint to Mary's weeping and the Judge's severity.

492 *scho sal se.* T: *that scho sees*; W: *that she shall se.*

494 *dole.* W: *mournynge.*

494   *sal be*. T: *es*.

495   *space*. ATW: *tym*. *Tym* appears to substitute for this synonym supplying alliteration.

           whoso. W: *them that wyll*.

496   *And for to seke socoure, and folys to flee*. T: *And for to seke socoure and folys for to fle*; W: *And seke after socoure and foly to flee*. G and GW omit the second *for* in T.

498   *sall*. W: *wyll*.

499   *dere Lady*. W; AT: *Lady Mary*. W preserves the alliterating word lost in AT.

499–500   GW comment upon Mary's passive role here: "In this poem, Mary is not so much the queen, sure of her request being granted and saving her clients in spite of her Son's anger (as she is represented so often in medieval literature), but rather the gentle feminine advocate, influential indeed, but finally appalled into silence before the Judge's wrath" (p. 35).

500   *to*. T: *till*.

501   *How may we axe mercy fore our mysded*. Taken from W. The other texts read:

           A: How myght thai have mercy fore thar mysdedes;
           T: How may thay hafe mercy for thaire mydede.

           Only W maintains the first-person plural pronouns of the rest of the stanza. It also possesses the more vivid verb *axe*. The rhyme in A is disrupted by the plural *mysdedes*.

502   *when*. T: *when that*.

503   *yare*. A (adopted by G and GW); T: *thare*; W: *thore*. A has the better reading; T's *thare* is redundant after *tharto*. W links the bob to line 504 for an entirely different meaning: *There is no waye but two thore*. On the confusion between thorn and yogh, see note to line 57.

505–06   These lines are transposed in W.

506   *Wheder-swa sall we ga.* AW: *Wheder that we schall ga*; T: *Whethir so sall to ga*; G and GW emend: *Whethir-so sall we ga.* The evidence of both A and T must be combined to recover the sparkling soundplay of lines 504–07. The original word *swa* is discernible in both T's *so* and A's *that we.* See *OED whitherso* adv., and notes to lines 178 and 216–17. On the original northern *sall*, see note to line 57.

507   *fore.* Omitted in T.

508   *hys.* T: *this*; W: *the. Hys* is a plausible and interesting reading, which reinforces the pastoral quality of the bird's speech. The maiden's blessing of the turtle-dove's "body, bones, and blood" (line 509) brings into focus its typological likeness to Christ. The word *hys* suggests the maiden's acquisition of the Truelove (i.e., Christ as Lover and Physician) through the bird's instructive words. Several situations of reciprocal verbal graciousness occur in this stanza: the bird counsels the girl, who, in turn, blesses the bird; repentant readers are bid to pray devoutly to Mary, who may, in turn, intercede for them. The line in W differs verbally: *Thus the bryght byrde taught the true maye.*

510   *Unto this ilk.* T: *Unto that ilke*; W: *Unto the.* The poet shifts from the sermon and story to the moral, which justifies the use of *ilk* here. The monotonous repetition in A and T of *ilk* is probably, however, part scribal addition. It appears in lines 512 (A only), 513 (both texts), and 515 (T only); compare notes to lines 79, 80, and 415. The word never appears in W.

    red I. TW: *I rede that.*

511   *That.* A: *At. At* is a northern form of "that," which also appears in A at line 514, and in T at line 460. Because the texts lack other evidence of this form, it is here emended.

    may do oure message. A: *wyll do oure message.* T: *will bere oure message*; W: *wolde our message do.* An *m*-word seems lacking in the a-verse; the most probable place for loss lies in the substitution of *wyll* for *may.* Note the similar usage in line 514, and compare the variants in line 41.

512   *And.* T: *And that scho.*

    oure. T; A: *that ilk*; W: *the.* See note to line 510.

512   *the*. T: *that*.

513   *thase ilk thre lefes*. W: *the thyrde lefe*. The reading in W harms the conceit by illogically having Mary appeal solely to the Holy Ghost (the third leaf).

513–15 T reads:

> Unto thase ilke thre leves that we may wyn with mode
> That grace grauntede grete God that dyede on Gud Fryday
> Unto that ilke ferthe lefe gracyouse and gude.

The reading found in T is a clear example of *homoeteleuton*: A scribe preceding Thornton omitted the words *gracyous . . . lefes* (lines 513–14) because of the repeated word *lefes*. Then he or a later scribe compensated for the error by tacking appropriate rhymes onto what he had and copying the omitted section in inverted form as a final line to the stanza. There is no physical evidence of revision in T. The resulting two final lines have different meanings. A and W end with a valedictory prayer, asking God's grace in winning the truelove and appropiately invoking the Cross (symbolic counterpart to the truelove). T ends with the special dispensation granted to Mary to act as intercessor on behalf of mortal sinners. The poor syntactic link between octave and bob in T supports the superiority of A.

gode. AT: *gud*; W: *good*. See note to line 310.

514   *thase*. W: *the*.

that. TW; A: *at*. See note to line 511.

515   *grace*. On the medicinal pun latent in this word ("herb" and "divine grace"), set up by the poet's botanical conceit, see Fein (1991), pp. 308–09. An analogous, if simpler, instance of putative herbal cures for spiritual diseases occurs in the interesting, highly alliterated lyric "As I Walked upon a Day" (ed. Brown, *Rel. Lyr. XV*, pp. 273–77, 347–48).

517   *walay*. T: *lay*; W: *valaye*. The variants are all of interest. *Walay* is an unrecorded form of *wellaway*, "lament" (see *OED wellaway* sb., sense B). It is the strongest reading. T has the word *lay*, "song," a genre that seems less specific to *Truelove* than *walay*. The exemplar of W must have read *walay*, too, but the sixteenth-century reviser changed its meaning and context: *This I herde in a valaye walkynge* (*walkynge* derives from the bob being affixed to the wheel-line).

The Bird with Four Feathers

Introduction

Many Middle English moral lyrics open with an ambling narrator. Strolling in an outdoor place, unconfined by the walls of constructed dwellings, this person sets aside his daily affairs and momentarily locates the sacramental in the midst of a leafy "church," with an architrave of tree branches and a choir of birdsong. The man who is responsive will learn something here that the hubbub of human commerce normally obscures from understanding. He will listen to the language of birds, and properly attuned to its chirpy, cryptic repetitions, his heart will absorb and retain sacred truths.

Such a premise underlies *The Bird with Four Feathers*. The sound pattern of the Latin refrain *"Parce michi, Domine!"* mimics a birdsong tweeted to the auditor at regular intervals. As a sound different from English, the Latin words of penance — at the heart of the poet's message — can masquerade as chirps from an avian plaintiff. Upon hearing the words uttered in a mournful fashion, the auditor is curious: who has harmed the bird by plucking her four feathers, and why does she sing this song? The bird's response insists that the answer cannot be a simple verbal translation of the song; it may be uttered only with heartfelt pain, and the auditor must likewise feel the pain in order to comprehend the meaning. The words represent a deeply experienced condition, and one's utterance of them requires devotion and sentient understanding.

A penitential poem, *The Bird with Four Feathers* is designed to stir Christian contrition in a reader who will use it to meditate upon mankind's need of God's mercy. The bird, who is female in the fictional prologue, becomes an entirely human male in its sad, moralized account of four lost feathers. The bird's tale allows the poet to teach behind an avian mask, while the narrator taking his outdoor stroll becomes a figure for the reader. The bracketed structure of [narrator {bird} narrator] puts the heart of the painful experience at some distance from the reader, that is, within the life of the bird, but the process of reading and understanding the unfolding, ever-deepening meaning of *parce* is intended to bring the message home to the reader, who will see that he intimately shares the condition of the everyman bird.

Compared to the bird, the narrator projects a consciousness barren of experience, a naïveté in the natural world that must be informed so that a newly acquired knowledge of his own life, death, and sinfulness will henceforth guide his self-conscious actions. He too will lose his four worldly attributes — youth, beauty, strength, and riches. Possessing them, he is distracted from true self-knowledge; only in losing them will he finally understand that they kept him from God. The poet asks that the reader consider this fact in advance, lest it take him unawares. The poet assumes, too, that every bearer of such wisdom will perforce sing the charm-like incantation "*Parce mihi, Domine!*" — "Spare me, Lord!" The song is taken to be the spontaneous reflex of a Christian awareness of one's primal condition, that is, of knowing one exists not just in the moment but as part of an expansive and purposeful plan.

The author of *The Bird with Four Feathers* assumes that emotions have the power to effect spiritual change. The bird is reluctant to reveal her inner pain because verbal expression will renew it. But she agrees to speak if the listener promises to absorb the message inwardly. An understanding of pathos that is both aesthetic and psychological is in evidence here. Words serve merely as vehicles to transport emotion from speaker to listener. They are not therapy for the speaker so much as for the hearer, who is expected to consume inwardly the content. The words are efficacious and healing in the most literal sense. It is quite clear, moreover, that the human capacity to respond emotionally — which is central to the redemptive process — derives ultimately from God. The first epithet for the Deity is, significantly, "Kyng of Pytee" (line 13), and the poet's penultimate line expresses the point of "*parce*" — to win divine pity. The speaker's sincerity is designed to move not just human listeners, but also God, the source of all compassion.

Outdoors, away from human society, the narrator learns about his true inner nature. His forested surroundings suggest the primal quality of this experience, and even his listening pose foreshadows the message he will hear. Supine amidst the flowers, he hears the cry of the featherless bird, and the lesson turns out to be about man's likeness to the ephemeral spring flower (stanza 19). The poem circles from the physical floral landscape engulfing the narrator to a moral symbolism of each individual withering like a blossom.[1] The supine narrator is both man refreshed by

---

[1] The associations must have been commonplace to an audience closely familiar with the Nine Lessons from Job found in the Dirge (the source for the refrain here and for *Pety Job*). Walter Skirlaw, bishop of Durham (1370–1410), prefixed to his will a typical lamentation that "all knowledge and glory, like flowers in the field, was [sic] destined to die and . . . all rational creatures, after the flowing of the course of their lives, come back to the sad thought of fearful death" (paraphrased by Jonathan Hughes, *Pastors and Visionaries: Religion and Secular Life in Late Medieval Yorkshire* [Woodbridge, Suffolk: Boydell, 1988], p. 268).

life and man doomed to die and return to the earth. In the only two illustrations of the poem found in manuscripts, the narrator's reclining pose is prominent (Plates 3 and 4).

In its lyric and religious conception *The Bird with Four Feathers* is carefully crafted, and its technical aspects display a similar artistic precision. As a refrain poem its stanzas of varying length (eight, twelve, sixteen, and twenty lines) are unusual. Overall there are twenty stanzas, an interesting round number; the bird's disquisition centers upon the number four; and the poem totals 240 lines. One might well suspect numerological ordering within the poem, or, at the least, some degree of symmetrical construction. The end of stanza 10 clearly marks a midpoint that is both numerical and rhetorical: at 120 lines the bird has described two feathers and begins an account of the third one. A. Kent Hieatt and Constance Hieatt have proposed a full

Plate 3. *The Bird with Four Feathers*, an illustration of the bird and the reclining listener (MS Douce 322, fol. 15a). The banner between them bears the refrain, "*Parce michi . . .*" The colophon to *Pety Job*, which precedes the text of *Bird*, appears above the drawing. For the illustration to *Pety Job* found in the same manuscript, see Plate 5. (Reproduced by permission of the Bodleian Library, University of Oxford.)

257

numerical structure (pp. 24–25), suggesting that the poem is organized in:o two "wings" with symmetrical bipartite structures (stanzas 1–7 and 14–20). The structure of each "two-feathered" wing, in terms of stanzaic line lengths, is: 12,8,8 / 12,12, 12,12; and 12,12,12,12 / 12,8,8. By this analysis the remaining central section consists of 88 lines (stanzas 8–13). The numerical arrangement of lines is, then, 28:48:88: 48:28, four feathers on two wings, one on either side of a central "body" of text.

What meaning the poet may have intended by these symmetries remains an open question. He apparently expected the poetry to "embody" the woeful bird and her lost feathers. Symmetrical structures are not uncommon in medieval verse, and often there is a real correspondence of verbal shape to the content, as, for example, in an allegorical poem on the periods of human life. The eighty-two-stanza poem seems loosely composed as it rambles through "mankind's" successive stages, foibles, and temptations over a lifespan of one hundred yeras. Nonetheless, his fiftieth year occurs percisely at stanza 41, midway in the poem.[2] A central depiction of kingship also not uncommon at the middle of poems with symmetries of structure.[3] In such works the poet invites a reader to see the midpoint as a sovereign moment, a pinnacle of power, human or divine. In two other works appearing here, *The Four Leaves of the Truelove* and *The Dispute between Mary and the Cross*, the strophic arrangement of ideas seems designed to recreate the shape of the Cross, with Christ's redemptives powers made manifest at the central point. Both of these poems, unlike *The Bird with Four Feathers*, are explicitly about the Crucifixion.

Nonetheless, the similarities between *The Bird with Four Feathers* and *The Four Leaves of the Truelove* are many: both pieces are *chansons d'aventure* with loquacious birds and meditative sermons upon a four-fold idea. Both develop a structure of two bilateral parts that straddle a middle section, leading one to surmise that, in each instance, a central metaphor is being physically "worded" out — four feathers on a bird's body or four leaves on a stem. For both visualized metaphors the typological source would be the shape of the Cross, or its correspondent, Christ's wounded body. It may be that the general set-up of a bird in a tree prepares a devout medieval reader for a christological meaning and pattern. Even though the bird here is primarily a figure for mankind struck down by age and fortune, her suffering in four

---

[2]*The Mirror of the Periods of Man's Life*, ed. F. J. Furnivall, *Hymns to the Virgin and Christ*, EETS o.s. 24 (1868; rpt. New York: Greenwood, 1969), pp. 58–78.

[3]See A. C. Spearing, "Central and Displaced Sovereignty in Three Medieval Poems," *Review of English Studies*, n.s. 33 (1982), 247–61; for the form in Renaissance works, see Alistair Fowler, *Triumphal Forms: Structural Patterns in Elizabethan Poetry* (Cambridge: Cambridge University Press, 1970).

extremities and her added heartache would recall in faint outline the wounds of Christ.

This meaning exists as a shadow behind the bird's lament over her loss of four worldly attributes to the ravages of time and fortune. The complaint maintains a mournful, entirely human perspective. There is, however, buried in the bird's words of devotion to God, a deeper pattern that seems to complement the structural symmetries. Just as the first reference to God, "Kyng of Pytee," is especially meaningful, subsequent calls to God allude to the four mourned attributes as understood in divine terms, and together they sequentially construct Christ's life as a man and role as Savior. Lamenting her lost Youth, the bird appeals to Christ incarnate as human infant, "Hym . . . that Marie bare" (line 63). Bracketing this appeal at the other end of the complaint, when the bird mourns lost Riches, she appeals to Christ's rich gift to mankind — "Jhesu, for Thi precious blood" (line 187). The theme is Christ's Incarnation, the demonstration of God's mercy that forms the basis of the penitent's hopeful petition, "*Parce michi, Domine!*"

These calls to God occur at symmetrical points, the one to Jesus as Infant in stanza 6, the other to Jesus as Crucified in stanza 15. These stanzas each occur six in from the endpoints. Counting in two more stanzas in each direction (stanzas 8 and 13), one finds God initially called upon in His might, an attribute that is softened in the second reference to include God's mercy.[4] Again there is a sequence, from Might, to Might and Mercy, the change wrought by Christ's living as a man.

Moving inward again, to the two central stanzas (10 and 11), one discovers a midpoint exemplum on sovereignty: Solomon was a fair and worthy king (lines 105–08), but as any mortal will, he eventually fell (in his case, to concupiscence); the narrating everyman bird was also at one time "a man of mochel myght" (line 123), but he too fell away from God; God alone is the ultimate "Kyng, corowned in hevenne blys" (line 131).

The various terms for God, always strategically placed in an appropriate context, create a composite portrait of God in the sequential roles adopted by Christ: King of Pity, Son of Mary, God of Might, King of Heaven, God of Mercy, Crucified Man. These hidden signs complement the "winged" shape of the poem: Divine Kingship in the middle, flanked by Divine Power and the Incarnation on one side, Divine Mercy and the Crucifixion on the other. Framing the whole is a conception of God

---

[4]The naming of God's power and mercy occurs at either end of the "middle" section of 88 lines. The first one accompanies the bird's description of her second feather, Beauty (line 91). The second reference to God's "Myghtes Most" comes, appropriately, in the discussion on Strength (line 153); the additional mention of mercy (line 159) implies a strength greater than brute power.

as font of "pytee," ever responsive to a heartfelt cry of "*parce*." Ultimately, the poem
— if read repeatedly, learned by heart, or meditated upon devoutly — would come to
reveal an emanation of the divine within its lines. The well-attuned meditant would
experience something approaching a fulfillment of the pious petition in the last lines:

> And *parce* geteth Godis pyté,
> And scheweth to us His blessed face. (lines 239–40)

God's "face" is enigmatically present to be discovered by the literaté meditant whose
search for God's "pytee" is earnestly pursued.[5]

By the end of the poem the guise of an innocent narrator gives way to a tone of
newfound sagacity. Lee Patterson observes that, in general, penitential lyrics tend to
dilute the personal pain of a confession by shifting, in the end, to a conventional
didactic stance:

> . . . possessed of his bitter wisdom, he [the speaker] is self-evidently no longer the man he
> once was, and in the very course of the poem he is transformed from penitent into sage,
> directing his words to an audience that has not yet learned the lesson he knows so well. He
> becomes, in effect, an agent of the institutional authority from which he was originally
> alienated, and his assumption of these familiar tones marks his assimilation into the body
> of the saved. (p. 389)

Patterson observes that the typical movement from needing to repent to preaching
the need to repent "is bought at the price of what seems to be a self-alienation. . . .
Penitential feelings . . . are thus simply set aside in favor of a consoling self-
righteousness" (p. 389).

However, looked at in light of Patterson's views, *The Bird with Four Feathers*
appears not to settle, finally, into comfortable self-complacency. The narrator's initial
naïveté is born of his careless youth, and listening to the penitential bird is at first
a casual, curious diversion. But the words will, in actuality, penetrate his soul as the
bird advises in stanza 4. His final stance is that of a penitent, while, interestingly, the
bird herself seems stuck in a mood of complaint. Despite the example of Job's patient
piety, the bird's final words express nothing more than the universal fact of death:

> Alle that lyveth, bothe powre and ryche,
> Shall deye unknowyng of her day. (lines 231–32)

The bird's pain remains the pain of a simple bird whose feathers are plucked; her
lament is over what she has lost. The embedded signs of God seem to lie outside her

---

[5]The poet's structural use of the number eight might also participate in this naming of God;
see Peck, pp. 9–21.

perception. The bird without reason is ultimately excluded, while the wit-endowed narrator learns a valuable lesson about the human condition. His last words to the reader are to heed the lesson he has newly absorbed, to sing with inner comprehension *"parce,"* and to seek the godly vision that is implicit in the verses sung by the bird. Penitential *aventure* is both "bale and bote" (painful effect and remedy; line 236), an ongoing experience of sorrow, reward, and sorrow renewed.

The pairing of *The Bird with Four Feathers* with *Pety Job* in three manuscripts was the logical inspiration of some fifteenth-century compiler. Sharing the same refrain, the two long, penitential lyric complaints are both products of serious poets. All three volumes are from the London area, as is a fourth one, Bodley 596 (used for the copy-text here), connected with Westminster Abbey.[6] Hope Emily Allen mentions that several works appearing in manuscript with *Pety Job,* such as *The Bird with Four Feathers,* "resemble each other in style, metre, and cadence, and they probably all emanate from the same source" (p. 370), and she refers specifically to the French literary fashions current in the capital in the mid-fifteenth century, which is about when *Pety Job* was written. While *The Bird with Four Feathers* would have similarly appealed to cosmopolitan readers with cultivated, devotional tastes, its time of composition preceded that of *Pety Job* by many years. Its relationship to lyrics in the Vernon series and to the alliterative *Four Leaves of the Truelove* points to the period 1390–1410,[7] a date allowing sufficient time for several variant texts — altered or abridged — to crop up in manuscripts of the mid-fifteenth century and later.

These doctored texts reveal that not every fifteenth-century reader was alert to the niceties of form matched to meaning, since several editors felt free to obliterate the poem's artistic, devotional structure in preference for a tighter narrative or for stanzas of uniform length. The least drastic alteration occurs in Royal 18 A.x, where an editor decided that the poem should end with the exemplum on Job, the biblical author of the refrain. This person simply left out the last two stanzas, removing the

---

[6]The pairing of *Bird* and *Pety Job* may have come about through William Baron, who is associated with two manuscripts. The Baron arms appear on the present first leaf of Bodley 596 (the earliest manuscript of *Bird*), added there apparently after it had lost its opening 127 folios. William Baron was a feoffee of John Shirley in 1444, and his granddaughter was professed into the nunnery at Dartford in 1478. Sometime between then and his death in 1484 William bestowed Douce 322 to Dartford for her use. (I am grateful to Doyle for providing this information.) A discussion of the cultural setting for Douce 322, Harley 1706, and Trinity R.3.21 appears in the Introduction to *Pety Job.*

[7]Praising its "pithy phrase and vigorous description," Brown places *The Bird with Four Feathers* in an anthology of fourteenth-century verse, beside the Vernon series, and comments that, despite the poem's allegorical quality, "its refrain and its moral observations relate it . . . closely to many of the Vernon poems" (p. xxi).

Plate 4. *The Bird with Four Feathers*, the incipit and initial B decorated with foliage (TCC MS R.3.21, fol. 34a). Four birds (the speaking one has a banner in its beak) perch above the reclining listener, whose hand is raised in a sign of benediction. The upper banner wrongly assigns authorship to John Lydgate. *Pety Job* follows *Bird* in this manuscript and is likewise illustrated (Plate 6). (Reproduced by permission of the Master and Fellows of Trinity College, Cambridge.)

bird and narrator's final words and creating a situation in which the principal protagonists have vanished from the poem. Two other variants were much more destructive: zealous revisers attempted at least twice to give the poem the metrical uniformity of either eight-line stanzas or twelve-line stanzas. Moreover, in the revised copies that survive many whole stanzas have been excised or inadvertently omitted, leaving the original argument blurred beyond recognition. These revisers and copyists were evidently blind to the carefully numbered, shaped structure and the embedded namings of God that are to be found in the original poem. One compiler, a Glastonbury monk of about 1450, shows a collector's taste for proverbs and moral *chansons d'aventure* in his commonplace book. To judge from the garbled form of his redaction of *Bird*, he was attracted to the poem for its sententious wisdom — expounded in its refrain and moral exemplums — without much attention paid to the narrative logic of the bird's lament. His careless transcription entirely omits the third feather.[8] The editor of the eight-line stanzaic version (found in Harley 2380) has substituted a rather pedestrian structure; after a five-stanza prologue, the laments for individual feathers fall in place methodically: Feather One in stanza 6; Feather Two in stanza 8; Feather Three in stanza 10; and Feather Four in stanza 12. By the conclusion in stanza 13 the narrator has been forgotten, but nonetheless the penultimate line seems a gloss designed to provide the hidden name of God, who "ys Fader and Sun and the Holy Gast."[9]

There remained, however, an audience for the poem in its original form, readers who were undeterred, apparently, by the stanzas of irregular length and who would have wanted to grasp the appeal from bird to "Man!" as a serious poeticized message in touch with the sacred realm. The continued copying of the twenty-stanza poem in London through the later fifteenth century, next to other serious devotional texts, indicates a respect for the poet's effort to supply an innovative aid for readers in their private meditations. In particular, one may note the neat layout of the piece in Harley 1706, which helps to showcase the poem's symmetry. Copied in six even columns of forty lines, the midpoint occurs, appropriately, at the top of the fourth column.

If there had not been readers who understood the method of the verse, its survival fully intact in several copies of a generation or two later would be remarkable. A well-educated, very pious, aristocratic society, customers of the booktrade in London with close ties through family and patronage to several religious houses, appears to have promoted a demand for texts that promised both moral edification and mental challenge. *The Bird with Four Feathers* is the kind of text that asks one to meditate

---

[8]The monk may have had before him a complete version that had been edited into 12-line stanzas; the fragment preserved in Bodl. Lat. misc. e 85 — which appears to derive from the same version — ends imperfectly, but for what it has, it includes the stanzas omitted in the commonplace book. Rigg comments that the abridgement in the Trinity O.2.38 copy "may have been intentional, but the omission of [lines] 121–32 [the account of the third feather] . . . was certainly a mistake" ([1968], p. 53).

[9]The text of a late sixteen-line lyric (*Parce mihi O Lord Moste Excellent*) suggests that one's hope in repeating the refrain is to see God's hidden face. Job does in fact see it in the illustrations to *Pety Job* (Plates 5 and 6). Compare the gloss by Chaucer's Parson, *CT* X(1) 183–84 (*Riverside Chaucer*, p. 291).

upon it, offering the reward of hidden truths. Since the densely structured poem appealed to the tastes of this audience, it seems very likely that at least some readers knew the work to contain secret patterns, and that a pleasure in working out the hidden mystery in this and similar works fostered an art of meditational reading in a self-consciously literate culture.

Select Bibliography

Manuscripts

Oxford, Bodleian Library MS Bodley 596, fols. 21b–24b. London, c. 1421–22. [Base text; connected to Westminster Abbey; owned by Baron family.]

Stonyhurst, Stonyhurst College MS 23, fols. 60b–63b. C. 1450. [Ends imperfectly at line 218.]

Oxford, Bodleian Library MS Douce 322, fols. 15a–16b. London, c. 1475. [Apparently given to Dartford Priory by William Baron.]

Cambridge, Trinity College MS R.3.21, fols. 34a–37b. London, c. 1475. [Associated with Shirleian booktrade of St. Bartholomew's Close.]

London, British Library MS Harley 1706, fols. 16a–17a. London, c. 1500. [A copy of Douce 322 or from the same exemplar.]

Abridged Version

London, British Library MS Royal 18 A.x, fols. 119b–123a. C. 1450. [Ends with Job exemplum; lacks stanzas 19–20.]

Version in Twelve-Line Stanzas

Cambridge, Trinity College MS O.9.38, fols. 24a–25a. Glastonbury, c. 1450. [Monk's commonplace book; rhymes *ababcdcdefef*; lacks stanzas 2, 6, 11, 13–14, 16–17; third stanza has 8 lines.]

Oxford, Bodleian Library MS Lat. misc. e 85, fols. 79a–81a. C. 1550. [Contains Easter sermons and anti-Protestant verse; ends imperfectly at line 122; lacks stanzas 10, 12–20.]

Version in Eight-Line Stanzas

London, British Library MS Harley 2380, fols. 72b–74a. Northern, c. 1500. [Rhymes *ababbcbc* imperfectly, with variant ending; lacks stanzas 9, 12–13, 17–20.]

Fragment

San Marino, Huntington Library HM 906, fol. 60v. C. 1400–50. [Imperfect, possibly prosaicized version of vv. 1–3.]

Editions

Brown, Carleton, ed. *Religious Lyrics of the XIVth Century.* Second ed. Rev. G. V. Smithers. Oxford: Clarendon, 1957. Pp. xxi, 208–15, 283. [Bodley 596.]

Hanna, Ralph, III, ed. *"The Index of Middle English Verse* and Huntington Library Collections: a Checklist of Addenda." *Papers of the Bibliograpical Society of America* 74 (1980), 241. [Huntington 906 fragment.]

Kail, J., ed. *Twenty-Six Political and Other Poems.* EETS o.s. 124. London, 1904. Pp. 143–49. [Douce 322.]

Rigg, A. G., ed. *An Edition of a Fifteenth-Century Commonplace Book (Trinity College, Cambridge, MS. O.9.38).* 2 vols. D.Phil. Thesis (unpublished), Oxford, 1966. Pp. 1.38–43, 2.259–65. [Trinity O.9.38.]

Related Middle English Works

The Abbey of the Holy Ghost. Ed. N. F. Blake. In *Middle English Religious Prose.* Evanston: Northwestern University Press, 1972. Pp. 88–102. [Allegorical text preceding *Bird* in Stonyhurst 23.]

Chansons d'aventure with birdsong refrains:

Asay Thi Frend or Thou Haf Nede. Ed. R. Dyboski. In *Songs, Carols, and Other Miscellaneous Poems from the Balliol MS. 354*. EETS e.s. 101. Oxford, 1907. P. 3.

Do for Thyself While That Thou Art Here. Ed. Sandison (see below, under "Criticism"). Pp. 113–15.

Fortis ut mors dileccio. Ed. R. Dyboski. In *Songs, Carols and Other Miscellaneous Poems from the Balliol MS. 354*. EETS e.s. 101. Oxford: Oxford University Press, 1907. Pp. 84–85.

Lydgate, John. *To Find a Frend at Nede*. Ed. H. N. MacCracken. In *The Minor Poems of John Lydgate*. Part 2. EETS o.s. 192. 1934; rpt. London: Oxford University Press, 1961. Pp. 755–59.

Mercy Passes All Things. Ed. Carleton Brown. In *Religious Lyrics of the XIVth Century*. Second ed. Rev. G. V. Smithers. Oxford: Clarendon, 1957. Pp. 125–31.

Make Amends. Ed. Carleton Brown. In *Religious Lyrics of the XIVth Century*. Second ed. Rev. G. V. Smithers. Oxford: Clarendon, 1957. Pp. 196–99.

Timor mortis conturbat me. Ed. R. Dyboski. In *Songs, Carols and Other Miscellaneous Poems from the Balliol MS. 354*. EETS e.s. 101. Oxford: Oxford University Press, 1907. Pp. 88–89.

Welfare Hath No Sikernes. Ed. R. Dyboski. In *Songs, Carols and Other Miscellaneous Poems from the Balliol MS. 354*. EETS e.s. 101. Oxford: Oxford University Press, 1907. Pp. 47–48.

The Dispute between Mary and the Cross. Printed in this edition. [Bird-in-tree image is Christ borne of Mary and Cross; appears in Royal 18 A.x.]

Fader and Sone and Holy Gost. Ed. Carleton Brown. *Religious Lyrics of the XVth Century*. Oxford: Clarendon, 1939. Pp. 210–11, 336. [Lyric with some refrain.]

Forma confitendi. Ed. Carl Horstmann. In *Yorkshire Writers*. Vol. 2. London: Swan Sonnenschein, 1896. Pp. 340–45. [Prose confession that ends with a list of the Four Principal Virtues (righteousness, temperance, prudence, strength); appears in Bodley 596; similar, but abbreviated confession follows *Bird* in Douce 322 and Harley 1706.]

The Four Leaves of the Truelove. Printed in this edition. [*Chanson d'aventure* with bird sermon; structural use of number four.]

The Lamentacion of Oure Lady. Ed. Carl Horstmann. *Archiv für das Studien der Neueren Sprachen und Litteraturen* 79 (1897), 454–59. [Prose complaint; precedes *Bird* in Bodley 596.]

Introduction

Parce mihi O Lord Moste Excellent. Ed. Edward Bliss Reed. "The Sixteenth Century Lyrics in Add. MS. 18,752." *Anglia* 33 (1910), 353.

Pety Job. Printed in this edition. [Same refrain; precedes *Bird* in Douce 322 and Harley 1706; follows *Bird* in Trinity R.3.21.]

Revertere. Ed. R. Dyboski. In *Songs, Carols and Other Miscellaneous Poems from the Balliol MS. 354*. EETS e.s. 101. Oxford: Oxford University Press, 1907. P. 80. [*Chanson d'aventure* on sins of youth; cryptic refrain written on briar leaves; appears in Trinity O.9.38.]

The Seven Deadly Sins. Ed. Nita Scudder Baugh. In *A Worcestershire Miscellany Compiled by John Northwood, c. 1400, edited from British Musuem MS. Add. 37,787*. Philadelphia: no publ., 1956. Pp. 87–95.

Syng We to the Trinite. Ed. Richard Leighton Greene. In *The Early English Carols*. Second ed. Oxford: Clarendon, 1977. Pp. 214, 439. [Carol with some refrain.]

Criticism of *The Bird with Four Feathers*

Hieatt, A. Kent, and Constance Hiaett. "'The Bird with Four Feathers': Numerical Analysis of a Fourteenth-Century Poem." *Papers on Language and Literature* 6 (1970), 18–35.

Louis, Cameron. "Proverbs, Precepts, and Monitory Pieces." In *A Manual of Writings in Middle English, 1050–1500*. Ed. Albert E. Hartung. Vol. 9. New Haven: Connecticut Academy of Arts and Sciences, 1993. Pp. 3009, 3379.

Sandison, Helen Estabrook. *The "Chanson d'Aventure" in Middle English*. Bryn Mawr College Monograph 12. Bryn Mawr: Bryn Mawr College, 1913. Pp. 84–85.

Related Studies

Alford, John. "A Note on *Piers Plowman* B.xviii.390: 'Til *parce* it hote.'" *Modern Philology* 69 (1971–72), 323–25.

Allen, Hope Emily. *Writings Ascribed to Richard Rolle, Hermit of Hampole*. New York: Heath, 1927. Pp. 369–70.

Fein, Susanna Greer. "Twelve-Line Stanza Forms in Middle English and the Date of *Pearl*." *Speculum* 72 (1997), 388–90, 392, 397.

Gray, Douglas. *Themes and Images in the Medieval English Religious Lyric*. London: Routledge & Kegan Paul, 1972. Pp. 171–75.

Keiser, George R. "'Noght How Lang Man Lifs; Bot How Wele': The Laity and the Ladder of Perfection." In *De Cella in Seculum: Religious and Secular Life and Devotion in Medieval England*. Ed. Michael G. Sargent. Cambridge: D. S. Brewer, 1989. Pp. 145–59.

Patterson, Lee. "The Subject of Confession." In *Chaucer and the Subject of History*. Madison: University of Wisconsin Press, 1991. Pp. 367–94.

Peck, Russell A. "Number Structure in *St. Erkenwald*." *Annuale Mediaevale* 14 (1973), 9–21.

Rigg, A. G. "'*Gregory's Garden*': A Latin Dream-Allegory [in TCC O.9.38]." *Medium Ævum* 35 (1966), 29–37.

———. *A Glastonbury Miscellany of the Fifteenth Century: A Descriptive Index of Trinity College, Cambridge, MS. O.9.38*. Oxford: Oxford University Press, 1968. Pp. 53–54.

The Bird with Four Feathers

1

By a forest syde, walking as I went,
Disport to take in o mornyng,   *Amusement; a morning*
A place I fond schaded with bowes ybent,   *arching tree boughs*
Iset aboute with flowrs so swete smellyng.   *Covered*
5   I leyde me down upon that grene,   *meadow*
And kast myn eyyen me aboute: *eyes*
I fond there breddes with fedres schene,   *birds; feathers shining*
Many on sitting upon a rowte.   *Many a one; in a group*
O brid therby sat on a brere —   *One bird; briar*
10   Hir fedres were pulled! Sche myght not fle!   *plucked*
She sat and song with mornyng chere: *sang; sad countenance (see note)*
    "Parce michi, Domine!"   *Spare me, Lord!*

2

"Spare me, Lorde, Kyng of Pytee!"   *compassion*
(Thus sang this bryd in pouer array)   *pitiful dress*
15   "My myrthe is goo, and my jolyté!   *gone; happiness*
I may not flee as othir may!
My fedres schene ben pulled me fro,   *lovely*
My Yowthe, my Strengthe, and my Bewté!   *Beauty*
Wherthorgh I take this song me too: *For which reason I take up*
20   *Parce michi, Domine!"*

3

When I herd this mornyng song,   *sad/morning (pun)*
I drew this brid nere and nere,   *nearer and nearer*
And asked who had don this wrong,
And brought here in so drowpyng chere,   *her; downcast appearance*
25   And who had pulled here fedres away,
That schuld here bere fro tre to tre,   *which should bear her*
And why sche song in her lay,   *sang; poetic song*
    "Parce michi, Domine!"

4

30	The bryd answerd and seid me till,	*to me*
	"Man, be in pees, for Cristes sake!	*be still*
	Yif I schewe the myn hertis will,	*thee; emotions*
	Peynes sore me wolle awake!	*will disturb me*
	Yif thow wilt take my word in mynde,	*mentally absorb my words*
	Ther shal no sorow be my letting	*prevent me*
35	That I nyl holy myn herte unbynde,	*From wholly unbinding my heart to you*
	And sothly telle the thyn asking,	*truly tell you*
	Which were my fedres that were so clere,	*what; bright*
	And who hath pulled hem all fro me,	*them*
	And why I sitte singging on brere,	*briar*
40	'Parce michi, Domine!'	

5

	"Fedres fowre I had ywis! —	*indeed*
	The two were set on every wynge —	*each*
	Thei bare me breme to my blys,	*speedily*
	Where me lust be at my lykyng.	*Wherever I desired to find my pleasure*
45	The first was Yowthe, the secunde Bewté,	
	Strengthe and Ryches the other two.	
	And now thei ben as thow maist se —	*may see*
	All foure fedres ifalle me fro!	*fallen off of me*
	My principal fedre Yowthe it was:	
50	He bare me ofte to nyseté!	*It; wantonness*
	Wherfore my song is now, allas!,	*For which reason*
	Parce michi, Domine!	

6

	"In yowthe I wrought folies fele,	*committed many follies*
	Myn herte was set so hye in pride;	
55	To synne Y yaf me every dele,	*I entirely gave myself to sin*
	Spared I neither tyme ne tyde.	*I was heedless of time and event*
	I was redy to make debate;	*be quarrelsome*
	My lyf stood ofte in mochel drede	*at great risk*
	And my lyking to walke late,	*Because of my desire to*
60	And have my lust of synful dede.	*fill of sinful deeds*
	I was now here, I was now there.	
	Unstable I was in al degré.	*in every way*

The Bird with Four Feathers

To Hym I crye that Marie bare,   *whom; bore*
    Parce michi, Domine!

7

65 "For Salamon seith in his poysé,   *poetry*
'Thre weyes ther beth ful hard to knowe: *are very hard to understand*
Oon is a schep that sailleth in the see,   *ship*
An egle in hey, a worme in lowe.'   *on high*
And of the ferthe telle he ne kan —   *he cannot tell*
70 It is so wondirful in his hering! —   *understanding*
'The weyes of a yong man
Whiche that ben here at her lyking.'   *their (i.e., his)*
And now hath Age ismyte me fro   *struck*
My pryncypal fedre of jolyté!
75 For al that ever I have misdoo,   *misdone (i.e., sinned)*
    Parce michi, Domine!

8

"My secunde fedre height Bewté.   *is called*
I held myself so clere of schap,   *handsome in form*
That al the peple scholde loke on me,   *would*
80 And worschip me with hoode and cap!   *praise; (see note)*
My rud was reed, my colour clere —   *complexion*
Me thought never non so faire as I,
In al a contré, feer ne nere! —   *country; far*
In fetewrs and schap so comely,   *features*
85 My forhed large, my browes bent,   *curved*
Myn eyyen cleer, and corage bolde,   *manner*
My schap ne myght no man ament.   *improve*
Me thought myself so fayre to beholde!
And yet I was begyled in syght:
90 The myrrour, Lorde, deseyved me!
Wherfore I aske, Lord, of Thi myght,
    Parce michi, Domine!

9

"This fedir me bare ful ofte to synne,
And, principally, to leccherye.
95 Clipping and kessing cowth I not blynne,   *Embracing; resist*

271

Me thought it craft of curteseye.   *a required art of courtesy*

A cusse! It is the develis gynne!   *kiss; trap*

Oft of it ariseth woo and wrake!   *woe and ruin*

The devel with cusse many doth wynne!

100   I counseil the: thow synne forsake.

Sampson lost his strengthe therfore,   *by that means (i.e. kissing)*

David his grace for Bersabee,   *[lost] his grace*

Til he cried with wordes sore,

     'Parce michi, Domine!'

10

105   "Salamon, that worthy king,

Ful fayr he was fro top to too;   *toe*

Wherfore, in his age yyng,   *young*

He was *amabilis domino*!   *lovable to the lord (i.e., God)*

And after he fel fowle and sore   *afterward; unhappy*

110   For lust of women that was him neygh;   *who were nigh about him*

Thei fonned him in his age hore,   *made a fool of; white-haired*

That he forsoke his God on heygh.   *So that; high*

Nought onlich thise, but many moo,   *Not only these; more*

Bewté hath begiled iwys.

115   I woot wel I am on of thoo —   *know; one of those*

I can the better telle this!

Now hath Age ysmyte me fro

My secunde fedre that height Bewté;

For al that ever I have misdoo,

120   Parce michi, Domine!

11

"My thridde fedre Strengthe height.   *was called*

My name was knowe on every syde,   *known*

For I was man of mochel myght,

And many on spak of me ful wide.

125   To prike and praunce I was ful preste,   *put on airs; eager*

My strengthe to kepe in every place,   *maintain*

And evermore I had the best —

Such was myn hap! Such was my grace!   *fortune*

My strengthe ful ofte me drowgh amys   *drew*

130   And torned me, Lord, clene fro The;   *entirely*

The Bird with Four Feathers

Now, Kyng corowned in hevenne blys,   *the bliss of heaven*
    Parce michi, Domine!

12

"This feder me bare beyonde the see
To gete me name in uncowth londe;   *reputation; foreign*
135   To robbe and slee had I deyntee,   *slay; delight*
Ne spared I neither fre ne bonde.   *freemen nor bound servants*
Of holy chirche took I no yeme,   *consideration*
Bokes to take, ne vestement;
Ther myght no thing so moche me queme   *please*
140   As robbe or see an abbey brent!   *burnt*
With strengthe I gat me gret aray,   *looted possessions*
Precious clothes, gold, and fee;   *wealth*
I thougth ful litel on thilke day.   *this very day*
    Parce michi, Domine!

13

145   "When Nabugodonosor fers in fight   *fierce*
Jerusalem had thought to wynne,   *conquer*
And so he dede with mayn and myght,   *did; power*
And brent the temples ther withinne.
And al the gold that he there fonde
150   He toke with hym, and hom gan ryde.   *did*
Him thought ther scholde nothing withstonde —   *withstand [him]*
His herte was set so heigh in pryde! —
Till the King of Myghtes Most
Browght him there that lowest was,
155   And caught him fro his real oost,   *royal host*
And drof him to a wildirnesse;   *drove*
And there he lyved with erbe and rote,   *herb and root*
Walkyng ever on foot and on honde,
Till God of mercy dede him bote,   *gave him a remedy*
160   And brought his prisoun out of bonde.   *freed him from prison*
Thanne seide this kyng thise wordes iwis:
'Al thing be, Lord, at Thi powsté;   *might*
Mercy I crie! I have do mys!   *done amiss*
    Parce michi, Domine!'

14

165 "While I had my strengthe at will,
Ful many a man I dede unrest;   *abused*
Thei that wolde not myn heste fulfill   *command*
My knyf was redy to his brest.
And now I sitte here blynde and lame
170 And croked beth my lymes alle.   *limbs*
I was ful wilde, I am now tame:
This ffedre of Strengthe is fro me falle!   *fallen from me*
And now hath Age ysmyte me fro
My thridde fedre of jolyté!
175 For al that ever I have misdo,
    Parce michi, Domine!

15

"My ferthe feder Ryches was.
To make it schyne, I travailled sore;   *labored hard*
I wente in many a perilous place;
180 Wel oft my lyf was neigh forlore!   *almost lost*
By dale, by downe, by wode syde,   *by the side of woods*
I bood many a bitter schowr;   *endured, hardship*
In salt see I sailled wel wide,
For to multiplie my tresowr;
185 With fals sleightes I gat my gode;   *deceptions; gained my goods*
In covetise I grownded me!   *avarice*
Jhesu, for Thi precious blood,
    Parce michi, Domine!

16

"Whan I was siker of gold ynow,   *assured; enough*
190 I gan to ride aboute wel fast;   *began*
I purchaced moche and — God wot how! —   *knows*
I wende this lyf wolde ever have last.   *thought; would always last*
I let me bilde castell and towres,   *arranged to build*
Without iwarded with stronge dyche,   *Protected without by a great moat*
195 Withinne ibildet halles and bowres —   *Constructed within with; small chambers*
Ther was no towr my castel liche!   *that was like my castle*
In this was yset al my lyking,   *All my pleasure was set in this*
And turned me, Lord, holich fro The!   *I was turned; wholly away from*

To The I crye now, Heven Kyng,
200   *Parce michi, Domine*!

17

"Whan I was most in al my flours,   *most vigorous; prime of life*
And had aboute me wif and childe,
I lost my catel and my tours —   *possessions; towers*
Thanne wex myn herte in party mylde! —   *grew; somewhat humbled*
205   Catell fel fro me sodeynly,
Ryght as it come, it went away!   *Just*
Men seith, 'Good gete untrewly   *Goods gained impurely*
The thridde heire broke it ne may.'   *heir (i.e., grandchild) may not retain it*
I was ful wilde, I am now tame;
210   Fortune hath pulled Ryches fro me;
Yowre wreche, Lorde, I cannot blame: *punishment*
      Parce michi, Domine!

18

"Job was richer thanne ever was I
Of gold, silver, and other good;
215   It fel hym fro, and that scharply,   *abruptly*
As dede the water owt of the flood.   *sea*
Hym was not left so mochel a clothe,   *so much as*
His naked body for to hele;   *cover*
Hym lakkyd crostes of a loffe   *He lacked crusts of bread*
220   When him lest ete in tyme of mele.   *When he wished to eat*
And yet he held up thanne his honde,
And seide, 'Heigh God, in magesté,
I thank The of Thy swete sonde;   *gift*
      Parce michi, Domine!'

19

225   "Now *Parce michi, Domine*!
My joye, my merthe is al agoo!   *gone*
Yowthe, Strengthe, and my Bewté,
My fetheres faire be falle me froo!
Wherto is a man more liche   *Is a man more like to anything*
230   Thanne to a flowr that springes in May?   *Than to a flower that blooms in May?*

275

Alle that lyveth, bothe powre and ryche,   *poor*
Shall deye unknowyng of her day."   *not expecting 'heir time*

20

I sette me down upon my knee,
And thanked this bryd of here gode lore.   *for her good teaching*
235   It thought me wele this word *"parce"*   *I meditated deeply [on how]*
Was bale and bote of gostly sore.[1]
Now *parce*, Lord, and spare Thow me;
This is a worde that sone gat grace;   *obtained*
And *parce* geteth Godis pyté,   *compassion*
240   And scheweth to us His blessed face. Amen.   *reveals*

---

[1] *Was both the painful effect and remedy of spiritual distress*

Notes

Abbreviations:

B   MS Bodley 596. [Base text.]
D   MS Douce 322.
S   Stonyhurst College MS 23.
T   Trinity College, Cambridge MS R.3.21.
R   MS Royal 18 A.x.
H   MS Harley 1706.
T*   Trinity College, Cambridge MS O.9.38.
H*   MS Harley 2380.
L*   MS Lat. misc. e 85.

B preserves the earliest and best text of the poem. S and R are related, with S the better version. D, T, and H form a distinct group of affiliated MSS (all produced in or near London in the late fifteenth century), with D the earliest and best copy in this group of texts. (For a possible stemma, see Rigg [1968], p. 54.) B agrees with RS more often than with DTH, but points of agreement with DTH are especially interesting. For this edition emendation of B has been conservatively undertaken by collation with D, S, T, R, and H, considered in that order. The notes record the significant variants from these five MSS. Variants that are merely orthographical are not recorded. Variants unique to one MS are also not recorded, unless they provide evidence for an editorial judgment.

The three altered versions of the poem (T*, H*, and L*) can be collated only sporadically with B. Readings from these MSS are given only where they may be of interest. On the fragment attributed to *Bird* by Hanna, see the note to line 1.

1   S, a generally reliable copy, reverts to a *chanson d'aventure* formula — the narrator on horseback — at the expense of the rhyme: *By a fforest as I gan ryde*. The sixteenth-century Welles Anthology contains a ballad opening that seems to recall *The Bird with Four Feathers*: "Throughe a forest as I can ryde / to take my sporte yn on mornyng / I cast my eye on every syde / I was ware of a bryde syngynge" (ed. Sharon L. Jansen and Kathleen H. Jordan, *The Welles Anthology*, Medieval and Renaissance Texts & Studies 75 [Binghamton: SUNY Binghamton, 1991], pp. 216–19).

The Bird with Four Feathers

1   Ralph Hanna III identified a lyric scrap in Huntington Library MS 906 fol. 60a, as vv. 1–3 in "prosaicized" form, but this identification is dubious. The fragment, in an early fifteenth-century hand, reads: *Be on fayre forest syde and by the wase wandryng / os that I went, / My sportes be forto take thus in a May mornyng, / Forand I fond a place of gentyll bowris gay* (p. 241). The long, looser, and more alliterative line is unlike the style of *Bird*. The scrap is, in fact, little more than a blend of formulaic tags, the first line recalling also the Vernon lyric *Thank God of All*, which opens: "Bi a wey wanderyng as I went" (ed. Brown, *Rel. Lyr. XIV*, p. 157).

3   *ybent*. S: *bent*. On the past participle with *i-*, see note to line 4.

4   *Iset*. R: *Sette*. Here BDSTH agree, but at line 197 *yset* appears only in B. Compare also *set* at lines 42, 54, and 152. The past particle formed with *i-* is more prevalent in B than in the other manuscripts. See also notes to lines 48 and 73.

4–5   The narrator's supine pose among the flowers will be, in retrospect, emblematic of his mortality. Compare lines 229–30.

9   The collocation "bird on briar" appears in *The Sinner's Lament* (line 34) and elsewhere; see Bartlett Jere Whiting, *Proverbs, Sentences, and Proverbial Phrases* (Cambridge, Mass.: Belknap, 1968), B290, B296. The scene of a bird upon a briar may be faintly emblematic of Christ on the Cross (as is the bird upon a tree in *The Four Leaves of the Truelove*). The Vernon MS contains a list of similitudes, among them "Hou a brid wan he fleth maket a Cros" (fol. 223b); ed. Carl Horstmann, "Proprium Sanctorum: Zusatz-Homilien des Ms. Vernon fol. CCXV ff. zur nördlichen Sammlung der Dominicalia evangelia," *Archiv für das Studium der Neueren Sprachen und Literaturen* 81 (1888), 301. This bird — not one of the "rowte" — has endured bodily damage in four places (? Christ's hands and feet) and heartache (? Christ's side wound). The bird is primarily a figure for mankind's mortality, but its hard-won wisdoms are gleaned through suffering. For the briar as an emblem, compare the poem *Revertere*.

10   The bird's gender is female throughout the poem, but its lament reflects the experience of a human male. The H* reviser changed the bird's gender to male.

11   *song*. DSTH: *sang(e)*. Compare the variants at lines 14 and 27.

11   *mornyng chere*. The word *mornyng* is a pun (repeated at line 21) upon two meanings: "morning" (as in line 2) and "mournful" (because the bird's song is one of sorrow and loss). The same pun appears in line 21 and the first stanza of *The Four Leaves of the Truelove*.

12   *Parce michi, Domine*! The bird immediately provides a translation in the next line. The Latin phrase (from Job 7.16) begins the first lesson of Matins of the Office of the Dead. *Pety Job* — the companion to this poem in D, T, and H — has the same refrain. The refrain appears, too, in a short lyric (*Fader and Sone and Holy Gost*, ed. Brown, pp. 210–11) and a carol (*Syng We to the Trinite*, ed. Greene, p. 214). On the currency of the phrase, see Alford, pp. 323–25.

13   *Kyng*. Omitted in SR.

        Pytee. The poem features compassion among God's attributes. God's capacity for pity validates the emotionalism of the bird's lament, which can provide an aesthetic and psychological curative for the responsive narrator/reader. After receiving the lesson, the narrator defines *parce* as a means of access to God's pity (line 239). For a fuller discussion, see the Introduction.

14   *sang*. D: *seyng*; T: *saide*; R: *song*; H: *saying*. The spelling in D probably led to the variants in T and H.

        pouer array. The word *pouer* completes the list of missing feathers in this stanza by alluding to the fourth one, Riches. *Array* is a theme in the poem, each feather bringing to the bird a different kind of gaudy "array" (see, for example, line 141).

15   *and*. Omitted in SR. The idea in this line is repeated at line 226. The repetition is part of a larger design that brings stanza 19 around in full circle to the ideas that opened the poem.

19   *Wherthorgh*. SR: *Wherfore*.

22   *drew*. DTH: *drew(e) to*; compare T*: *wente to*; H*: *drowe to*.

23   *asked*. B: *askesd* (an error).

        don. S: *do*; R: *do hir*.

26   *fro*. SR; BDTH: *from*. *Fro* is the form confirmed by rhyme (lines 16, 48, 73, 117, 173, 210, and 227). The manuscripts intermix the two forms, but *fro* predominates, and at no line do all manuscripts read *from*. (In T* *fro* appears consistently.) B has been emended in the same manner at lines 106, 155, and 198.

27   *song*. DSTRH: *sang(e)*.

30   *Man, be in pees*. The bird rebukes the inquisitive narrator, who has just asked three questions in breathless succession. The strolling narrator has come to a physical stop under the tree, but his questions reveal a continued mental restlessness and impatience, which the bird seeks to quell. The double-layered address to "Man" parallels other *chansons d'aventure* (*In a Valley of This Restless Mind*, for example): while the discourse is ostensibly given to a narrator inside the fiction, the generic term of address directs it outward, to the reader. The rebuke to "hold still" prepares the reader for a lengthy discourse.

32   *sore me wolle*. DH: *me sore woll*; T: *me sore than wil*; R: *sore wil me*.

37   *my*. DSTRH; B: *myn*. The text has been emended according to what seems to be a consistent usage by the poet: -*n* only before vowels and aspirant *h*, as at lines 6, 31, 35, and 86. This practice affects lines 54, 128, 167, and 204.

43   *blys*. The word has an entirely earthbound meaning; the attributes and actions the feathers represent are turnings from God. Compare lines 129–31.

44   *lust*. ST: *list*.

46   *the*. SR: *that*.

48   *ifalle*. SR: *falle*; DTH: *fallen*. The past participle of *fallen* appears elsewhere without the prefix; see lines 172 and 228. The form with *i-* is characteristic of B elsewhere: see notes to lines 4 and 73.

53   *wrought*. DSTRH; B: *wrowth*. The spellings *height/myght/fight* found in rhyme positions in all manuscripts suggest the original spelling. Compare B's *heith* at line 77.

54   *Myn*. T; BDSRH: *my*. See note to line 37.

59   *lyking*. SR: *likyng was*.

59–62   Youth's predilection for wandering about identifies the strolling narrator with this attribute. The plucked bird is, in contrast, grounded and stationary.

63   *Hym . . . that Marie bare*. The invocation evokes Christ in his youth.

65   Compare Vernon lyric *Think on Yesterday*, line 73: "Salamon seide in his poysi" (ed. Brown, *Rel. Lyr. XIV*, p. 145). In these unusual occurrences, *poysé* to proverbs rather than to poetry.

66–72   Proverbs 30.18–19: "Three things are hard to me; and the fourth I am utterly ignorant of. The way of an eagle in the air, the way of a serpent upon a rock, and the way of a ship in the midst of the sea, and the way of a man in youth." The list of four reflects the form of the poem. It may be, too, that the poet associates the other three "things" with the remaining three attributes: the soaring eagle with Strength (lines 133–34); the low serpent with Beauty (lines 97–99, 109–12); and the sea-faring ship with Riches (lines 183–84).

68   *in*. DSTH: *an*; R: *a*; T*: *on*. Compare the Vulgate: *Viam aquilae in caelo*.

72   *her*. DTH: *theyr(e)*.

73   *ismyte*. STR: *smyte*. In B the past participle of *smyten* always appears with the prefix *y-*. This line is repeated three times (see lines 117 and 173), giving the first three answers to the narrator's question of "Who has plucked your four feathers?" The bird answers that "Age" is responsible for lost Youth, Beauty, and Strength.

75   This line becomes a tag, used elsewhere, to introduce the refrain; see lines 119 and 175.

77   *height*. DSTRH; B: *heith*. Compare *height* in rhyme position at line 121.

80   *hoode and cap*. Refers to the practice of removing headgear before persons of superior rank. The *MED* cites this line as an example of the meaning "hood and cape," but the more likely sense is an inclusive phrase for any head covering,

that is, "hood and/or cap." See *MED cappe* n. and *hod* n. The reading found in the abridged text of L*, "hod and hatt," supports this interpretation.

83   *ne.* DSTR; B: *no*; H: *ner.*

85   *browes bent.* Arched eyebrows are conventional attributes of beauty. The feature belongs, for example, to Alisoun of Chaucer's Miller's Tale, *CT* I 3245–46 (*Riverside Chaucer*, p. 69) and to the ruling king in *Summer Sunday*, line 68 (ed. Rossell Hope Robbins, *Historical Poems of the XIVth and XVth Centuries* [New York: Columbia University Press, 1959], pp. 98–102).

86   *Myn.* SDH: *My.*

87   *ament.* DTRH: *amend(e).*

95   *cowth.* DTH: *cowde.*

98   *woo and.* Omitted in SR.

101   Alludes to the story of Samson, Delilah, and the Philistines (Judges 16). The exempla that appear in stanzas 9–13 (Samson, David, Solomon, and Nebuchadnezzar) are in biblical sequence. These historical exempla are typical of medieval moralizing; see Morton W. Bloomfield, *The Seven Deadly Sins* (East Lansing: Michigan State University Press, 1952), who cites a similar list by Nicholas Bozon (p. 144). Bozon's list is longer, but it includes Samson's strength, Solomon's wisdom, and Nebuchadnezzar's wealth (instead of pride) (c. 1320; *Les Contes moralisés de Nicole Bozon, Frère Mineur*, ed. Lucy Toulin Smith and Paul Meyer, Société des anciens textes français [1889; rpt. New York: Johnson Reprint, 1968], p. 18).

102   Alludes to the story of David and Bathsheba (2 Kings 11). By tradition Psalm 51 (50 in the Vulgate) was David's penitential prayer after his act of adultery with Uriah's wife. As one of the Seven Penitiential Psalms, its opening words were familiar in the Middle Ages, and they justify the poet's placement of the refrain in David's mouth: *"Miserere mei, Deus"* ("God, have mercy on me"). The psalm was frequently paraphrased from Latin to Middle English; see, for example, Brown, *Rel. Lyr. XV*, pp. 222–30, and Susanna Greer Fein, *"Haue Mercy of Me* (Psalm 51): An Unedited Alliterative Poem from the London Thornton Manuscript," *Modern Philology* 86 (1989), 226–32.

106   *fro*. SR; BDTH: *from*. See note to line 22.

107   *yyng*. DH: *yong*; T: *yeng*.

108   *amabilis domino*. Solomon's remarkable gifts from God are recounted in 3 Kings 3.12–13: "Behold, I have . . . given thee a wise and understanding heart. . . . Yea, and the things also which thou didst not ask, I have given thee: to wit, riches and glory, so that no one hath been like thee among the kings in all days heretofore." See also 3 Kings 4.29–34 and 10.23.

109   *And after*. DH: *That after*; T: *After that*; R: *And aftirward*. The variants attest to scribal confusion, perhaps derived from an abbreviation (*and, ther*, or *that*) that opened the line.

109–12   3 Kings 11.4: "And when [Solomon] was now old, his heart was turned away by women to follow strange gods; and his heart was not perfect with the Lord his God."

113   *onlich*. DTH: *(o)only*. The adverbial ending *-lich* has support elsewhere in the poem. See note to line 229.

        thise. The antecedents are Sampson, David, and Solomon.

117   *Now*. SR: *And now*.

        ysmyte. SR: *smyte*. The second part of the bird's answer to the question "who?" See note to line 73.

125   *prike and praunce*. An idiomatic expression. See *MED priken* v.

127   *best*. DSTRH; B: *beest*.

128   *Such . . . such*. SR: *Swich . . . swich*.

        myn hap. T; BDSRH: *my hap(p)*. See note to line 37. B inverts *grace* and *hap*.

130   *fro*. T: *from*.

131   *corowned*. DTRH: *crouned*.

       hevenne blys. Compare line 43. The bird used the feathers to fly to a "bliss" of the wrong kind.

133   *feder*. DSTRH; B: *fader*.

       me bare. DTRH: *bare me*.

136   *fre ne*. DH: *for no(o)*.

141   *gret aray*. A reversal of the bird's *pouer array* (line 14).

143   *thilke*. DSTH: *that*; R: *on domesday*.

145–63 The story of Nebuchadnezzar is recounted in Daniel 1–4. On Nebuchadnezzar's madness as a medieval exemplum, see Penelope B. R. Doob, *Nebuchadnezzar's Children: Conventions of Madness in Middle English Literature* (New Haven: Yale University Press, 1974), pp. 54–94, especially pp. 78–79.

148   *ther withinne*. SR; BDTH: *that were therinne*. The longer phrase appears to be a corruption of the shorter phrase, which can be explained by a confusion of the abbreviations for *ther* and *that*, with and *were*.

149   *fonde*. STR; BDH: *founde*.

151   *Him*. T: *He*. The line is suspect in metrics and weak in sense. Perhaps it should read: *Him thought nothing scholde him withstonde*.

153   *King of Myghtes Most*. The epithet stresses, appropriately, God's strength. On the technique elsewhere, compare notes to lines 13 and 63.

155   *fro*. SR; BDTH: *from*. See note to line 22.

159   *God*. DSTRH: *Cryst(e)*.

160   *brought*. SR; Omitted in BDTH.

163–65   The prayer of praise derives from Daniel 4.31; the penitential plea does not, however, correspond to any specific scriptural passage.

167   *myn*. DT; BSRH: *my*. See note to line 37.

168   *his*. T*: *her*. The reviser has made the pronoun plural to agree with *Thei* in line 167.

173   *ysmyte*. D: *smetyn*; SR: *smyte*; TH: *smyten*. The third part of the bird's answer to the question "who?" See note to line 73.

179   *a*. Omitted in SR.

181   *wode*. DTH: *wodes*. The final *e* is pronounced.

187   *Jhesu*. Brown mistakenly prints *Ihesus*.

         precious blood. Again, the appeal is to a specific feature of Christ that suits the bird's theme (here, riches). See notes to lines 13, 63, and 153.

191   *moche*. SR: *moche(l) good*.

193   *castell*. DH: *castelles*.

194   *dyche*. STR; BDH: *dyches*.

195   *ibildet*. D: *ybylde*; R: *bildide with*.

197   *yset*. DSTRH: *set(te)*. See note to line 4.

198   *holich*. DTH: *holy*. On the adverbial ending in -*lich*, characteristic of BSR, see note to line 229. The form *holy* appears in line 35.

         fro. SR; BDTH: *from*. See note to line 22.

201   *flours*. The word is another subtle (and punning) identification of the bird's former life to the narrator's present one (literally, lying in the flowers). Compare note to lines 59–62.

204   *wex*. DTH: *wexed*.

        myn. DTH; BSR: *my*. See note to line 37.

205   *fro*. T: *from*.

206   *come*. DTH: *cam(e)*. Compare Job 1.21.

207   *seith*. DTH: *seyen*; R: *seye*.

        gete. DH: *geten*; S: *gote*; T: *goten*.

207–08 This proverb was current until at least the eighteenth century; in Whiting's earliest citation it appears three times in Mannyng's *Handling Sin* (c. 1303). See Whiting G333, and Morris Palmer Tilley, *A Dictionary of the Proverbs in England* (Ann Arbor: University of Michigan Press, 1950), G305.

208   *broke*. The verb is *brouken*, "to have the benefit of something, enjoy." See *MED*, sense 1(a).

210   *fro me*. DS; BTRH: *me fro*. The rhyme calls for the emendation. The exemplar of S apparently shared the error; the scribe copied *me fro* and then corrected the phrase.

210–11 These lines represent the fourth and final part of the bird's answer to the question "who?" While Age led to the other three losses, Fortune is responsible for the loss of Riches. The second line can be read two ways: (1) I cannot blame you, Lord, for punishing me; or (2) You, Lord, are not responsible for the punishments I receive (i.e., I bring them on myself). Both (overlapping) understandings are plausible and both suit the Job exemplum of the next stanza, which informs the entire poem and supplies the refrain. The bird's laments her losses, but she stays devoted to God.

213   On Job's afflictions, see Job 1–2.

216   The origin and purpose of this unusual simile of water pouring torrentially "out of" the sea is not clear. Perhaps it is intended to call up the sublime imagery for God's powers in Job 38 — much of it expressed in terms of floods, tempests, and seas. T* reads: *As doth the water of salte floode*.

217 *so mochel*. DTH: *so mekyll*; omitted in R.

217–18 The poet is returning now to his opening concepts: Job's "array" was "poorer" than the bird's *pouer array* in stanza 2.

218 *hele*. DSTRH; B: *hille*. This is S's last line.

221 *thanne*. T: *that tyme*; omitted in RH.

222 Line repeated in H after line 223.

222–23 Job's praise of God even in adversity appears at Job 1.21 and 2.10.

223 Line omitted in T.

224 R ends at this line, after the last stanza with the refrain. The refrain is uttered by Job, its biblical author. The scriptural context is, however, quite different: "I have done with hope, and I shall now live no longer: spare me, for my days are nothing" (Job 7.16). The poet's message is that *parce* brings comfort, a message derived from the Church's Office of the Dead.

225–32 This stanza wraps up ideas introduced in stanzas 1 and 2: the four attributes are named (Riches is now the "powre and ryche"; compare line 14); the lament is repeated (see line 15); and the flower imagery returns with a glossed meaning (see lines 4–5, 201; compare Job 14.2 and *Pety Job*, lines 301–04).

226 *agoo*. BDTH: *agoon*. Emendation is indicated by the rhyme. Compare line 15.

228 This line echoes line 48.

229 *liche*. DTH: *lyke*. The word also appears in a rhyming position at line 196 (where all MSS agree).

230 *springes*. DTH: *spryngeth*.

231 *lyveth*. DTH: *lyven*.

235 *It thought me wele*. DTH: *I bethought me well of*.

236   *bale and bote. Parce* represents both the need for mercy and the verbal manner in which it is obtained. The line is omitted in T.

238   *gat.* DTH *geteth.*

238–40   The T* reviser has refashioned the last 8-line stanza into twelve lines with a refrain. The final three lines have been rewritten as seven:

> Thys they askyth to speke well
> *Parce* steryth God to pyte
> And voydeth the fowle fendys of hell
> *Parce* ys a woorde that soone getyth grace
> And openyth the yatis of heven syte
> God grawnte us all to se thy blessyd face
> That seyth *Parce michi Domine.*

239   On the theme of God's compassion, see note to line 13.

Pety Job

Introduction

The poem *Pety Job* is a passionate penitential monologue that uses as its meditative base the liturgical text intoned daily for the souls of the dead. In the mid-fifteenth century (the approximate date for the composition of *Pety Job*), the Matins of the Office of the Dead, also called the Nine Lessons of the Dirge,[1] was a long-established sequence of verses drawn from Job's speeches to God.[2] The Matins service contained three nocturns, each made up of three psalms (read with antiphons) and three lessons from Job. Cloistered religious would have heard the Office read every day, and, increasingly in the fifteenth century, a devout and literate laity imitated monastic practice by daily attendance at mass and disciplined private devotions at home. Laypersons adopting a personal regimen of worship were instructed to recite their devotions daily; the Office of the Dead was often one of the prescribed offices (Pantin, pp. 405, 413–14). Along with the Little Office of Our Lady and the Hours of the Cross and of the Holy Ghost, the Office of the Dead was among the regular items in primers and in private books of hours.[3]

Pety Job must, then, be read in recognition of a culture that fully embraced the Office of the Dead as a ritualized way to enclose and confront death, or at least to accept its mystery through time-honored words of earnest entreaty, rebellion, questioning, and submission. The speeches of the long-suffering Job provided the *Pety Job* poet a lyrical departure point, and the universality of the liturgy offered an emotionally charged context. Repetition of the Latin — whether fully understood or not by auditors — would most likely have been a somber but comforting experience,

---

[1] Called Dirge, or *Dirige*, from the antiphon that begins the first nocturn of Matins: *Dirige, Domine Deus meus, in conspectu tua viam meam*, "Direct my path, O Lord my God, in your sight" (*Breviarium Sarum*, ed. Proctor and Wordsworth, p. 274). Vespers of the same office was commonly known as *Placebo* from its opening antiphon. Line 550 of *Pety Job* assumes an audience familiar with these terms.

[2] (1) Job 7.16–21, (2) Job 10.1–7, (3) Job 10.8–12, (4) Job 13.22–28, (5) Job 14.1–6, (6) Job 14.13–16, (7) Job 17.1–3, 11–25, (8) Job 19.20–27, and (9) Job 10.18–22.

[3] Littlehales, pp. xi–xxii; McSparran and Robinson, pp. viii–ix.

a memorial to the departed and a prayerful remembrance of one's own fate. Through vernacular translation and gloss the Middle English poet aligns the ancient words of Job to a medieval reader's desire to comprehend his or her own mortal condition, investing words already fraught with the power of long usage with a contemporary fervor and immediacy.

In three of the five *Pety Job* manuscripts scribes have prefaced the poem with a discursive *incipit*:

> Here begynneth the nyne lessons of the Dirige, whych Job made in hys tribulacioun lying on the donghyll, and ben declared more opynly to lewde mennes understanding by a solempne, worthy, and discrete clerke Rychard Hampole, and ys cleped Pety Job, and ys full profitable to stere synners to compunccioun.[4]

The other two manuscripts have no such rubric. While the long introduction has no authorial basis, it does offer a glimpse of the work's appeal to a contemporary reader, mingled, probably, with a bookseller's commercialism. The three manuscripts (Douce 322, Harley 1706, and Trinity R.3.21) all appear to have been produced in or near London, with one of them (Trinity R.3.21) copied by a scribe known to have had access to volumes that had belonged to John Shirley (c. 1366–1456). This scribe's work is datable to the reign of Edward IV (1460–83). Historians have gathered evidence that points to a "setting of John Shirley and his successors in the business of compiling manuscript miscellanies, based in a shop in St. Batholomew's Close and employing local resources, aided by a network of personal relationships."[5] There is no proof that the book business of St. Bartholomew's had a role in producing Douce 322 and Harley 1706, but circumstantial evidence — early patrons or owners — points to connections within the same neighborhood and social circles.

The chatty rubric that introduces *Pety Job* is characteristic of volumes produced by John Shirley, and the feature derives, perhaps, from a desire to imitate contemporary

---

[4]Plates 5 and 6 present the illustrations for *Pety Job* that appear in two of these manuscripts. The rubric appears in full in Plate 6.

[5]A. I. Doyle, "An Unrecognized Piece of *Piers the Ploughman's Creed* and Other Works by Its Scribe," *Speculum* 34 (1959), 434. The known records on this scribe are summarized by Linne Mooney, "A Middle English Text on the Seven Liberal Arts," *Speculum* 68 (1993), 1028 nn. 7–8 and "More Manuscripts Written by a Chaucer Scribe," *Chaucer Review* 30 (1996), 401–07. He is the copyist for most of one booklet of R.3.21, a portion containing *The Bird with Four Feathers* and most of *Pety Job* (fols. 34r to 49v [top four lines only]). See also Julia Boffey and John J. Thompson, "Anthologies and Miscellanies: Production and Choice of Texts," in Jeremy Griffiths and Derek Pearsall, eds., *Book Production and Publishing in Britain 1375–1475* (Cambridge: Cambridge University Press, 1989), p. 308 n. 57.

French fashion, where such rubrics were common. In France the vernacular translation of Scripture was not restricted (as it was in England after 1408), and expositions upon the Book of Job and the Dirge were very popular. The fashion extended into French-speaking circles in England, particularly in London.[6] Two French plays about Job rely heavily upon the Office of the Dead for dialogue,[7] and there was also a stylish, philosophic poem, *Vigillus de la mort*, or *Paraphrase des neufs leçons de Job*, in wide circulation, written by Pierre Nesson (1383–1442/3), "a poet conspicuous in the higher circles of his time."[8] The illustrations appearing near two of the long rubrics (Plates 5 and 6) also suggest French fashion. A. I. Doyle believes the source of the Douce illustration to be a similar P for *Parce mihi* on fol. 22 of Oxford, St. John's College MS 208, a Sarum book of hours.[9] This exemplar is by the Master of Sir John Falstolf, a French illuminator working in England and Normandy in the 1440s and 1450s.

The long rubric gives the poem two titles. Both are also found in the simpler rubric appearing in CUL Ff.2.38 and Pepys 1584:

> Here . . . begynneth the ix lessons of dyryge whych ys clepyd Pety Job.

The first title, *The Nyne Lessons of the Dirige*, is purely descriptive and it defines the work's liturgical status as paraphrase of the Dirge. The scribe or compiler assumes an audience that would easily recognize the reference. The second title is to be taken, however, as the primary one: *Pety Job*. Middle English *pety* derives from Old French *petit*, and the phrase means "little Job," in other words, an abridgement of the Job

---

[6] See Allen, p. 370; Crawford, pp. 138–46; Parkes, pp. 564–70; and C. A. Robson, "Vernacular Scriptures in France," *Cambridge History of the Bible*, ed. G. W. H. Lampe, vol. 2 (Cambridge: Cambridge University Press, 1969), pp. 448–51.

[7] *Le Mistère du Viel Testament* (ed. James de Rothschild, Société des anciens textes français 5 [Paris: Firmin Didot, 1885], pp. iii–xii, 1–51) and *La Patience de Job* (ed. Albert Meiller [Paris: Klincksieck, 1971]); see Crawford, pp. 141–43.

[8] Allen, p. 370. Nesson's poem is more than twice the length of *Pety Job*; for a comparison, especially of the consolation and mortality themes, see Crawford, pp. 143–58. On Nesson's poem, see C. S. Shapley, "Pierre de Nesson's *Les Vigilles de la mort*," in *Studies in French Poetry of the Fifteenth Century* (The Hague: Martinus Nijhoff, 1970), pp. 1–31.

[9] I am grateful to Dr. Doyle for providing this information. An illumination from the St. John manuscript is reproduced in J. J. G. Alexander and Elżbieta Temple, *Illuminated Manuscripts in Oxford College Libraries, the University Archives and the Taylor Institution* (Oxford: Clarendon, 1985), plate 763. On the iconography typically associated with the figure of Job, see Meyer; Von der Osten; and Garmonsway and Raymo, eds., *A Middle English Metrical Life of Job*.

story. Strictly speaking, the phrase is a misnomer because its use in French referred to résumés of the Job *narrative*, with the long speeches omitted, but here the verses are drawn from dialogue only. Apparently, "any highly-abridged version of the Book of Job . . . could be classed as a 'petit Job' by scribes of the fifteenth century."[10]

The long rubric's ascription of authorship to the early fourteenth-century Yorkshire mystic, Richard Rolle, hermit of Hampole, cannot be accurate. Neither the dialect (southeast midland) nor the date of composition fits the facts known about Rolle. There also exists a marked difference in tone and style. Hope Emily Allen observes that *Pety Job*'s lyric qualities are wholly unmatched in Rolle's writings:

> [*Pety Job*] is a very beautiful commentary, of a sustained poetical and metrical power quite beyond what Rolle has shown in any other work; and, though very devout, it is quite unmystical. It seems to speak in a detached way of those sanctified in this life (among whom Rolle ranged himself). (p. 370)

Richard Rolle did write a commentary upon the Office of the Dead, *Postillae super novem lectiones*, a work whose aims were quite different from those of *Pety Job*. Rolle's gloss absorbed and transformed the solemn mood of the Office within his own mystical doctrine, in which the penitent "was open to receive the foretaste of salvation in warmth, sweetness and song" (Hughes, p. 265). *Pety Job*, on the other hand, "from beginning to end preserves the tone of proud, and even bitter submissiveness found in the original texts" (Allen, p. 370). Nonetheless, Rolle's popularity was at its height in the fifteenth century, and works attached to his name were in demand. The false ascription of *Pety Job* to Richard Rolle in the three London-area manuscripts bespeaks a bookdealer's interest in catering to a strong popular taste for a certain kind of devotional reading.

The conscious, subtle, and sophisticated style of *Pety Job* devolves from a particular social milieu, in which "literature" was seen as cognate with devotional values, and poetic "translation" did not demand the word-for-word reenactment of a text. One manuscript of *Pety Job* (Harley 1706) contains a brief note explaining how reading is a pious engagement of the mind to devotional pursuits:

---

[10]Crawford, p. 127; see also pp. 137, 140. Compare, however, the different usage of Besserman, who refers to all ME texts of the Dirge as "*Pety Job*," grouping the present poem with the prose translation found in the Prymer and a shorter poetic version (p. 81). In his analysis the liturgy remains the text of central importance, and in all variants the voice is understood to be that of Job. In *Pety Job*, however, Besserman acknowledges that the words "are best thought of as . . . spoken for a penitent fifteenth-century audience by and through the biblical protagonist" (p. 82).

Introduction

> We schulde rede and use bokes into this ende and entente: For formys of preysynge and preyynge to God, to oure lady Seynte Marye, and to alle the seyntes, that we myghte have by the forseyd use of redynge understondynge of God, of hys benyfetys, of hys lawe, of hys servyce, or sume orther goodly and gostely trowthis, or ellys that we myghte have good affeccyon toward God and hys seyntes and hys servyce to be gendryd and geten. (fol. 212b; quoted by Doyle, p. 231)

A book's purpose is to provide a path to understanding God, God's law, and God's service. *Pety Job* as paraphrase of a liturgical service offers such understanding and (as in the long rubric) is "full profitable to stere synners to compunccioun." As A. I. Doyle remarks, the notion of literature here expressed carries a peculiarly medieval

Plate 5. *Pety Job*, illustrated initial P (MS Douce 322, fol. 10a). The figure of Job lies abject before God, who peers on him from heaven. Job's hands are in a pose of prayer or supplication. The shaded areas under and around the male figure comprise the dunghill associated with Job iconography. For another drawing from this manuscript, see Plate 3. (Reproduced by permission of the Bodleian Library, University of Oxford.)

293

sense, that is, reading becomes an activity pursued solely for spiritual improvement, as part of "a regular habit of mind and living, shared by solitaries and widows in vows, . . . besides monks, nuns, and friars, and accepted as something to be emulated, so far as possible, by earnest seculars, clerks and layfolk" (p. 231). To help this wide community of the devout reach a better understanding of God, the vernacular poet-translator would have understood that his role was to convey the "truth" — not merely the words — embedded in the original. The source is used nonrestrictively to

Plate 6. *Pety Job*, illustrated initial P (TCC MS R.3.21, fol. 38a). The prostrate figure of Job is similar to that in Douce 322 (Plate 5), but here his hands seem to indicate petition rather than prayer. God, too, has expressive hands with one raised in a sign of benediction. Compare the illustration by the artist for *The Bird with Four Feathers* (Plate 4). (Reproduced by permission of the Master and Fellows of Trinity College, Cambridge.)

beget an independent work that remains, nevertheless, a translation. An expansion of the original material is to be expected — it is to be "declared more opynly to lewde mennes understandyng" — and such expansion, when handled skillfully, was regarded highly as a sign of inspiration.[11]

Within this devotional aesthetic the *Pety Job* poet produces an exceptionally fine piece of contritional writing. Surprisingly, given its rare power of expression, *Pety Job*'s lyric lament has garnered little modern critical attention other than some brief praise in scattered quarters. In agreement with Allen's remarks, Laurence Muir voices an opinion that "the poetry has power and beauty" (p. 383), and E. V. Gordon's observes that *Pety Job* is closer, metrically, to *Pearl* than any other surviving poem in the same stanza and may even contain verbal echoes (p. 87). Against these discernments stands the more usual reflex that puts *Pety Job*, without closer discrimination of style or form, into a vast class of penitential and didactic literature. For example, Frances McSparran's description of CUL Ff.2.38 explains the genre's dry appeal: "The various items [in a group including *Pety Job*] are not lyrical or affective; there is little emotional warmth, no mysticism or exaltation; instead, they are sober, religious, didactic and chastening" (p. viii). *Pety Job* deserves, however, to be separated from conventional penitential poems and tracts and to become better recognized. The poetic voice resonates with an intensity of emotion both sustained and insistent. Translating Job loosely, the poet scrutinizes the quintessential condition of each individual, who by his own nature could not be redeemed but by an undeserved gift of grace. As a lyrical expression of monumental contrasts — human insufficiency juxtaposed to divine omnipotence — the poem ultimately transcends its own theme of human unworthiness, becoming a powerful artistic successor to the sublimity of its biblical source.

The poet adopts the difficult stanza form of *Pearl*, twelve lines in a complex rhyme-scheme that uses only three rhymes. As in the group of Vernon lyrics with the same stanzaic pattern, each stanza of *Pety Job* ends with a refrain, here drawn from the opening words of the First Lesson, *Parce michi, Domine*, "Spare me, Lorde" (Job 7.16). Since these words also stand as the poem's first line, the refrain delivers a circular effect, from stanza to stanza and from end back to beginning.[12] The poet has

---

[11]On fifteenth-century translational methods, see Jerome Mitchell, *Thomas Hoccleve* (Urbana: University of Illinois Press, 1968), pp. 75–77; and Barratt, p. 275.

[12]The refrain follows a formula described by Stephen Manning, the liturgically based "address plus petition" (*Wisdom and Number: Toward a Critical Appraisal of the Middle English Religious Lyric* [Lincoln: University of Nebraska Press, 1962], p. 64). According to Manning, a refrain poem creates its own kind of structure, based not on "progression" but rather on "sheer force of repetition."

charged what could have been mere perfunctory tags with a sense of urgent entreaty. William Langland's casual shorthanding of the phrase to *parce* (in *Piers Plowman* B 18.390) and its use as a refrain in at least three other surviving poems point to its widespread familiarity.[13] In *Pety Job* the translation stresses the speaker's desired intimacy with God: *Domine* is rendered "*dear* Lord," *michi* expanded to "my *soul*," and the imperative *parce* rendered emphatically with its subject "*Thou* spare!" The resultant phrase in English, "Lyef Lord, my soule Thow spare!," invigorates the hypnotically familiar Latin.

In the three London-based manuscripts each stanza of *Pety Job* is headed by a Vulgate verse from Job, in the same nonsequential order used for the Nine Lessons. The scribes of the remaining two copies reproduced *Pety Job* as a more exclusively English lyric, the Latin headings omitted. These two manuscripts, CUL Ff.2.38 and Pepys 1584, closely overlap in contents, and although they were not copied from the same exemplar, the scribes "likely had access to some standard source in which these related texts were already associated."[14] The former of these manuscripts is a volume compiled for private use within a secular household. It is instructive to see here the poem presented for a lay audience without its Latin counterpart. Indeed, it is possible that the original poem did not possess the Latin headings. Often the poet will extend a thought or rhetorical figure over a series of stanzas, seeming to assume a reader's light recall of the Latin without any actual interruption of the English verses.

Evidence in two of the London-based manuscripts (Douce 322 and Harley 1706) connects them with Dartford Priory and Barking Abbey, two London houses closely associated with prominent, wealthy families (Doyle, pp. 222–43). From such evidence, Crawford postulates an early audience that was primarily in orders. Along with Syon Monastery, these religious foundations "were at the center of the fifteenth-century movement for more devotional literature and must have been involved with considerable book-commissioning and book-lending" (p. 108). Crawford speculates that the free renderings of the Nine Lessons in the vernacular "could have supplied, for instance, nine days of the required readings in English during meals" for nuns who "were by the fifteenth century urged to learn the meaning of the texts they

---

[13]Alford, pp. 323–25. The other poems are *The Bird with Four Feathers* (printed in this edition and a companion to *Pety Job* in three manuscripts); a verse prayer *Fader and Sone and Holy Gost*; and a carol *Syng We to the Trinite*. On other poems taking refrains from the liturgy, see F. A. Patterson, pp. 22–24. The insertion of the word "*Domine*" in popular usage indicates the common source to be the liturgy, not the Vulgate directly, where the word of address does not appear.

[14]McSparran and Robinson, p. xvi. Kreuzer summarizes some of the MS corresponcences: (1938), pp. 78–80, (1949), pp. 359–63.

recited" (pp. 107–08).[15] The later of the two manuscripts, Harley 1706 (c. 1475–1500; a copy of Douce 322 or its replica) retains the signature of one of its early owners, Elizabeth Beaumont, a noblewoman with substantial family ties to Dartford (her husband's aunt and then her own aunt or cousin had been prioress in the years 1442–58 and 1471–72, respectively) and to Barking (where her sister was a nun). About a year after her husband William's death in 1507, Elizabeth married John Vere, 13th Earl of Oxford. Her signature appears six times in the volume, twice as "Beaumount" and four times as "Oxynforde." One of the earlier Beaumont signatures appears on fol. 11a below the text of *Pety Job*. By all accounts this early "reader" of *Pety Job* lived a devout life:

> [S]he died [in 1537] in the Benedictine nunnery of Stratford (at Bow), another not-far-distant community of gentle birth and breeding, and was buried, along with her husband, in the church of the London Austin friars' convent. . . . [I]n the preamble of [her] extremely pious [will] the Countess speaks of herself as being then in her 'pure widowhede', a phrase which might be interpreted to mean that she had actually taken, as was quite frequent with ladies of her condition in the Middle Ages, special vows to remain in such a state, pursuing a quasi religious manner of life. (Doyle, pp. 235–37)

What evidence exists, then, as to an early audience for *Pety Job* suggests it included women of noble birth and high religious observance, some in orders and some secular but with close family ties to religious houses. It is fair to assume, as well, an audience of some men — those who served as spiritual counselors to such women and family members who, like the Earl of Oxford, would have shared some of this devotional practice.[16]

The theory that the original audience was substantially composed of women may give one pause, for the poem *Pety Job* is avowedly masculine in its theological philosophizing, as is the Book of Job. The question posed in the second stanza of the poem, that is, the vexed query of Job 7.17 (*Quid est homo, quia magnificas eum?*,

---

[15]On the general question of women as the audience of texts, see Carol M. Meale, "'alle the bokes that I haue of latyn, englisch, and frensch': Laywomen and Their Books in Late Medieval England," and Julia Boffey, "Women Authors and Women's Literacy in Fourteenth- and Fifteenth-Century England," in *Women and Literature in Britain 1150–1500*, ed. Carol M. Meale (Cambridge: Cambridge University Press, 1993), pp. 128–58, 159–82.

[16]See Pantin, and Armstrong. Evidence of early ownership in Trinity R.3.21, CUL Ff.2.38, and Pepys 1584 suggests, moreover, that a class of devout bourgeois also read *Pety Job*. The latter two volumes, especially, appear to have been "household books" in general use within middle-class families. All five MSS contain full *pastoralia* — expositions of the basic tenets of Christian doctrine — designed to educate the laity.

"What is a man that thou shouldst magnify him?"), opens an inquiry that is framed in gendered terms. By the term *man* the poet means "the condition of each soul born into the world from a woman." The rhetorical stance separates "man" (the status of the voice and his audience) from "woman" (the contaminating source of a material life cursed by constant sinning and a *consciousness* of sinning). There is little doubt that a house of religious women could accept this metaphorically gendered definition, just as Chaucer's Second Nun could term herself an "unworthy sone of Eve" (*CT* VIII 62), an interesting inversion of ordinary gendered terms, making the original ancestor a woman, and each penitent descendent, like the narrating Nun, a male child. The *Pety Job* poet underscores the distinction, as though the dual-gendered world symbolizes the essence of the human predicament of separation from God. One's troubles begin at the moment of birth (lines 625–33). The poet adds to his Latin source the self-negating wish that he had been absorbed into his mother's body. He wishes that his eyes — part of his enemy flesh — might never have looked upon the enticements of the enemy world.

The lyric voice thus speaks of a misery shared by all who have (or have had) voices to speak and ears to listen. The poet provides a generic name for the verses of *Pety Job*: they are a song of truth (lines 2–3, 9–12). The words of the poem represent a speech-act that is conscious of its own vocal essence, that is, of the power and dangers inherent in speaking. It becomes the collective voice of all dead and all living, individualized but sharing the universal experience, and wishing, paradoxically, for the status of the unborn, the only condition that could have prevented the speaker from knowing and saying terrible truths. It is utterance reduced to a basic sentence: the soul stands in need of God's grace; he cannot achieve salvation on his own merits. With nuanced subtlety and a sense of anguish, the poet of *Pety Job* explores the complex psychology of sin, penance, and verbal confession. Lee Patterson has described the delicate tightrope act that contrition had become in late medieval religious life: "an uneasy balance of negation and assertion, a radical self-hatred and fear of God that is paradoxically joined to *spes triplex* [the threefold hope of pardon, grace, and glory] and a reliance on divine mercy" (pp. 378–79). In style and substance *Pety Job* is expressive of such inner conflict.

The insistently intimate tone portrays a voice mature in self-knowledge but also pathetically childlike, alternately petitioning, praising, fearing, questioning, even reproaching the Deity addressed as majestic Father-Figure. A mood of prayer and confession prevails. The reader is soon invited to be more than an eavesdropper and to accept the interiorized lament as his own (lines 31–34). Eventually the speaker asks that his words be written down as an example to others. Given that the poem exists on the page, the written verses become the fulfillment of the verbally enacted petition (stanzas 48–49, expanding upon Job 19.23–24). Nevertheless, the request and its embodiment in writing run counter to the verbal self-consciousness of the prayer-lament, which the voice offers as a *spoken* utterance to be written down by *someone else*, that is, a compassionate friend of the speaker, who ought, after the lyricist's death, to remember and pity his plight (stanzas 46–47, an expansion of Job 19.21–22). Such a friend will remember him with the prescribed prayer, fasting, and almsgiving, as well as with recitation of the Office of the Dead on his behalf (lines 547–50). The poem thus enacts the very liturgy that will someday serve for the voice who speaks it, or perhaps it already has.[17] The oral rituals of petition, confession, and the intoned Office of the Dead coexist, consciously and paradoxically, with their material representation as a written text.

The lyric voice is itself in a sense disembodied, but it returns, often and obsessively, to the subject of corporeality, for the sounding tongue is enclosed by the body (stanza 45). Salvation, if it is to come, depends upon the sinner's confessional voice, yet speaking is itself a reflex of the corrupt body. The paradox creates a powerful tension between verbal form and penitential meaning, leading to a subtle exploration of the difficulties inherent in any confession that emerges from a man still mortally enclosed within the brittle clay of life. Man is caught in sin even as he speaks.

The theme of man as shaped from clay derives from Job 10.9 (see stanza 14), but the voice of *Pety Job* reiterates this theme even more insistently than the source, making it a metaphor that defines human nothingness.[18] For example, in the seventh stanza, where Job complains, "I shall sleep now in the dust: and if thou seek me in the morning, I shall not be" (7.21), the lyricist's voice takes the thought further by lamenting his *origin* in dust:

> Loo, in pouder I shall slepe,
> For owte of poudere furst I cam,
> And into poudere must I crepe,
> For of that same kynde I am.
> That I ne am pouder I may not threpe,
> For erthe I am as was Adam,
> And nowe my pytte ys dolven depe;
> Though men me seke, ryght nought I am! (lines 73–80)

---

[17]The poem contains a subtle and progressive "subnarrative" that positions the voice initially with the living but seems gradually to move past the point of death (see note to line 203).

[18]This theme was also favored by Gregory the Great in the *Moralia in Job*. In general, though, the author of *Pety Job* shows little dependence upon Gregory's important commentary. On this emphasis on human nothingness, see especially the note to lines 13–16, and the evocative imagery of stanza 24 (note to lines 277–80).

He makes literal Job's implied equation between dirt, human corporeality, the grave, and death's oblivion.

While the voice sings of how the body's weighted flesh drags down the soul, he also bewails another punishment that comes through intellect: man lives in knowledge of his constantly flawed state. The voice, in a state of conflict, is deeply repentant but still "dived" deep in sin (stanza 4). The unfairness of the struggle sometimes rankles the penitent: it was God who endowed man with his substance; why did He make man's flesh have desires contrary to His will (lines 51–52; see Job 7.20)? And is it not a great hardship to have such faulty vision that man may see only outward things, and not the spiritual ways of God (lines 295–99; see stanza 10)? For the penitent soul, punishment seems to come arbitrarily for sins enacted unconsciously or over which he had no control (lines 457–64). The ways of God are inscrutable, and despite the hope for mercy, man's subjugated condition seems unbearably cruel treatment from a Father.

The psychological and metaphysical dilemma takes on an existential dimension. God has endowed man with an unasked-for awareness of his own unworthiness and has also made him subject to a never-ending surveillance. Quoting, paraphrasing, and freely expanding upon Job, the lyric voice complains that man may not hide himself from God, who knows all his movements, private deeds, and thoughts (stanzas 22–23); he pleads for a brief respite (stanza 31); and he expects no relief from correction even in the afterlife (lines 373–82). He complains especially of his tormented thoughts, which cannot make sense of this predicament. These thoughts — a mark of his humanity — keep him awake, turning night into day (stanzas 40–41; see Job 17.11–12). At last, in a remarkable shifting of the images of sleeplessness and troubled thoughts, the voice reduces the life of the soul to a little bed of personal consciousness:

> In derkenesse dymme, all oute of ese,
> My lytell bed spred I have:
> That bed shall I never lese,
> Though I wolde for angor rave,
> Tyll the Day of Dome that, of my grave,
> I shall aryse, and mo with me.
> My soule, Lorde, I pray, Thow save
> With *Parce michi, Domine*! (lines 497–504)

The soul's "lytell bed" is its enclosure within the body, and in this small space the mind is afflicted with the tormenting "thoughts" of personal guilt and future doom that the voice of *Pety Job* records with precision. And these thoughts will pass to

300

another small space, the grave, where the still troubled soul will await the Day of Judgment.

The voice's self-negating impulses — a wish to be unborn, an utterance of misery, a preoccupation with death — translate into a desire to be released from consciousness, from speech, and, logically extended, even from the production of a religious art of the kind created here. A profound, black irony would seem to rest at the heart of a poem composed to express a desire to undo God's creation of self-aware humanity: the logic behind the lyric complaint would seemingly repudiate the human power to create the beautiful artifact of earnest devotion that *Pety Job* becomes. Nevertheless, subject always to God, the voice carries on.

Crawford accurately characterizes *Pety Job* as "not a dogmatic treatise on the sacrament of penance," but "rather the emotional expression of a poetic 'I' in which the audience could participate" (p. 176). She goes on to evaluate the seeming absence of a transcendent, mystical goal:

> [While] he seeks to motivate [his audience] to do their duty[, t]here is no penetrating assessment of the value of repentance, no mystical fervor, no tender devotion in the *Pety Job*: in short, no achievement of sublimity. (p. 177; compare Allen, p. 370, and Hughes, p. 265)

This assessment, put in negative terms, does not quite do justice to the poet's accomplishment. While perhaps there is nothing in *Pety Job* that is like Richard Rolle's assurance of "warmth, sweetness, and song," the poet does achieve what might be called a sublime revelation without ever losing the meditative focus upon human smallness and unworthiness. The penultimate lesson, Lesson 8, provided opportunity, for here the words of Job extend the promise that one may personally glimpse the Godhead:

> For I know that my Redeemer liveth; and in the last day I shall rise out of the earth. And I shall be clothed again with my skin, and in my flesh I shall see my God: whom I myself shall see, and my eyes shall behold, and not another. This my hope is laid up in my bosom. (19.25–27)

The soulful voice of *Pety Job* affirms his faith in this experience, praising God's magnificence in his transported account of what wondrous sights he will see. The burden of the isolated consciousness will be rewarded by the promised directness and non-vicariousness of this experience (lines 605–08). The penitent voice imagines that he shall see this sight *himself*, as was promised, with his own spiritually transformed eyes.

The last lesson, Lesson 9, returns the voice, even with this hope, to his enduring condition of sin and penitence, now with the wish (already cited) that his mother's flesh had consumed him before his birth so that his eyes might never have seen the world. The hoped-for reward will be ineffably splendid, but the fact of day-to-day existence remains still a discouragement (lines 639–42). The song now becomes one of weeping, that is, the penitent's gift of tears, and the poem closes with an admonitory vision of "the derke lande . . . / That kevered ys with black alway" (lines 667–68). The final imagery of death and hell is stark, powerful, and utterly bereaved in its frightening evocation of where the sinner without God would be abandoned:

> The londe of myschefe and of derknes,
> Whereas dampned soules dwell,
> The londe of woo and of wrechednesse,
> Where ben mo peynes *than tonge may telle,*
> The londe of dethe and of duresse,
> In whyche noon order may dwelle,
> The londe of wepyng and of drerynesse,
> And stynkyng sorow on to smelle! (lines 673–80; italics added)

This place with more pains "than tonge may telle" possesses a horror as bluntly inexpressible as is the majesty of the Godhead. Lyricism somehow conveys the untold terror of this place of black abandonment, the poet's tongue succeeding both in expression of what cannot be said and in utterance of the only plea that may save him, "*Parce michi, Domine!*"

Note on the Edited Text

In three manuscripts (Douce 322, Harley 1706, and Trinity Coll. Camb. R.3.21) each stanza of *Pety Job* is headed by the corresponding Latin verse from the Office of the Dead. Two manuscripts (Camb. Univ. Lib. Ff.2.38 and Pepys 1584) omit Latin headings. I have used the latter format, supplying the Vulgate text as it is written by the Douce 322 scribe (and the corresponding Douay-Rheims translation) at the foot of each page of text. For a medieval reader the Latin text of the Office of the Dead was familiar; many would have known it by heart. For a modern reader not likely to have this facility, inclusion of Latin headings tends to obstruct the vigor of the vernacular poem. Moreover, one cannot be certain that the poem originally had the headings, especially since inclusion of the Latin led those three scribes to omit the poem's first line. In several instances, moreover, the English syntax flows across stanza breaks. Other editors have printed the poem with liturgical stanza headings, but Crawford acknowledges that they could have been "added by a very clever copyist" (p. 44).

Introduction

Select Bibliography

Manuscripts

Oxford, Bodleian Library MS Douce 322, fols. 10a–15a. London, c. 1475. [Base text; connected to Dartford Priory.]

Cambridge, Trinity College MS R.3.21, fols. 38a–50b. London, c. 1475. [Copied by a London scribe (fl. 1460–83) who is known to have had access to Shirley manuscripts after John Shirley's death; an early owner, who perhaps commissioned it, was a well-to-do London mercer, Roger Thorney (c. 1450–1515).]

London, British Library MS Harley 1706, fols. 10b–15b. London, c. 1500. [A copy of Douce 322 or from the same exemplar; connected to Elizabeth Beaumont, Countess of Oxford, and to Barking Abbey.]

Cambridge, Cambridge University Library MS Ff.2.38, fols. 6a–10a. C. 1490. [Designed for use in a middle-class household; contains works of religious instruction and several romances.]

Cambridge, Magdalene College MS Pepys 1584, fols. 48a–62a. C. 1490. [Contents similar to religious portion of CUL Ff.2.38.]

Facsimile

McSparran, Frances, and P. R. Robinson, intro. *Cambridge University Library MS Ff.2.38*. London: Scolar, 1979.

Editions

Crawford, Karis Ann, ed. *The Middle English Pety Job: A Critical Edition with a Study of Its Place in Late Medieval Religious Literature*. Ph.D. Thesis (unpublished). University of Toronto, 1977. [Douce 322 as base text.]

Horstmann, Carl, ed. *Yorkshire Writers*. Vol. 2. London: Swan Sonnenschein, 1896. Pp. 381–89. [Harley 1706 as base text.]

Kail, J., ed. *Twenty-Six Political and Other Poems*. EETS o.s. 124. London: Kegan Paul, Trench, Trübner & Co., 1904. Pp. xxiii, 120–43. [Douce 322.]

Lessons from the Dirge

Day, Mabel, ed. *The Wheatley Manuscript*. EETS o.s. 155. 1921. Pp. xviii–xix, 59–64. [Middle English prose text found in some primers.]

Kail, J., ed. *Twenty-Six Political and Other Poems*. EETS o.s. 124. London: Kegan Paul, Trench, Trübner & Co., 1904. Pp. 107–20. [Middle English verse paraphrase, in 52 8-line stanzas, based on primer translation.]

Littlehales, Henry, ed. *The Prymer or Lay Folks' Prayer Book*. EETS o.s. 105, 109. 1895, 1897; rpt. as one vol. Millwood, N.Y.: Kraus, 1975. Pp. 56–70. [Standard prose translation of liturgy.]

Procter, Francis, and Christopher Wordsworth, eds. *Breviarium ad usum insignis ecclesiae Sarum*. Vol. 2. Cambridge: Cambridge University Press, 1879. Pp. 274–79. [Latin liturgy.]

Related Middle English Works

The Bird with Four Feathers. Printed in this edition. [Same refrain; follows *Pety Job* in Douce 322 and Harley 1706; precedes it in Trinity R.3.21.]

Brampton, Thomas. *Metrical Paraphrase of the Seven Penitential Psalms*. Ed. James R. Kreuzer. *Traditio* 7 (1949), 359–403. [Paraphrase of liturgical Scripture; companion to *Pety Job* in Pepys 1584; also found in CUL Ff.2.38.]

Fader and Sone and Holy Gost. Ed Carleton Brown. *Religious Lyrics of the XVth Century*. Oxford: Clarendon, 1939. Pp. 210–11, 336. [Lyric with same refrain.]

God Send Us Patience in Our Old Age. Ed. Carleton Brown. In *Religious Lyrics of the XVth Century*. Oxford: Clarendon, 1939. Pp. 233–36. [Refrain poem in same stanza; appears in Harley 1706.]

Introduction

Lichfield, William. *The Complaint of God to Sinful Man*. Ed. E. Bergström. *Anglia* 34 (1911), 498–525. [Companion to *Pety Job* in CUL Ff.2.38; also found in Trinity R.3.21 and Pepys 1584.]

A Middle English Metrical Life of Job. Ed. G. N. Garmonsway and R. R. Raymo. In *Early English and Norse Studies Presented to Hugh Smith in Honour of His Sixtieth Birthday*. Ed. Arthur Brown and Peter Foote. London: Methuen, 1963. Pp. 77–98.

Parce mihi O Lorde Moste Excellent. Ed. Edward Bliss Reed. "The Sixteenth-Century Lyrics in Add. MS. 18,752." *Anglia* 33 (1910), 353.

Pearl. Ed. E. V. Gordon. Oxford: Clarendon, 1953. [Same stanza; perhaps some verbal echoes (see p. 87).]

Syng We to the Trinite. Ed. Richard Leighton Greene. In *The Early English Carols*. Second ed. Oxford: Clarendon, 1977. Pp. 214, 439. [Carol with the same refrian.]

The Twelve Profits of Anger. Ed. James R. Kreuzer. *PMLA* 53 (1938), 78–85. [Poem on the virtues of affliction, found in both CUL Ff.2.38 and Pepys 1584.]

Vernon Lyrics. Ed. Carleton Brown. In *Religious Lyrics of the XIVth Century*. Second ed. Rev. G. V. Smithers. Oxford: Clarendon, 1957. Nos. 95, 100, 101, 103, 106, 110, 118, 120. [Refrain poems in same stanza.]

Criticism of *Pety Job*

Allen, Hope Emily. *Writings Ascribed to Richard Rolle, Hermit of Hampole*. New York: Heath, 1927. Pp. 369–70.

Besserman, Lawrence L. *The Legend of Job in the Middle Ages*. Cambridge, Mass.: Harvard University Press, 1979. Pp. 79–84.

Muir, Laurence. "Translations and Paraphrases of the Bible, and Commentaries." In *A Manual of the Writings in Middle English, 1050–1500*. Ed. J. Burke Severs. Vol. 2. Hamden, Conn.: Connecticut Academy of Arts and Sciences, 1970. Pp. 383–84, 536.

Related Studies

Alford, John. "A Note on *Piers Plowman* B.xviii.390: 'Til *parce* it hote.'" *Modern Philology* 69 (1971–72), 323–25.

Armstrong, C. A. J. "The Piety of Cicely, Duchess of York: A Study in Late Mediaeval Culture." In *For Hilaire Belloc: Essays in Honour of His 72nd Birthday*. Ed. Douglas Woodruff. London: Sheed & Ward, 1942. Pp. 73–94.

Astell, Ann W. *Job, Boethius, and Epic Truth*. Ithaca: Cornell University Press, 1994. Pp. 70–96.

Barratt, Alexandra. "The Prymer and Its Influence on Fifteenth-Century English Passion Lyrics." *Medium Ævum* 44 (1975), 264–79.

Doyle, A. I. "Books Connected with the Vere Family and Barking Abbey." *Transactions of the Essex Archaeological Society*, n.s. 25 (1958), 222–43.

Fein, Susanna Greer. "Twelve-Line Stanza Forms in Middle English and the Date of *Pearl*." *Speculum* 72 (1997), 367, 383–85, 389–90, 397.

Hughes, Jonathan. *Pastors and Visionaries: Religion and Secular Life in Medieval Yorkshire*. Woodbridge, Suffolk: Boydell, 1988. Pp. 265–69.

Keiser, George R. "'Noght How Lang Man Lifs; Bot How Wele': The Laity and the Ladder of Perfection." In *De Cella in Seculum: Religious and Secular Life and Devotion in Medieval England*. Ed. Michael G. Sargent. Cambridge: D. S. Brewer, 1989. Pp. 145–59.

Meyer, Kathi. "St. Job as a Patron of Music." *Art Bulletin* 36 (1954), 21–31.

Pantin, W. A. "Instructions for a Devout and Literate Layman." In *Medieval Learning and Literature: Essays Presented to Richard William Hunt*. Ed. J. J. G. Alexander and M. T. Gibson. Oxford: Clarendon, 1976. Pp. 398–422.

Parkes, M. B. "The Literacy of the Laity." In *The Medieval World*. Ed. David Daiches and Anthony Thorlby. London: Unwin Brothers, 1973. Pp. 555–76.

Patterson, Frank Allen. *The Middle English Penitential Lyric*. 1911; rpt. New York: AMS, 1966.

Patterson, Lee. "The Subject of Confession." In *Chaucer and the Subject of History*. Madison: University of Wisconsin Press, 1991. Pp. 367–94.

Scattergood, V. J. "Unpublished Middle English Poems from British Museum MS Harley 1706." *English Philological Studies* 12 (1970), 35–41.

Spitzig, Joseph A. *Sacramental Penance in the Twelfth and Thirteenth Centuries*. Washington, D.C.: Catholic University of America Press, 1947.

Von der Osten, G. "Job and Christ: The Development of a Devotional Image." *Journal of the Warburg and Courtauld Institutes* 16 (1953), 133–58.

Pety Job

Here begynneth the nyne lessons of the Dirige, whych Job made in hys tribulacioun lying on the donghyll, and ben declared more opynly to lewde mennes understanding by a solempne, worthy, and discrete clerke Rychard Hampole, and ys cleped Pety Job, and ys full profitable to stere synners to compunccioun.

1

	Parce michi, Domine! [1]	*Spare me, Lord!*
	Lyef Lord, my soule Thow spare!	*Dear*
	The sothe I sey now sykerly:	*truth· certainly*
	That my dayes nought they are,	*nothing*
5	For though I be bryght of ble —	*complexion*
	The fayrest man that ys oughware —	*anywhere*
	Yet shall my fayrenesse fade and fle,	*disappear*
	And I shal be but wormes ware.	*food for worms*
	And when my body ys all bare,	
10	And on a bere brought shal be,	*bier*
	I not what I may synge thare	*do not know*
	But *Parce michi, Domine.*	

2

	What ys a man, wete I wolde, [2]	*understand*
	That magnifyeth hymself alway,	
15	But a marke made in molde	*a molded impression made*
	Of a clyngyng clot of clay?	*From a sticky clod*
	Thow shopest us for that we shulde	*shape us in order that*
	Have ben in blysse forever and ay —	*ever*
	But nowe — allas! — bothe yong and olde	

---

[1] *Parce michi, Domine, nichil enim sunt dies mei.* Job 7.16: Spare me, for my days are nothing. The Latin passgaes which mark the first line of each stanza refer to each complete stanza as it paraphrases the Biblical text.

[2] *Quid est homo, quia magnificas eum?* Job 7.17: What is a man that thou shouldst magnify him?

20	Foryetyn hit bothe nyght and day!	*forget*
	A, good Lord! What shall I say?	
	I that stande in thys degré?	*condition*
	I wote nothyng that helpe may	*know of*
	But *Parce michi, Domine*.	

3

25	Or why puttist Thow thyn hert ayene [1]	*against*
	That Thow hast so dere bought?	*That one whom*
	Thow vysyteste hym, and art full fayne	*eager*
	Sodenly to preve yef he be ought.	*determine if; anything*
	To longe in synne we have layne,	
30	For synne hath so oure soule thorow sought;	*thoroughly pervaded*
	To helpe oureself have we no mayne —	*strength*
	So moche woo hit hath us wrought!	*made for us*
	But to the pyt when we be brought,	*pit [of hell]*
	Then men woll wepe for the and me,	*thee (the reader)*
35	But certes all that helpeth nought,	*certainly*
	But *Parce michi, Domine*.	

4

	O why so longe or Thow wolt spare [2]	*before*
	Me in synne, that depe dyve?	*Who am delved so deeply in sin*
	Thow woldest suffer never mare	
40	Me to swolowe my salyve?	*saliva*
	I have The gylt and grevyd sare,	*offended and sorely grieved You*
	For synne with me hathe ben to ryve;	*too rife*
	But, Lord, now lere me with Thy lare	*teach; lore*
	That dedly synne fro me may dryve.	*Which may drive deadly sin from me*
45	And, Jhesu, for Thy woundes fyve,	
	As Thow becammest man for me,	
	When I shall passe oute of lyve,	
	Than *Parce michi, Domine*.	

---

[1] *Aut quid apponis erga eum cor tuum? Visitas cum diluculo, et subito probas illum.* Job 7.17–18: Or why dost thou set thy heart upon him? Thou visitest him early in the morning, and thou provest him suddenly.

[2] *Usquequo non parcis michi, nec dimittas me, ut glutiam salivam meam? Peccavi.* Job 7.19–20: How long wilt thou not spare me, nor suffer me to swallow down my spittle? I have sinned.

5

	What shall I do unto The,[1]	*How shall I serve*
50	O Thow Kepar of all mankynde?	
	Of suche a matiere why madest Thow me	*substance*
	To The contrarious me for to fynde?	*that causes me to be contrary*
	O Fader of Heven, fayre and fre,	
	As Thow art bothe good and hende,	*gentle*
55	Yet be kynde, as Thow hast be,	*kind (natural)*
	And spare me, Lorde, that am unkynde.	*unkind (unnatural)*
	Thy frenshyp, Fader, late me fynde,	
	As Thow art God in Trinité.	
	Of Thy mercy make me have mynde	
60	Wyth *Parce michi, Domine*.	

6

	Why takest Thow nat my syn away,[2]	
	A Thow God of all goodnesse?	*O*
	And why, also, as I The say,	
	Dost nat awey my wykednesse?	
65	Thow madest me of a clot of clay	*lump*
	That breketh ofte thorough brotylnesse:	*brittleness (i.e., weakness)*
	Full brotyll I am — hit ys no nay! —	*I cannot deny it!*
	That maketh me ofte to do amysse.	
	But, good Jhesu, I pray The thys,	
70	For thy grete benygnyté,	*mildness*
	Thy mercy, Lorde, late me nat mys,	
	But *Parce michi, Domine*.	

7

	Loo, in pouder I shall slepe,[3]	*dust*
	For owte of poudere furst I cam,	

---

[1] *Quid faciam tibi, o custos hominum? Quare posuisti me contrarium tibi, et factus sum michimet ipsi gravis?* Job 7.20: What shall I do to thee, O keeper of men? why hast thou set me opposite to thee, and I am become burdensome to myself?

[2] *Cur non tollis peccatum meum, et quare non aufers iniquitatem meam?* Job 7.21: Why dost thou not remove my sin, and why dost thou not take away mine iniquity?

[3] *Ecce nunc in pulvere dormio; et si mane me quesieris, non subsistam.* Job 7.21: Behold now, I shall sleep in the dust: and if thou seek me in the morning, I shall not be.

75	And into poudere must I crepe,
	For of that same kynde I am.
	That I ne am pouder I may not threpe,
	For erthe I am as was Adam,
	And nowe my pytte ys dolven depe;
80	Though men me seke, ryght nought I am!
	O Thow, Fader Abraham,
	For Mary love, that mayde so fre
	In whos blode thy Son swame,
	So *Parce michi, Domine*.

nature (line 76)
dispute (line 77)
grave; dug deeply (line 79)
Mary's; generous (line 82)

8

85	Hyt forthynketh my soule, ywys,[1]
	The lyfe that I have lad alway;
	For now my speche ayenst me ys;
	Sothly my lyfe I shall dysplay.
	In sorow and in bytternesse,
90	Of myn oune soule, thus shall I say:
	"Now, good Jhesu, Kynge of Blysse,
	Dampne me nat at Domesday!"
	And, good Jhesu — to The I pray! —
	Telle how thus Thow demest me.
95	Nowe yeve me mercy, and say nat nay,
	Wyth *Parce michi, Domine*!

My soul repents, indeed (line 85)
led (line 86)
Truly (line 88)
own (line 90)
Damn (line 92)
judge (line 94)
give; do not deny [me] (line 95)

9

	Semeth hit good, Lord, unto The,[2]
	To thryste me doune, and me accuse?
	I am Thy werke, Thow madest me:
100	Thyne oune handwerk Thow nat refuse.
	Wythyn the close of cheryté,

thrust (line 97)
do not refuse (line 100)
enclosure of charity (line 101)

---

[1] *Tedet animam meam vite mee; dimittam adversum me eloquium meum, loquar in amaritudine anime mee. Dicam Deo: Noli me condempnare; indica michi cur me ita judices.* Job 10.1–2: My soul is weary of my life, I will let go my speech against myself, I will speak in the bitterness of my soul. I will say to God: Do not condemn me: tell me why thou judgest me so.

[2] *Nunquid tibi bonum videtur, si calumpnieris me, et oprimas me opus manuum tuarum, et consilium impiorum adives?* Job 10.3: Doth it seem good to thee that thou shouldst calumniate me, and oppress me, the work of thy own hands, and help the counsel of the wicked?

Good God, Thow me recluse,   *make me a recluse*
And yef I gylte The in any degré,   *if I offend*
With Thy mercy Thow me excuse.
105   Ne late me never of maters muse   *dwell on*
That fallen unto dyshonesté.   *tend toward dishonesty*
Thys prayer Thow nat recuse,   *refuse*
But *Parce michi, Domine.*

10

Whether Thyne eyen flesshly be,[1]   *[How can I know] Whether*
110   Or yef Thow seest as seeth a man?   *if*
Nay, forsoth, but oonly we
Of outeward thynges beholdyng han;   *have the power to behold*
But inward thynges dost Thow se,
That non other may se ne can.
115   Therfore, Lorde, I pray to The,
Warne me when I am mystan,   *mistaken*
That I may flee fro foule Sathan,
That ys aboute to perysshe me.   *destroy*
Lese nat that Thow ones wan,   *Lose not what You once won*
120   But *Parce michi, Domine.*

11

Whether Thy dayes, Lord, be lyke[2]   *[How can I know] Whether*
As mennys dayes, that dwellen here,
Or Thy yeres be ought lyke   *anything*
To the tymes of mannes yere?   *duration*
125   That day a man ys fresshe and fryke,   *vigorous*
And sheweth forth a gladsom chere;   *face*
But tomorow he wexeth syke,   *becomes ill*
And haply borne forthe on a bere.   *will perchance be borne; bier*
Thus mannes tyme ys in a were,   *state of uncertainty*
130   But Thy tyme stondeth in oo degré.   *one*

---

[1] *Nunquid oculi carnei tibi sunt? aut sicut videt homo, et tu vides?* Job 10.4: Hast thou eyes of flesh: or shalt thou see as man seeth?

[2] *Nunquid sicut dies hominis dies tui, et anni tui sicut humana sunt tempora?* Job 10 5: Are thy days as the days of man, and are thy years as the times of men?

Therfore, I pray in thys manere:
Lorde, *Parce michi, Domine*.

12

	For to seche my wyckednesse, [1]	*examine*
	And for to serche thus all my synne,	
135	Methynketh hit cometh of grete hardnes	*comes from great obstinancy*
	With me, Lorde, so to begynne.	*[and] so begins [there]*
	Shewe Thow forth thy grete goodnes,	
	And Thyne hardshyp up Thow pynne;	*restrain*
	Thynke opon the brytylnesse	
140	That alwey worcheth me withynne,	*works entirely*
	And sythen I may nat fro The twyn,	*since; part*
	Ne from Thyne hande warysshed be,	*protected*
	Though I offende more or mynne,	*less*
	Ever *Parce michi, Domine*.	

13

145	Thyne handes, Lorde, have made me [2]	
	And formed me in shap of man,	
	And me Thow settest in degré	*rank*
	Of grete nobley after than.	*worthiness*
	But whan I, thorough the sotylté,	*subtlety*
150	Deceyved was of foule Sathan,	*by*
	Thow puttedyst me fro that dignité	*cast*
	Hedlyng doune on my brayn pan.	*Headlong; skull*
	Noon other cause alege I can	
	But that synne hathe depryved me.	
155	Now for the blood that from The ranne,	*for the sake of the blood*
	So *Parce michi, Domine*!	

---

[1] *Ut queras iniquitatem meam, et peccatum meum scruteris, et scias quia nichil impium fecerim, cum sit nemo qui de manu tua possit eruere?* Job 10.6–7: That thou shouldst enquire after my iniquity, and search after my sin? And shouldst know that I have done no wicked thing, whereas there is no man that can deliver out of thy hand.

[2] *Manus tue fecerunt me, et plasmaverunt me totum in circuitu: et sic repente precipitas me?* Job 10.8: Thy hands have made me, and fashioned me wholly round about, and dost thou cast me down headlong on a sudden?

14

Have mynde, therfore, I The pray,[1]
O Thow God, Almighty Kynge,
Thynke Thow madest me of clay,
160   And into clay Thow shalt me brynge.
Suche ys Thy myght, and hath be ay,   *been forever*
And sythen Thow madest furst all thynge,   *since You created*
Who dare sey ayene The nay,   *say no to You*
To lette Thy wyll or Thy lykyng?   *To prevent*
165   There ys no man, olde ne yonge,   *nor*
That stryve dar ayenst The;   *dares to strive*
Therfore nede maketh me synge,
Lorde, *Parce michi, Domine*.

15

Mylkedest nat me, Lorde, as mylke,[2]
170   With nesshe blood, whan Thow me made?   *soft blood*
And sythen, Lord, Thow madest that ylke,   *then; same [blood]*
Ryght as the hardnesse of chese ys hade?   *Harden like cheese*
My bloode ys nessher than ys sylke,   *softer*
In reyny weder that sone woll fade,
175   And thus me made do dedys swylke   *I am made to do such deeds*
With whyche my goste ys ofte unglade.   *spirit; sorry*
And thus in sinne full depe I wade
That nygh I droune thorow freelté!   *almost; frailty*
Although I can of synne nat sade,   *be satiated*
180   Yet *Parce michi, Domine*.

16

With flesshe and felle Thow hast me cladde,[3]   *skin*
With bones and synewes togeder knyt;
Lyfe and mercy of The I hadde;   *from*

---

[1] *Memento, queso, quod sicut lutum feceris me, et in pulverem reduces me.* Job 10.9: Remember, I beseech thee, that thou hast made me as the clay, and thou wilt bring me into dust again.

[2] *Nonne sicut lac mulsisti me, et sicut caseum me coagulasti?* Job 10.10: Hast thou not milked me as milk, and curdled me like cheese?

[3] *Pelle et carnibus vestisti me; ossibus et nervis compegisti me.* Job 10.11: Thou hast clothed me with skin and flesh: thou hast put me together with bones and sinews.

	To governe me Thow yave me wyt.	*gave me intelligence*
185	To kepe Thyne hestes Thow me bade,	*commands; ordered*
	And seydest that I shuld, for hit,	
	In heven blysse be ever gladde.	
	And yet I woll nat fro syn flytte,	*flee*
	But freelté, Lord, so me smytte,	*frailty; has so smitten me*
190	Unnethe kepte ys oone for me!	*Scarcely; one [command] by me*
	Nat for than I pray The yet	*Despite that [failure]*
	For *Parce michi, Domine.*	

17

	Lyfe and mercy Thow yave me, ay! [1]	
	When I wold Thy mercy crave,	
195	Thow seydest to me nat ones nay,	*never once no*
	But glad was when I wold hit have.	
	Thow were redy, nyght and day,	
	With mercy, Lord, me to save!	
	But I denyed hit alwey,	
200	So woodly syn made me to rave;	*madly*
	I servyd syn, and was hys knave;	
	I dyd that was ayenst me.	*that which was against*
	Now, Lord, when I am leyde in grave,	
	Than *Parce michi, Domine!*	

18

205	Thy vysitacion, Lorde, hath kepte [2]	*preserved*
	My spyryte that ys me withyn,	
	For when I wolde to syn have lepte,	
	Than holy grace made me to blyn;	*desist*
	And ofte tyme I have sore wept	
210	The more grace of The to wyn;	
	And thus with wepyng have I wypt	*whipped*
	My soule, Lord, from dedly synne.	
	Lord, late me never werke begynne	*let*

---

[1] *Vitam et misericordiam tribuisti michi.* Job 10.12: Thou hast granted me life and mercy.

[2] *Et visitacio tua custodivit spiritum meum.* Job 10.12: And thy visitation hath preserved my spirit.

That in any wyse may displese The; *any way*
215   And, somtyme, though I from The twyn, *separate*
Yet, Lord, *Parce michi, Domine*.

19

What wykednes — all that I have! — [1]
With my synnes — all on an hepe! —
Shewe me hem or I go to grave, *Show them to me before*
220   That I for hem may sore wepe, *grievously*
My soule, Lord, that I may save
From the pyt of hell so depe,
Where synful soules tumble and rave
In endeles woo — ataketh good kepe! — *beware!*
225   Toodes on hem doth crowde and crepe — *Toads upon them*
In suche peynes the soules be!
From that place I may nat kepe *keep myself*
Withouten *Parce michi, Domine*.

20

Why hydest Thow fro me Thy face,[2]
230   That ys so full of all fayrenesse?
I mene thys: Somtyme Thy grace
That Thow withdrawest, and yevest me lesse.
As Thyne enemy Thow dost me chace, *chase*
Demyng me in grete hardnesse; *Judging; obstinacy [in sin]*
235   Thy love fayne wold I purchase *earnestly*
Yef Thow wolt me hit graunte of thy goodnes. *If*
Now graunte me, Lord, suche stedfastnes *persistence*
That I may stande in oo degré,
And though I fall thorow brotylnes,
240   Lorde, *Parce michi, Domine*.

---

[1] *Quantas habeo iniquitates et peccata? Scelera mea atque delicta ostende michi.* Job 13.23: How many are my iniquities and sins? Make me know my crimes and offenses.

[2] *Cur faciem tuam abscondis, et arbitraris me inimicum tuum?* Job 13.24: Why hidest thou thy face, and thinkest me thy enemy?

21

Ayenst a leefe, that lyght ys to blowe,[1]   *As [the wind] against a leaf*
To me, that am freel of kynde,   *frail by nature*
Thy myght and power dost Thow showe;
Although I myght beres bynde,   *[be bold enough to] bind bears*
245 With wyndes ofte I overthrowe.   *By [Your] winds; am overthrown*
Suche fondyng of The I fynde.   *testing from You*
I renne forthe fro rowe to rowe,
Somtyme before, somtyme behynde;
I grope as a man that ys full blynde,   *fully blind*
250 But though I stomble, Thow folowest me:
A, Lord! Though I to The be unkynde,
Yet *Parce michi, Domine!*

22

Thow wrytest, Lord, ayenst me [2]
Bytternesse, that I shall rede   *Bitter things*
255 At Domesday, in syght of The   *in Your sight*
And all the worlde in length and brede;
That I dyd in pryvyté   *That which; private*
There opynly hit owte shall sprede.
And thys Thow wylt full well yse,   *see*
260 And distroy me for my wyked dede!
But, Lorde, to The I clepe and grede,   *call and cry out*
As Thow art Lorde of all pyté,   *compassion*
That day when I shall drope and drede,   *be abject and afraid*
Than *Parce michi, Domine!*

---

[1] *Contra folium quod vento rapitur, ostendis potenciam tuam, et stipulam siccam persequeris.* Job 13.25: Against a leaf, that is carried away with the wind, thou shewest thy power; and thou pursuest a dry straw.

[2] *Scribis enim contra me amaritudines, et consumere me vis peccatis adolescencie mee.* Job 13.26: For thou writest bitter things against me, and wilt consume me for the sins of my youth.

317

23

265 In a synew Thow hast my feet sette,[1]   *snare*
　　With the whyche that I go shall,
　　And all the pathes Thow hast mette   *have watched (L. observati)*
　　That ever I yede in wey or walle;   *walked in open or walled places*
　　There ys nothyng that The may lette   *may prevent You from knowing*
270 To knowe my steppes, grete and smalle,
　　Wycked and worse, good and bette —   *better*
　　I wote well, Thow considerest alle!
　　But, Lorde, to The I clepe and calle: *speak*
　　When I slyde, supporte Thow me,
275 And though somtyme I take a falle,
　　Yet *Parce michi, Domine!*

24

　　The whyche, as rotyng shall consume,[2]   *That which rotting*
　　And fare as mowthe-eten cloth,
　　And as from the fyre departeth fume,   *smoke*
280 So body and soule asundre goth.   *[do] body; go asunder*
　　I am made of a lothly hume —   *loathly compost (humus)*
　　Hit ys a thyng to man most loth!   *loathsome*
　　Wherof than shulde I presume   *For what reason then*
　　To be hygh-herted or lyghtly wroth?   *proud or playfully angry*
285 Though I be he that ofte mysdoth,   *acts wrongfully*
　　Of mercy art Thow large and fre;   *generous*
　　As I leve that thys ys soth,   *believe; true*
　　So *Parce michi, Domine!*

25

　　A man that ys of a woman bore[3]   *born of a woman*
290 But lytell whyle he lyveth here,   *lives here but a little while*

---

[1] *Posuisti in nervo pedem meum, et observasti omnes semitas meas, et vestigia pedum meorum considerasti.* Job 13.27: Thou hast put my feet in the stocks, and hast observed all my paths, and hast considered the steps of my feet.

[2] *Qui quasi putredo consumendus sum, et quasi vestimentum quod commeditur a tinea.* Job 13.28: Who am to be consumed in rottenness, and as a garment that is moth-eaten.

[3] *Homo, natus de muliere, brevi vivens tempore, repletur multis miseriis.* Job 14.1: Man born of a woman, living for a short time, is filled with many miseries.

And every day, more and more,
Replenysshed ys with synnes sere;   *diverse*
With hote and colde, and hungor sore,
Turmented ys from yere to yere,
295 And ofte hym wanteth Goddys lore,   *desires; teachings*
That gostly wey he shuld lere.   *So that the spiritual way; learn*
And thus he wandreth in a were,   *state of uncertainty*
As a man blynd, and may nat se!
Therfore I pray The, with lovely chere,   *loving countenance*
300 For *Parce michi, Domine!*

26

The whyche spryngeth oute as a floure [1]   *That which*
That groweth fresshe, all men to glade,   *please*
But when he with a sharpe shoure   *shower [of rain or afflictions]*
Ys smyten, begynneth sone to fade.
305 So lese I the fayre coloure
That God Almyghty furst in me made,
And thus I chaunge in every houre,
And fle away ryght as a shade;   *ghost*
And herewith I am full lade   *laden*
310 With synnes of diverse degré —   *diverse kinds*
Of heven blysse me nought degrade,   *From; do not demote me*
But *Parce michi, Domine!*

27

And, Lord, Thow lettest that hit be dygne [2]   *may you allow; worthy*
Thyne eyen to opene uppon suche on,   *such a one*
315 And hym Thow shewest, by that sygne,
That he, with The, to dome shall gone.   *shall go with You to judgment*
Have mercy on me, Jhesu benygne!   *kind*
Methynketh myn hert ys harder than ston,

---

[1] *Qui quasi flos egreditur et conteritur, et fugit velud umbra, et nunquam in eodem statu permanet.* Job 14.2: Who cometh forth like a flower, and is destroyed, and fleeth as a shadow, and never continueth in the same state.

[2] *Et dignam ducis super huiuscemodi aperire oculos tuos, et adducere eum tecum in judicium?* Job 14.3: And dost thou think it meet to open thy eyes upon such a one, and to bring him into judgment with thee?

And besyed with a spiryte maligne,   *occupied by; evil*
320 My flesshe, the worlde, they ben my fone!   *are my foes*
These ben myn enemyes, Lord, echone,   *each one*
Ever aboute to perysshe me!   *destroy*
Lorde, for the love of Mary and John,   *St. John the Evangelist*
Ever *Parce michi, Domine!*

28

325 But, Lord, who may clene make [1]   *undefiled*
Conceyved thyng of seede unclene?   *A thing conceived of unclean seed*
Nat Thow? A, yes, I undertake,   *I am sure [You may]*
Yef The lyste to make hit clene.   *If it pleases You*
Allas! I walke in a lake
330 Of dedly synne that doth me tene;   *does me harm*
But, Lorde, for the Love of Maryes sake,
Amende the harme that I of mene.   *complain about*
Ywys I am nat worthe a bene,   *bean*
Of my sylfe, to commendyd be.   *On my own merits*
335 Yet helpe me, Lorde, with thy grace shene,   *shining*
And ever *Parce michi, Domine!*

29

Mennes dayes ben shorte. Beware! [2]   *are*
And therto take good entente!   *heed*
For in respyte of tyme evermare,   *in comparison to eternity*
340 They beth nothyng equipolent.   *not at all equivalent*
The nombre of hys monthes are
Alwey at The, Lorde, verament;   *at Your will; truly*
Oure lyfe ys nought but sorow and care
Tyll we be passed jugement.
345 My wyttes, Lorde, I have myspent   *reasoning power*
That Thow me yave to rewle with me,   *gave to me to rule myself*

---

[1] *Quis potest [facere] mundum de immundo conceptum semine? Nonne tu qui solus es?* Job 14.4: Who can make him clean that is conceived of unclean seed? is it not thou who only art?

[2] *Breves dies hominis sunt; numerus mensium eius apud te est.* Job 14.5: The days of man are short, and the number of his months is with thee.

But that I may ryse up and here repent,
Lorde, *Parce michi, Domine!*

30

	Hys termes, Lord, Thow hast ordeyned:[1]	*His (A man's)*
350	How longe he shall now lyve here,	
	That may he nat passe, ne be refreyned,[2]	
	But by Thyne absolute power;	*Except by means of*
	Thys sentence may be well susteyned	*illustrated*
	By a story, as we may here.	
355	Howe Ezechye to dethward peyned	*Ezekiel declined to death*
	And yet God addyd over fiftene yere;	*added [to his life]*
	Hys kyndly tyme was comen full nere,	*His (Ezekiel's) natural*
	But for hys synnes tho wepte he!	*then*
	Lorde, yeve me grace that I may here	
360	Have *Parce michi, Domine!*	

31

	Therfore, Lord, a lytell go awey,[3]	
	Withdrawe Thyn hande, that man may rest,	
	Tyll he desyre hys dethe day	
	And wylne to be shut up in hys cheste;	*wishes; coffin*
365	And late hym lyve, yef hym lust ay;	*always as he pleases*
	Thys holde I, Lorde, for the beste.	*This I maintain is*
	All dysease from hym delay,	*withhold*
	Tyll the careyn in erthe be keste.	*body; cast*
	Allas, all thys world now ys myswrest	*misguided*
370	To carpe thys, Lorde, ayenst The!	*complain in this manner*
	Make me to Thy mercy trest	*trust*
	For *Parce michi, Domine!*	

---

[1] *Constituisti terminos eius, qui preteriri non poterunt.* Job 14.5: Thou has appointed his bounds which cannot be passed.

[2] *That [amount of time] he may neither surpass nor fall short of*

[3] *Recede ergo paululum ab eo, ut quiescat, donec optata veniat, et sicut mercenarii, dies eius.* Job 14.6: Depart a little from him, that he may rest, until his wished for day come, as that of the hireling.

32

Who to me may yeve or graunte,[1]
For love or any affeccioun,   *For the sake of*
375   Fro Thy wrathe that ys duraunte   *everlasting*
I may have my proteccioun?   *May I be protected*
In helle, yef I be concurraunte,   *prone to rebel*
There am I in subjeccioun;
In heven, though Thow woldest me haunte,   *stay near me*
380   Yet there am I at Thy correccioun.
I may nat from Thy respeccioun   *sight*
By no way, Lorde, hyde now me;
Therfore seye I thys leccioun   *lesson*
Of *Parce michi, Domine!*

33

385   And Thow woldest a tyme ordeyne[2]   *If*
In whyche Thow woldest of me have mynde,
With som solace me to susteyne,
That of Thy blysse am so fere behynde.   *Who from*
My woo from The can I nat leyne,   *conceal*
390   But telle hit The, for Thow art kynde: *I must tell it to You*
I am fast bounde here with a cheyne
Of dedly synne, full wele I fynde,
But woldest Thow, Lorde, me unbynde
Thorough the vertew of Thy pyté,   *compassion*
395   Than were I glad, and lyght as lynde,   *a linden tree*
To have *Parce michi, Domine!*

34

Trowest Thow nat that man shal ryse[3]   *Do You not believe*
Ayene to lyfe, that dyed onys?

---

[1] *Quis michi hoc tribuat ut in inferno protegas me, [et abscondas me,] donec pertranseat furor tuus?* Job 14.13: Who will grant me this, that thou mayst protect me in hell, and hide me till thy wrath pass?

[2] *Et constituas michi [tempus] in quo recorderis mei?* Job 14.13: And appoint me a time when thou wilt remember me?

[3] *Putasne, mortuus homo rursum vivat?* Job 14.14: Shall man that is dead, thinkest thou, live again?

Yes, and that in a wonderful wyse,   *wondrous manner*
400   With flesshe and felle, bloode and bones.   *skin*
         Than shal God Hys dome devyse,
         And to Hym take the good att ones;
         But dampned soules shullen sore gryse,   *complain*
         And yeve a shoute with hydous grones.   *hideous*
405   Thus make they shull wofull mones,
         All that shullen dampned be.
         That I may dwelle withyn the wones   *[Grant] that; place*
         Of *Parce michi, Domine!*

35

         All the dayes that I lyve here [1]
410   In thys wofull wepyng dale,
         I byde alwey, from yere to yere,   *remain always*
         Tyll I chaunge, as men do fale.   *fail*
         Change I shall withouten were,   *doubt*
         Nat ay be dwellyng in thys vale;   *valley*
415   But, Lorde, whan I am leyde on bere,
         Hye up to heven my soule hale —   *pull*
         For there commyn neyther grete ne smale,   *comes*
         But Thow drawe hem, Lorde, to The —
         That my soule be not in bale,
420   But *Parce michi, Domine!*

36

         Thow shalt me call at Domesday, [2]
         When Thow art set on jugement,
         And I to The, wythouten delay,
         Shall yeve myn answere verament.   *truly*
425   But, good Jhesu, to The I pray,
         Thynke alwey with full entent;   *attention*
         Thow madest me of a clot of clay;

---

[1] *Cunctis diebus quibus nunc milito, expecto, donec veniat immutacio mea.* Job 14.14: All the days, in which I am now in warfare, I expect until my change come.

[2] *Vocabis me, et ego respondebo tibi; operi manuum tuarum porriges dexteram.* Job 14.15: Thou shalt call me, and I will answer thee: to the work of thy hands thou shalt reach out thy right hand.

Thyne handwerke helpe, as Thow furst ment!   *intended*
And my wittes though I have myspent   *which I have wasted*
430 Thorough malyce, here, of frealté,   *in my frailty*
Here, leef Lorde, late me repente,
Thorow *Parce michi, Domine*!

37

Forsothe, my steppys everychone [1]   *every one*
Thow nombred hast, and tolde hem all.   *numbered; tallied*
435 But, Lorde, to The I make my mone,
As Thow art Lord of heven and hell.
Vertues, Lorde, though I have none,
Late Thy grace in me now welle,   *Let; spring up*
For woo ys hym that stante alone,   *who stands*
440 And hathe noon helpe yef that he fall.
My syn ys bytterer than eysell or gall,   *more bitter; vinegar*
And stynketh, Lorde, in syght of The;
But nought for than to The I call   *for that reason*
For *Parce michi, Domine*!

38

445 My spyryt shal be feble and feynt [2]
When I am fallen in any age;   *at any age*
My dayes, make I never so queynt,   *no matter how carefully I live them*
Shullen abrege and somwhat swage.   *be cut short and somewhat abated*
And I ful sone shal be atteynt   *overcome*
450 Whan I have loste myn hote corage;   *fiery pride*
And though I dyed than as doth a seynt,
A pyt shal be myne herytage.
In erthe gete I non other wage   *payment*
Of all rychesse that man may se;
455 Whan I am closed in that cage,   *grave*
Than *Parce michi, Domine*!

---

[1] *Tu quidem gressus meos dinumerasti, sed parce peccatis meis.* Job 14.16: Thou indeed hast numbered my steps, but spare my sins.

[2] *Spiritus meus attenuabitur, dies mei breviabuntur, et solum michi superest sepulcrum.* Job 17.1: My spirit shall be wasted: my days shall be shortened; and only the grave remaineth for me.

39

I have nat synned wylfully[1]
Thorow my feynt, feble nature,
Ne greved The so grevosly,   *Nor aggrieved You*
460   Wherfore I shulde thys wo endure.   *That I should [deserve to]*
Thow punysshest me, and I not why,   *do not know*
Passing resoun and good mesure.   *beyond what is reasonable*
Hit ys my flessh, Lorde, and nat I,
That grocheth ayenst Thyn hard reddure.   *complains about; strictness*
465   But, Lorde, as I am Thy creature,
And Thow that ylke God that boughtest me,   *same*
So my care recovere and cure   *restore to health*
With *Parce michi, Domine*!

40

My dayes, Lorde, passed are,[2]
470   And olde I am, I am no faunt.   *infant*
My thoughtes wandre wyde whare,   *everywhere*
For they ben, Lorde, full variaunte.   *indecisive*
Myne herte they grevyn wonder sare,   *afflict*
For ever about hym they haunte;   *it*
475   Thys maketh me to drowpe and dare,   *droop and cower*
That I am lyke a pore penaunte!   *humble penitent*
Though I be, Lorde, unsuffisaunte   *unworthy*
Any helpe to gete of The,
Yet, for I am Thy creaunte,   *because; creature*
480   Lorde, *Parce michi, Domine*!

41

The nyght they turned into the day,[3]   *they = the thoughts*
For they maden me to wake all nyght;
I myght nat slepe by no way,   *by no means*

---

[1] *Non peccavi, et in amaritudinibus moratur oculus meus*. Job 17.2: I have not sinned, and my eye abideth in bitterness. (Job 17.3 is omitted; see note.)

[2] *Dies mei transierunt; cogitaciones mee dissipate sunt, torquentes cor meum*. Job 17.11: My days have passed away; my thoughts are dissipated, tormenting my heart.

[3] *Noctem verterunt in diem, et rursum post tenebras spero lucem*. Job 17.12: They have turned night into day; and after darkness I hope for light again.

	Suche thoughtes were in myn hert plyght.	*fastened*
485	In derkenesse dymme as I so lay,	
	Yet hoped I after the clere daylyght;	*I looked for*
	But thoughtys me so trobled ay,	
	That I was than a wofull wyght!	*creature*
	But, Lorde, as Thow art mekyl of myght,	*great*
490	All evyll thoughtes put fro me,	
	And that I of The may have a syght,	
	Lorde, *Parce michi, Domine!*	

42

	Lorde, yef I shall suffre thys grete disese,[1]	*unease*
	Hit woll me brynge unto my grave!	
495	And yet, ywys, I may nat chese,	*choose*
	Whether I be kyng, knyght, or knave.	
	In derkenesse dymme, all oute of ese,	
	My lytell bed spred I have:	
	That bed shall I never lese,	*lose*
500	Though I wolde for angor rave,	
	Tyll the Day of Dome that, of my grave,	*from*
	I shall aryse, and mo with me.	*more*
	My soule, Lorde, I pray, Thow save	
	With *Parce michi, Domine!*	

43

505	To roten erthe, ryght thus sayde I,[2]	
	"Thow art my fader of whom I cam,"	*father from*
	And unto wormes sekurly,	*certainly*
	"Thow art my moder, thy son I am;	*mother*
	My sustren all ye bene, forwhy	*sisters; because*
510	None other then ye, forsoth, I am."	*Nothing; than you, truly*
	I shall call hem sustres, lo, forthy	*for that reason*
	For I shall roote amonge ham.	

---

[1] *Si sustinuero, infernus domus mea est; in tenebris stravi lectulum meum.* Job 17.13: If I wait, hell is my house; and I have made my bed in darkness.

[2] *Putredini dixi: Pater meus es; mater mea, et soror mea, vermibus.* Job 17.14: I have said to rottenness: Thou art my father; to worms: my mother and my sister.

Of the lowest erthe God made Adam,
Of whyche my kynde I had, as he.   *nature*
515   Now, Lorde, that art lykened to a lambe,
So *Parce michi, Domine*!

44

Where ys myn abydyng nowe,[1]   *endurance*
And all my pacience therto?
They ben away, I wote never howe,
520   Forsothe me wanteth bothe two.   *Truly I am in need of*
Yef myn hert be styf and towe,   *If; firm and strong [enough]*
To thanke The in wele and woo,   *weal and woe*
Hit ys nat I, but only Thow.   *the credit is due only to You*
Thow art my Lord and God also.
525   O Thow, grete Lord, Alpha and Oo,   *Omega*
Helpe me, for Thy grete pyté!
I have ynowgh, I pray The hoo,   *have had enough; cease*
And *Parce michi, Domine*!

45

To my skyn my mouth ys lo,[2]   *[attached] low*
530   And cleved fast, as ye se may;
And wasted ys my flesshe also;
And bothe my lyppes ben away;
My whyte tethe, they ben full bloo —   *blackened*
Ye wolde be agaste yef ye me say!   *saw*
535   Myne heryng ys full clene ago;   *hearing is entirely gone*
Myne eyen ben dymme, that weren ful gray;
And I that was full stoute and gay,   *cheerful*
Full horyble am now opon to se!
Tyme ys that men now for me pray,
540   For *Parce michi, Domine*!

---

[1] *Ubi est ergo nunc prestolacio mea et paciencia mea? Tu es, Domine, Deus meus.* Job 17.15: Where is now then my expectation, and who considereth my patience?

[2] *Pelli mee, consumptis carnibus, adhesit os meum; et derelicta sunt tantummodo labia circa dentes meos.* Job 19.20: The flesh being consumed, my bone hath cleaved to my skin: and nothing but lips are left about my teeth.

46

Reweth on me, reweth on me! [1]   *Pity me, pity me!*
My frendes namly, now helpeth at nede!
For I am there I may nat fle;   *there where*
The hande of God ful sore I drede.
545   And frendes, seeth that I am he
Thys other day that on the erth yede.   *[Who] This; passed*
Now helpe, yef that youre wyll be,
With prayer, fastyng, and almesdede.   *almsgiving*
For these mowen best gete me mede   *might; reward*
550   With *Placebo* and *Dirige.*
Herewith my soule, I pray yow, fede
With *Parce michi, Domine!*

47

Why, as God, do ye pursewe [2]
Me that suffre these sharpe shoures?   *assaults*
555   Ye lat me peyne here in a peynfull pewe,   *suffer; allotted situation*
That ys a place of grete doloures.   *agonies*
Yow I chese for frendes trewe,
And made yow myne executoures.
But tyme shall come that ye shall rewe   *regret*
560   That ever ye were to me so false treytoures.   *traitors*
My good ys spent, as hit were youres,   *as if*
But nat a peny yevyn ye me.   *did you give to me*
Nowe for all suche faytoures,   *imposters*
Lorde, *Parce michi, Domine!*

48

565   Who may graunte me thys boone, [3]   *request*
That my wordes wreten were   *be written*

---

[1] *Miseremini [mei], miseremini mei, saltem vos, amici mei, quia manus Domini tetigit me.* Job 19.21: Have pity on me, have pity on me, at least you my friends; because the hand of the Lord hath touched me.

[2] *Quare persequimini me sicut Deus, et carnibus meis saturamini?* Job 19.22: Why do you persecute me as God, and glut yourselves with my flesh?

[3] *Quis michi tribuat ut scribantur sermones mei?* Job 19.23: Who will grant me that my words may be written?

Pety Job

	In ensample of everychon	*As example to everyone*
	That hap may to ben in care?	*Who may happen to be in care*
	For yef they wolden make moone,	*if; complaint*
570	Eyther groche with hert sare	*Or lament with heavy heart*
	Ayenst God that sytteth in troone,	*throne*
	Because yef they wolden spare	
	And make nat so ferly fare,	
	But take ensample wolden of me.[1]	
575	Now, Lorde, as I am but wormes ware,	*food for wormes*
	So *Parce michi, Domine!*	

49

	Who shall graunt me, or I be dede,[2]	
	To wryte hem by oon and oone,	*them (i.e., words)*
	My booke with ynke blak or rede,	
580	Made with gumme and vermylone?	*gum; vermilion (a pigment)*
	Or ellys yet in plate of lede,	*by lead impression*
	Or graven in harde flynte of stone,	*engraved in hard flintstone*
	That all men, whereever they yede,	*go*
	Myght otherwhyle loke theropon?	*in other times*
585	I wolde my frendys and my foon	*would like that; foes*
	Ensample take myght by me.	
	As Thow art Thre, and God al Oon,	
	Now *Parce michi, Domine!*	

50

	I wote ryght well that my Redemptour[3]	
590	Lyveth yet, and lyve shall aye!	*forever*
	And I shall ryse, I not what oure,	*do not know what hour*

---

[1] *Perhaps if instead (i.e., because of me) they will refrain / And not make so wondrous a disturbance, / But rather take me as an example (see note)*

[2] *Quis michi det ut exarentur in libro, stilo ferreo, plumbi lamina, vel celte sculpantur in silice?* Job 19.23–24: Who will grant me that they may be marked down in a book, with an iron pen, and in a plate of lead, or else be graven with an instrument in flint-stone?

[3] *Scio enim quod Redemptor meus vivit, et in novissimo die de terra surrecturus sum; et rursum circumdabor pelle mea, et in carne mea videbo Deum Salvatorem meum.* Job 19.25–26: For I know that my Redeemer liveth; and in the last day I shall rise out of the earth. And I shall be clothed again with my skin, and in my flesh I shall see my God.

Oute of the erthe on Domysdaye,
And take to me my furst coloure,   *coloring*
In flesshe and felle, clad on clay.   *in*
595   And so shall I see my Savyour
Deme the worlde in wondre aray.   *wondrous fashion*
The wikked than, withouten delay,
As arowes, to helle they shullen fle.
Lorde, that I go nat that way,
600   So *Parce michi, Domine*!

51

Whan I mysylfe shall see in syght,[1]
With eyen clere and hert stable,   *steadfast*
And knowe Hym as God Almyght,
That was forme man disparitable,   *in form unequal to man*
605   Shall ther fore me noon other wyght   *before me; person*
Se my God that ys durable,
But I mysylfe, with eyen bryght,   *gleaming eyes*
Shall Hym beholde most honorable: *[Who] is most honorable*
O Lord, that charyté that ys so amyable,   *whose charity is*
610   And bryght shynyng in Thy magesté!
That syght to se, Lord, make me able,
Thorow *Parce michi, Domine*!

52

Thys hope ys in myn hert sette,[2]
That never from me shall dyssevere.   *depart*
615   Thereyn my truste also ys knette,   *knit (i.e., bound)*
The whyche to have now ys me levere.   *I am eager*
I hope to God that I shall gete   *gain recovery from*
Of all diseases yet rekevere,
And se my Lorde in Hys turete,   *turret*
620   With whom I hope to dwelle ever!
Though I be synfull, Lorde, take me never

---

[1] *Quem visurus sum ego ipse, et oculi mei conspecturi sunt, et non alius.* Job 19.27: Whom I myself shall see, and my eyes shall behold, and not another.

[2] *Reposita est hec spes mea in sinu meo.* Job 19.27: This my hope is laid up in my bosom.

In any thyng that may displese The.
Thy blysse late me have forever
Thorough *Parce michi, Domine*!

53

625   A, Lord, why leddest Thow so me [1]
     Oute of the wombe that I was in?
     Wold God I had consumed be
     Within myn oune moders skynne!
     That the eye with whyche I se
630   Had nat seyn no more ne mynne!   *less*
     That I myght in that degré   *condition*
     Never have wyste what had be synne!
     For syn maketh me from The to twynne —   *separate*
     That of nought madest Thow me — [2]
635   Thy mercy, Lord, make me to wynne
     With *Parce michi, Domine*!

54

     And wold God that I be hadde [3]   *treated*
     As a thyng that never was —
     For all with synne I am bestadde,   *beset*
640   And every day I do trespas!
     No wonder though I be ungladde,   *despondent*
     And though I synge often "allas!"
     For pure woo I wexed madde,
     Nere Goddys mercy my solas —   *Were not*
645   Lo, Lorde, lo, I am ryght as   *just like*
     A wytles man withouten The!   *witless (i.e., unreasoning)*
     But, as Thow of plenté mercy has,
     So *Parce michi, Domine*!

---

[1] *Quare de vulva eduxisti me? Qui utinam consumptus essem, ne oculus me videret!* Job 10.18: Why didst thou bring me forth out of the womb? O that I had been consumed, that eye might not see me!

[2] *For sin makes me — whom You made from nothing — separate from You*

[3] *Fuissem quasi non essem, de utero translatus ad tumulum.* Job 10.19: I should have been as if I had not been, carried from the womb to the grave.

55

	Whether the fewnes of my dayes [1]	*[How may I know] Whether: scarcity*
650	Shull nat hastyly have an ende?	
	Sythen I can se by no worldly wayes,	*foresee*
	But oute of the world sone shal I wende,	*pass*
	The worldes wyles ryght nat me payes,	*do not pay me [justly]*
	For they ben false and full unthende.	*entirely unprofitable*
655	My flesshly lust my soule affrayes,	*frightens my soul*
	And I am tempted with the fende.	*by the fiend*
	Thys maketh me to bowe and bende	*This state*
	Alwey to syn, that woo ys me.	
	Lord, that art curteys and hende,	*gentle*
660	So *Parce michi, Domine!*	

56

	Therfore, Lord, suffer Thow me [2]	*allow*
	A lytell whyle that wepe I may	
	The tyme that ever I greved The	
	In ded or thought, by nyght or day,	
665	And graunt me, yef Thy wyl be,	
	That here in erthe wepe I may.	
	The derke lande that I never se,	
	That kevered ys with black alway,	*covered*
	Now, good Jhesu, to The I pray,	
670	As Thow art God in Trinité,	
	From that londe Thow kepe me ay,	
	Thorow *Parce michi, Domine!*	

---

[1] *Nunquid non paucitas dierum meorum finietur brevi?* Job 10.20: Shall not the fewness of my days be ended shortly?

[2] *Dimitte ergo me, Domine, ut plangam paululum dolorem meum; antequam vadam, et non revertar, ad terram tenebrosam, et opertam mortis caligine.* Job 10.20–21: Suffer me, therefore, that I may lament my sorrow a little: Before I go and return no more, to a land that is dark and covered with the mist of death.

57

The londe of myschyef and of derknes,[1]   *sinfulness*
Whereas dampned soules dwell,
675   The londe of woo and of wrechednesse,
Where ben mo peynes than tonge may telle,
The londe of dethe and of duresse,   *hardship*
In whyche noon order may dwelle,
The londe of wepyng and of drerynesse,
680   And stynkyng sorow on to smelle!
Now from that londe, that cleped ys helle,   *called*
Worthy Lord, rescue now Thow me,
So that I maye ever with The dwelle
Thorough *Parce michi, Domine!*

Here endeth the ix lessons of the Dirige, which Job made in his tribulacion.

---

[1] *Terram miserie et tenebrarum, ubi umbra mortis et nullus ordo, sed sempiternus horror inhabitans.* Job 10.22: A land of misery and darkness, where the shadow of death, and no order, but everlasting horror dwelleth.

Notes

Abbreviations:

D MS Douce 322. [Base text.]
T TCC MS R.3.21.
H MS Harley 1706.
C MS Camb. Univ. Lib. Ff.2.38.
P MS Pepys 1584.

D presents the best text in the DHT group of affiliated MSS. The other two MSS, C and P, are related to each other but are not from the same exemplar (McSparran and Robinson, p. xvi). Crawford's analysis persuasively shows that the DHT textual group is nearer to the original poem than the CP pair (pp. 43–55). The following notes list variants only where: (1) C and P agree (thereby providing the secondary tradition, for which the texts are unpublished); or (2) readings from H, T, C, or P shed light on a problematic reading in D. Inverted wordings and variant spellings or verbal endings are not listed.

Incipit   C: *Here endyth the Compleynte of God and begynneth the ix lessons of dyryge whych ys clepyd Pety Job*; P: *Here endith the Seale of Mercy or the vii Salmes and begynnyth the ix lessons of dyrige that is clepid Pety Jobe.*

1–84   Stanzas 1–7 paraphrase Lesson 1 of the Dirige: Job 7.16–21. DHTP indicate the beginning of each lesson by means of large initials at stanzas 1, 8, 13, 19, 25, 32, 38, 45, and 53. The rubricator of C erroneously inserted only three large capitals, at stanzas 1, 32, and 45, but marginal indicators for initials appear at stanzas 8, 13, 19, and 25, and spaces (each containing a small guide letter) were left at stanzas 19, 38, and 53.

1   *Parche michi, Domine*! Line supplied by CP; omitted in DHT, where the stanza is headed (as is normal in these three MSS) with the Vulgate verse *Parce michi domine nichil enim sunt dies mei.*

8   *be but.* CP (adopted by Horstmann); DHT: *be.* Compare the similar phrase at line 575, where (conversely) CP omit the word *but.*

11   *not.* Kail and Crawford read the word in D as *nat,* but the vowel appears to be an *o.* Crawford emended her reading to *not,* as found in the other MSS. The usual form in D for the negative adverb is *nat,* but the verb for *ne wot,* "does not know," would be *not* (compare lines 461 and 591, where all MSS agree).

12   The refrain is the same in *The Bird with Four Feathers,* a companion poem in DHT. See note to line 12 of that poem. The word *Domine* appears in the liturgy — and in the commentaries of Gregory the Great, Odo of Cluny, Rupert of Deutz, and Peter Riga (Alford, p. 324 n. 6) — but not in the Vulgate text.

13   *What.* CP: *But what.*

13–16   The syntax of this question displays the poet's artfulness, as he asks, in effect, three differently modulated questions, each one building from the last: What is a man? What is a man who always magnifies himself? What is he other than a mere mark made from a clod of clay? In stating that man magnifies *himself,* the speaker alters the Latin sense (God as magnifier of man), emphasizes human pride, and starkly contrasts it to man's "nothingness." The imagery depicts God as artistic sculptor of man's form, with an emphasis upon the earthiness of the medium. The poet's overall stress upon man's base make-up from "dust" surpasses even the source verses in Job. As Crawford comments, "the synonyms *clay, pouder, erth,* and *hume* come up again and again" (p. 155).

21   *good Lord.* CP: *Lord God.*

What shall I say? The speaker establishes a tone of primal questioning that drives the poem: "I have a need to know what is man. It is evident he is *nothing* but as Thou, God, formed him. Knowing this and being a man, I need to know how to speak to Thee." In its spirit of questioning, the poem might be compared to the Vernon lyric *This World Fares as a Fantasy* (ed. Brown, pp. 160–64); see discussion by Douglas Gray, *Themes and Images in the Medieval English Religious Lyric* (London: Routledge & Kegan Paul, 1972), pp. 212–16.

23   *wote.* CP: *knowe.*

               helpe. CP: *helpe me.*

25   Crawford cites the opening *Or* of this line, *they* in line 481, and *hem* in line 578 as evidence for the continuity of the English poem from stanza to stanza. It would appear that the poet did not expect the Latin Office (used as stanza headings in DHT) to interrupt the flow of English verse.

               ayene. DHTC: *ayenst man*; P: *man agayn.* Emendation (also adopted by Crawford) is indicated by the rhyme and meter. The form for the preposition "against" is generally *ayenst* (appearing eight times) but *ayene* is found at line 163 (in all MSS).

30–34   The voice here speaks for himself and the reader, hence, the plural first-person pronouns (and the mixed singular/plural *oureself*), culminating in the phrase *the and me.*

36   Crawford remarks that the refrain has a substantive force here and at stanzas 5, 8, 16, 19, 25, 30, 31, 33, 34, 35, 36, 37, 39, 42, 45, 46, 51, 52, 53, 56, and 57. Here and at those points she hyphenates the Latin phrase and defines it "God's mercy towards me." Occurrences of the phrase elsewhere in Middle English suggest that it had currency as a common prayer; see Alford, pp. 323–35.

37   *O.* HCP (adopted by Crawford); DT: *Or.*

39   *mare.* TC; DHP: *more.* The northern spellings of T are adopted for the rhyme here and in lines 41 and 43. On northern forms in *Pety Job*, see note to line 512.

40   *salyve.* CP: *spotull blyfe.* Crawford notes that the reading of CP is influenced by the Prymer, which always used "some form of the word *spotull*" (p. 114). On the larger question of Prymer influence, see Crawford's careful analysis (pp. 107–17).

41   *sare.* T; DHCP: *sore.*

43   *lare.* T; DHCP: *lore.*

44   *That*. CP: *That Y*.

45   The poet introduces a christological reference to Jesus's five wounds into the paraphrase of verses from Job. The devotional theme is not, however, integral to the poem, as it is, for example, in *The Valley of This Restless Mind*.

47   *of*. CP: *of thys* (adopted by Horstmann).

53   *O*. Omitted in CP.

55–57   These lines set God's mercifulness toward man against man's willful ingratitude toward his own Creator. Because God gave man his being, this ingratitude is taken to be unnatural (*unkynde*). On the lyric tradition of God as mankind's friend, see Rosemary Woolf, *The English Religious Lyric in the Middle Ages* (Oxford: Clarendon, 1968), pp. 214–18.

59   *make me have*. CP: *that Y may*.

69   *pray The*. TCP (adopted by Horstmann and Crawford); DH: *pray*. The meter of the TCP reading is better; the word *The* probably dropped out by confusion with the next word *thys*.

79   *pytte*. The word means "hell" in line 33, but here it is the grave, whether actual (the voice is a soul who has died) or potential (the voice is a living soul for whom a grave is reserved). The voice typically speaks from a vaguely timeless perspective, for all souls, dead and living. There is eventually, however, a subtly timed sequence given to the speaker's state; see note to line 203.

80   *Though men me seke*. Crawford notes that this phrase appears to be a mistranslation of the Latin *si mane me quesieris*, the poet rendering *mane* ("in the morning") as "men."

81   *Abraham*. CP: *fayre Abraham*.

84   *So*. CP: *Ever*.

85–144   Stanzas 8–12 paraphrase Lesson 2: Job 10.1–7.

88   *lyfe*. C: *selfe* (adopted by Horstmann).

90   *oune*. Omitted in CP.

94   *how*. CP: *whi*, a reading that translates Latin *cur*. But, as Crawford notes, the reading of DHT fits the penitential stance: "The poet knows why he is judged . . . he is asking how the judgment will be carried out" (p. 248).

97–108   The *Pety Job* poet omits the last phrase of the verse in Job, *et consilium impiorum adives* ("and help the counsel of the wicked"), an accusation of God's injustice that goes beyond the sinner's personal plight.

98   *accuse*. CP: *to accuse*.

105   *of*. CP: *on*.

107   *Thow*. TCP: *Lord Thow* (adopted by Horstmann and Crawford, for better meter). The extra syllable is not necessary; stress falls upon *Thys* and the second syllable of *prayer*.

114   *may se*. CP: *man may*.

119   *nat that*. TCP (adopted by Horstmann and Crawford); DH: *nat*. The variant reading is accepted for both sense and meter. The word *that* must have been omitted by confusion with either *nat* or *Thow*.

121   *lyke*. C: *slyke* ("such," adopted by Horstmann). The reading in C "could be an original Northern rime preserved or . . . a scribe's attempt to avoid the identical rime" (Crawford, p. 250). Kail erroneously prints *syke*.

125   *That*. TCP: *This* (adopted by Horstmann and Crawford, for sense). Emendation is unnecessary; *that* contrasts as well as *this* with *tomorow* in line 127.

126   *gladsom*. CP: *gladly*.

128   *borne*. Horstmann emends: *is borne*. Crawford notes, however, that *borne* can be read as parallel to *syke*, with both words serving as complements to the verb *wexeth* (line 127).

132   *Lorde.* CP: *Ever.*

133–44   The poet omits Job's protestation of innocence (*scias quia nichil impium fecerim*), in keeping with the poem's penitential emphasis. Compare stanza 39, where Job's "I have not sinned" is rendered by the poet "I have nat synned *wylfully.*"

134   *to serche thus.* C (adopted by Horstmann and Crawford); D: *suche thus*; H: *suche ys*; T: *to seche thus*; P: *to serche.* Crawford's analysis of this line is plausible: "The poet probably used *seche* in line 133 to translate Latin *queras*, and *serche* in line 134 to translate Latin *scruteris*" (p. 250). The errors of D and H support evidence elsewhere that H is a copy of D (p. 52).

135   *hardnes.* CP: *hardynesse.*

145–216   Stanzas 13–18 paraphrase Lesson 3: Job 10.8–12.

148   *nobley.* CP: *noble lord.*

150   The subject of Satan as deceiver and cause of man's fall is not found in the biblical verse. Compare note to line 246.

152   *Hedlyng.* C (adopted by Horstmann); DHT: *Heldyng*; *Heledyng*. It is likely that the poet used the word for "headlong" found in C; see *MED hedlyng* adv. (a), where in two citations the word is followed by the adverb *doun.* For Job 10.8 the Prymer has "thou castist me doun so sodeynli" (p. 60), and Douay (1609) has "thou cast me down headlong on a sudden." In DHT the image is curious — God holding down man by his skull — and does not correspond to the Latin.

155   *ranne.* CP: *down ran.*

156   *So.* CP: *Evyr.*

161   *be.* TCP: *ben* (adopted by Horstmann).

165   *ys no.* CP (adopted by Horstmann and Crawford); DH: *ys*; T: *nys.* The reading of CP is accepted for better sense and meter.

168   *Lorde*. CP: *Thus*.

169   *nat me, Lorde*. C: *not me*; P: *Thou not me*.

169–78   Springing from the biblical simile of milk, the poet builds up a sequence of "liquid" images. The milk, his blood, is softer (that is, weaker) than silk, which is vulnerable to rain; consequently it leads him to sin, so that he, who is filled with such blood, wades deeply in sin and nearly drowns in it.

171   *Thow madest that*. CP (adopted by Horstmann); DH: *that*; T: *of that*; Crawford emends: *thow cruddedest*. The reading of DH has obviously lost at least one word, and T appears to be a rough attempt to correct the DH reading. Crawford supplies the verb *crudden*, which, she states, is used to translate Latin *coagulare* "in all manuscripts of the Middle English Prymer, in the *Ten Lessons*, and in the Wycliffite Bible" (p. 252). Her speculation may be correct, but it is not needed for the sense, since the phrase in CP, *madest . . . ryght as the hardnesse*, supplies the meaning of *coagulare*. Moreover, the CP phrase continues the emphasis upon what God has "made" (compare lines 159, 162, and 170) and leads to stanza 16.

172   *chese ys*. CP: *flesche hyt*.

175   *thus*. TCP: *this*.

183   As Crawford notes, this line anticipates and translates the next verse, Job 10.12; compare line 193.

192   *For*. CP: *Of*.

195   *to me nat ones*. C: *not oones to me*; P: *oonis to me*.

202   *that*. C: *that that* (adopted by Horstmann).

203   The lyric monologue subtly dramatizes a sequence of events, moving from a state of contrition in life to the uncertain state of the soul after death. Here the speaker is still one of the living, praying for something before he is "laid in the grave." The progression past the point of death is gradual, occurring at about stanza 42.

206   *that ys.* CP: *that Y have*; omitted in T.

208   *Than.* TC: *Thyn* (adopted by Horstmann); P: *Thy.*

        grace. CP: *goste.*

211   *wypt.* P: *whypt.* The spelling in P helps to establish the meaning of this word, "whipped, driven with force." The rhymes in *-ept(e)* may indicate an original form *w(h)ept*, a northern variant spelling. Crawford follows the *OED* in defining *wypt* as "wiped" (*wipe* v., sense 4.). The phrase *wipe from* is, however, otherwise unattested, and parallel senses in the *OED* do not begin until 1535.

214   *in.* Omitted in CP.

216   *Lord.* Omitted in CP.

217–26 Ten lines form a long sentence jumbled in syntax by rapid mental associations and emotions. The poet seems to be reacting to the scriptural pile-up of Latin terms for his iniquity, *iniquitates, peccata, scelera,* and *delicta.* As the speaker acknowledges his heap of sins, he envisions the frightening pit of hell.

217–88 Stanzas 19–24 paraphrase Lesson 4: Job 13.23–28.

218   *an.* CP: *a.*

220   *may.* CP: *may heere* (adopted by Horstmann).

222   *so.* Omitted in TCP.

225   *on.* TCP (adopted by Horstmann and Crawford); DH: *of.* The emendation is needed for sense. For a similar image of hell, see *The Sinner's Lament,* line 66.

227   *may.* CP: *may me* (adopted by Horstmann).

232   *lesse*. TCP (adopted by Horstmann and Crawford); DH: *lace*. The rhyme shows that TCP preserve the correct reading. The shared error in DH was caused by attraction to the a-rhyme.

233   As Crawford notes, the poet here extends his biblical source, showing God to persecute the sinner as an enemy.

235   *fayne*. CP: *Lorde*.

236   *me*. The line would be better, metrically, without this word, but it is found in all MSS.

238   *oo*. CP: *good*.

240   *Lorde*. CP: *Evyr*.

241   *to*. CP: *to be*.

242   *freel*. CP: *full frele* (adopted by Horstmann).

244   *Although*. DHTCP: *As though*. Emendation is needed for sense.

        beres bynde. DHTCP; Crawford emends: *be berebynde*. The phrase is apparently a common expression for boldness. Compare the Vernon lyric *Think on Yesterday*, where *bynde* rhymes with *wynde*, a word used for the forces of the world:

> This wrecched world nis but a wynde,
> Ne non so stif to stunte ne stare,
> Ne non so bold beores to bynde,
> That he nath warnynges to beo ware.
>   (lines 52–55, ed. Brown, p. 144)

        S.v. *MED bere* n.(1), sense 1.(d). Crawford's emendation to *be berebynde* (a plant-name) is overly speculative.

246   *fondyng*. See *OED fanding* vbl. sb., "a testing or putting to the proof."

        of The. CP: *of the fende* (adopted by Horstmann and Crawford); T: *oft*. The phrase *fondyng of the fende* is well attested; see *MED fondinge* and *OED fanding*, sense 2. The CP phrase may therefore be the original, especially since the poet does add the agency of Satan elsewhere (compare lines 117, 150, and 656). I have, however, retained the DH reading because the idea that God does the testing accords with the scriptural source.

249 *grope*. CP: *graspe*.

    a. Omitted in CP.

250 *though I stomble*. Crawford emends: *through the stobble*, another editorial attempt to bring the poem closer to the Latin Job (see note to line 244). Her interpretation of the line is faulty: "if the poet stumbles God would not be following him but catching him." The point is that the speaker is blind to God's ways, even to God's tests, but God is nonetheless constantly watchful of him.

252 *Yet*. CP: *Evyr*.

258 *hit*. Omitted in CP.

259 *thys*. CP: *thus* (adopted by Horstmann).

    yse. Horstmann emends: *I see*.

260 *And distroy me for*. C: *Dyscrye me of*; P: *Discryve me of*; Horstmann emends: *Distroy me for*. Horstmann's rendition of lines 259–60 (*And thus thou wyllt, fulle welle I see, / distroy me ffor my wycked dede*) removes the idea that God sees private sins.

262 *Lorde*. CP: *welle*.

263 *drope*. TCP: *drowpe*.

265 *a synew*. CP: *stockes*. For the sense "snare," see *OED sinew* sb. sense 1.b. *Synew* to translate Latin *nervus* also occurs in some copies of the Prymer; the word *stockes* occurs in other copies and has once been inserted as a correction of *synew*. According to Crawford, the variants suggest "that the

poet or some of the scribes did have a verbal memory of at least parts of a Prymer or of some similar vernacular version of the Office of the Dead" (p. 112).

268   *in wey or walle*. The sense would seem to be "in open-ways and in walled enclosures." Crawford suggests a reference to "medieval wall-walks, such as those surviving in York today" (p. 257).

277–80   The syntactic conjoining of three images (the third one not found in the Vulgate) is magnificently evocative. Rotting shall consume *the body*, which fares just like moth-eaten cloth, or just like (the innovation) smoke departing from fire. The final image denotes the true transparency of the ephemeral body, and the burning life of the soul. The remarkable pile-up of images is then converted to a stark summation: "So body and soul asundre goth."

278   *mowthe-eten*. C: *moght eton*; P: *mothis etyng*; T: *mothis that eten*.

279   *And*. Omitted in CP.

281   *hume*. CP: *slyme*.

283   *than*. CP: *Lorde*.

287   *leve*. CP: *beleve*.

289   Human experience is gendered as male. "Woman" is the earth from which men spring, the material source to be abhorred and regretted. The androcentrism derives from Job (see Edwin M. Good, "Job," in *Harper's Bible Commentary*, gen. ed. James L. Mays [San Francisco: Harper & Row, 1988], p. 432), but in *Pety Job* it is strongly colored by medieval penitential ideas of the male soul birthed into errant female flesh (see stanza 53). *The Messengers of Death*, a poem found in the Vernon MS, opens with a paraphrase of this verse:

        The Mon that is of wommon i-bore,
        His lyf nis heere but a throwe [instant] —

So seith Job us heer bifore
Al in a Bok that I wel knowe. (lines 1–4)
> (ed. F. J. Furnivall, *The Minor Poems of the Vernon Manuscript*, Part 2, EETS
> o.s. 117 [1901; rpt. New York: Greenwood, 1969], p. 443)

289–372   Stanzas 25–31 paraphrase Lesson 5: Job 14.1–6.

293   *hote and colde, and hungor.* CP: *heete colde hungur and.*

294   *Turmented.* CP: *Turned he.*

298   *a.* Omitted in CP.

    and. TCP: *that.*

299   *The.* Omitted in CP.

    lovely. CP: *mylde.*

300   *For.* CP: *Of.*

301   *spryngeth oute.* CP: *owt spryngyth* (adopted by Horstmann).

307   *houre.* CP (adopted by Horstmann); DHT: *shoure.* The reading of CP is
better than the repeated rhyme of DHT. As soon as the Job text calls up the
ancient flower simile — a figure for man in time — and the poet establishes
an a-rhyme upon *-oure, houre* becomes the inevitable fourth rhyme word,
after *floure, shoure,* and *coloure.* It suits also the theme of growth after birth,
"from yere to yere," begun in stanza 25.

308   *ryght.* Omitted in C; P: *like.*

309   *full.* C: *all full*; P: *all foule.*

311   *Of heven blysse.* CP: *Lord of hevene.*

318   *ys harder than.* C: *ys harde as*; P: *as hard as*; T: *harder than.*

    ston. TCP (adopted by Crawford); DH: *a ston(e).*

320   In expanding his paraphrase of the Job verses, the poet often alludes to the traditional three foes of mankind, the flesh, the world, and the devil. On the addition of Satan elsewhere, see note to line 246.

       they. HTCP (adopted by Crawford); D: *then.* The error in D is caused by attraction to the following word *ben.*

321   *Lord.* Omitted in CP.

323   Passion literature often contained devotion to both Mary and John the Evangelist, derived from John 19.26–27. Compare *The Four Leaves of the Truelove*, lines 225–26, and the meditation addressed to St. John the Evangelist by the fourteenth-century monk John Whiterig (ed. Hugh Farmer, *The Monk of Farne* [Baltimore: Helicon, 1961], pp. 149–51).

325   *But.* C: *A*; P: *O.*

327   *A.* Omitted in CP.

       undertake. CP (adopted by Horstmann and Crawford); DH: *understande*; T: *undirstake.* Crawford explains the T reading as a scribal attempt to correct the faulty rhyme produced by the error in DH.

333   *Ywys.* CP: *Forsothe.*

335   *Lorde.* Omitted in CP.

336   *And ever.* CP: *Wyth.*

338   *take.* CP: *take thou* (adopted by Horstmann).

343–44 These lines summarize the speaker's attitude about the life of the soul before and after bodily death: it is only sorrow and care until God's Judgment, which may allow entry to heaven.

347   On the notion of actively rising up out of sin to repent, a move that requires willed energy, compare *The Sinner's Lament*, line 72.

348   *Lorde.* CP: *Evyr.*

350   *now*. Omitted in CP.

354–58   For the story of Ezechias, see 4 Kings 20 and Isaiah 38. The poet recasts the story into a penitential exemplum. The biblical Ezechias wept not for his sins, but for the fact that his life was being cut short. Rather than repent, he pleaded his righteousness. The reference to Ezechias at this verse in Job corresponds to Gregory's use of it in the *Moralia in Job* (Crawford, pp. 135–37; for Gregory, see J. P. Migne, ed., *Patrilogia Latina* 75.987). In general, there is little evidence that Gregory's work influenced the poet. The borrowing need not have been direct from Gregory but rather from a sermon or other reading. As usual, the English poet inserts a greater penitential emphasis.

359   *Lord, yeve*. CP: *So graunt*.

360   *Have*. CP: *Wyth*.

364   *hys*. CP: *a*.

365   *lust*. CP: *lyste*.

366–69   A rhetorical shift severs the complaint of the octave from the speaker's piety in the final quatrain. The speaker precariously balances two contrary perspectives: the plaintive "This holde I, Lorde, for the beste" and the repudiative "all thys worlde now ys myswrest."

369   *all*. Omitted in CP.

370   *thys*. TCP: *thus* (adopted by Horstmann).

372   *For*. CP: *Thorow*.

373–84   Crawford notes that in this stanza the poet departs from the primary sense of the Job verse: "The sense of hiding in the grave, expressed in the Latin *in inferno protegas me*, is turned by the poet into a stanza on the omnipresence of God" (p. 262).

373–444   Stanzas 32–37 paraphrase Lesson 6: Job 14.13–16.

375   *Fro*. T (adopted by Crawford); DHCP: *For*. Kail prints *Fro* without noting it as an emendation of D.

376   *my*. CP: *any*.

377   *concurraunte*. The rhymes in this stanza exhibit an aureate flair. This word would probably contain the earliest meaning in English for *concur*, "to run together violently, to collide," hence my definition, "prone to rebel." See *OED concur* v., which shows little currency for the word before the sixteenth century. The *MED* offers a tentative definition of the unusual usage in *Pety Job*, "? exist along with others," a definition adopted by Crawford.

378   *in*. CP: *in thy* (adopted by Horstmann).

379   *haunte*. C: *daunt*; P: *daund*. The word *haunt* means "frequent the company of, stay near" (*MED haunten* v., sense 3a), not "seek," as cited in the *MED* (sense 3b).

380   *Yet*. Omitted in CP.

382   *now*. Omitted in CP.

383   *leccioun*. CP; DHT: *lessoun*. The spelling of CP is adopted to accord with the aureate rhyme-words of the stanza. Although not found in the *MED* (compare *lecoun* n.), *leccioun* is an anglicized form of Latin *lectio*, "a reading, a lesson." The word *leccio* heads each lesson of the Dirige in the Prymer.

388   *of Thy blysse am so*. CP: *am of blysse full*.

391   *bounde here*. CP: *bownden*.

393   *Thow*. Omitted in CP.

393–94   On God's *pyté*, compare *The Bird with Four Feathers*, line 13.

395   *lyght as lynde*. A proverbial expression for carefree light-heartedness, derived from the linden tree's delicate leaves, which are easily set in rapid motion by the wind; see *MED lind(e)* n., sense 1b.

396	*To have.* CP: *Of.*
399	*in.* CP: *on.*
401–02	These two lines are omitted in T.
405	*Thus.* TCP (adopted by Horstmann); DH: *Thys.*
407	*That I may.* CP: *Graunt me to.* The variant helps to clarify that lines 407–08 are to be read as a petition.
	the. CP: *thy* (adopted by Horstmann).
408	*Of.* CP: *Wyth*; Horstmann emends: *Lord.*
409	*lyve.* CP: *leve.*
410	*wepyng.* C: *woopes*; P: *wopis.*
412	*fale.* TCP; DH: *fall(e).* The reading of TCP is adopted for the rhyme; the variant is not cited by Crawford.
416	*hale.* CP: *thou hale* (adopted by Horstmann).
420	*But.* CP: *Evyr.*
424	*myn.* T (adopted by Horstmann and Crawford); DH: *my*; CP: *an.* The emendation conforms to the D scribe's practice elsewhere of using *-n* on possessive pronouns preceding vowels. A similar emendation is adopted at line 589.
429	*And my wittes though.* P; DHT: *And with my thought*; C: *And wyttes myne thogh*; Crawford emends: *My wittes though.* The reading of P is adopted for better sense; compare similar phrasing at line 345.
432	*Thorow.* CP (adopted by Crawford); DH: *But*; T: *With.* The emendation complements the one at line 429 and is needed for logical sense.
436	*hell.* CP: *alle.*

438   *welle*. CP: *walle*.

441   *bytterer*. HTCP (adopted by Horstmann and Crawford); D: *bytter*. The D
         scribe neglected to add the hooked sign for *-er* to the end of the word.
         Crawford mistakenly reads *bytter* in H and takes this line as an instance of
         shared error in DH.

         eysell or gall. Vinegar and gall, the two bitter drinks offered to Jesus on the
         Cross, to increase his torment (Matthew 27.34).

445–528 Stanzas 38–44 paraphrase Lesson 7: Job 17.1–2, 11–15. The *Pety Job* poet
         omits one verse found in the Office of the Dead: *Libera me, Domine, et pone
         me iuxta te, et cuiusvis manus pugnet contra me*. (Job 17.3: Deliver me, O
         Lord, and set me beside thee, and let any man's hand fight against me.) The
         missing verse would have come between stanzas 39 and 40.

446   *I am fallen in any*. CP: *that Y am fall(en) yn* (adopted by Crawford). Craw-
         ford's adoption of the CP reading is based on a belief that the poet is
         describing the weakness of old age. The context, however, suggests that his
         weakness remains a fact regardless of age and of how cautiously he might try
         to live.

447   *never*. Crawford emends: *hit never*, in order "to complete the phrase *make hit
         queynt*" (p. 265). For the idiom, see *OED quaint* a., sense 11, and *MED
         queinte* adj., sense 2(e). The emendation is not needed, however, because the
         subject *dayes* supplies the implied object for the idiom. Another example of
         the idiom without *hit* appears in the Vernon lyric *Who Says the Sooth, He
         Shall Be Shent*, line 14 (ed. Brown, p. 152).

455   *cage*. A figurative term for the grave. Compare the similar use of a cage
         image in *The Sinner's Lament*, line 56.

461   *not*. In D the *o* is written over an *a*.

465   This line is omitted in H.

466   *Thow*. The word is omitted in DHT, but supplied by comparison of the line
         with the two variants, that is, C: *And Thou that yche God that madyst me*, and
         P: *And Thou God aloan that madist me*. Both Horstmann and Crawford

adopt the emendation, which is needed to supply an antecedent for *that ylke God*.

471   *wandre*. C: *wandren* (adopted by Horstmann); P: *wanderith*.

             whare. The word has the generalized sense, "wherever, whither"; see *OED where* adv., sense 9.

472   *Lorde*. CP: *ofte*.

479   *Thy*. CP: *thus*.

480   *Lorde*. CP: *Evyr*.

481   *they*. Refers to the thoughts described in the preceding stanza. See note to line 25.

484   *myn*. CP: *my*.

             plyght. CP: *pyght* (adopted by Horstmann and Crawford). Crawford states that "none of the *OED* definitions of *plyght* (DHT) fits the context of this line." (p. 267). The word is, however, the past participle of *pleiten*, meaning "fastened" (*MED*, sense [c]) or "turned over in one's mind" (sense [a]).

489   *mekyl*. CP: *moche*.

491   *a*. Omitted in CP.

492   *Lorde*. CP: *Thorow*; T: *With*.

493–94   The poet emphasizes disease and death, not hell as in the Latin source. Here the poet initiates a series of stanzas that meditate upon the experience of the soul after death. In the poem as a whole this series occurs within a larger sequence from life to death; see note to line 203.

496   *Whether I be*. CP: *Be Y*.

497   The imagery of a bed and sleeplessness, begun in the last stanza, evokes now multiple meanings: birth, individual consciousness, a deathbed, the grave.

501   *that, of my.* CP: *owt of that.*

503   *Thow.* CP: *The Thou*; HT: *The.*

504   *With.* CP: *Thorow.*

508   *I am.* CP (adopted by Kail, Horstmann, and Crawford, for the rhyme); DHT: *am I,* an error caused by attraction the a-rhyme.

509–12 Note how the poet plays with the sounds of *for* and *I* within these lines.

510   *then.* D; HTCP: *than* (adopted by Crawford). The form is merely a spelling variant; compare *than* at lines 318 and 441.

        am. C: *name*; P: *ne am*; Horstmann emends: *nam.*

511   *sustres.* CP: *systren.*

512   *ham.* CP; DHT: *hem.* The spelling, either northern or Midland, is accepted for the rhyme. The D scribe's usual form is *hem.* The poet's dialect is difficult to ascertain because the evidence in the poem is mixed. On the frequent presence of northern forms, Crawford writes:

> By the mid to late fifteenth century, when the *Pety Job* poet was working, many Northern forms had no doubt become part of the literary language at the command of any poet looking for appropriate rimes. Desire that their works be associated with the popular Northern devotional poems (especially those of Richard Rolle) may also have prompted authors whose dialect was non-Northern to use Northern forms. Although determination of dialect from mixed rime evidence is difficult, it may be conjectured that the *Pety Job* poet used a Southeast-Midlands dialect. (p. 57)

515   On Christ likened to a lamb, see John 1.29.

527   *hoo.* CP: *sey hoo.* The variant takes the word to be the exclamation, "hoo," used to attract someone's attention. But it is a verb; see *OED ho* v.[2], "to cease, pause." The speaker is asking God for a brief respite from his oppressive human condition.

528   *And.* CP: *Wyth.*

529   *skyn my mouth*. C: *mouthe me skynne*; P: *skyn my bone*. Crawford points out that the poet has apparently mistranslated *os meum* (Douay "my bone") as *my mouth*. The result is a stanza entirely about the mouth, teeth, and lips (in a free rendering of the Latin), and then about senses (hearing and eyesight) also located in the head. The P scribe tried to correct the error of *os meum*, possibly from a memory of "my boon" in the Prymer.

    lo. The meaning is possibly "lo!" (Crawford).

529–52 The persons addressed in these two stanzas are other men, a shift from the intimate address to God that characterizes most of the poem.

529–624 Stanzas 45–52 paraphrase Lesson 8: Job 19.20–27.

530   *And cleved*. C: *Cleved* (adopted by Crawford); P: *Clevyng*; T: *And clevith*. CP (and Crawford) read *ys cleved* as a single verb; DHT have a compound verb, *ys* (attached low) and (is) *cleved*.

533   *they*. Omitted in CP.

536   Gray eyes, often used to describe heroines in romance, were considered beautiful. *Gray* probably refers to the eye color one would now term light blue.

538   *Full*. Omitted in CP.

539   *that*. Omitted in CP.

540   *For*. CP: *Wyth*.

542   *now*. CP: *ye*.

    helpeth. HTCP: *helpe*. See note to line 547.

545   *And*. CP: *Now*.

    seeth. TCP: *syth*.

546   *that*. Omitted in CP.

547   *helpe*. This apparently plural imperative does not agree in form with *reweth*, *helpeth*, and *seeth* in the same stanza. Alternation of form was not uncommon in Middle English; see Tauno F. Mustanoja, *A Middle English Syntax*, Part I. Parts of Speech (Helsinki: Société néophilologique, 1960), p. 474.

          that. Omitted in CP.

548   Refers to the three classes of pentiential deeds required in the satisfaction of the sacrament of penance. See Matthew 6.1–18; and Spitzig, p. 179.

550   *Placebo* and *Dirige*. The opening words, respectively, of Vespers and Matins of the Office of the Dead (see *Breviarium Sarum*, ed. Procter and Wordsworth). The phrase appears in the refrain of a political poem (ed. Robbins, *Historical Poems of the XIVth and XVth Centuries* [New York: Columbia University Press, 1959], pp. 187–88).

551   *Herewith my*. CP: *My hungery*.

555   *peyne*. TCP: *pyne* (either a spelling variant, or the verb "pine").

          pewe. Cited in the *OED* as the first usage of the word with the sense "station, situation, allotted place." See *pew* n., sense 3.b. The *MED* tentatively assigns this unusual usage to the noun (found in place-names) meaning "hill, knoll" (*peue* n.[2]).

561   Crawford suggests that this line approximates a translation (otherwise absent) of the Latin *et carnibus meis saturamini*, noting that the poet "changes the verbal persecution of the biblical Job by his 'comforters' into robbery" (p. 270).

563   *faytoures*. C: *false factowres*; P: *false faytours*. In C the scribe has interlined the word *false*, which may indicate that it was added to fill out the line in an earlier exemplar. In meaning *factowres* (C) does not differ from *faytours* (DHTP).

564   *Lorde*. CP: *Evyr*.

569–74   Given that *Pety Job* is itself an extended complaint over the human condition, the thought expressed in this stanza becomes (perhaps unconsciously) paradoxical. The speaker states that he would like to be an example, after death, to others so that they might "spare" their own complaining. The idea that the speaker becomes a "mirror" by which others may learn and thereby contain their own grief is similar in point to *The Sinner's Lament*, but the *Pety Job* speaker has offered scarce comfort to the reader (other than what the refrain may suggest), and his own example might be said to be one of unrestrained lament (see note to lines 665–66). The poet seems to play, nonetheless, upon the idea that learning to "spare" one's lament is a worthy reflection of God's "sparing" mercy.

570   *Eyther*. CP: *Or*.

           with hert. CP: *ofte wyth hertys*.

572   *Because yef*. Horstmann emends: *Percase yet*; Crawford emends: *Percase then*. But the agreement of all MSS on this reading and on *Fore yef* at line 569 suggests a grammatical construction of hypothesis that the scribes could understand: "for if something is liable to occur, (yet) by (another) cause perhaps something else will come about." *Yef* can encompass the meaning "perhaps" (see *MED if* conj., sense 5).

573   *nat so*. CP: *no soche*.

575   *but*. Omitted in CP. Compare line 8.

578   *hem*. Refers to the words mentioned in line 566 in the preceding stanza. See note to line 25.

579   *My*. DHTCP; Horstmann and Crawford emend: *In*. The editors' emendation is based on the Latin *in libro* and the plausibility of such an error on paleographical grounds. But *In* is not necessary for sense (it is understood in context), it has no basis in any MS, and the phrase *My booke* becomes a figure for "my life made into a tangible example for others," something that is quite significant and personal to the speaker.

580   *gumme*. The *MED* does not cite this use of the word in the art of bookmaking. Besserman notes the presence in this stanza of "the anachronistic vocabulary of the medieval scribe" (p. 81).

581   *yet*. Omitted in CP.

583   *whereever*. CP: *where*.

588   *Now*. CP: *So*.

589   *my*. HTCP (adopted by Crawford); D: *myn*. Compare line 424.

592   *on Domysdaye*. These words represent the poet's translation of *in novissimo die* and are part of the general addition of judgment to the ideas found in the Latin verse. The Last Judgment is a recurring theme; compare stanzas 22 and 34.

594   *In*. CP: *And*.

601   *Whan*. DHTCP; Horstmann emends: *Whame*; Crawford emends: *Whom*. The emendation derives from Latin *Quem*, but it is not necessary, nor does it help the sense or syntax of the complex Middle English sentence that runs for eight lines.

602   *hert*. Kail emends: *herte*, for meter.

604   *disparitable*. Horstmann suggests *despitable*, but does not emend. Another example of aureate rhyme, the word is perhaps a coinage by the poet. No other examples are cited in the *MED*.

607   *bryght*. The word connotes the speaker's visual capacity and also the brightness of the sight of God's majesty, as envisioned at line 610.

609   *charyté that ys*. CP: *arte* (adopted by Crawford). This hypermetric line suggests the speaker's imagined rapture at the sight of the Godhead.

622   *In any thyng*. C: *Wyth oghe*; P: *With oute*.

624   *Thorough*. CP: *Wyth*.

625–26 In William Lichfield's *The Complaint of God to Sinful Man* (preserved with *Pety Job* in TCP) man answers God:

> I wolde my motheris wombe had be my grave.
> For what profityth my lyvyng here,
> But if I do so that Thou wylt me save? (lines 164–66)
>   (ed. E. Borgström, p. 513; see note to line 289)

625–84   Stanzas 53–57 paraphrase Lesson 9: Job 10.18–22.

628   *Within.* CP: *In.*

629–30   The poet changes the sense of the Latin, perhaps in mistranslation, and greatly expands the penitential sense of regret at having seen the temptations of the world. While the verse in Job is a plea that God might never have seen the unfortunate Job, the *Pety Job* version has the eye belonging to the speaker and its sight is focused upon the world.

630   *no more.* CP: *me more*; Crawford emends: *ne more.* Crawford derives her emendation from a blend of the two readings "to make the negatives parallel" (p. 274). The change is not needed. The CP reading appears to be a partial attempt to correct the mistranslation of lines 629–30.

    ne. C: *or*; P: *of.*

633   *from.* CP: *Lorde fro.*

634   CP: *Ye from the Lorde that madyste me.* Crawford points out that the word *That* in DHT could refer to either *me* or *The* in line 633, and that the sense is the same either way. CP represents a scribal rewording.

635   *make me to.* CP: *graunt that Y may.*

636   *With.* CP: *Thorow.*

637–48   The poet omits the second half of the verse from Job (in Douay, "carried from womb to the grave"). Job expresses the wish to have never been, that is, to be as if conveyed immediately from womb to grave; the clause negates not birth but the experience that comes with life. In *Pety Job* the wish is stronger: *never* to have been born.

644   *Nere.* CP: *Ne were*; T: *Nor.*

647   *of plenté*. CP: *Lorde all*.

652   *oute of*. CP: *fro*.

653–56   On the poet's insertion of the theme of the world, the flesh, and the devil, see notes to line 246 and 320.

660   *So*. CP: *Evyr*; omitted in T.

661   *Thow*. CP: *now*.

661–84   Chaucer's Parson draws upon this passage (Job 10.20–22) to exemplify the third cause of contrition, the fear of judgment and dread of hell, "the derke lond, covered with the derknesse of deeth" (*CT* X(1) 175). See especially *CT* X(1) 180–85 (*Riverside Chaucer*, p. 291).

662   *whyle that wepe*. C; DHT: *what that whyl(l)*; P: *what that whaile and wepe*; Crawford emends: *whyle that whaile*. The reading of C is adopted for sense, and for its translation of the Latin phrase *ut plangam paululum*.

663   *greved*. CP: *gyltyd*.

665–66   The petition is for an allowance of time to lament and for permission to use one's earthly life in lament. In retrospect, these lines are expressive of the speaker's mode of poetic utterance, which figures profitable living as a verbal song of perpetual complaint and appeal, sorrow and repentance. On the problematic psychological balance required of the penitent (acknowledgment of sin without despair), see Lee Patterson, pp. 374–84.

667   *never*. C: *ne*; P: *not*.

669   *good*. Omitted in CP.

678   *may*. CP: *may there*.

679   *of*[2]. Omitted in CP.

680   *sorow*. CP: *orrour*. The reading in CP seems to derive from the Latin word *horror*, but it should also be noted that the poet's rendition of Job is rather free in this stanza.

681   *cleped*. CP: *named*.

682   *Worthy*. CP: *Worschypfull*.

     now Thow. Omitted in CP.

Colophon CP: *Here endyth Pety Joob and begynnyth the Proverbis of Salamon*.

The Sinner's Lament

Introduction

What sorow, qwat dred hopes thon the weryed wrycches sal hafe whene God sal say: "*Ite maledicti in ignem eternam.*" . . . Than sal the foule deevells dryfe thase wrytches in til hell als wod lyouns, withouten end thare forto dwele. Than sal thay wery the tyme that thai eever ylle wrogth. . . . Nedderes, snakis, tadis and other venemous beestis, ma than I can neevene, sal lif in that fyre als fysshes duse in the flode, to pyne thase wrytches.[1]

An editorial misjudgment made in the nineteenth century and becoming, over time, an accepted tradition has obscured the true nature of the poem appearing here. In 1866 F. J. Furnivall misdesignated it the prologue to a longer work, *The Adulterous Falmouth Squire*, but, in doing so, he relied on the evidence of only one of its six manuscripts, Ashmole 61, where *The Sinner's Lament* immediately precedes *The Adulterous Falmouth Squire* and is copied continuously with it. Nowhere else are the two works related. They appear separately in every other manuscript, five others for *Lament*, seven for *Squire*. In one copy, moreover, *Lament* appears under a contemporary title: *Lamentacio peccatoris*.

Proof that the link in Ashmole is spurious can be readily demonstrated. Someone — most likely "Rate," the Ashmole scribe and compiler — doctored the first stanza in order to join the two works and to give a name and locale to the sinner: he is identified, satirically, as Sir William Basterdfeld of England. Three verses were added to this stanza, and its eight-line length was consequently altered to eleven lines. The ascription can therefore be dismissed as an extrapolation by someone who wished to join two originally separate pieces. Nevertheless, Furnivall's designation appears in virtually every index and catalogue. Even where *Squire* is absent (as it is everywhere but Ashmole), *The Sinner's Lament* has been consigned to the anonymity conferred by a lifeless title, *Prologue to The Adulterous Falmouth Squire*.[2]

---

[1]*Meditation on the Passion; and of Three Arrows on Doomsday* (MS Rawlinson C.285, fols. 64a–68b), a work associated with Richard Rolle (ed. Horstmann, pp. 120–21).

[2] Woolf attempted to correct the error in 1966 (p. 321 n.3), but to no avail. The effect of the title has been to disappoint some who expect a better match for the sensational tale of a son who witnesses the hell-torments of his libidinous father. For example, Brian Stone curtly

The Sinner's Lament

The surviving evidence warrants a more accurate appraisal. What the manuscripts preserve is not the prologue to a particular story but rather a penitential lyric that beckons a fifteenth-century audience to contrition through the assumed voice and bodily torment of a doomed, already dead sinner. The manuscripts show, moreover, that the poem survives in two distinct versions, with no record made before now of the second one. While the copies that have been published all derive from the same tradition, the text found in Oxford, Corpus Christi College MS 237 (CCC 237) preserves a version that has a greater length, a finer structure of parallel halves, and a more inclusive social orientation. This version is the one printed here — designated "A" — with the other manuscripts representing "B." Version A emphasizes the need of general humanity — men and women, rich and poor — to repent before they die. Version B, surviving at its most complete in Ashmole 61, points its poetic finger at rich, indolent noblemen, singling out lechery as their chief vice.

The Sinner's Lament belongs to a widespread class of penitential lyrics in which the dead speak from the grave and deliver a warning to the living. The sinner expresses sorrow for his sins, and (in Version A only) he follows doctrine and convention in enumerating his guilt in all seven deadly sins. Being located, however, outside the efficacy of a standard confession, this speaker will be neither purged of sin nor saved from hell. His cry for sympathy comes from the place beyond purification: the realm of the damned. In life he was immersed in worldly desire, and he fatally delayed in seeking God. Now God has abandoned him. His emotional plea is therefore not for himself (as one expects in an act of penance), but for the reader: "Look upon me! See my pain! Help yourself before it is too late!" The sinner's chance has passed; the reader's is now. The rhetoric of the poem posits an unlikely act of virtue from an unvirtuous man. It also grants a glimpse of the experience beyond the grave: unnerving tortures that would extract belated confession from a hardened sinner. Were the reader to see his or her own life for what it is — a living suicide of impious behavior — he or she might repent while there is time. The poem is thus structured upon a set of implicit contrasts — living/dead, here/there, now/then, light/dark — that reconfigure time on earth as a living death in sin, while death becomes an afterlife devoid of hope but of potential redemptive value to others. Horror and empathy may lead the reader to contrition and God while time exists.

The Sinner's Lament conjures for the receptive reader what Woolf terms "a

---

dismisses the "prologue" as a "prolix and repetitive harangue" (*Medieval English Verse*, second ed. [New York: Penguin, 1971], p. 83), while Andrea Hopkins mistakenly assumes the existence of several shared manuscripts (*The Sinful Knights: A Study of Middle English Penitential Romance* [Oxford: Clarendon, 1990], p. 220).

warning meditative image" (p. 323), a visual imaging of the speaker's body and its condition. Other graphic warnings from the suffering dead exist in Middle English (many enumerated by Woolf, pp. 315–21), and the opening call to those who pass by is itself a convention (from Lamentations 1.12, "*O vos omnes qui transitis per viam*"). The call to behold and learn can be found both in death lyrics and in meditative lyrics with a somewhat different orientation. It opens, for example, a poem asking the passers-by to contemplate Christ's wounded body:

> Abyde, gud men, and hald yhour pays
> And here what God Himselven says,
> > Hyngand on the rode:
>
> . . . .
> Behald my body or thou gang,
> And think opon my payns strang . . .[3]

Both types of appeal (from the dead, from Christ wounded) are calls to visualize a body in its suffering, and the similarity says something about medieval devotional habits. The values of the body become the route for spiritual change. Such poems appeal directly to the emotions, to innate trust in what one sees, to sensorial knowledge of pain, and to each individual's primal sense of corporeal wholeness. The meditant is asked to empathize with a human sufferer whose body is undergoing an arduous trial. By feeling the wretched condition of another in one's normally complacent flesh, one might be drawn closer to adopting the salvational instruction in one's spiritual life.

It is possible, too, that the original version of *The Sinner's Lament*, with its bold visual opening ("Behold and see!"), had some sort of pictorial representation to aid the meditant, either a manuscript illustration or a wall painting. Its content accords with other popular subjects commonly displayed in public places. In allowing a dead man to speak to the living, it is reminiscent of the widespread motif of the Three Dead and the Three Living, often found painted upon the sanctuary walls of medieval English churches.[4] Similarly, John Lydgate's *Dance of Death*, commissioned in 1426

---

[3]*Abyde, Ye Who Pass By* (lines 1–3, 7–8), ed. Carleton Brown, *Religious Lyrics of the XIVth Century*, p. 59. On the devotional image of Christ's body, see Gillespie, especially pp. 111–15; and Gray, pp. 140–41.

[4]Twenty-one of these paintings still survive, and a few carry inscriptions; see Tristram, pp. 234–35 nn. 60, 62, 68; Gray, pp. 208–09. On the motif of the Three Living and the Three Dead, see Tristram, pp. 162–67, and the English poem *De tribus regibus mortuis*. On medieval images of death as "salutory warning" rather than morbid interest in decay, see Pearsall, especially p. 66.

by John Carpenter, City Clerk of London (c. 1370?–1441?), accompanied rich paintings along the wall of the north cloister of Saint Paul's Cathedral.[5] Death was a popular subject for such representation: in life-sized public display, the stasis of image (the dead) could serve as forcible contrast to those who move by. Some of the affective power may also have rested in a wry reversal of who comes and goes. As Philippa Tristram observes, "it is the dead, paradoxically, who dance, whilst the living are frozen in fear" (p. 168).

The visceral effect in *Lament*, if experienced with the sinner, is one of shattered boundaries.[6] Those well delineated in life — body versus soul, self versus external world — crumble away in death. The wretched sinner speaks from a realm where hardfast worldly verities have shifted, his former states of luxury and dominance vastly altered to pain and servitude. The sinner's physical suffering is made gruesomely palpable to the reader: toads and snakes "lap" him both outside and inside his body, which is evidently losing its determinant shape, deteriorating first to a "cage," and then to "fire," and all the while devils rip him from "toppe to too."

The image of body as cage occupies the middle stanza of the poem, followed by various types of confinement noticeably cruder and more open than is a living person's normal sense of body. The damned soul is caged by fire, fettered by fiends, confined as a beast in a stall. What develops is a tactile sense of the soul lost, not merely abandoned metaphysically but also homeless in a space without its accustomed fleshly enclosure. The poet shatters the reader's worldly sense of time and space by forcing a sensation of the sinner's corporeal open-endedness. The rhetorical contrasts deployed in the speaker's warnings thus challenge the reader's sense of distance from the next world: "Such as I am shall you be." The verbal structure, at times loose, repetitive, distracted, is like the sinner in pain, and like his increasingly unstructured body, with its unwanted reptilian appendages.[7]

---

[5]*The Dance of Death*, intro. White, pp. xxii–xxiv; Tristram, pp. 168–70; Gray, pp. 50–51, 208; and E. Carleton Williams, "The Dance of Death in Painting and Sculpture in the Middle Ages," *Journal of the British Archaeological Association*, 3rd series, I (1937), 229–57. See also Thomas Brewer, *Memoir of the Life and Times of John Carpenter, Town Clerk of London* (London: Arthur Taylor, 1856), pp. 29–36.

[6]For some strong images of the damned suffering bodily fragmentation, see Bynum, plates 12, 15, 31; and also Kren and Wieck.

[7]In noting the poem's "lack of steady progression," Woolf neglects to consider that what seems a flaw may in fact be part of an affective design. She detects a similar looseness in what may be a Latin source, the *Speculum peccatorum* (p. 322). Admittedly, the lyric that survives does contain — in both textual traditions — repetitions and tag phrases, and the manuscripts reveal scribes at work reconstructing the poem, willing to use familiar phrases as filler (see note

Introduction

Remarkably, given the frequent vagaries of medieval lyric survival, most of the six manuscripts that preserve *The Sinner's Lament* were copied by men identifiable by name, locale, and compilational habits, allowing us to glimpse some early readers of this lyric and to guess at the reasons for its inclusion in their collections. In general, these copyists treated the poem casually: it never appears with the same number of strophes in any two manuscripts; lines or groups of lines have a tendency to be repeated or misplaced; and frequently (in four manuscripts) it seems to have been used as a filler in a blank space left between copies of longer works. Always it fits thematically with adjacent material, and how it fits can be informative. Probably because the piece had some sort of public (and possibly oral) life, it was seen as available for plunder by compilers wishing to adapt it for a contextual purpose, much as a well-known song or saying might now be used. Often chosen to complement longer pieces, *Lament* was apt to be placed so as to become a meditational epilogue or preface to another devotional lament or narrative about someone's fall from grandeur to death.

In MS Ashmole 61 the northeast midland scribe Rate formally affixed *Lament* to *The Adulterous Falmouth Squire*. Rate, who was selecting and editing a variety of works for "family audiences of mixed age and gender,"[8] handles texts in ways both idiosyncratic and purposeful. He adapted works to enhance their appeal to his audience and to fit his own biases. Thus it was probably Rate who gave the doomed sinner the allegorical name "Sir Will(ia)m Basterdfeld" — a droll sign of his willful lechery. Rate signs the work preceding *Lament*, but he does not sign *Lament*, which is followed by *Squire* without any break other than a slightly enlarged first capital. Another Rate signature appears after *Squire*. Elsewhere the compiler shows a devotional interest in meditations upon Christ's wounds and in family tales that mix demons and adulterous sinning, such as *The Knight and His Jealous Wife* and *The Tale of an Incestuous Daughter*.[9]

Advocates MS 19.3.1, a manuscript now in Scotland, was also copied for family use

---

to lines 25–32). The merits evident in Version A indicate, however, an original that was effectively constructed and phrased.

[8]Lynne S. Blanchfield, "The Romances in MS Ashmole 61: An Idiosyncratic Scribe," in *Romance in Medieval England*, ed. Maldwyn Mills, Jennifer Fellows, and Carol M. Meale (Cambridge: D. S. Brewer, 1991), p. 86, who postulates that Rate collected texts to entertain family audiences gathered for feasts of the Corpus Christi Guild in Leicester. See also Boffey and Thompson, pp. 297–99, 313–14 nn. 101–04; A. J. Bliss, ed., *Sir Orfeo* (Oxford: Clarendon, 1966), p. xvii; and M. B. Parkes, "The Literacy of the Laity," in *The Mediaeval World*, ed. David Daiches and Anthony Thorlby (London: Unwin Brothers, 1973), pp. 569, 576 nn. 82–83.

[9]See Blanchfield, pp. 79, 82.

in the northeast midlands. The primary scribe identifies himself by the signature "Recardum Heege." Other hands appear in the volume, and one of them, signed "John Hawghton," collaborates with Heege in two quires.[10] Hawghton is the copyist of *Lament*, which appears in the tenth quire. Heege's hand opens this gathering with a long lament poem, Lichfield's *Complaint of God*, and the lyric *The Sweetness of Jesus*.[11] Beginning on the next available recto, Hawghton copies *Lament*, Lydgate's *Four Things That Make a Man a Fool* (worship, women, wine, and old age), maxims for daily conduct, and a hand-shaped device for teaching Guidonian musical notation. The maxims, current in a number of versions, were often incorporated into Lydgate's *Dietary* and taught to children:

> Serve thou God truly,
> And the world besely;
> Ete thy mete merely ["merrily"],
>   And ever lyf in rest.
> Thank God mekly,
> Thoughe he veset the poorly,
> For he may mende it lyghtly
>   Wen hym likthe best.[12]

This piece and the seven-line Lydgate poem carry the air of common wisdoms to be committed to memory and recited at appropriate moments. Given Hawghton's interest in musical instruction, they may well have had accompanying tunes, as may *Lament*, which breaks off in this manuscript after eight stanzas. The tenth quire forms one of several entertaining and edifying booklets collected into this large volume, Adv. 19.3.1, which apparently formed the household library of a late fifteenth-century family, possibly the Sherbrookes of Derbyshire.[13] The arrangement of booklets in the bound manuscript divides into halves, so that *Lament* becomes

---

[10]Phillipa Hardman, "A Mediaeval Library *in parvo*," *Medium Ævum* 47 (1988), 262–73. See also Boffey and Thompson, pp. 295–97.

[11]On the joining of these two works in a sequence elsewhere (MS Lambeth 853), see the Introduction to *In a Valley of This Restless Mind*. On quire 10 specifically, see Hardman, pp. 265, 272.

[12]See F. J. Furnivall, ed., *The Babees Book*, EETS o.s. 32 (Oxford: N. Trübner & Co., 1868), pp. 58; see also Gray, pp. 48, 240 n. 54.

[13]Thorlac Turville-Petre, "Some Medieval English Manuscripts in the North-East Midlands," in *Manuscripts and Readers in Fifteenth Century England*, ed. Derek Pearsall (Cambridge: D. S. Brewer, 1983), pp. 133–40.

appropriately grouped not only with Lichfield's *Complaint*, but also with visionary tales similarly warning of the afterlife, *The Vision of Tundale* and *The Trental of Saint Gregory*.

The Sinner's Lament also appears in the important manuscript of romances copied by Robert Thornton of Yorkshire, Lincoln Cathedral MS 91. The arrangement of this volume falls into three subject areas: (1) narrative texts, with ten romances, (2) religious and devotional writings, and (3) a medical tract. *Lament* appears early in the first section of romances, wedged between the prose *Life of Alexander* and the alliterative *Morte Arthure*. The first two quires and most of the third contain *Alexander*. The fourth through sixth quires contain *Morte Arthure*, beginning on the first recto (fol. 53a). The third quire originally possessed more leaves than Thornton needed for the prose narrative; he excised some, but space remained on fols. 49b–51b. On these folios appear:

49b	Late pen-trials, including names of Thornton's son and grandson; otherwise blank.
50a–b	Prognostications of weather.
51a	A few more late pen trials, but otherwise blank.
51b–52a	*Lamentacio peccatoris*, and a crude sketch of a head and torso.
52b	Crude sketches of knights and a charger; a catchword for fol. 53 (joining this quire to the first *Morte* quire).[14]

The script on these leaves is uneven, but most scholars have agreed that Robert Thornton wrote all the items (other than the scribbles) here and elsewhere in the volume, where the handwriting varies considerably.[15] Given that *Lament* appears on folios left at the end of a long work, its copying must have occurred after *Alexander* had been copied, possibly even after the *Alexander* quires had been joined to the *Morte Arthure* quires. For a scribe who often sought thematic development in the

---

[14]Owen, in Brewer and Owen, p. xiv. Stylized dragons appear on fol. 51b with the catchword and on fol. 52a with the explicit ("Explicit lamentacio"); a similar one appears on fol. 162a as part of the explicit for *The Awntyrs off Arthure*.

[15]Gisela Guddat-Figge claims that the prognostications are later and in a different hand (*Catalogue of Manuscripts Containing Middle English Romances* [Munich: W. Fink, 1976], pp. 140, 141 n. 6), but both Brewer (Brewer and Owen, p. vii) and R. M. Thomson (*Catalogue of the Manuscripts of Lincoln Cathedral Chapter Library* [Cambridge: D. S. Brewer, 1989], p. 68) assert the hand to be consistent. James Orchard Halliwell took *Lament* to be in a later and different hand (*The Thornton Romances*, Camden Society 1.30 [1844; rpt. New York: AMS, 1968], p. xxvii).

sequencing of material,[16] the position of *Lament* between the narratives of exemplary but flawed men could be significant: *Lament* seems to follow as a comment upon *Alexander*, which ends somberly with the hero's death, or as a meditative prelude to *Morte Arthure*, a *casus* with its own share of worldly pride and laments over the dead.[17] Elsewhere, Thornton displays an interest in visions of the afterlife by inscribing *A Revelation of Purgatory Shown to a Holy Woman* (fols. 250b–58a).

Thornton's possible association of *Lament* with *de casibus* narrative may be further illuminated by the interests of a later compiler. Humphrey Welles, a Tudor administrative official and recusant, whose career was tied to the court of Henry VIII, created what is now MS Rawlinson C.813 (the Welles Anthology). This book is a gathering of lyrics, several of which are lamentations for the deaths of the once politically powerful. Appearing near the beginning of the collection, *Lament* helps to establish a subject that must have been vitally interesting to Welles: that tragedy can unexpectedly afflict the proud lives of those close to the court.[18]

To varying degrees, these four manuscript settings support the class bias of Version B, in which a pointed reference to "lords" rather than "men" (line 97) targets wealthy aristocrats as particularly susceptible to the sinner's fate because they

---

[16]See Phillipa Hardman, "Reading the Spaces: Pictorial Intentions in the Thornton MSS, Lincoln Cathedral MS 91, and BL MS Add. 31042," *Medium Ævum* 53 (1994), 250–74, who notes that elsewhere Thornton places a devotional lament of Christ before the *Northern Passion* (p. 262); she further argues that Thornton intended meditational images to be drawn next to two poems of Christ's lament (pp. 261–67). If she is right, then *Lament*, which is also accompanied by adequate space for an image, may have been intended to provide another meditational site in the manuscript. The sequence of Thornton's copying has been much studied. It appears that he originally planned to place *Morte Arthure* first in the manuscript, but later gaining access to the prose *Alexander*, he positioned it before the already completed *Morte*. See John J. Thompson, *Robert Thornton and the London Thornton Manuscript* (Cambridge: D. S. Brewer, 1987), pp. 61–62; Ralph Hanna III, "The Growth of Robert Thornton's Books," *Studies in Bibliography* 40 (1987), 51–61.

[17]Renate Haas, "The Laments for the Dead," in Karl Heinz Göller, *The "Alliterative Morte Arthure": A Reassessment of the Poem* (Cambridge: D. S. Brewer, 1981), 117–29, 176–77; and also Russell A. Peck, "Willfulness and Wonders: Boethian Tragedy in the Alliterative *Morte Arthure*," in *The Alliterative Tradition in the Fourteenth Century*, ed. Bernard S. Levy and Paul E. Szarmach [Kent, Ohio: Kent State University Press, 1981], p. 170. For the death of Alexander, see *The Prose Life of Alexander*, ed. Westlake, pp. 113–15.

[18]Edward Wilson, "Local Habitations and Names in MS Rawlinson C 813 in the Bodleian Library, Oxford," *Review of English Studies*, n.s. 41 (1990), 12–44 (especially pp. 32–37); and Jansen and Jordan, pp. 33–35.

practice his crimes of gluttony, sloth, and (in Ashmole 61 especially) lechery.[19] While in agreement as to the order of stanzas, these manuscripts differ in number of stanzas, with Ashmole being the longest (see chart in Notes). A fifth manuscript of *Lament* cannot be classed as either A or B because it preserves only the first eighteen lines, which are the same in both versions. However, the copy here follows the pattern of being placed with contextually appropriate material and of representing a later addition. Here the associations are with an Office of the Dead and an Hours of the Virgin's Compassion (both in Latin) and an English rime royal poem on the Sorrows of the Virgin. Mixed with these elevated laments, *Lament* — a less doctrinal *planctus* — would seem to be chosen for its affective appeal. The late hand that began its inscription on a last quire leaf after the Virgin's compassion used a formal book script to fill seventeen of the page's twenty-two ruled lines. Prayers to Saint Cuthberga suggest Wimborne as the provenance of this volume.[20]

MS CCC 237, the sole book preserving Version A, presents *The Sinner's Lament* in thirteen stanzas in an entirely different order. As with the other volumes, CCC 237 contains works compatible with *Lament* (especially with this version). Situated among more laments and *The Pilgrimage of the Soul* (a translation of Guillaume de Deguileville's *Pèlerinage de l'âme*), *Lament* precedes Lydgate's *Dance of Death*. A scribe who signed himself "E. C." copied lives of Sts. Katherine and Margaret and the Deguileville translation. The same scribe (or one with a very similar hand) later added William Lichfield's *Complaint of God* and Lydgate's *Dance of Death* (under the heading "Daunce of Powlys," a title tying the poem to its public life at the Church of St. Paul's). This copyist was most likely Edmund Carpenter, the first known owner of CCC 237. He may have been a younger relative of John Carpenter, the London town clerk who commissioned Lydgate's poem (McGerr, p. lxvii). Edmund Carpenter (if he is "E. C.") did not, however, copy *Lament*. A second hand, one that does not appear elsewhere in the volume, has written the lyric on one and a half pages left blank between the Lichfield and Lydgate pieces. The lyric has been carefully laid out to fill the open space attractively: four large, eye-catching stanzas on the lower half of fol. 146a and the remaining nine in two neat columns (four and a half stanzas per column) on fol. 146b. It is clear that the piece was selected to complement its longer companions on either side.

---

[19] See also Woolf: "[the speaker] insists on the deadly sins that he committed, which are characteristically those of the rich" (p. 322).

[20] Montague Rhodes James, *A Descriptive Catalogue of the MSS in the Library of Lambeth Palace: The Mediaeval MSS* (Cambridge: Cambridge University Press, 1932), p. 769. The volume also contains a list of itemized expenses incurred by a "John Semon" in purchasing books and parchment.

The Sinner's Lament

The message of Version A targets all readers, not merely the rich. Directly addressed is an audience of rich and poor (line 73), men and women (line 31), all who need to heed the devotional call to repentance. The universalized message especially suits the juxtaposition in CCC 237 with Lydgate's inscription-poem *The Dance of Death*, where the figure of Death leads men and women of every estate and age to the grave. Philippa Tristram believes that the Dance of Death motif developed chronologically from the Three Living and Three Dead Legend. Since *Lament* is, like the Legend, a warning from the dead, her comparison of the two motifs sheds light on the apparent grouping in CCC 237:

> The Legend is initially a warning to men to reform in this life; it has its relation to that instructive fear which ends in redemptive action. The Dance, which may possibly develop from it, no longer prompts men to choose, but forces them to submit to the inevitable. (p. 167)

Version A is well paired with *Dance* because it shares the same social perspective and its message is a prelude to that of the *Dance*.

Moreover, compared to B, Version A is structurally more coherent, being patterned in parallel, chronologically sequenced halves. The first half presents the sinner's memory of his youth and his past life, with a confession of all seven sins. The seventh stanza (the middle one) is a turning point that pivots upon images of eating, where the sinner's comfortable gluttony is inverted into the worms that dine upon him, while he mourns his lost chance to fast in penance. The second half of the poem develops his physical agonies after death, starting with the image of the cage (which follows from his youthful lightness as a bird) and progressing to a wish never to have been born into his now disintegrating body. In B this symmetry is blurred beyond recognition. First of all, the stanza that completes the confession of seven sins (stanza 6) is missing, so that the three named — lechery, sloth, gluttony — come to dominate a lament from a nobleman. The complaint of wasted youth (stanzas 2–5) is interrupted by the stanza about snakes and toads (stanza 9), blunting the logic of parallel halves in the A text. The eating stanza comes eighth out of twelve stanzas, so its effectiveness as a turning-point is also gone.

Thus, on the basis of how the ideas are patterned, Version A is superior to Version B. Whereas the poet of A intends to warn "man and wife" (line 31), the poet of the adapted B constructs a decidedly male sinner who views women with hostility: she is a maiden or wife to be sexually used (line 15), or she is his mother who ought not have borne him (lines 81–82). Hence, the poet of B leans toward an understanding of the exclusively male human condition as circular and bearing a punishment that fits the crime: indifferently born of a woman through another man's fornication, one lives to fornicate, indiscriminately begetting more bastards, and finally one ends

370

up in the hell of one's own actions. *The Adulterous Falmouth Squire* is about this subject, the clerical poet dutifully explaining how adultery causes the damnation of three souls, the man and woman who defy holy wedlock *and* the misbegotten heir, who will be barred from the priesthood. The Squire's lawful son — destined himself to become a priest — must learn the lesson by witnessing his father's torture by fiends.

Neither version offers much traditional imagery of the grave — only, perhaps, the toads and snakes — but the aura of a hellish place engulfs the sinner's speech: Lucifer and cohorts appear to have him well ensnared (lines 32, 80, 86–88) and the blast of a distant horn serves as his fateful summons (line 103). As he thus stands fleetingly before the living, the doomed sinner offers to all a lesson on grace: A person is to seek it while he or she is alive, grace being defined as the capacity, obtainable through God, to recognize one's own sinful condition and need for mercy. Even though the sinner himself failed to find this balm (line 14), he petitions God to provide it to everyone living, regardless of rank (line 101, Version A only). The signs of grace are defined in the tenth stanza: an ability to see in this lost soul a warning for oneself, the ability to know good from evil, a concern for the poor (expressed negatively as not killing them for their faults), and a refraining from overindulgence in physical desires. Themes raised in the opening stanzas — the acceptance of grace, the prevalence and meaninglessness of "debate" among the living, and an all-important sense for things drawing to an end — are all concluded in the last ones.

In general, the highly malleable text of *The Sinner's Lament* and its secondary addition to two-thirds of its manuscripts (Adv. 19.3.1, Thornton, Lambeth 560, CCC 237) suggest that the lyric enjoyed a popular and probably ephemeral existence — as either song or inscription to a devotional image — from about 1430 to 1530, an existence lively enough to cause it to come to mind when one heard, read, or recalled other mournful devotions or narrative laments of the great brought low. Perhaps Version A originated as an inscription and Version B was a popular, lightly satirical song that followed. While an oral source certainly does not underlie every surviving text, the currency of such a source would help to explain much of the wide variation seen from copy to copy.

Note on the Edited Text

Because the text preserved in CCC 237 is so valuable for recovering a more coherent version of this lyric of a lost soul, I have edited it with a minimal amount of emendation. The Notes present the variants of Version B and include a comparative table of the surviving stanzas in each manuscript.

Select Bibliography

Manuscripts

A-Text

Oxford, Corpus Christi College MS 237, fóls. 146a–146b. London, c. 1450. [Base text; 13 stanzas.]

B-Text

Oxford, Bodleian Library MS Ashmole 61, fols. 136a–136b. Northeast midlands (Leicestershire), c. 1479–88. [Scribe/compiler named Rate; 12 stanzas copied as 24 quatrains; lacks stanza 6; 3 spurious lines in stanza 1.]

Welles Anthology: Oxford, Bodleian Library MS Rawlinson C.813, fols. 4b–6b. London, c. 1530. [Made by or for Humphrey Welles, Tudor courtier-lawyer; copied as 23 quatrains; lacks stanzas 6, 7a.]

Thornton MS: Lincoln, Lincoln Cathedral MS 91, fols. 51b–52a. Yorkshire, c. 1440. [Scribe/compiler is Robert Thornton, gentryman of East Newton, Yorkshire; poem entitled *Lamentacio Peccatoris*; copied as 20 quatrains; lacks stanzas 3b, 6, 9a, 11.]

Edinburgh, National Library of Scotland MS Advocates 19.3.1, fols. 174a–175a. Northeast midlands, c. 1450. [Compiler named Recardum Heege; scribes are Heege, John Howghton (copyist of *Lament*), and others; lacks stanzas 6, 8, 11, 12, 13.]

Fragment

London, Lambeth Palace Library MS 560, fol. 98b. Possibly Wimborne, c. 1475. [17 lines: vv. 1–12, 14–18.]

Introduction

Facsimile

Brewer, D. S., and A. E. B. Owen, intro. *The Thornton Manuscript (Lincoln Cathedral MS 91)*. London: Scolar, 1977.

Editions

Bolle, Wilhelm, ed. "Zur Lyrik der Rawlinson-Hs. C. 813." *Anglia* 34 (1911), 292–96. [Ashmole 61, Welles.]

Furnivall, F. J., ed. *Political, Religious, and Love Poems*. EETS o.s. 15. Second ed. 1903; rpt. Bungay, Suffolk: Richard Clay, 1965. Pp. 123–26. [Ashmole 61.]

Horstmann, Carl, ed. *Altenglische Legenden: Neue Folge*. Heilbronn: Henninger, 1881. Pp. 367–68, 529–30. [Ashmole 61, Thornton.]

Jansen, Sharon L., and Kathleen H. Jordan, eds. *The Welles Anthology, MS. Rawlinson C. 813: A Critical Edition*. Medieval and Renaissance Texts & Studies 75. Binghamton: SUNY Binghamton, 1991. Pp. 96–100. [Welles.]

Leonard, Anne L., ed. *Zwei Mittelenglische Geschichten aus der Hölle*. Zurich: Orell Füssli, 1891. [Collation of Ashmole 61, Welles, Thornton, Lambeth.]

Padelford, Frederick Morgan, ed. "The Songs in Manuscript Rawlinson C.813." *Anglia* 31 (1908), 317–20. [Welles.]

Perry, George G., ed. *Religious Pieces in Prose and Verse*. EETS o.s. 26. 1905; rpt. New York: Greenwood, 1969. Pp. 115–18. [Thornton.]

Latin Analogue

Speculum peccatorum. Ed. Clemens Blume and Guido M. Dreves. In *Analecta hymnica medii aevi*. Vol. 46. 1905; rpt. New York: Johnson, 1961. Pp. 349–51.

Related Middle English Works

The Adulterous Falmouth Squire. Ed. Carl Horstmann. In *Altenglische Legenden, neue Folge.* Heilbronn: Henninger, 1881. Pp. 368–70. [Vision of a sinner's afterlife; companion poem in Ashmole 61.]

De tribus regibus mortuis. Ed. Ella Keats Whiting. In *The Poems of John Audelay.* EETS o.s. 184. 1931; rpt. Millwood, N. Y.: Kraus, 1988. Pp. xxiv–xxvii, 217–23. [Only Middle English poem on Three Dead and Three Living.]

The Knight and His Jealous Wife. Ed. Carl Horstmann. In *Altenglische Legenden, neue Folge.* Heilbronn: Henninger, 1881. Pp. 329–33. [Legend of Mary and devils vying for soul of sinful woman; appears in Ashmole 61.]

Lydgate, John. *The Dance of Death.* Ed. Florence Warren and Beatrice White. EETS o.s. 181. 1931; rpt. Oxford: Humphrey Milford, 1971. [Follows *Lament* in CCC 237.]

———. *Four Things That Make a Man a Fool.* Ed. Henry Noble MacCracken. In *The Minor Poems of John Lydgate.* Part 2. EETS o.s. 192. 1934; rpt. London: Oxford University Press, 1961. P. 709 [III]. [Follows *Lament* in Adv. 19.3.1.]

Meditation on the Passion; and of the Three Arrows on Doomsday. Ed. Carl Horstmann. In *Yorkshire Writers.* Vol. 1. London: Swan Sonnenschein, 1895. Pp. 112–21.

Morte Arthure. Ed. Larry D. Benson. *King Arthur's Death: The Middle English Stanzaic Morte Arthur and Alliterative Morte Arthure.* Second ed. Rev. Edward E. Foster. TEAMS Middle English Texts Series. Kalamazoo, Mich.: Medieval Institute Publications, 1994. Pp. 129–284. [Alliterative poem; follows *Lament* in Thornton MS.]

The Pilgrimage of the Soul. Ed. Rosemarie Potz McGerr. New York: Garland, 1990. [Contains "Pitouse Compleynte of the Soul"; appears in CCC 237.]

The Prose Life of Alexander. Ed J. S. Westlake. EETS o.s. 143. 1913; rpt. New York: Kraus, 1971. [Precedes *Lament* in Thorton MS.]

The Trental of Saint Gregory. Ed. K. D. Bülbring. "Das 'Trentale Sancti Gregorii' in der Edinburgher Handschrift." *Anglia* 13 (1891), 303–08. [Lament of saint's deceased sinful mother; appears in Adv. 19.3.1.]

Introduction

The Vision of Tundale. Ed. W. B. D. D. Turnbull. Edinburgh: T. G. Stevenson, 1843. [Vision of afterlife; appears in Adv. 19.3.1.]

Criticism of *The Sinner's Lament*

Cooke, Thomas D. "Tales." In *A Manual of Writings in Middle English, 1050–1500.* Ed. Albert E. Hartung. Vol. 9. New Haven: Connecticut Academy of Arts and Sciences, 1993. Pp. 3259–60, 3552–53.

Louis, Cameron. "Proverbs, Precepts, and Monitory Pieces." In *A Manual of Writings in Middle English, 1050–1500.* Ed. Albert E. Hartung. Vol. 9. New Haven: Connecticut Academy of Arts and Sciences, 1993. Pp. 3035–36, 3395.

Woolf, Rosemary. *The English Religious Lyric in the Middle Ages.* Oxford: Clarendon, 1968. Pp. 321–22, 325. [Related lyrics discussed on pp. 67–113, 309–55, 401–04.]

Related Studies

Boffey, Julia, and John J. Thompson. "Anthologies and Miscellanies: Production and Choice of Texts." In *Book Production and Publishing in Britain 1375–1475.* Ed. Jeremy Griffiths and Derek Pearsall. Cambridge: Cambridge University Press, 1989. Pp. 279–315.

Bynum, Caroline Walker. *The Resurrection of the Body in Western Christianity, 200–1336.* New York: Columbia University Press, 1995.

Duffy, Eamon. "The Pains of Purgatory." In *The Stripping of the Altars: Traditional Religion in England 1400–1580.* New Haven: Yale University Press, 1992. Pp. 338–76. [*Lament* cited, p. 340.]

Gillespie, Vincent. "Strange Images of Death: The Passion in Later Medieval English Devotional and Mystical Writing." In *Zeit, Tod und Ewigkeit in der Renaissance Literatur.* Ed. James Hogg. Salzburg: Institut für Anglistik und Amerikanistik, Universität Salzburg, 1987. Pp. 111–59.

Gray, Douglas. "Death and the Last Things." In *Themes and Images in the Medieval English Religious Lyric.* London: Routledge & Kegan Paul, 1972. Pp. 176–220.

Keiser, George. "The Progress of Purgatory: Visions of the Afterlife in Later Middle English Literature." In *Zeit, Tod und Ewigkeit* (see Gillespie). Pp. 72–100.

Kren, Thomas, and Roger S. Wieck. *The Visions of Tondal from the Library of Margaret of York*. Malibu: J. Paul Getty Museum, 1990.

Le Goff, Jacques. *The Birth of Purgatory*. Trans. Arthur Goldhammer. Chicago University of Chicago Press, 1981.

Patterson, Frank Allen. *The Middle English Penitential Lyric*. 1911; rpt. New York: AMS, 1966.

Pearsall, Derek. "Signs of Life in Lydgate's *Danse Macabre*." In *Zeit, Tod und Ewigkeit* (see Gillespie). Pp. 59–71.

Tristram, Philippa. "Mortality and the Grave." In *Figures of Life and Death in Medieval English Literature*. New York: New York University Press, 1976. Pp. 152–83.

Wenzel, Siegfried. *The Sin of Sloth: Acedia in Medieval Thought and Literature*. Chapel Hill: University of North Carolina Press, 1960. Pp. 88–96.

The Sinner's Lament

1

All Cristen men that walkys me by,	*walk by me*
Behold and see this dolefull sight!	*sorrowful*
Hit happith me noght to call and crye,	*It is no use to me*
For I am dampned a woofull wight.	*damned; creature*
5 Beware by me, both kyng and knyght,	
And amend you here while ye have space,	*opportunity*
For I have lost everlastyng light —	
Mercy is goon! I gete no grace.	

2

When I was yong, as nowe be ye,	
10 I kepyd never to have oder lif;	*imagined; a different*
I spendid my yeres in vanité,	*spent*
In veynglory, debate, and strif.	*quarrel*
Gret othis they wer with me full rif;	*oaths; numerous*
I had no grace for to amend;	
15 I sparid neyther maydyn ne wif;[1]	
And that hath brought me to this end.	

3

I had no grace when I was here	*fair occasion*
For to arise and me repent	
Unto the tyme that I lay on bere —	*Until; bier*
20 Then was to late, for I was shent!	*too; ruined*
This ffendes ffell they have me hent,	*Thus; wicked fiends; taken*
Awey with them I am conveyed —	
In balefull fire I shal be brent!	*painful; shall be burnt*
Alas! This world hath me disseyvid!	*deceived*

---

[1] *I spared neither maiden nor wife (a reference to his sexual rapaciousness)*

4

25   Of gloteny I had my ffyll;   *gluttony*
        In slewith alwey I led my lif;   *sloth*
        Lechery pley I lovid full well;   *Lecherous*
        All synnes in me they war full rif!
        I slewe myself withoutyn knyf!
30   Dolefull deth this hath me dight.   *Grief-inflicting; assailed*
        Beware by me, both man and wif,
        Lest that ye with Lucifer light.   *alight (i.e. end up)*

5

        For when that I was in my fflouris,   *youthful prime*
        Then was I light as bird on brere!   *briar*
35   Therfor I suffer here sharp showris,   *afflictions*
        And bye that bargeyn wunder dere —   *pay dearly for that bargain*
        I abyde in paynes many and sere!   *various*
        Therfor this I make my mone,   *thus; complaint*
        For nowe may help me no prayer,
40   For I had no god but gold alone.

6

        Example take ye all at me   *from*
        Of your mysdedes for to amend!
        Ther was no vice that ever myght be
        But part of theym I had an ende —   *I made my goal*
45   My pride and wreth myght ever be kend;   *wrath; known*
        Envy and covetise lovyd I ay!   *cupidity; always*
        Nowe it is wors than I wend!   *thought*
        Therfor my song is "Well-a-wey!"

7

        In delicat metes I had delite,   *foods*
50   And myghty wynes unto my pay;   *strong; pleasure*
        That makes the wormys on me to bite —
        Therfor my song is "Well-a-wey!"
        I myght not fast. I wold not pray.
        I thought to amendyd me in myn age.   *to [have] amended; old age*
55   I drowe on forth from day to day.   *carried on*
        Therfor I abide here in this cage!

The Sinner's Lament

8

This cage is everlastyng fire
That I am ordeynid in to dwell.   *destined*
Hit is me gevyn unto my hire,   *given to me as my reward*
60   Evyr to bren in the fyre of hell.   *burn*
This am I feterd with fendes fell,   *Thus; fettered by*
And ther to abide as best in stall.   *beast*
Ther is no tonge my care can tell —
Beware ye have not such a fall!

9

65   This am I lappid all aboute   *Thus*
With todys and snakes, as ye may see;   *toads*
They gnawe my body in and oute —
Alas! Alas! Full woo is me!
Hit is to late! It will not be!
70   I knowe that we will nevyr twyn! [1]
For Hym that died for you and me,
Ryse up and rest not in your synne!

10

Woo be to theym, whatever they be,   *whatever rank*
That hath ther five wittes at will,   *senses*
75   And will not example take by me,
And knowe the good from the ill.   *And will not know*
The pore for faute lat theym not spill — [2]
For and ye do, your deth is dight;   *For if; appointed*
Your fflesly lust you not fulfill,
80   For then with Lucyfer shall ye light!

11

Alas, that ever I gotyn was,   *begotten*
Or modyr me bare! Whi did she soo?   *mother bore me*
For I am lost for my trespas,   *sins*
And ever to abide in endles woo!   *will forever abide*

---

[1] *we will never separate (i.e., the toads and snakes will always be with him)*

[2] *Let them not condemn the poor for their faults (due to poverty)*

85 I have no frendes, but many a foo!
Behold howe I am all totorne —   *completely torn*
They rif me this ffrom toppe to too!   *rip me thus; toe*
Alas, that ever was I borne!

12

Good brother, have this eft in mynd,   *hereafter*
90 And thynk that thou shall die awey:
Unto thy soule be not unkynd.
Remembyr hit both nyght and day.
And besely loke that thou praye,   *actively*
Besechyng Hym that is Hevyn Kyng
95 To save the at the dredefull day,   *you*
When every soule shall geve rekenyng.   *give an account [of its sins]*

13

Ther is no man for the shall pray,
Nother justice ne man of lawe.   *Neither*
Thy charter helpith the not that day.
100 Thy pletyng is not worth an hawe.   *Thy legal pleading is worthless*
God geve the grace thyself to knowe,
And every man in his degré.[1]
Farewell! I here an horne blowe.
All Cristyn men, beware by me!

---

[1] *And [may God give such grace to] every man of whatever rank*

Abbreviations:

CCC   Oxford, Corpus Christi College MS 237. [Base text.]
Adv   MS Advocates 19.3.1.
L   Lambeth Palace Library MS 560.
A   MS Ashmole 61.
W   Welles Anthology (MS Rawlinson C.813).
T   Thornton MS (Lincoln Cathedral MS 91).

Among the MSS there is a great deal of variation. The following notes cite all variants except those of minor significance (such as orthographical or dialectal variation). The following table exhibits the number and order of the stanzas in each of the six extant MSS (**a** and **b** indicate halves of stanzas; * marks a variant stanza):

A-Text:	CCC	1	2	3	4	5	6	7	8	9	10	11	12	13
B-Text:	A	1*	2	3	4*	9	[ ]	5	10	7	8	11	12	13
	W	1	2	3	4*	9	[ ]	5	10	[7b]	8	11	12	13
	T	1	[2a3a2b]		4*	[9b]	[ ]	5ba	10	7	8	[ ]	12*	13*
	Adv	1	2	3	4*	9	[ ]	5	10	7	[ ]	[ ]	[ ]	[ ]
Fragment:	L	1	2	3a	[ ]	[ ]	[ ]	[ ]	[ ]	[ ]	[ ]	[ ]	[ ]	[ ]

1   Based on Lamentations 1.12, "O all ye that pass by the way, attend, and see if there be any sorrow like to my sorrow," which is used as part of the liturgy for Good Friday. The *O vos omnes* opening is conventional in medieval literature. See, for example, the Latin hymn *Speculum peccatorum*, and the epitaph stanza *All Ye That Passe be Thys Holy Place* (ed. Theodore Silverstein, *Medieval English Lyrics* [London, 1971], p. 123).

walkys. LAW: *walke*.

The Sinner's Lament

1 *me by.* A: *by me.*

3 *Hit happith me noght.* Adv: *Hyt helpes me noder*; L: *It helpeth me not*; A: *It helpys not*; W: *Ytt bootes me nott*;   T: *I beyd nother.* On the impersonal usage of *happen*, the verb unique to CCC, see *MED happen* v.(1), sense 2.(c).

 and. AdvLW: *nor*; A: *ne*; T: *nor to.* The CCC reading is possibly a scribal error for *nor* or *ne.*

4 *am.* T: *am so.*

 woofull. A: *dollfole.*

 wight. In CCC the scribe wrote *si* and deleted it before this word.

 After this line A inserts three spurious verses that identify by name and place the lamenting sinner:

> Sometyme in Inglond duellyng
> Thys was trew withouten lesyng
> I was callyd Sir William Basterdfeld knyght.

 The name appears to be allegorical: "the lord who, following his lecherous will, creates a field of bastards." The attribution helps to link *Lament* to *The Adulterous Falmouth Squire*, the next piece in A (fols. 107a–10a).

5 *Beware by.* W: *Take hede to*; T: *Tayk heyd of.*

 both. Omitted in LT.

6 *amend you.* AdvT: *mend yow*; L: *amend*; W: *mend yourselfe.*

 here. Omitted in AdvLAW. *Here* refers to the the world of the living, which the dead sinner is merely visiting. *Space* indicates time and physical dimension, parameters in which the living may act.

 ye. Adv: *that he.*

7   *For I have.* W: *Thys have I*; T: *Fore qwen ye.* This line refers to "the recurrent verse and response in the burial liturgy, 'V: Requiem aeternum dona es Domine; R: Et lux perpetua luceat eis'" (Jansen and Jordan, p. 100).

8   *Mercy is goon! I.* A: *And thus of mercy can I*; T: *Fro mercy be gone ye.*

    no. L: *never.*

9   *yong, as nowe be ye.* A: *now as ye be*; T: *yowyng es now er ye.* An instance of the ancient warning phrase *Quod tu es, ego fui* ("such as I am shall you be") common in funerary verse inscriptions; see Gray, pp. 200–20, and Woolf, pp. 401–04.

10   *I kepyd.* T: *Than beyd I.*

    to have. Omitted in AdvLAWT.

    oder. L: *none other*; W: *better*; T: *a fayrer.*

11   *I.* L: *But.*

    spendid. AdvLW: *spende*; T: *spent.*

12   *debate, and.* A: *bate and*; T: *and in.* T (copied in quatrains) places lines 17–20 after this line.

13   *they wer with me.* AdvAW: *with me wer*; T: *to me tha war.* Compare the syntax of line 28. L omits this line.

14   *grace.* The word here has the sense of "self-knowledge, especially of one's sinfulness, as obtainable through God," a meaning defined at the end of the poem (line 101). The lamenting sinner could have availed himself of this grace (a knowledge of God and goodness that rested within him), but he neglected it — and thereby refused it — in his lifetime. Analogous definitions appear in an English prose treatise entitled *De gracia dei*, associated with Richard Rolle, which appears in the Thornton MS (fols. 240a–43a; ed. Horstmann, *Yorkshire Writers*, vol. 1 [London: Swan Sonnenschein, 1895], pp. 305–10).

    for. L: *me for*; AW: *me.*

15   *neyther*. AdvW: *noder*; LA: *nother*; T: *never noder*.

       ne. AdvLW: *nor*.

16   L substitutes a new line to complete the rhyme disrupted by the omission of line 13: *The whiche hath broughte me to this lyfe*.

       hath. AdvT: *hase* (both T and Adv are in a northern dialect).

17   *grace when*. LAWT: *hap(e) whyle*; Adv: *hape when*.

18   *For to arise*. AdvW: *For to ryse*; T: *To ryes*. This is the last line that appears in L (where the text fills one folio side).

19   One of many lines that vary from MS to MS. The variant lines read:

       Adv: Tull I was broght in a bere;
       W: Tyll I was dede and leyd on beyre;
       A: Tyll that I was brought on bere;
       T: Now am I broght apon a beyre.

20   *Then was*. T: *Itt ys*.

       I was. Adv: *was I*; W: *sore was I*; T: *I am*.

21   *this*. Adv: *Yesd*. The scribe of CCC often writes *this* for "thus." The spelling recurs at lines 30, 38, 61 (also in W), and 65. The form is well attested; see *OED this* adv.

21–24   T lacks these lines. A omits line 21 (disrupting the rhyme) and substitutes a new concluding line:

       All wey with them I ame aweyde   (= 22)
       In fyre of hell I schall ever be brent   (= 23)
       Alas this werld hath me deseyvede   (= 24)
       Fore I had no grace me to amende.

22   *I am conveyed*. Adv: *I ham avemede*; W: *thys am I wayvyde*.

23   Two MSS have variant lines:

Adv: In halle ever my be brentt;
W: In hell evermore to be brente.

24   *This*. W: *the*.

     disseyvid. Adv: *defend*.

25–32   Stanza 4 differs in B-Text, where the sinner's lechery receives prominence. A colorful last line, ending on *had-I-wyst* ("if only I had known") appears in this version, too, and in T an echoing link to the next line is created upon this word. Here is the variant stanza as it appears in Adv:

In lechere I lad my lyfe,	(= 27/26)
For I hade gold and gud att wyll.	(compare 40)
I schlue myselfe withowtyn a knyfe.	(= 29)
Of glotene I had my fyll.	(= 25)
In scloth I lye and sclepyd full styll.	(compare 26)
I was desevud in a tryst,	
Delfull deth dyd me kyll —	(= 30)
Theyn was to late yf "I-had-wyst!"	(AW: of had I wyst)

One may note the interesting verbal enactments of the sins evident in the two versions, taken together: the sinner "had his fill" of gluttony (A- and B-Texts), "lay and slept" in sloth (B-Text), and "loved to play" in lechery (A-Text). The original stanza may well have been some blend of these two versions. Compare a similar description of the vices in Harley Lyric 13, *An Old Man's Prayer*: Lechery was his mistress, Liar his interpreter, Sloth and Sleep his bedfellows, and so on (ed. G. L. Brook, *The Harley Lyrics* fourth ed. [Manchester: Manchester University Press, 1968], p. 47). The quatrain link in T is effective:

And all ys tornyd to adywyst
Add-Y-wyst yt wyll not bee. (substitutes for line 69)

27   *Lechery*. This word appears as an adjective elsewhere in ME. The *MED* cites *Piers Plowman* C. 7.194 (Huntington MS): "lecherye tales."

29   *knyf*. In CCC the scribe wrote *ky* and deleted it before this word.

30   *deth*. Here and at line 78 the word refers to spiritual death and damnation, a more frightening prospect than mere bodily death.

31 *both man and wif.* This address to an audience of both men and women does not appear anywhere in the other MSS (see note to lines 25–32).

32 Compare line 80 and its variants.

33 *For when that.* AdvA: *For when*; W: *When.* The variant line in T reads: *Qwen I was yown and in my flowres.* The B-Text follows a variant order from this point on. See the chart that appears at the beginning of these notes. In T lines 33–36 and lines 37–40 are reversed.

34 *light.* AdvWT: *blythe.* The bird-on-briar simile for carefree youth might be compared to *The Bird with Four Feathers* (line 9; see note), where such a bird has come to lament his losses much in the manner of this sinner.

   on brere. Adv: ? *in on bres.*

35 *Therfor I suffer.* T: *That garrys me.*

   here. W: *mony*; T: *thes*; omitted in A.

35–36 CCC reverses these two lines, causing a disruption in sense and rhyme; they appear in correct order in the other MSS.

36 *bye.* From AdvAWT; CCC: *byes.*

   that. Adv: ? *theth* or *thep*; WT: *thys.*

   wunder. From AdvAWT; CCC: *under.*

37 *I abyde in.* A: *And byde in*; W: *I suffer.* The variant line in T reads: *Qwen I was lapyd in synnys seyre.*

   sere. Adv: *fre.*

38 *Therfor this.* AdvA: *Therefor thus*; W: *Wherfore thys*; T: *Sore to yow.*

39 *For.* Omitted in AdvAWT. The variant line in T reads: *Ther meght me help no gud prayer.*

39   *help me.* Adv: *help*; WT: *me help(e)*.

40   *For.* Omitted in AdvAT.

       gold. AdvAWT: *go(o)d, gode, gud*, a variant that verbally plays upon the idea of material goods becoming one's god. An echo of this line occurs in B-Text, stanza 4, second line (cited above, note to lines 25–32). There, the same variant appears in T: *god and gude.*

41–48   This stanza appears only in CCC. It completes the list of seven deadly sins begun in stanza 4.

48   This line, appearing only in the A-Text, repeats line 52.

49   *had delite.* A: *sette my delyte*; T: *had gret delytt.*

49–52   W lacks these lines.

50   *And myghty.* T: *So had I.*

       wynes. Adv: *wynn*; T: *wyne.*

51   *makes the.* Adv: *makes there*; A: *make this*; T: *garres thes.*

52   *Therfor my.* Adv: *An therffor my* ; T: *And ever ther.*

53   *fast.* T: *fast nor.*

54   *to amendyd me.* Adv: *I woll amend me*; AW: *to amend me*; T: *to amendyd.*

55   *I.* Adv: *And*; W: *Soo I.*

       drowe on forth. Adv: *drof an furght*; A: *droffe ever forth*; W: *drove off*; T: *drave ever of.*

56   *abide.* AdvAW: *byd(e)*. Compare T: *And now am I lokyk in a kage.* The text in Adv, following B-Text order, ends on this line, the sinner immobile in his "cage."

57   *This cage is.* W: *Thys cage ytt ys of*; T: *The kage yt be on*.

       everlastyng. T: *byrnyng*.

58   *That I am ordeynid in*. A: *I ame ordeynd therin*.

59   *Hit is me gevyn*. W: *Ytt ys gevyn me*; T: *Thys have tha gyvyn me*.

       unto. A: *fore*; T: *to*.

60   *bren*. T: *last*.

       fyre. AW: *pytte*; T: *panes*.

61   *This am I*. A: *I ame*.

       fendes. A: *the fendes*; T: *fendys so*.

62   *to*. A: *I*. The other two MSS have variant lines:

         W: And as a beest bounden in a stalle;
         T: As qwo bynd besse into a stall.

63   *care*. T: *woo*. The visual image is of a gruesome, decomposing corpse, for the toads and snakes "lap" him both inside and outside his body, which is losing its former physical boundaries.

64   T seems to direct the admonition at gentlemen: *Bywar, gud serys, of syche a fall*.

65   *am I*. Adv: *I ham*.

65–68   T lacks these lines.

66   *may*. Adv: *wyll*.

67   *gnawe*. Adv: *hnafe*.

       in and oute. AdvW: *thoroowt*. Compare A: *I ame gnawyne my body aboute*.

69   For the line substituted in T, see the note to lines 25–32.

70   *I knowe that we will nevyr twyn.* The variants read:

> Adv: I know wele me ne mon ous tweyn;
> A: I knaw welle women mour and mynne;
> T: I wot I mune never more thweyn.

This line seems to have confused the scribes, who construed it several ways, but the reading in CCC and W makes the best sense. The body of the wretched sinner is now eternally intertwined with snakes, worms, and toads — and the corruption they symbolize. Adv is similar in meaning, and T is garbled. A substitutes a new line that stresses adultery (entirely out of context here, but appropriate, perhaps, when the poem is used as a prologue to *Adulterous Falmouth Squire*).

71   *and.* From AdvAWT; omitted in CCC.

72   *Ryse up.* AdvT: *Ryse*; AW: *Aryse.* Compare line 18. This line is written twice in T, at the end of a column. The concept of "rising up" against vice, of actively combatting sloth and the other sins, is central to the poet's idea of sin as something one falls into by nature, if one remains unaware and unvigilant. The fall into bodily sin is natural prelude to the spirit's fall into hell's fire. Christ's active dying for mankind works as contrast to man's innate sloth, and as an example for willed virtue. On the sin of sloth, see Wenzel, pp. 88–96.

73   *be*[1]. Omitted in T.

theym, whatever they be. A: *th[e]i whosoever th[e]i be*; W: *them whatsooever they be*; T: *thes werever tha bee.* These words in all versions imply that the warning is aimed at persons of all ranks, but line 77 suggests that the poorest class (those who would need alms and are not to be oppressed) is somehow outside of the injunction.

74   *wittes.* T: *inwyttes.*

at. From AdvAW; CCC: *and* (an ampersand, easily confused with *at*); T: *to.* Compare the same phrase (a commonplace) in the B-Text, stanza 4, 2nd line (cited above, note to lines 25–32).

75   *And*. T: *That*.

75–79   The speaker lists four injunctions for his auditors: to take to heart his message
          as a potent warning, to distinguish good from evil, not to harm the poor, and
          not to follow one's fleshly desires.

          example take by. AdvW: *bewarre by*; A: *bewer be*; T: *now tayk tent to*.

77   *The pore for faute lat theym not spill*. W and T have variant lines:

          > W: Lett never the pore for faute spyll;
          > T: Pure for fawt ye lat not spyll.

          The provision for the poor is stated negatively: Do not condemn (or kill) them
          for their faults. For a similar sentiment about how the wealthy ought not to
          oppress the poor, who in turn should not rise up, see Lydgate's envoy to *The
          Debate of the Horse, Goose, and Sheep*, ed. Henry Noble MacCracken, *The Minor
          Poems of John Lydgate*, part 2, EETS o.s. 192 (1934; rpt. London: Oxford
          University Press, 1961), pp. 563–65.

78   The rhetorical shift from third-person (*theym*) to second-person (*ye*) is startling
          and effective.

79   *Your fflesly lust you not fufill*. The B-Text variants are:

          > AdvA: Yowr fals flese yow nott fullfyll;
          > W: Ye shal be jugged ageynst your wyll;
          > T: The lust of yowr fleych wyl never fulfylle.

80   *For then with Lucyfer shall ye light*. Compare line 32 (A-Text only). The B-Text
          variants are:

          > Adv: Leyst with Lucifere that ye lygth;
          > A: Lost with Lucyfere fro the lyght;
          > W: Frome the place of everlastyng lyght;
          > T: Bywar in Luscefer not at the lyght.

81   *gotyn*. A: *borne*. On the wish never to have been born, compare *Pety Job*, lines
          625–28.

81–88   T lacks this stanza.

390

84   *And ever to abide in endles woo!* A and W have variant lines:

        A: And abyde in everlastyng wo;
        W: Soo shall I byde everlastyng woo.

85   *frendes.* A: *frend.*

86   *Behold howe I am all totorne.* A and W have variant lines:

        A: Behold me how that I ame tourne;
        W: Beholde and see howe I am lorne.

87   *They rif me this ffrom.* A: *Fore I ame rente fro;* W: *They reve me from the.*

89   *Good brother.* W: *Good ffrendes;* T: *Gentyll brother.* W changes the singular second-person pronouns in lines 91, 95, 97, 99, 100, and 101 to plurals. The first and last lines address a plural audience, but all texts except W particularize the admonition to one "brother" listener.

    this eft. A: *me;* W: *itt;* omitted in T.

90   *And thynk that.* A: *And thinke how;* T: *Hyen qwen.*

    die awey. AW: *dye alwaye;* T: *weynd away.*

91   *Unto thy.* A: *And to;* T: *To thi.*

    thy soule. W: *your sollys.*

    be not. WT: *be never.*

92   *hit.* W: *thys;* T: *that.*

93   *And.* Omitted in AW.

    thou. W: *you doo.*

93–96   T has a different version:

> Full derly to hym that ye pray
> To hym that was don apon a tre
> To safe yowr sallis on dowymysday
> Qwen all salles savyd mon be.

94 *Besechyng Hym that is.* A: *And beseke thou.*

95 *the¹.* W: *you.*

at. A: *on.*

the². AW: *that.*

96 *soule.* The CCC scribe wrote and deleted *bod* before this word. A maintains male gender: *That every man shall gyffe rekenyng.* The usage agrees with the last stanza.

geve. W: *make.*

97 *Ther is no man for the shall pray.* The variants read:

> A: Fore ther no lordes schall fore the praye;
> W: Ther shall noo lordes ffor you praye;
> T: Than may ther na luyd men for yow mute.

Only CCC uses the classless term *man*. A and W state the uselessness of having noblemen of worldly wealth and power pray for a lost sinner, and T dismisses the petitions of "lewd" (ignorant) men. On the uselessness of earthly judicial power before the Supreme Judge, compare *The Four Leaves of the Truelove*, stanza 35.

97–104 The last stanza returns to three themes introduced in the second stanza: (1) "debate," or legal quarreling; (2) accepting God's grace to amend oneself spiritually; and (3) coming to an end (previously, it was the sinner's fate in hell; now, it is the end of the sinner's speech — and, with it, a warning about the reader's imminent end).

98 *Nother . . . ne.* A: *Ne . . . nother;* WT: *Noo . . . nor noo.*

99   *Thy charter helpith the not*. A: *Ther charter helpys the not*; W: *Your charter shall nott helpe*.

        that day. So all MSS except T; the CCC scribe wrote and deleted *an hawe* and interlined *that day*.

99–101   T reads:

        Fore and tha tha be no buyt
        Ther charter wyll not preyf worthe a hawe
        Thus every man ye tayk gud tent.

100   *Thy*. A: *There*; W: *Your*.

        an. W: *a*.

101   *the . . . thyself*. W: *you . . . yourselffe*.

        grace. See note to line 14.

        knowe. Original of this word and *blowe* (line 103) may have been Northern forms *knawe* and *blawe* to rhyme with *lawe* and *hawe*. These forms do not appear in any of the MSS.

102   *And*. Omitted in T.

103   *Farewell*. W: *Adewe*; T: *Me thynk*. The sounding horn is a spectral call to the dead or dying. Compare the end of *The Parlement of the Thre Ages*, lines 654–56 (ed. M. Y. Offord, EETS o.s. 246 [London: Oxford University Press, 1959]); the words of Tutivillus in the Wakefield play *The Judgement*, "My horne is blawen" (*The Towneley Plays*, ed. Martin Stevens and A. C. Cawley, EETS s.s. 13, vol. 1 [Oxford: Oxford University Press, 1994], p. 410); and the warning from a dying man, "I sey no more but beware of ane horne!" in *Farewell, This World*, line 21 (ed. Carleton Brown, *Religious Lyrics of the XVth Century* [Oxford: Clarendon, 1939], p. 237). Woolf believes that a larger narrative may once have enclosed *Sinner's Lament*: "the speaker bids farewell on the blowing of a horn, as though this were a return from the dead made to a specific person as in so many *exempla*" (p. 319).

103   *an.* WT: *a.*

104   A: *I may no lenger byde with the.*

Glossary

abyd(e), abide *abide, endure, wait for*
agoo *gone*
al (adv.) *entirely*
al so *as, just as*
an ende, on ende *in the end*
apill, apyll, appill *apple*
apon *(up)on*
art *are*
awn *own*
awr(e) *our*
ay *ever, always*
ayene, ayeyn, ayein, agayne *again*
ayenst *against*

bale *sorrow, pain*
bar(e) (v.) *bore*
be, beo, bi *by*
ben(e), beo(n) *be*
beoth, byth *is, are*
bere, beere (v.) *bear*
bere *bier*
beste, beest *beast*
beten, beoten, betyn *beat*
betere *better*
bewté *beauty*
bit, byt *asks, bids, commands; asked, commanded*
blak(e) *black; sinful*
ble *complexion*
blede *bleed*
blys(se), blis *heavenly bliss*

blyssed, blyssyd *blessed*
blod(e) *blood*
blodi, blody *bloody*
bodi *body*
bold(e) *bold, brash; castle, fortress*
bondes *bonds, fetters*
bord *board*
bot (v.) took a bite
bot(t) *but, however, yet; except for*
bot if *unless*
bounde(n) *bound*
brac, brak *broke, broken*
brede *bread; tablet; spread broadly; book cover*
brest *breast*
brid *child*
bryd *bird*
bryht, briht, bryght *bright, beautiful*
brytylnesse, brotylnesse *brittleness*
brotyl *brittle*
bur, bour *bower*

certes *certainly*
chambir *bed chamber*
chere *countenance, face; happiness*
chese *choose*
chyld, cheld *child*
chylder, childer *children*
clarke, clerk *scholar*
clene *entirely*
cleped *called*

395

clere *lovely; bright; virtuous*
clot *clod*
comforth *comfort, console*
comly *comely, beautiful; fair one*
con *can, to be able*
cristenyng *baptism*
Cros, Crois *Cross*
cumen *to come*

dampne *damn*
dampned *damned*
ded *death*
dede *did*
degré *condition*
dem(e) *judge, sentence*
der(e) *dear, beloved*
deth *death*
devel *devil*
deye, dy(e) *die*
dole *sorrow*
dom(e) *judgment, sentence*
dred *fear, awe*
dredfull *inspiring fear and awe*
dude *did*
dunt *blow*

efter *after*
ende See **an ende**
ensample *example*
eny *any*
er *before*
everychone *everyone*
eyyen, eyn *eyes*

fader *father; father's*
fadres, faderes *fathers; father's*
fare, fayre (v.) *go, proceed*
fare, fayre, feir(e) (adj.) *fair, pleasant, excellent, fortunate*
fedre *feather*
fela, felawe *close companion*
fell, feol(l)e *wicked; harmful*

fell(e) *skin*
fend(e), feond *fiend*
fere, feere *companion, friend,* (**in fere**) *together*
flesch, flech *flesh*
flour *flower*
folk(e) *people*
forsoth *indeed*
forthy *for this reason*
foule *bird*
fourme(n) *form, make*
fourte *fourth*
frealte *frailty*
fro, fra *from*
ful(l) *very*
furst(e), fyrst *first*
fynd(e) *find*

ga, gan(e), gon *go*
gan, gon *did*
gane *gone*
god(e) *good, kind*
goo *gone*
gret(e), grett *great; high in rank; powerful*
gylt(e) *sin against*

hafe *have*
haly *holy*
haly, hally *entirely*
handwark(e) *handiwork; mankind as God's creation*
hard, herde *heard*
hart(e), herte, heorte *heart; will, desire*
hath *has*
hed(e), heved *head*
hedde *had*
heerde *shepherd*
height *is called*
hem *them; him*
heo *she*
heor(e) *their*

Glossary

her *here*
here *hear, respond*
heven(e), heovene *heaven; heaven's*
hi, heo *they*
hir(e), hyre, here *her*
hit, hire *it*
hond *hand*
hwan(ne), hwen(ne) *when*
hwat *what*
hwile *while*
hy(e), hihe, hiye, heih *high*

Ich, Ic *I*
ilk(e), ilka, ilk a *same, each, every*
iwys *indeed*

jolyte *happiness*
justes, justyse *judge; judges*

kynde, kuynde, kende (n.) *nature;
    creature; wits; kindred; heritage; person*
kynde (adj.) *natural*
kyn *kinsfolk*
kyng(e) *king*

ladi *lady*
lang(e) *for a long time*
lat(e) (v.) *let*
leche *physician*
leef, lyef, leof, leove *dear*
lef(e) *leaf*
lefe *believe*
lefed (pp.) *left*
lefmon, leofmon, leovemon *lover*
leid(e) *laid*
lese *lose*
lette *prevent*
leve *believe*
leve *leave, cease*
loked, looked *locked, bound*
lomb *lamb*
luf(e), luve *love*

lust *desire*
lyf(e) *life*
lykyng *pleasure, desire*
lyon, lyoun *lion*

mai (v.) *may*
mare *more*
may *maiden, young girl; virgin*
mayde *virgin*
mayden, madyn *virgin*
mede, meode *reward; sweet drink (mead)*
mekyl(l) *great, much*
merveille, mervayle *marvel*
mery *pleasant, delightful*
mest(e) *most*
mete *food*
mett(e) *met, joined*
mi *my*
mid, myd *with*
mihte, mayht (v.) *might*
minne, mynne *make a sound*
misdoo (pp.) *sinned*
misdoth *sin*
mo, moo *more*
mochel, muchel *great, much*
mod(e) *mien, bearing*
moder *mother*
mon *man; one*
mon(e) *moan, lament*
mony, moni *many*
mowen *might*
myht(e), myght(e) (v.) *might*
myld(e) *gentle; gracious; compasionate*
myn(ne) *less*
myrth *spiritual joy, happiness*

na, ne, non (adj.) *no*
nan (adv.) *not at all*
nan(e) (pron.) *none*
nayl(e), nale *nail*
ne (conj.) *nor*
ne (adv.) *not*

neer, nere *near; nearer*
nere *were not*
nis, nys *(there) is not*
noght(e), nouht *not*
not *do not know*
nou, nu *now*

o, oo, on *one, a*
on ende See **an ende**
ones, onys, oonys *once*
or *before*
other, othre *other, or*
ought *anything*
oughware *anywhere*
oure *houre*
owr(e) *our*

pardoun *pardon*
payn, peyne, pyne *pain, suffering*
pité *compassion*
presse *wine press*
putt(e), pute, puiten *put*

quen(e), qween *queen*

red (v.) *advise, guide; command, decree*
red(e) (v.) *tell, relate, expound*
red(e) (adj.) *red*
riche, rych(e) *powerful; wealthy*
rife, ryf *numerous*
riht, ryght *right*
rihtful *rightful; righteous*
Rod(e), Roode *Cross*

sad *profound*
sald *sold, betrayed*
sal(l) *shall*
sare *sorrowfully; intensely*
sauh, saih, say, sigh *saw*
saule *soul*
schal, schul *shall*
scharp(e) *sharp*

schaw, schew *show*
schene, shene *beautiful*
scho *she*
schulde *should*
seche, seke *seek*
seid(e), seyde *said*
seint(e), sa(y)nte *saint*
sekurly, sykerly *certainly*
seo(n) *see*
serwe *sorrow, distress*
sett(e) *set*
shalbe *shall be*
shoure *assault*
shul(e) *shall*
sith, sythen, sin *since*
soght(e) *sought, searched (for)*
son (adv.) *soon*
son(e) (n.) *son*
son(ne) (n.) *sun*
sore (adj.) *grievously*
sorwe, sorow *sorrow, distress*
soth (adj.) *true*
sothe (n.) *truth*
sothly, sothliche *truly*
spac, spak(e) *spoke*
speche *speech*
spek(e) *speak*
sprad, spred *spread*
springe, sprynge (trans.) *bring forth;* (intrans.) *grow vigorously*
staf *staff*
stod(e) *stood*
suld *should*
swerd *sword*
swylk(e) *such*
syd(e) *side*
syker(e) *sure, secure*
syn(e), syen *directly after that, next*
syn(ne), sinne *sin*

tech(e) *teach*
teye, ty(e) *tie, bind*

thai, thay, thei *they*
tham, thaim *them*
than *then*
thar(e), ther *their*
thar(e), ther *there*
thar(e) *these*
thase *those*
the *you*
theih *though*
these *this*
thes, theos(e) *these*
theves, theoves *thieves*
thi *thy*
thine *your*
this *thus*
tho *then*
thorw(h), thurght *through, by*
thouht(e), thoght *thought; distress of mind*
thre, threo *three*
thu, thow *you*
til(l) *until*
tre, treo, trene *tree; Cross*
treowe, trew *true, constant*
treson, tresun *treason*
treuth, trewth, trouthe *truth; troth*
trew, trow *believe*
trewluf(e) *herb paris; true love; God*
twa *two; both*
twyn(ne) *part, be separated*
tym *time*

uche, uich, uych(e), uychon *each, every*
uch a, uych o *each*
unkynde *unnatural*
uppon *upon*
ur(e) *our*

vergeous *acidic juice of green grapes or apples*

wa, wo *woe; damnation*
wald, wold(e) *would*
war(e), weor(e), whar *were*
warkes, werkes *works, acts*
warld, werld *world*
wei(e), weye *way*
wele, wel(l) (n.) *prosperity, fortune*
well(e) (n.) *well, fountain; source*
wepe, weop *weep*
were *uncertainty, doubt*
wete *understand*
whar(e), ware, wher *where*
whi *why*
whon *when*
whoso *whoever*
wil(e), wyll, wol(l), wole, wule (v.) *will*
wite(n), wyte(n) *know, advise; guard, defend; think; teach*
withowt(yn), withute(n), withouten, wythute *without*
wondes *wounds*
wondir, wunder *very*
wote *know (of)*
write(n), wretyn *written*
wroght, wrouht *made, created; behaved*
wyd(e) *wide, large*
wyf(e), wyve *wife*
wyght, wight *creature; person*
wyld(e), wyled, wild *natural; rough; distracted; wayward, sinful*
wyll (n.) *longing; divine purpose*
wyn *wine*
wyn(ne), winne *win*
wyse *manner*
wyste (pp.) *known*

yaf, yave *gave*
yare (adj.) *elaborate; available*
yare (adv.) *quickly; readily; thoroughly*
ye *you*
yf, yef, yif *if*
yeve, yive *give*

yifte *gift*
yit, yitt(e) *yet*
ymston(e) *gemstone*
yode, yede *went*
yow *you*
ysmyte *taken*
ywys *indeed*

Other Volumes in the Middle English Texts Series

The Floure and the Leafe, The Assemblie of Ladies, and *The Isle of Ladies*, ed. Derek Pearsall (1990)

Three Middle English Charlemagne Romances, ed. Alan Lupack (1990)

Six Ecclesiastical Satires, ed. James M. Dean (1991)

Heroic Women from the Old Testament in Middle English Verse, ed. Russell A. Peck (1991)

The Canterbury Tales: Fifteenth-Century Continuations and Additions, ed. John M. Bowers (1992)

Gavin Douglas, *The Palis of Honoure*, ed. David J. Parkinson (1992)

Wynnere and Wastoure and The Parlement of the Thre Ages, ed. Warren Ginsberg (1992)

The Shewings of Julian of Norwich, ed. Georgia Ronan Crampton (1993)

King Arthur's Death: The Middle English Stanzaic Morte Arthur and Alliterative Morte Arthure, ed. Larry D. Benson and Edward E. Foster (1994)

Lancelot of the Laik and Sir Tristrem, ed. Alan Lupack (1994)

Sir Gawain: Eleven Romances and Tales, ed. Thomas Hahn (1995)

Sir Perceval of Galles and Ywain and Gawain, ed. Mary Flowers Braswell (1995)

Four Middle English Romances: Sir Isumbras, Octavian, Sir Eglamour of Artois, Sir Tryamour, ed. Harriet Hudson (1996)

The Poems of Laurence Minot (1333–1352), ed. Richard H. Osberg (1996)

Medieval English Political Writings, ed. James M. Dean (1996)

The Book of Margery Kempe, ed. Lynn Staley (1996)

Amis and Amiloun, Robert of Ciseyle, and Sir Amadace, ed. Edward E. Foster (1997)

The Cloud of Unknowing, ed. Patrick Gallacher (1997)

Robin Hood and Other Outlaw Tales, ed. Stephen Knight and Thomas H. Ohlgren (1997)

The Poems of Robert Henryson, ed. Robert Kindrick (1997)

To order please contact:

MEDIEVAL INSTITUTE PUBLICATIONS
Western Michigan University
Kalamazoo, MI 49008–3801
Phone (616) 387–8755
FAX (616) 387–8750